THE STEPMOTHER TONGUE

Also by John Skinner

TELL-TALE STORIES: Essays in Narrative Poetics
THE FICTIONS OF ANITA BROOKNER: Illusions of Romance
CONSTRUCTIONS OF SMOLLETT: A Study of Genre and Gender

The Stepmother Tongue

An Introduction to New Anglophone Fiction

John Skinner

© John Skinner 1998

First published 1998 by
MACMILLAN PRESS LTD
Houndmills, Basingstoke, Hampshire RG21 6XS
and London
Companies and representatives
throughout the world

ISBN 0–333–67613–0 hardcover
ISBN 0–333–67614–9 paperback

A catalogue record for this book is available
from the British Library.

This book is printed on paper suitable for recycling and
made from fully managed and sustained forest sources.

10   9   8   7   6   5   4   3   2   1
07   06   05   04   03   02   01   00   99   98

Typeset by EXPO Holdings, Malaysia

Printed in Hong Kong

Published in the United States of America 1998 by
ST. MARTIN'S PRESS, INC.,
Scholarly and Reference Division,
175 Fifth Avenue, New York, N.Y. 10010

ISBN 0–312–21176–7 cloth
ISBN 0–312–21177–5 paperback

Indifferent language of an alien shore,
the journey was troubled but I am here:
register me among your stepchildren

Debjani Chatterjee

one should never pass over in silence the question of the tongue in
which the question of the tongue is raised

Jacques Derrida

For Carla

Contents

Preface   viii

Introduction   1

Part I   New Literatures in Old Worlds   29
1   Asia   31
2   Africa   77
3   The South Pacific   119

Part II   New Literatures in New Worlds   131
4   Afro-America   133
5   The Caribbean   160

Part III   Old Literatures in New Worlds   197
   Introduction   199

6   Australia and New Zealand   211
7   South Africa and Canada   239

Part IV   Old Literatures in Old Worlds   269
   Introduction   271

8   The British Isles   276
9   North America   294

Extroduction   308

Afterword   332

Works Discussed   339

Author Index   343

General Index   350

Preface

The Stepmother Tongue: An Introduction to New Anglophone Fiction is intended for the student, critic and general reader. It does not provide a new theoretical model for post-colonial literature, but merely a broad and modestly innovative taxonomy of new fiction in English.

Each element of the title already implies a certain critical bias. There are countless twentieth-century writers (beginning with Conrad and Nabokov) whose relation to the English language is in some way exceptional, whether ambivalent, problematic, or in some cases even hostile: one may, in various senses, speak of a "stepmother tongue". These are the authors who receive particular emphasis in the following pages.

More practically, a study of this kind demands rigorous selection. I began in search of a term which would include all literature written in the various "world englishes", but exclude native English writers (although not Black British ones) and American writers (but not African Americans, or any of the other minority literatures of the United States). It is a complex but fairly precise job description, although there may, surprisingly, be no satisfactory candidate. The composite term "New Anglophone" draws on connotations currently familiar in Europe – the Anglo-Saxon world generally preferring "post-colonial".

Unfortunately, the word "anglophone" itself is anomalous, as it should logically include *all* literature written in English, Margaret Drabble as well as Ngũgĩ wa Thiong'o. Some preliminary justification for *de facto* omissions is offered here. On a practical level, even the sketchiest account of "mainstream" English and American fiction would have drastically curtailed the space available for other authors less familiar to many readers; whilst the existence of excellent single-volume surveys of both fields (those of Malcolm Bradbury spring immediately to mind) is a further deterrent.

At a slightly higher conceptual level, one may recall two vignettes in Salman Rushdie's seminal essay "Commonwealth Literature Does Not Exist": the "lady from the British Council" who reassured him that "English studies are taken to include Commonwealth literature" and the Cambridge don who asked whether he experienced "a kind of liberty, certain advantages, in

occupying ... a position on the periphery". The date of both incidents is 1983, since which the "empire" has been writing back with
increasing insistence. It is nevertheless noticeable how many perspectives on fiction in English start at the so-called "centre" and
never quite reach the "periphery". The present study could therefore be ironically regarded as a simple act of restitution, starting at
the "periphery" but never quite reaching the "centre". Quotation
marks are everything here, of course, since both of the concepts
placed inside them have been progressively invalidated by the
post-colonial theorist and the contemporary general reader.

The final justification for the present format derives, however,
from the concept of the stepmother tongue: the four sections of the
book reflect the diminishing degrees of literalness with which this
trope could be applied. If it seems paradoxical in the context of
"white writing" from Australia, New Zealand, South Africa or
Canada, then it is surely inapplicable to mainstream English or
American writing. These issues are explored more fully in the
Introduction proper.

A brief comment is also necessary on the hitherto careless elision
of "literature" and "fiction". The former is too vast a field for this
book, which therefore limits itself to the twentieth century's dom-
inant literary genre. Where fiction is concerned, moreover, most
examples are chosen from the last fifty years, and almost all among
full-length novels; the early twentieth century and the short story
are two more victims of an enforced selection process.

The Stepmother Tongue does not claim to be exhaustive. Omissions
range from individual novels and novelists to entire literary traditions (e.g. Malta), whilst other countries – such as the Philippines –
are unfortunately not represented among the eighty texts treated in
greater detail. The book is simply a personal attempt to fill, as usefully as possible, the space that was made available: space, incidentally, which seemed more than generous, for, if the novels
discussed never seemed too long, the relevant critical or theoretical
works rarely seemed too short.

A broad survey of this kind is clearly indebted to many standard
secondary sources. These are normally acknowledged at the end of
the appropriate section, although certain consistently useful works
should be mentioned here. The relevant volumes of the *Dictionary
of Literary Biography* (on Caribbean, Black African, Afro-American,
Euro-American and Canadian writers) are invariably helpful,
although there are as yet (regrettably) no volumes on Asian,

Australasian, or white South African writers. More comprehensive, although obviously smaller in scale, is the invaluable Routledge *Encyclopedia of Post-Colonial Literatures in English*. The leading scholarly journals in the field are the long-running *Journal of Commonwealth Literature* (with its excellent annual bibliographies), together with the more recent *Kunapipi*, *Wasafiri*, *World Literature Written in English* and *Ariel*. To all of these sources I am naturally indebted. For simple issues of selection or exclusion, it was also of great benefit to have worked as consulting editor (with responsibility for Africa and Asia) on the new *Cambridge Guide to Fiction in English*. The policies of Ian Ousby and his other regional editors about who to include were particularly instructive. On matters of demographic and linguistic data, finally, Kenneth Katzner's *The Languages of the World* (1995 edition) was most useful.

It is also a pleasure to record more personal debts. I am grateful, above all, for the practical support of my department Chair, Risto Hiltunen, and to the Academy of Finland for an Advanced Research Fellowship for 1995–6, which enabled me to make additional study or research trips to the University of Cambridge (England), the University of the West Indies (Jamaica, Barbados, and Trinidad), and the Universities of Kerala and Mysore (India).

I would like to thank friends and colleagues who have offered good advice, shared their expertise, and/or helped obtain urgently needed materials. They include Victor Chang, Edward Baugh and Mervyn Morris (Jamaica); Kenneth Ramchand (Trinidad); K. C. Belliappa, Anil Kumar and K. Radha (India); D. C. R. A. Goonetilleke (Sri Lanka); S. K. Okleme (Ghana); Ian Ousby, Alastair Niven and Gilian Gorle (England); Bernth Lindfors (United States); Adrian Mitchell, Glen Philips and Cynthia vanden Driesen (Australia); Ralph Crane (New Zealand); Carla Raule (Italy); and Gerald Doherty (Finland). With these and many others who kindly answered all my queries, I can only hope that I asked some of the right questions.

Naantali, Nådendal,   JOHN SKINNER
Valles Gratiae, Finland

John.Skinner@utu.fi

Introduction

COMING TO TERMS WITH MODERN ANGLOPHONE FICTION

In 1995, the Nobel Prize for Literature was awarded to an Irish poet, Seamus Heaney; in 1993, it was won by an African American novelist, Toni Morrison, and in 1992, by a poet and dramatist from St Lucia, Derek Walcott. The 1991 award went to South African novelist Nadine Gordimer, the 1986 one to Nigerian dramatist Wole Soyinka. Having once honoured Winston Churchill and Pearl Buck, but never Joyce, Proust, or Kafka, the Swedish Academy is by no means infallible, although there are welcome signs of critical sophistication and cultural awareness in the recent recognition of English-language writers outside the mainstream British and American traditions. All of the authors in question may be placed within the broad literary category variously known as World Literature in English, the New Literatures in English, Post-Colonial Literature, or (with certain exceptions) Commonwealth Literature.

The field in question is coherent and identifiable (however vast), although still without a universally acceptable general label. The most useful introduction to the subject here may be a brief review of the competing terms used to describe it.

Commonwealth Literature

To begin in reverse order: the traditionally favoured label of *Commonwealth Literature*, acquiring prominence in the 1960s, refers explicitly to the loose political association of some fifty countries linked to Britain by a common colonial past. There are obvious anomalies in the term. Britain is an official member of the original Commonwealth, although English, Scottish, or Welsh authors would never normally be regarded as "Commonwealth" writers. There is clearly a hidden agenda here, whether paternalistic or protectionist, with its hints of marginality or subordination. It is an ironic situation, moreover, since it is hard to find a contemporary British-born novelist with the international stature of the so-called Commonwealth writers Salman Rushdie or V. S. Naipaul.

1

The term Commonwealth would, of course, exclude American and Irish literature, as well as such major English-language writers as the Somali Nuruddin Farah, or the Filipino F. Sionil José. Within the Commonwealth itself, moreover, the label generally seems reserved for writers in English, and ignores francophone Canada or Afrikaans-speaking South Africa, not to mention the indigenous languages of Africa and the Indian subcontinent. Other writers, such as Gordimer and Coetzee (South Africa), Ghose and Sidhwa (Pakistan), and most recently, Soyinka and Achebe (Nigeria), presumably move in and out of the category "Commonwealth" as their respective countries join, leave, or are suspended from this august body. Of the five Nobel laureates cited in the first paragraph, then, only Walcott, despite having spent much of his creative life in the United States, has impeccable Commonwealth credentials. And at this point, one might incidentally remember the many writers who themselves find the label "Commonwealth writer" either demeaning (Roy Heath) or simply offensive (Salman Rushdie).

In defence of the term, it may be pointed out that its users are almost invariably aware of these terminological problems, but stick with a convenient name for want of something better. On a similarly practical level, the major conferences on the subject are organized by ACLALS, the Association for Commonwealth Literature and Language Studies, together with its regional offshoots; while the longest-running (and most substantial) scholarly journal in the field is called precisely the *Journal of Commonwealth Literature* (an original justification for the name was that librarians could hardly ignore such a solidly respectable title). Both conferences and journal, need it be added, regularly feature such potentially unclassifiable figures as Farah.

Post-Colonial Literature

The more recent term for a frequently overlapping, if rarely identical, area is *Post-Colonial Literature*, its scholars often adding theoretical rigour to what occasionally seemed a peaceful literary backwater. Post-colonial studies are presently a modish field, although it is worth remembering that today's boom may be tomorrow's bubble. Approaches that were the avant-garde of the 1980s and the orthodoxy of the 1990s may one day become the theoretical equivalent of flared trousers. Despite its ambiguous and contradictory nature, however, "post-colonial literature" (or more broadly, "post-colonial studies") is the term currently favoured by American and British scholars – but not by their European counterparts, who often prefer "New Literatures in English". The problems of post-colonial literature as a discipline are connected with both its historical parameters and its present academic scope. Of the two questions, the second is more easily dealt with.

It is fair to suggest that the field of "post-colonial studies" in the English-speaking world is arbitrarily limited (or perhaps potentially unlimited) and ill-defined. Its prophets include an ex-patriate Martinican, Frantz Fanon, and a francophone Tunisian, Albert Memmi; its high priest(esse)s are a Palestinian, Edward Said, and two Indians, Homi Bhabha and Gayatri Chakravorty Spivak, the last three impressively cosmopolitan if ultimately entrenched in Anglo-American academia. Its storm-troopers, however, are frequently Anglo-Saxon, politically correct, but conspicuously monoglot, academics from "English Departments" in British, North American, or Australasian universities. This is by no means a protest against current politicization of "English Literature", a process which may be seen as a useful corrective to so many previously unquestioned ideological assumptions. But an increased emphasis on the "post-colonial" dimension has meant a corresponding indifference to the significance of "English", in either its literary or its linguistic aspects. The terminological dichotomy is worth pursuing.

An essential point here is that the experiences of ex-British colonies are often duplicated in the territories appropriated by other colonial powers, most notably France, Spain and Portugal. The range and expression of African literature in English is justly celebrated, although that of francophone writing in the same area may be even more remarkable. In the light of colonial history, moreover, the value of a comparative approach might seem self-evident, although anglophone and francophone African literature, for example, are normally segregated. The concept of *literature* itself, on the other hand, imposes an additional limitation, if insufficient attention is paid to history or the social and political sciences. A "post-colonial studies" dominated by the reading of imaginative *literature* in *English* (paying mere lip service to other subjects and disciplines, or to other languages and cultures) can thus become an unbalanced or dangerously truncated pseudo-subject. Or, perhaps worse, post-colonial studies risks becoming no more than a politically correct version of "Eng. Lit."

The other, broader, issue requiring attention here is that of historical parameters. Post-colonial literature (among English-speaking academics at least) is often defined as the literature produced since independence by the ex-colonies of Britain (or any other imperial power). In such reductive terms, it would presumably exclude India before 1947, although this country's three major anglophone novelists, Anand, Rao, and Narayan, were already writing in the 1930s; or even Nigeria prior to 1963 – Achebe's great classic *Things Fall Apart* dates from 1957.

"Post-colonial" is, of course, sometimes given a broader definition and assumed to include relevant writing from any period since initial colonial contact. Conrad's *Heart of Darkness* and Defoe's *Robinson Crusoe* are thus widely recognized as central texts, whilst the major themes of post-colonialism (in English literature at least) are considered to have been anticipated in Shakespeare's *The Tempest*, particularly in the figure of Caliban. The heart of the issue may lie in the apparently harmless phrase "relevant text": the relevance of the colonial theme to *Robinson Crusoe* or *Heart of Darkness* would be obvious even if post-colonial studies had never existed. The light thrown by the new theory on a novel such as *Mansfield Park* is, however, startling. Sir Thomas Bertram's unexpected delay on his Antigua plantation (a slave insurrection perhaps) can never again be read as mere narrative expediency. Post-colonial theory has shown how gaps and silences can be as eloquent as the text itself.

But the term "post-colonial literature" has other problematic aspects. The chief of these is a monolithic or homogenizing tendency, according to which the colonial experience (uniformly negative) is seen as the common denominator of all post-colonial discourse. Some theorists thus merely invert, rather than deconstruct, certain notorious binary models. This process has been much facilitated by a broad elision of colonialism and patriarchy – man's colonization of New Worlds is equated with his exploitation of woman; not least because of this powerful analogy, the Canadian feminist Margaret Atwood is as much a post-colonial writer as the Nigerian novelist Buchi Emecheta. Such questions are clearly related to current debates about "settlers" and "indigenes", where representatives of the former sometimes perform intellectual acrobatics to legitimize their own position. There is no suggestion, on the other hand, that colonial or post-colonial subjects, however defined, produce many defences of colonialism; and yet, however iniquitous its respective regimes, the old British and current American empires carry little direct responsibility for such practices as the caste system (the subject of Anand's *Untouchable*) or various forms of female mutilation (at the centre of numerous novels from Farah's *Sardines* to Nwapa's *Efuru*).

A quite different problem inherent in the term simply concerns the psychological associations of definitions used for certain categories of authors: for how long will writers of Africa, the Caribbean, or the Indian subcontinent remain content to be identified in exclusively derivative or subordinate terms? It is simply nicer to be *"pre-*this" than *"post-*that", and perhaps nicest of all to belong to an autonomous category in one's own right. Without undue reductivism, a small parable may be extracted here from the novels of Narayan. In many of the latter, the only reminder of the British Raj is the (admittedly substantial) English-language medium. In the imperial heyday, the merchant, the missionary, or the administrator were the yardstick by which the so-called benefits of empire could be judged by a metropolitan establishment; whilst in the post-colonial era, the same people become the bogey-men or scapegoats of academic critics and theorists in what one is tempted to call a new metropolitan establishment. In more abstract terms, this might be described as the obsession with "otherness". In both contexts, however, these emblems of Empire remain *central*, whereas in Narayan they are normally just *irrelevant*, such is the ability of Indian civilization to ignore or absorb external influences, whether Persian, Mogul, or British. In claiming to displace the imperial centre, but only managing to demonize it, then, the *post-*colonial comes dangerously close to the *neo-*colonial.

The New Literatures in English and World Literature in English

The two other terms mentioned at the beginning of this exposition do not require such lengthy discussion. *The New Literatures in English* seems, on first sight, ideologically unexceptionable, and is the term often preferred in continental Europe. John Thieme, editor of the large Arnold anthology in the field, describes a survey conducted among international scholars to canvass a name for his collection. Anglo-American academics generally favoured a title incorporating the term "post-colonial", whereas their European counterparts preferred a formula based on "New Literatures in English". Thieme's publishers were shrewd enough to prefer

Anglo-American political confrontation to European intellectual detachment, and went for post-colonial.

But is the term "New Literatures in English" so neutral? The word "new" is troubling in the light of its implied comparisons with other presumably normative literatures ("English", British, or American) which are "old"; in the present context, of course, the concepts of "new" and "old" may have some historical justification, but the constant implication that one literature is in subordinate or derivative relation to another is undesirable, and increasingly without objective basis. The actual concept of a national "literature in English", on the other hand, with all its suggestion of breadth and comprehensiveness, may well be applicable to Nigeria or India, but perhaps less so to Pakistan or Sri Lanka.

The term *World Literature in English*, finally, which perhaps will strike some as a pernicious example of linguistic or cultural imperialism, may in fact be the most anodyne formula of all. Theorists have surely exaggerated the cultural pretensions of a term which has all the bland neutrality of another modern cross-cultural institution: international airline food.

ANGLOPHONE LITERATURE

All four terms then – Commonwealth Literature, Post-Colonial Literature, the New Literatures in English, and World Literature in English – have clear disadvantages. The field appears to offer scope for an alternative label, particularly if accompanied by a new methodological approach. The latter would be based on linguistic, stylistic, and socio-cultural factors, rather than political platforms or ideological prejudice: the label itself would be *anglophone literature*. A survey of literature in English along these lines could learn much from the highly successful (if already somewhat dated) recent *linguistic* survey entitled The *Story of English*. The latter is an even-handed, highly accessible (if under-theorized) account of varieties of English ("world englishes" would be the preferred term of many post-colonial theorists).

The actual label proposed, "anglophone literature", has an obvious analogy in "littérature francophone", which is related in turn to the concept of "francophonie": all those countries where French has official status, that is to say a kind of cultural or linguistic equivalent to the Commonwealth. The issue of terminology is, incidentally, conditioned at this point by a kind of semantic blind spot in English itself. The term "English literature" normally refers either to "literature written in the English language" or to "literature written by English people". English thus lacks a distinction such as that separating "Arabic literature" (or literature written in the Arabic language) from "Arab literature" (literature written by Arabs).

Things are better in French, where one may distinguish between "la littérature française" (ambiguous, but referring primarily to ethnically French writers) and "la littérature d'expression française" (all literature written in French). The concept of "ethnicity" has become another theoretical minefield, since Werner Sollors asked so pointedly who *is* ethnic, but the linguistic referent of the second term, at least, is fairly precise. A pioneering academic conference in Nairobi in 1963 actually defined its topic as "African Writers of English Expression", although this formulation has subsequently been little used, presumably because it seems clumsy. The other Germanic languages have at least one comprehensive and self-explanatory term: *englischsprachig Literatur* (German) or *engelskspråkig litteratur* (Swedish), but the nearest English equivalent of "English-speaking literature" (outside the context of talking-books for the visually handicapped) sounds distinctly odd. Back, then, to anglophone.

LAND OF MANY LANGUAGES / LANGUAGE OF MANY LANDS

There are other distinct advantages in using the term *anglophone* (with its stress on the linguistic constant), rather than post-colonial (implying a monolithic and homogenizing reading of history) or even Commonwealth (often unfortunately suggesting little more than imperial nostalgia). Above all, it allows a new emphasis on the simultaneous emergence of the modern English language and the first colonial enterprises of the English themselves. Historical analogies in the present context are instructive.

The evolution of English is conventionally divided into three distinct periods: Old English, Middle English, and Modern English. All three phases were initially marked by vigorous colonial expansion. When the Angles, Saxons, and Jutes arrived in Britain in the fifth century, they supplanted the Celtic language (then presumably used

by all but a Latin-speaking elite) as comprehensively as they dispossessed the Celts themselves. The modern form of this Celtic language, with the descendants of its banished speakers, is today of
course found in Wales. The strength of the division between
Germanic and Celtic culture is suggested by the fact that Old
English has scarcely a single loan from its linguistic predecessor; by
a final irony, moreover, even the term "Welsh" is derived from a
Germanic word meaning "foreigner".

The advent of Middle English (*c.*1100) also coincides with a
period of invasion, annexation, and colonial expansion, although
the English are now on the receiving end. The arrival of the
Normans in 1066 led to the suppression, perhaps even to the virtual
extinction, of the English language: for roughly three centuries, the
written languages of England were Norman French and Latin,
making it correspondingly difficult to gauge the true fate of *spoken*
English. The early history of the conquerors is easier to trace,
however, and it is known that Norman knights also began the colonization of Ireland, thereby challenging popular assumptions of
eight centuries of "English" oppression in that country. There is
a significant revisionist narrative here, according to which the
English and Irish were originally common victims of Norman oppression. But even if this is so, one can only reduce the period of
English mayhem in Ireland by a couple of centuries, since it is hard
to deny that the emergent English eventually showed greater
capacity for ruthlessness and far less talent for assimilation than
their Norman predecessors.

In a literary survey based on linguistic parameters, moreover, the
early Norman period is also significant for the numbers of English
refugees in Scotland, where they were instrumental in founding the
medieval Scottish *burgs*, the fortified towns of which Edinburgh is
the most notable example. They also introduced that Germanic
dialect (several centuries before the existence of Modern English)
which was to be the linguistic predecessor of modern Scots.

The "re-emergence" of English (or perhaps the simple emergence
of Middle English) south of the border is not without controversy.
Traditional scholarship insists on a continuity between Old,
Middle, and Modern English, a thesis which doubtless reflects a
strong ideological investment in terms of national mythology.
Similarly questionable genealogies have been proposed at various
times for the "British Constitution" (said to date from the pre-
Roman period) and the Anglican Church (traced directly to the

days of primitive Christianity). The English can never be accused of indifference to historical precedent. Some linguists nevertheless now suggest that, far from being a direct descendant of Anglo-Saxon, Middle English may be more accurately regarded as a "creolization" of French. This hypothesis, with its implication of an initial stage when the new English was a mere contact language, in effect a kind of pidgin French, is probably less flattering to English national sensibilities than traditional theories. It nevertheless has the attractive corollary of bringing the "mother of englishes" conceptually closer to the contact pidgins and vernaculars of Africa and the South Pacific.

But the most relevant example of simultaneous linguistic and territorial expansion concerns the rise of Modern English, conventionally dated from 1500. English transatlantic exploration begins in exactly the same period, under the Genoese navigator John Cabot, who made his (personal) discovery of Newfoundland in the service of Henry VII. A later expedition to the "New World" was an obvious inspiration for Shakespeare's final play. But since the allegorical potential of *The Tempest* has been well mined by postcolonial theorists and writers alike, it may be worth recalling the less familiar *locus classicus* of John Donne's nineteenth elegy:

O my America, my new found land,
My Kingdom, safeliest when with one man manned,
My mine of precious stones, my Empery,
How blessed am I in this discovering thee!

And since the elegy is subtitled "To His Mistress Going to Bed", while the referent is the woman's body, the parallels between colonial and sexual appropriation are as clear as might be expected in a poet who described men–women relations as "fitting Actives to Passives".

Also significant in the present context, however, is the more widespread colonization of Ireland that occurred in the sixteenth century, followed by the unification of the Scottish and English crowns in 1603, and the founding of the first Ulster plantations a mere five years later. The emergence and eventual territorial expansion of Modern English, from 1500 onwards, is exactly coterminous, then, with the new economic and political expansion of Modern England. One advantage of the term "anglophone" (within the primarily linguistic parameters of this discussion) lies in its compatibility with this link. One may even view the evolution of the England / English complex in terms of a huge parabola, moving broadly from "land of many languages" (as in sixteenth-century Britain) to "language of many lands" (the case of twentieth-century English).

If we thus briefly regard Britain as identical with the entire "British Isles" (as it was, with varying degrees of legitimacy, for much of the Modern English period), then its linguistic profile has changed dramatically. During the sixteenth century, the following languages were widely written or spoken over this area: English, Scots, Scots Gaelic, Irish, Welsh, and Latin; to this should be added more local tongues such as Cornish, Manx (on the Isle of Man), Norn (the variety of Old Norse spoken in the Shetlands), and French (in the Channel Islands): in other words, "land of many languages". The story of twentieth-century English, on the other hand, is probably too familiar to need repeating here. In the British Isles today, Welsh hangs on grimly, whilst the other indigenous languages have either disappeared or become threatened species; English, however, is recognized as an official language by almost a third of the 190-odd member states of the United Nations: in a nutshell, "language of many lands". The concept of post-colonial writing, then, or whatever the category one chooses to complement or replace it, should also take these "stories of English" into account.

In spite of all these considerations, however, the term "anglophone literature" also has one grave disadvantage. The present study, like those of so many earlier critics and theorists, began in search of a term which would include all literature written in the many varieties of English, but exclude "native English" writers (although probably not Black British ones) and American writers (although arguably not African Americans, or any of the various minority literatures of the United States). These are complex but precise parameters, although it may be hard to find a suitable term.

"Anglophone literature" would thus presumably denote all creative writing in the English language, unless one is to succumb once again to the kind of double standard implied by the term "Commonwealth literature". Whether we like it or not, then, anglophone literature must surely include Lawrence, Golding, and Faulkner, as well as Gordimer, Atwood, and Frame. It logically extends from Earl Lovelace to Anita Brookner. The problem is how – without special pleading or arbitrary value judgements (however tempting) – to bypass two vast literary traditions in order to find more space for the fine writers located outside them. In the crudest terms, how does one attain the goal (which many would doubtless approve) of more Ngũgĩ wa Thiong'o and less Kingsley Amis?

A simple response, on the basis of careful examination, might be that there is no entirely suitable label for the concept, not even "anglophone literature" itself. The latter nevertheless seems an advance on any of the other four terms reviewed. Beyond the purely practical considerations advanced in the Preface, moreover, the supplementary trope of the "stepmother tongue" may offer a means of displacing or excluding (without recourse to double standards) the two oldest literary traditions of writing in English.

To begin at the beginning: the conventional concept of writing in the *mother tongue* may seem self-explanatory, even if – on closer inspection – this often proves not to be the case. There are, on the other hand, an enormous number of writers who have consciously chosen, accepted, modified, subverted, and even rejected or abandoned the English language. English, for many, was never a tongue automatically possessed; it was laboriously learned rather than painlessly acquired. By a simple kinship analogy, one may therefore speak of the *stepmother tongue*. In folk-tales from many cultures, moreover, relations between children and stepmothers are almost invariably fraught; the corresponding connections in the field of anglophone literature are often no easier.

The above analogy does not imply that individual "stepmother-tongue" writers necessarily experienced practical difficulties at the simple level of English usage (although this is certainly the case with a Tutuola, and even a Conrad). But there are countless other writers who express narratives of ambivalence or even resistance to the language, from Jamaica Kincaid (who comments in her novel *Lucy* on the irony of the ex-slave reduced to using the very language of the master) to James Joyce (whose hero Stephen in *Portrait of the Artist as a Young Man* undergoes a sense of linguistic alienation before his English Dean of Studies). It is in fact possible to record a virtually infinite range of strategies by which writers have first *adopted* and then *adapted* the "stepmother tongue". Since these same writers are now widely read and appreciated, moreover, they may also be assumed to have found viable solutions to the linguistic dilemmas confronting them. Risking accusations of slickness, then, one may even posit a kind of three-stage evolutionary process in terms of "adopt", "adapt", and "adept".

One could actually construct a broad taxonomy for all modern writing in English, in terms of "mother" and "stepmother tongue". Such a model would at some points supplant divisions by geographical regions, an approach that is often banal and unwieldy, for cultural hybridity and physical displacement are endemic in the modern anglophone writer. The amount of cross-reference required in a survey arranged on purely regional lines is daunting. The alternative model would need to be sensitive to both historico-geographical dimensions and current socio-linguistic realities. To emphasize the latter, one could introduce the terms "land" and "language" (which is either "ours" or "theirs"), where the first noun denotes a sense of place and the second a cultural identity. To emphasize the former, one might use the admittedly Eurocentric categories of "New" or "Old" literatures in "New" or "Old" worlds. The parallel sets of co-ordinates each allow four different combinations, and thus four broad categories of English-language writers. The taxonomy would correspond to the table as set out below and elaborated in the pages that follow:

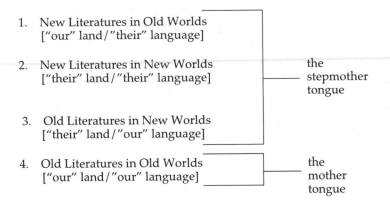

1. New Literatures in Old Worlds
    ["our" land / "their" language]

2. New Literatures in New Worlds
    ["their" land / "their" language]   the
                                                         stepmother
                                                         tongue

3. Old Literatures in New Worlds
    ["their" land / "our" language]

4. Old Literatures in Old Worlds   the
    ["our" land / "our" language]   mother
                                                         tongue

The paradigms proposed here are tentative, and certain initial reservations should be entered at once for each of the three sets of co-ordinates from which they are constructed. The concepts of "our" / "their" and "land" / "language" probably lack the force of a coherent theoretical model. Merely the high dependence on quotation marks hints at the problematic nature of these four combinations as objective cultural or linguistic markers. It is nevertheless impossible to ignore the frequency and prominence of "land" and "language" as simple *leitmotiv* in the eighty novels analysed in this study; had space permitted, moreover, it would have been possible to provide eighty more texts (and perhaps even eighty more authors) where the two dimensions have the same thematic significance.

The analogous co-ordinates of "old" or "new" literatures in "old" or "new" worlds would seem more conceptually viable, although the labels should be used with an ironic awareness of the Eurocentric perspective they imply – the terms are not far removed, after all, from the kind of cultural solecism that has Columbus "discovering" America. They are surely justified by definition in the present context, however, since the constant referent is the English language (evolving in its early modern version on a damp little North *European* island five centuries ago). The first explicit anticipation of this paradigm in post-colonial studies seems to occur in an essay from 1984 by Stephen Gray referring (in a predominantly South African context) to "Old Literatures in New Places" and "New Literatures in Old Places", although Gray does not develop this classification further.

The four logical combinations available here find more recent parallels in the readiness of some post-colonial theorists to think in terms of "First", "Second", "Third" or "Fourth-World" literatures. Critics such as Alan Lawson and Stephen Slemon have thus borrowed and modified the three original categories (for Lawson, "Second-World" applies to white settler-colonial writing), whilst the neologism "Fourth-World" commonly refers to indigenous or *first-nation* authors anywhere. "First" and "Third" World, on the other hand, have retained their original political sense, although Aijaz Ahmad (most notably) has attacked this particular binary construct. Precise demarcation lines between "old" and "new" literatures and worlds, then, are understandably complex, but the divisions themselves are helpful and therefore retained as section headings in this study.

The model will nevertheless stand or fall on the concept of the stepmother tongue, although the latter might at first glance seem suspiciously like yet another binary construct, now privileging the "white" writing of England or the United States (the biological children, as it were) as more "natural", "authentic" or "validated". For various reasons, however, this would be a myopic and reductive reading. It is a fact that the stepmothers of fairy-tales have a universally bad image, but it is equally true that poet and children's author Debjani Chatterjee (quite literally) and various other postcolonial writers (indirectly) have cheerfully drawn on the same metaphor to express their relation to the English language.

Of greater interest here, however, are the potential revisions of the stepmother trope. With the new fluidity and flexibility of family structures in the West at the end of the millennium, for example, there is no reason why the "stepmother" should not be a positive force, and why the child of divorced parents should not have *two* largely undifferentiated mother (or indeed father) figures: the comparable sense of cultural enrichment for an anglophone writer possessing "mother" and "stepmother" *tongues* hardly requires further emphasis.

More relevant still are the literary recuperations of the stepmother, such as that offered by Indian author Suniti Namjoshi's "The Little Prince" (*Feminist Fables*, 1983). Here, rather than undergo some trite mutation from "wicked stepmother" to "paragon of virtue", Namjoshi's protagonist simply attempts to replace the king's incompetent and decadent heir with her own highly gifted biological daughter. Or, to complete the analogy, the vernacular feminism of a Merle Hodge or Erna Brodber challenges the corresponding forms of literary succession.

The most significant revision of all in the context of the stepmother tongue may nevertheless regard modern responses to the fairy-tales themselves. Both Bruno Bettelheim's psychoanalytical readings in *The Uses of Enchantment* (1976) and Maria Tatar's structural analyses in *The Hard Facts of the Grimms' Fairy Tales* (1987) argue conclusively that the mother and the stepmother of traditional fairy-tales are in fact one and the same person; or more precisely, that the child projects onto the stepmother unresolved feelings of hostility towards the biological mother. The corresponding literary analogy could apply quite literally to a writer such as the Nigerian Zaynab Alkali ("I find writing in English is agonizing, to say the least"); for it is perhaps the act of *writing* itself, (in either English or Alkali's native Hausa which is really agonizing. In a broader perspective, however, the now widely perceived unity of mother and stepmother in the fairy tale may be taken to (pre)figure the merging of mother and stepmother tongue in present or future literary practice. In the title essay of *Imaginary Homelands*, Rushdie views the issue with his customary penetration:

> Those of us who do use English do so in spite of our ambiguity towards it, or perhaps because of that, perhaps because we can find in that linguistic struggle a reflection of other struggles taking place in the real world, struggles between the cultures

within ourselves and the influences at work upon our societies. To conquer English may be to complete the process of making ourselves free.   (p. 17)

But, as Rushdie goes on to explain, the British Indian writer, at least, does not have the option of rejecting English, anyway. His, or her, children probably speak it as a first language, which then becomes central in the forging of a British Indian identity. Mother and stepmother are indeed identical.

The remainder of the Introduction attempts a brief taxonomy of anglophone fiction according to the terms proposed and reviewed here.

*   *   *

1.   NEW LITERATURES IN OLD WORLDS
[*our land/their language*]

This category would cover all those writers for whom English is truly an alternative language, whether second, third or more. It would thus include three broad groups: Asian writers; African writers; and indigenous writers of Canada, South Africa, Australia, New Zealand and the South Pacific. In every case, stable and long-established local societies (in present terminology, "our" land or *Old Worlds*) were disrupted by Anglo-Saxon (predominantly British) imperial enterprises. For historical reasons that require no elaboration here, every writer in this category should possess (theoretically at least) one or more indigenous languages beside English, in which he or she could have written. Some actually did or now do so, but most of them use "their" language (English) to produce the *New Literatures* which arouse such widespread interest today. Whether adopted or rejected, then, English may here quite seriously be considered as a kind of stepmother tongue.

The two major literary traditions of anglophone writing in this context are those of India and Nigeria, with other South Asian countries standing in a subordinate relationship to India much as

the rest of anglophone Africa does to Nigeria. India, as a federation
of twenty-five states and seven union territories, originally recog-
nizing fifteen constitutional languages beside English, has a demographic and linguistic complexity which ensures a continuing role
for this language, even fifty years after independence. It is not possible to calculate exactly how many people use English daily, or
how many are able to read it. Some estimates on either score,
however, yield a figure in excess of the corresponding numbers for
Britain itself. Any consideration of anglophone Indian authors
should therefore emphasize their precise individual relations with
the English language.

Instructive examples, here, are provided by the three giants of
Indian anglophone fiction: Narayan, Rao, and Anand. R. K.
Narayan, on his own affirmation, speaks and writes Kannada well
(and Tamil even better), but never found time to write in either
(although, in a literary career spanning some sixty years, such
claims may seem ingenuous). Raja Rao has a partly similar South
Indian linguistic background, and speakers of Kannada are
constantly aware of the language's presence behind a novel such
as *Kanthapura*. Mulk Raj Anand, finally, explains that the dialogue
of *Untouchable* is almost completely translated from Punjabi or
Hindustani. Among other writers, Bhabani Bhattacharya cites
Bengali as the medium of his thoughts and dreams, whilst English
is an *alien* language to struggle with. For Anita Desai, with a multi-
lingual background of Bengali, German, Hindi, and Urdu, English
is a less traumatic alternative. The stepmother tongue trope cannot,
of course, be applied uniformly or literally – Rushdie is unlikely to
produce a novel in Urdu or any other Indian language – but its
varying degrees of applicability to so many writers is highly suggestive: they show a high correlation, for example, with Bharati
Mukherjee's well-known categories of "expatriate", "immigrant"
and "semi-assimilated" authors.

Whether because of historical reasons, linguistic policies, or mere
lack of numbers, no other Asian country can rival the depth and
variety of Indian fiction in English, although this does not diminish
the interest or importance of anglophone writing in, say, Pakistan,
Sri Lanka, Singapore, or the Philippines. The prominence of India
in Asian anglophone writing is, moreover, broadly analogous to
that of Nigeria on the African continent. This country is a federation of fifteen states, and although considerably smaller than India
in area and population, not far behind it in ethnic and linguistic

complexity. The major difference from India in this particular context, however, may lie in the socio-linguistic profile of the English (or "englishes") used in the country: English is thus the medium of instruction for virtually all higher education, but at the same time – if in very different forms – it has long provided a highly functional *lingua franca* for trade throughout much of West Africa. This linguistic diversity is reflected in Nigerian novels in English.

The latter have an enormous stylistic range. At one extreme may be found the popular Onitsha market literature, the folkloristic idiosyncrasies of Amos Tutuola, and, more recently, the linguistic experiments of Ken Saro-Wiwa. Cyprian Ekwensi is the most versatile in his presentation of various *englishes*, Gabriel Okara the most uncompromising in his attempt to suggest an African language in English. Elechi Amadi and Flora Nwapa are celebrated for novels of African life in the pre-colonial phase; T. M. Aluko for novels of disillusion set after independence. The versatile Buchi Emecheta also deals on occasion with the colonial period, although historical setting for her is generally subordinate to gender relations. Achebe provides masterly syntheses of European and African fictional techniques, while Soyinka's narratives (particularly *The Interpreters*) come closest to the existential novel of European tradition. Other countries of so-called anglophone Africa, except perhaps South Africa itself, tend to fall under the shadow of Nigeria, just as the rest of South Asia is dwarfed by India.

Attitudes to English among African anglophone writers – from Achebe's easy acceptance to Ngũgĩ's categorical rejection of the language – vary even more than among their Asian counterparts. In South Africa alone, Mongane Wally Serote admits frankly that he is not "English-speaking", a fact brought home to him clearly by his reading of the English press; whereas the short-story writer Can Themba claimed that he knew no indigenous African language.

This subgroup would also feature the growing number of indigenous writers from the old "settler" colonies. Black South African writers could logically be placed in this category, although one thinks more readily of Australia's Mudrooroo Narogin or New Zealand's Witi Ihimaera and Patricia Grace in this context. Other writers from the South Pacific include Papua New Guinea's foremost novelist Russell Soaba, and writers of Polynesian origin such as Albert Wendt (Samoa/New Zealand) or Epeli Hau'ofa (Tonga). Here, too, the co-ordinates of "our" land/"their" language should be applied with restraint: Ihimaera (like most Maori authors) writes in English, the language he knows best, although one of the strongest challenges to the hegemony of English comes paradoxically from the controversial Keri Hulme, whose links with New Zealand's minority culture are based on total cultural solidarity but one-eighth Maori ancestry. Such anomalies need not, however, invalidate the potential of the model.

2.   NEW LITERATURES IN NEW WORLDS
[*their land/their language*]

One category conspicuously privileged by post-colonial theory is the extensive literature of exile and diaspora, a writing which thus implicitly suggests, at least in the Eurocentric view, *New Literatures* in *New Worlds* and also corresponds, in some sense, to the co-ordinates of "their" land/"their" language. Its two main sub-divisions, according to the present model, are Afro-American and Afro-Caribbean fiction. To these groups, however, one should also add many writers of the Indian diaspora, drawn chiefly from the Caribbean, the South Pacific, and East Africa. The question of which writers in these groups can genuinely call on a second language as a potential literary medium is extremely complex. Hurston and Walker have used Black English Vernacular; Afro-Caribbean novelists from V. S. Reid and Earl Lovelace to Merle Hodge and Olive Senior have introduced, with varying success, representations of Caribbean creole; writers of the Indian diaspora, finally, from Moyez Vassanji to Ismith Khan, show different degrees of proximity to their own cultural and linguistic heritage.

The majority of writers in this category nevertheless have no other language, in a literal sense, as a potential alternative medium. In view of the traumatic experience of slavery, however, with segregation on ethnic lines and the historical suppression of African languages, it seems ironic to speak of English unreservedly as a mother tongue. Pursued to its logical extreme, the implication is that even for a Toni Morrison, the greatest contemporary black American author, English might *symbolically* be seen as an alien one. Paradoxically then, even those writers of the longest and greatest diaspora, the Afro-American exile, could be aligned with varying degrees of literalness within the co-ordinates of "their" land/"their" language.

Afro-Caribbean fiction is presumably less controversial with regard to the present model. "Their" language in this context is clearly the metropolitan English of colonial officialdom; "our" language, on the other hand, is best applied not to African or pre-Columbian traces, but to the remoter points on the creole continuum celebrated by countless contemporary Caribbean novelists. Edward Kamau Brathwaite has written at length of a Caribbean *nation language* that is only English in terms of certain lexical features; the alternative medium of standard English, on the other hand, is for Jamaica Kincaid simply "the language of the criminal who committed the crime", truly a stepmother tongue. The significance of "their" land, on the other hand, bearing in mind a two-hundred-year-old prose tradition of exilic writing from Olaudah Equiano to Caryl Phillips, hardly needs further discussion here.

There is, however, an additional body of writers who are the product of a "double exile". After the abolition of slavery, Caribbean plantation owners solved the resulting labour crisis by introducing contract workers from India under the so-called "indenture system". It is this movement which largely accounts for the particular ethnic mix of Trinidad and Guyana, with Fiji, Mauritius and South Africa, among other countries, also acquiring large Indian populations by the same process. When writers with this diasporic background then migrate to Britain, North America, or Australia, therefore, one could speak of a "double exile". The category would include Samuel Selvon (from Trinidad to Britain and eventually to Canada); Ismith Khan (from Trinidad to the United States); V. S. Naipaul (from Trinidad to Britain); or Satendra Nandan (from Fiji to Australia). In every case, one may continue to use (if less literally than with African or Asian writers) the trope of the stepmother tongue. In the following category, too, the term is still applicable, although it must now undergo a radical semantic shift.

3. OLD LITERATURES IN NEW WORLDS
[*their land/our language*]

This category applies broadly to writers of European descent in what were once called the "Dominions" and are now sometimes akwardly referred to as the old "settler colonies": Australia, New

Zealand, Canada, and South Africa. The four countries, in certain respects, divide conveniently into pairs.

Australia and New Zealand are similar in their geographical situation, their large white English-speaking majorities, their now correspondingly small aboriginal populations, and their history of European settlement in the nineteenth and twentieth centuries. Canada and South Africa are less homogeneous (not least for the latter's large black majority), although they each contain, in addition to one mainly anglophone population of European origin, another substantial white ethnic group, speaking an Indo-European language and claiming a colonial history considerably longer than that of their English-speaking neighbours. Here, however, similarities end. Culturally speaking, there is little cross-fertilization between francophone Quebec and English-speaking Canada (the classic image here is that of the "two solitudes"). Yet paradoxically, Afrikaans-speaking South Africans, after nearly two centuries of political or military conflict, have – in literary terms at least – important links with their anglophone counterparts. Breytenbach, for example, translates his own work into English, whilst Brink, who originally wrote only in Afrikaans, now publishes in both languages.

The great majority of anglophone writers in these countries nevertheless possess English as a mother tongue, by any current definition, although (particularly in Canada) there are fascinating exceptions to the rule: Rudy Wiebe is the child of German-speaking Russian Mennonites and began studying English at school; Frederick Grove, born Felix Greve in Germany, learned the language as an adult; for both of these authors, then, English is in some sense a stepmother tongue. For most white writers in all four countries, however, the significance of the trope is that English was an alien language *not* to those who used it, but rather to the *new environment on which it was imposed*. The "stepmother tongue" thus becomes an epistemological rather than a merely linguistic concept. The classic *topos* here is that of the nightingale: sub-Keatsian romantic effusions were difficult in countries – like Australia or New Zealand – where the bird was unknown. Brathwaite's surreal equivalent is the colonial school essay in which snow falls on the canefields. Such reductive examples are also, of course, the most literal illustrations of *Old Literatures* in *New Worlds*. But even a contemporary poet such as Canada's Dennis Lee speaks of "beginning with a resistant, external language"; while, in the context of prose

fiction, Canadian novelist Robert Kroetsch has described the experience of inhabiting a "mandarin language" that lacks roots in the
New World landscape, or quite simply of "writing a new country
in an old language". The same discrepancy between "land" and
"language" is also an important subtext in the fiction of David
Malouf, Randolph Stow, and – above all – Keri Hulme.

These metaphorical extensions apart, however, many older classics of Australia, New Zealand, Canada, or South Africa fit quite
convincingly into a European, or even metropolitan English, tradition. Many writers would have been flattered at the suggestion that
they were perpetuating the traditions of an Old Literature in a New
World. Such critical arguments are not intended as exercises in neo-
colonial expropriation, but merely indicate that, among many
writers themselves, the notion of the *stepmother* tongue may be irrelevant, and that of the *mother* tongue self-evident. The Australian
novelist Henry Handel Richardson thus spent most of her creative
life outside Australia, and aspired quite consciously to the native-
English realist tradition. Only a handful of Katherine Mansfield's
short stories have a New Zealand setting, and the writer herself
(outside her own country at least) is seen more frequently as a
European modernist than as a New Zealand regionalist.

In contrast to the upholders of transplanted European traditions,
on the other hand, there emerge key authors in each of these countries who are more conspicuously indigenous talents: Henry
Lawson in Australia; Frank Sargeson in New Zealand; H. C.
Bosman in South Africa; and, to a lesser extent, Stephen Leacock in
Canada. All of these figures have a particular local appeal, and variously emphasize the vernacular or the proletarian, the anecdotal or
the humorous. In every case, there are strong analogies with Mark
Twain and what the latter achieved for the American West. Or, in
present terminology, "their" land for these writers very soon
becomes "our" land; whilst the concept of the "stepmother tongue"
– never meaningful in a purely linguistic sense – fast loses its epistemological application, too, as the writer successfully inscribes the
high veld, the prairie, or the bush.

As the first section of this model suggested, however, all four of
the settler colonies also have major indigenous writers for whom
English was, once at least, quite literally "their" (i.e. a foreign)
language, just as the country was quite literally "our" land (before
European expropriation). It is therefore tempting to regard the
(*ex*-European) Australian, New Zealand, Canadian or South

African literature of "contact" – with the land, and most crucially, with the peoples already inhabiting it – as somehow particularly central to the respective literary traditions of these countries. The list of writers with a strong double awareness of this kind is impressive. It includes Xavier Herbert, Patrick White, David Malouf and Thomas Keneally in Australia; Noel Hilliard and Keri Hulme in New Zealand; Rudy Wiebe and W. O. Mitchell in Canada; and (inevitably) every white writer in South Africa.

4. OLD LITERATURES IN OLD WORLDS
[*our land/our language*]

The concept of the stepmother tongue holds good for Asian, African, Caribbean, and African-American writers, and can even (with a little ingenuity) be applied to the "white writing" of the old settler colonies. It is surely *a priori* inapplicable, however, within the category suggested by the co-ordinates of *Old Literature* in *Old Worlds*, or, more loosely, "our" land / "our" language: the latter terms, in fact, are surely no more than equivalents of *mother* country and *mother* tongue. The present section is not, however, aimed at merely disqualifying the mainstream British and American literary traditions. It attempts instead to challenge certain commonly held assumptions about the centrality of "English Literature"; and also to deconstruct national identities, whether by examining the traditional elision of England and Britain, or by actually separating out Scotland, Ireland, and Wales.

In Scottish fiction, for example, Scott and Stevenson are effectively bilingual writers, and have their modern counterparts in Irvine Welsh (English and Scots) or Iain Crichton Smith (English and Gaelic). Central to this discussion, too, is Lewis Grassic Gibbon's trilogy, *A Scots Quair*, offering the paradox of a work which may be read in either of two languages, English or Scots. Bilingualism among Irish novelists, on the other hand, is less common, with the exception of Flann O'Brien and Liam O'Flaherty, although many writers, from Joyce onwards, have expressed their ambivalence towards the English language. The Anglo-Welsh tradition, finally, has been strongest in poetry, although Caradoc Evans and Glyn Jones – whilst only publishing in English – open fascinating perspectives on the language in terms of an alien tongue.

For most Scottish, Welsh, or Irish twentieth-century novelists, of course, bilingualism in the strictest sense is not an issue; English is the only feasible language, although in many cases it may still be regarded, psychologically at least, as a foreign one. Poets seem to have understood the situation most clearly, with Edwin Muir suggesting that "Scotsmen feel in one language and think in another", or John Montague describing the Irish countryside as "a manuscript / We had lost the skill to read". Brian Friel's play "Translations" is the seminal text here. Whether or not they are included in the first section with their Asian and African counterparts, therefore, Scottish, Welsh or Irish writers are also effectively operating in "our" land (Scotland, Wales or Ireland) with "their" language (English). For in this respect, I see no essential difference between Joyce and Rushdie, or – through their common rejection of the English language – Beckett and Ngũgĩ.

The United States has always been characterized by a far greater ethnic diversity than Britain, and as different groups have become increasingly articulate in recent years, traditional concepts of a unified American literature have been further challenged. Within this broad field, a new prominence has been attained not merely by African American literature, but by Chicano, Native American, and various Asian American literatures. Among these constellations, only Chicano literature has a number of major writers regularly using another language (although even here, Spanish is increasingly giving way to English). For none of these groups, however, does the English language have the nature of a cultural given, as it does for a privileged white Anglo-Saxon establishment.

The Black English Vernacular (BEV) used by such African American authors as Zora Neale Hurston and Alice Walker is regarded by many scholars as having had a parallel but independent development from standard American English. (Its position would thus be broadly analogous to that of Scots in relation to the English of England.) Other black writers are ostensibly monoglot, but since (as previously suggested) their ancestral languages were suppressed through linguistic segregation and forced assimilation during slavery, the notion of English as a "mother tongue" has a certain ambivalence. Native and Asian Americans, on the other hand, have often "only" been forced to abandon English for economic reasons; *chicanos* are frequently bilingual (or as likely to be monolingual in Spanish as in English). For all of these groups, however, it is justifiable to speak in terms of the stepmother tongue.

The lessons of American literature invite us, incidentally, to reconsider the apparently holistic concept of (native) English litera-ture. The King's English is one of several broadly equivalent terms once used to describe a particular form of English. The point of res-urrecting an obsolete and discredited label is to emphasize that this variety was certainly never that used by the majority of his sub-jects. One may thus question to what extent the King's (or Queen's) English was truly the "mother tongue" of a regional novelist such as Hardy or a proletarian one like Lawrence. Both writers spoke and wrote local dialects fluently, and would not have acquired their metropolitan English without effort. Among contemporary novelists, Alex Miller, winner of the prestigious Commonwealth Writers' Prize for his novel *The Ancestor Game* (1993), describes (from the distance of Australia) the disadvantages of growing up speaking Cockney in the English underclass.

POSTSCRIPT: INTERNATIONAL AND TRANSCULTURAL

The four previous sections will have difficulty in accommodating certain novelists. Salman Rushdie (an Indian who finally emigrated to Britain in 1965) and V. S. Naipaul (a Trinidad Indian who arrived in 1950) are among the most distinguished novelists writing in English today. Both are often regarded as "British writers", and yet neither fits unambiguously into the present model. They are by no means the most complex examples of international or transcultural identity. Where, otherwise, should one place a novelist born in Persia (now Iran), raised in Southern Rhodesia (now Zimbabwe), living intermittently in South Africa, and finally settling in England; or a writer of Dutch extraction, born and raised in Sri Lanka, but educated in England before eventually moving to Canada? (The writers in question are, of course, Doris Lessing and Michael Ondaatje.) Rushdie himself has referred to cosmopolitan writers of "modern migrant tales".

A final category, then, would be a tentative list of novelists who, because of their transnational affiliations, do not fit easily into any of the previous sections. The British and American prototypes of this tendency are Conrad and Nabokov, respectively, but there are numerous more recent examples. Readers will doubtless create and justify their own lists, although the epilogue to this study suggests two broad categories around which most of these transnational writers, or tellers of "modern migrant tales", could be conveniently grouped. Within these parameters, a token ten representative novels have been chosen, culminating with Rushdie's *Midnight's Children*, in so many ways an exemplary text.

In conclusion, it is worth returning briefly to the semantic anomaly noted earlier in this section (according to which "English" refers both to a literary language *and* to an ethnic identity). Instructive parallels may be drawn at this point with the cultural history of another imperial power: ancient Rome. *Latin literature* refers objectively to literature written in the Latin language rather than literature written by "Latins" (a people originally occupying part of the Tiber valley from the early Iron Age); the term is particularly attractive since the referent is now almost exclusively linguistic. It thus includes writers of such widely varying ethnic origins as Seneca, Martial and Lucan (Spain), Ausonius (Gaul), Apuleius (Africa) and Phaedrus (Thrace), besides Lucretius and Petronius (birthplace happily unknown); the major common denominator of these writers is the fact of their having written in Latin, in most cases a learned language, if not a "stepmother tongue". One longs for a term as neutral as "Latin literature" for the present context, in which *England* – to paraphrase its greatest writer – is too much with us.

An equally striking analogy may be drawn from the cultural history of the English Renaissance. Some scholars of the period regard the literature in English from the Age of Shakespeare as belonging to a subsidiary tradition. The intellectual mainstream appears in another, less familiar body of literature, written in Latin. More's *Utopia* is virtually the only work from this corpus to have infiltrated the traditional English canon. If Modern English (in terms of dissemination and prestige) has something of the privileged position of Latin, then, Renaissance English may have had more in common than is generally allowed with such vernacular languages as Yoruba or Gikuyu. The tables may yet turn again (in a country like Malaysia, they have already done so), with English once more being relegated to a marginal role.

A combination of these two historical perspectives offers a final useful lesson. "English" literature could one day follow its Latin predecessor, although not in terms of dissemination or cultural significance (this it may have done already) but by a similar semantic shift: for the linguistic referent of "English" is already surely outstripping the "cultural" or "ethnic" one, and could one day supplant it entirely; or, in other words, "English literature" may yet come to refer primarily, if not exclusively, to literature written in the English language, rather than literature produced within a specific area or by a particular ethnic group. Even the English themselves, incidentally, could soon go the way of the original Latins. Until then, the term anglophone (modified by the concept of the *stepmother* tongue) remains a viable alternative.

FURTHER READING

The classic introduction to post-colonial literature is *The Empire Writes Back* (Routledge, 1989) by Bill Ashcroft, Gareth Griffiths and Helen Tiffin; the same authors have also produced a compendium of texts (many heavily abridged) entitled *The Post-Colonial Studies Reader* (Routledge, 1995). Elleke Boehmer's *Colonial and Postcolonial Literature* (Oxford, 1995) is ultimately more "colonial" than "post-colonial" in scope, and complements rather than supplants *The Empire Writes Back*.

The two leading theorists in the field are still Homi K. Bhabha, editor of the essay collection *Nation and Narration* (Routledge, 1990), and author in his own right of *The Location of Culture* (Routledge, 1994); and Gayatri Chakravorty Spivak, author of *In Other Worlds* (Routledge, 1988) and *The Post-Colonial Critic: Interviews, Strategies, Dialogues*, ed. Sarah Harasym (Routledge, 1990). If one reads only one critical study in the field, however, this must be Edward Said's highly accessible *Culture and Imperialism* (Vintage, 1993).

The hegemony of current theoretical orthodoxy is challenged both by Aijad Ahmad's *In Theory: Classes, Nations, Literatures* (Verso, 1992), which drives a few neat wedges between (so-called) "post-" and (*de facto*) "neo" colonial studies; and by Sara Suleri's *The Rhetoric of English India* (Chicago, 1992), emphasizing complicity rather than conflict in colonial and post-colonial relations.

The comprehensive *From Commonwealth to Post-Colonial*, edited by Anna Rutherford (Sydney: Dangaroo Press, 1992) is not, as its title might suggest, a record of changing theoretical paradigms, but a fine selection of papers from the Silver Jubilee conference of the Association for Commonwealth Literature and Language Studies (University of Kent at Canterbury, 1989). It gives a good idea of the range and depth of scholarly activity in the field. A more representative collection of essays generated by post-colonial theory is the recent *New National and Post-Colonial Literatures. An Introduction*, edited by Bruce King (Oxford University Press, 1996).

In an explicitly linguistic context, *The Story of English* (Faber, 1988) may be supplemented by the more specialised *English Around the World*, edited by Jenny Cheshire (Cambridge University Press, 1991) and *A Survey of Modern English*, by Stephan Gramley and Kurt-Michael Pätzold (Routledge, 1992). An invaluable source book is Kenneth Katzner's *The Languages of the*

World (Routledge, 1986); a useful additional guide is Suzanne Romaine's *Language in Society* (Oxford University Press, 1994).

The present study draws frequently on interviews with writers themselves, whether read with or against the grain. Collections from specific regions are noted in the appropriate section, but the finest global collection is Feroza Jussawalla and Reed Way Dasenbrock's *Interviews with Writers of the Post-Colonial World* (Jackson: University Press of Mississippi, 1992), with anglophone novelists from five continents.

[Please note that the Afterword contains more extended discussion of some of the works mentioned here.]

Part I
New Literatures in
Old Worlds

1

Asia

INDIAN FICTION

An appreciation of Indian fiction in English is enhanced by an awareness of certain historical, cultural, and linguistic factors often unfamiliar to readers outside South Asia. Of these three elements, the most fundamental is certainly the linguistic one, particularly with respect to the English language.

For a population of about 900 million, India has sixteen constitutional languages, including Hindi, the official language since 1965, and Sanskrit, the ancient liturgical language of Hinduism. Almost a third of the population (mostly in north-central India) speak Hindi, which may be linked with nine other constitutional languages, all Indo-Aryan like Hindi and derived from Sanskrit. These include Punjabi (with 25 million speakers), Kashmiri (3 million), and Sindhi (2.5 million) in the north-west; Gujarati (45 million) in the state of Gujarat, and Marathi (65 million) in Maharashtra – including Bombay – in the west; Bengali (70 million speakers) in West Bengal, with the closely related languages of Oriya (30 million) in Orissa, and Assamese (15 million) in Assam, all in the east. Less localized is Urdu, state language of Jammu and Kashmir but also spoken by some 50 million Indian Muslims. Until independence, and the calculated "sanskritization" of India's "national" language, Hindi and Urdu were virtually identical (apart from their different alphabets), and known collectively as Hindustani.

The south of India has four major languages belonging to the Dravidian group: Telugu (70 million speakers), official language of Andhra Pradesh in south-east India; Kannada or Kanarese (35 million) in Karnataka in the south-west; Malayalam (35 million) in Kerala on the Malabar coast; and Tamil (60 million), spoken in the southern state of Tamil Nadu, including Madras. These last three languages are to some extent mutually intelligible, although Telugu is more distant, whereas all four are quite remote from Hindi and the other Indo-Aryan languages of the north.

There is no space to mention India's several hundred other languages, but a passing comment is necessary on the *written* forms of the major fifteen. Hindi, like Marathi, uses the Devanagari alphabet of Sanskrit. Bengali and Assamese employ a slightly modified version, Gujarati a more distant one, of the same script. Punjabi and Oriya both have quite distinctive alphabets. Urdu is written in a Perso-Arabic script, whilst Kashmiri and Sindhi use either the latter or Devanagari. In the south, Telugu, Kannada, and Malayalam have different versions of the ancient Grantha script, while Tamil relies on an alphabet quite unlike any of these.

The consequences of such a complex linguistic situation are easy to imagine. A Kanarese shopkeeper or Keralan taxi-driver may understand something of the language spoken in neighbouring Tamil Nadu, but will certainly not read it. Educated southern Indians will have studied Hindi, but probably prefer to speak English in Delhi. A Bengali or Gujarati is highly unlikely to know a Dravidian language. Such factors may help to explain the practical value of India's sixteenth constitutional language: English.

English in India is still the main language of higher education, the media, or international (and sometimes inter-state) communication. It is difficult to calculate how many Indians effectively use it as a "major language" (such terms as "native language" or "mother tongue" are not very useful here), but estimates vary between 1 and 10 per cent. The latter suggestion sounds absurdly inflated, and would make English India's most widely spoken language after Hindi. A figure of 5 per cent, on the other hand, would place it together with Gujarati and above Punjabi at the exact half-way point in a table of the constitutional languages (with Sanskrit excluded). Even a 1 per cent tally would mean three times as many English as Kashmiri or Sindhi speakers. On the other hand, its significance as a first language is small: with only 1.3 million people claiming it as their mother tongue (according to the 1980 census), English occupies in the scale of Indian languages a modest 67th place.

Ultimately, of course, such data are unhelpful, since English is almost invariably a *second* language in India and a knowledge of it is a function of social class and educational level, rather than national or geographical origin. More relevant is the fact that virtually all Indian writers can (and many *do*) write in an indigenous language. And even if they do not, their fictional characters certainly could. The writer therefore faces the technical problem of indicating (and even representing) one or more Indian languages, together with the complex shifts between these and perhaps English ("code-switiching" in the jargon) which characterize Indian social life.

Several major Indian writers have made illuminating remarks about English and their relation to it. Mulk Raj Anand thus recalls a comment of H. G. Wells on hearing nationalist politician Krishna Menon speak in London in the 1930s:

> A very eloquent man! I can't speak as well as he does, I am a mere Kentish man; once a haberdasher's assistant; learnt to speak and write English the hard way. But you fellows speak very clearly, and for all to hear. We mumble, bumble, grumble.[1]

Anand recalled this meeting almost fifty years later, but neither personal nostalgia nor characteristic Wellsian obtuseness can obscure the point: there is often a hyper-correctness and conservatism in Indian English which goes hand-in-hand with highly idiosyncratic local usage.

An apparent easy mastery of the language may, however, be deceptive. Anand's great contemporary Bhabani Bhattacharya notes ironically:

> I have heard of Indian writers who not only write in English but think and dream in English! I have never been blessed with such an attainment. Bengali is the medium of my thoughts and dreams. When I seek to express myself in the alien tongue, I am unconsciously deep in the process of translation.[2]

Bhattacharya explains his practice of using literal translations of Bengali or Hindi words, "even if it is contrary to English usage or idiom". In his student years, in fact, he normally wrote in Bengali. Anand, too, describes writing in a language "in which the echo of my mother tongue, of my native speech, and of native consciousness could be heard". He cites the example of replacing the English idiom "Get the Hell out of here" with a literal translation from the Punjabi, "Go and eat the air." Of his novel *Untouchable* (1935), for example, up to 90 per cent of the dialogue is allegedly translated from Punjabi or Hindustani.

R. K. Narayan, although choice of language rarely seems an issue in his fiction, claimed in an interview that he wrote Kannada well (and Tamil even better), but had simply never found time to produce a novel in either. Kannada is also the language of Raja Rao, the third great classic author of the Indian English novel; Rao nevertheless thought that his native Kannada was "never adequate", and would have liked to write in Sanskrit. He confessed to Feroza Jussawalla and Reed Way Dasenbrock that he had once written a novel in Kannada, but then translated it into English ("and it seemed much better").[3] Speakers of Kannada find Rao's first novel, *Kanthapura* (1938), a virtual translation from the indigenous language, in the manner of Anand's *Untouchable*.

Language is but one issue illustrating the complexity of Indian life; one could discover a similar diversity in other contexts, religion being only the most obvious example. After the increasingly secular West, India will always strike the visitor (or reader) as a profoundly spiritual country. This is not the place for a long disquisition on Indian religions, but a number of the country's anglophone writers are unequivocally Hindu, Muslim, or Sikh; there are classic novels about the trauma of partition, for example, from each of these perspectives. The novelist Sudhindra Ghose was born into an established Christian family; Nissim Ezekiel, perhaps India's finest contemporary English-language poet, is Jewish. A feature of the modern Indian novel in English, on the other hand, is the number of writers with a Parsi background. These include Rohinton Mistry, Farrukh Dhondy, Firdaus Kanga and Boman Desai.

A broader view of Indian history and culture over the last fifty years brings a similar sense of distance from other countries with an anglophone literary tradition. Although there is interesting historical fiction, the vast majority of Indian novels deal with twentieth-century life. And here, it is remarkable how distinct Indian perspectives remain from British, American, or Australasian ones. The Second World War (occasionally referred to dismissively as "Churchill's war against Hitler") is thus relatively marginal; a few Indians served with the Allied forces; a few more took the opportunity of fighting in a liberation army under the Japanese; a larger number probably noted with interest how the seemingly impregnable Britain was humiliated in Asia by another non-Western nation (undoubtedly a further stimulus to the drive for independence); the vast majority of the population can have barely registered these events at all, however, their conditions of poverty and exploitation remaining largely unaltered.

Far more important in Indian eyes than the "world" war, of course, was the rising nationalism of Gandhi and his supporters in the 1930s, with the *Quit India* movement that began a decade later. And yet it has been plausibly suggested that even the idea of independence to many Indians, who had after all absorbed the British as creatively as they had assimilated earlier occupying powers, must have been less sensational than Gandhi's call for the abolition of the caste system. And in more recent times, the historical events that seem to have left the greatest impression on Indian English fiction (partition apart) are the two wars with Pakistan, the conflict with China, and Indira Gandhi's "State of Emergency" in the 1970s: events about which most non-Indian readers remain profoundly ignorant.

Similar cultural gaps between the Indian and non-Indian reader also open in other contexts. A knowledge of the Sanskrit Vedic tradition is as important for a full appreciation of Raja Rao's *The Serpent and the Rope* as Christianity is to understanding many European classics. Shashi Tharoor's masterpiece, *The Great Indian Novel*, has a far closer and more ingenious relationship to the Indian epic of the *Mahabharata* than Joyce's *Ulysses* has to Homer's *Odyssey*. But these specific instances of major literary models are ultimately less significant than the constant lesser analogies and associations that come naturally to all Indian writers and their characters. Saleem Sinai, Rushdie's protagonist in *Midnight's Children*, thus proudly displays his knowledge of the other great Hindu epic, the *Ramayana* (even if he actually confuses the myth of its origin with that of the *Mahabharata*); Mrs Rupa Mehra regularly interrupts her search for a "suitable boy", in Vikram Seth's novel of the same name, to take consolation from the *Bhagavad Gita*.

In a final gesture towards the wealth and variety of Indian English fiction, however, one inevitably returns to the language issue. In the more gruesome fairy-tales (and India has plenty of them), the ugly stepmother is eventually killed off. Many assumed that this would be the fate of English in India after the country's independence. And yet for reasons already suggested it remains as important as ever in both literature and public life. In drama, India has never had a viable English-language tradition. Its poets, in turn, must always be prepared to defend their choice of writing in an "alien" language; there is an implied parallel with Scotland here (although English is obviously closer to Scots than to any Indian language), where writers have been said to think in one language but feel in another. But the prose tradition flourishes, even if an increasing number of the most celebrated contemporary anglophone novelists now belong to the great Indian diaspora.

The prestigious *Sahitya Akademi*, India's national academy of letters founded in 1954, awards annual prizes to literary works of great merit in any of twenty-two languages. Anglophone novelists already honoured include Anand, Rao, Narayan, Bhattacharya, Nahal, Anita Desai, Joshi, Sahgal, Seth, Ghosh, Deshpande, Sealy and Bond (the last two being Anglo-Indian). By an ironic twist, however, short-listed works in the less accessible languages are often translated into English for the judges' benefit.

The outsider finds it difficult to gauge the strength of literature in the Indian languages. It is nevertheless common to hear Indian colleagues (even those with a vested interest in English) claim in general terms that Indian literature in the indigenous languages is "better", "greater", or "more interesting" than that in English. There is certainly an older fictional tradition in these languages, admirably surveyed in Meenakshi Mukherjee's *Realism and Reality: The Novel and Society in India* (1985). Two fairly short and easily available anthologies of modern Indian writing allow the non-Indian reader to go a little way towards forming independent judgements: the *Penguin Book of Modern Indian Short Stories*, where three items are English originals and the remaining fifteen have been translated; and the *Penguin New Writing in India* (covering prose and verse), where just a dozen of fifty-five authors are represented by pieces originally written in English.

And yet, if not another word were ever written by an Indian in English, the wealth, variety and significance of writing already available would ensure that Indian English writing never ceased to be a serious object of study.

THREE INDIAN NOVELISTS

The three classic representatives of twentieth-century Indian English fiction are Anand, Rao and Narayan. Having begun publishing in the 1930s and continued over six decades, all three writers remain a constant presence. If Anand is strongly political and Rao essentially metaphysical, then Narayan – perhaps the most famous of the three – is also the hardest to classify: regarded variously as moralist, satirist, or regionalist, he is also capable of inspiring the most patronizing and absurdly ethnocentric comparisons, as when he is regarded as a kind of Indian Jane Austen.

An obvious starting-point is **Mulk Raj Anand**; for although all three authors have been productive for so long, the most significant fiction of Narayan and Rao is comparatively recent, whilst the

Anand novels often regarded as his best are also the earliest. Anand differs most obviously from his great contemporaries in his humbler social background and North Indian origins. Born in Peshawar (now Pakistan) into a family of Hindu coppersmiths, he studied at the University of the Punjab and later at the University of London. As a writer, he is always sensitive to his double cultural heritage, a point that emerges nowhere more clearly than in his first and most accessible novel, *Untouchable* (1935).

The narrative follows twenty-four hours in the life of the young Bakha, camp cleaner with a British regiment in the Punjab. An existence only occasionally lightened by the sympathy of a regimental sporting hero or a British Salvation Army officer is later briefly transformed at a political rally attended by the great Gandhi.

Anand resolves the issue of speech presentation (his characters are primarily Punjabi or Hindustani speakers) by regularly transliterating proverbs, curses, or insults, and having occasional recourse to Punjabi or Hindustani words. A hint of Indian English phonology appears, too, in Bakha's awe for European "fashun" or in his desire to become an English "gentreman". There is a certain poignancy when Bakha finds even in a British military barracks "glimpses of another world, strange and beautiful"; but more than having a simple "English-apeing mind", Bakha has a thirst for literacy that could be satisfied by being able to read even his native Punjabi, far less English. Deprivation is not seen entirely in terms of colonial exploitation, and in one passage of authorial intrusion, Anand allows an intellectual bystander at the Gandhi rally to draw an analogy between British suppression of India, and the higher Indian castes' own repression of the lower castes.

The ideology behind the novel, in fact, is often as much Marxist as nationalist. The narrative focus fluctuates deftly between the naive perspective of the young Bakha and the sharper vision of informed political analysis. Only at the end of the novel is the balance between analysis and action disturbed, when Anand allows first a long political harangue from a bystander for the benefit of a listening peasant, and finally a debate between an Oxford-educated lawyer with a monocle and a local poet in flowing robes: a not particularly subtle confrontation of traditional and Westernized Indian attitudes. What began as an effective and highly concentrated naturalist narrative (condensed into the space of twenty-four hours) now turns into a rather verbose and self-consciously clever kind of Shavian debate.

After studying in London, Anand came into contact with Gandhi in the 1930s. *Untouchable* was partly written at the latter's Sabarmati Ashram, and later revised and shortened on Gandhi's advice. Here and in the two following novels, *Coolie* (1936), an epic of proletarian labour, and *Two Leaves and a Bud* (1937), on the exploitation of Indian tea-workers, Anand remains a strongly politicized writer. The early novels were followed by a trilogy on the life of Lal Singh, a young Punjabi peasant, with *The Village* (1939), *Across the Black Waters* (1940) – a major war novel – and *The Sword and the Sickle* (1942). After *The Big Heart* (1945), about the pressures on traditional coppersmiths from the new factories, Anand began a series of auto-biographical novels including *Seven Summers* (1951) and *Confessions of a Lover* (1976).

Anand's constant awareness of both the European and the Indian intellectual traditions provoked his famous reference to "the double burden on my shoulders, the Alps of European tradition and the Himalaya of my Indian past". What is an elegant enough analogy, however, may have an unintended irony: as the more self-consciously Indian Rao would certainly have noted, some Himalayan passes are actually higher than many Alpine peaks.

Raja Rao is undoubtedly the least known outside his native country of the three great Indian English classics. Regrettably, critical reputations are not based exclusively on literary merit, however, and can sometimes be influenced by the sheer availability of a writer's work in the West. Narayan is more fortunate here, since most of his fiction is currently in print outside India; of Anand, on the other hand, it is difficult to find anything but the early *Untouchable* and *Coolie*. Rao, finally, is served worst of all, since locating any of his novels requires considerable investment in time and energy. This is unfortunate, since *Kanthapura* (1938) is even more interesting than *Untouchable*, to which it is partly analogous, both in its study of Gandhian influence on socially marginal groups, and in its consistent representation in English of an Indian language (Kannada for Rao; Punjabi for Anand). Rao has also produced the graceful metaphysical novella *The Cat and Shakespeare* (1965), the ironic portrait of an Indian communist, *Comrade Kirillov* (1976), and the massive trilogy, beginning with *The Chessmaster and His Moves* (1988), on which he is presently at work. But unless a future complete version of the *Chessmaster* removes current widespread critical perplexity, *The Serpent and the Rope* (1960) will remain Rao's most important, and perhaps also his most quintessentially Indian, narrative.

The protagonist of the latter refers to his "sad and uneven chronicle of a life" (p. 231), and, in one sense, the novel is pure autobiography. Ramaswamy, a "provincial Brahmin from Mysore" (like the author), is writing a thesis on the Cathar heresy, whilst living in Aix-en-Provence with a French wife, in a marriage which eventually fails through what officialdom crassly describes as "incompatibility of temperaments". The autobiographical element is primarily spiritual, however, and co-exists with a powerful, often mystical, sense of place. The significance here of Rama's visit to Benares for his father's funeral rites, or his pilgrimage to Hardiwar and the sources of the holy Ganges, is self-evident. The inclusion of Europe in this spiritual order, on the other hand, can seem overly systematic: Paris is thus a kind of Benares (equally holy because all roads begin from *Notre Dame*), the Rhône is a spiritual "sister" to the Ganges, whilst the South of France (Provence or Languedoc) is often equated on cultural and historical grounds with Rama's (and Rao's) native Southern India.

The same schematic quality reappears in the metaphysical structure of the novel. The symbolism of the title is normally read as the expression of a conflict between "East" and "West", or Indian and European systems of thought. As the novel's only extended reference to the symbolism of serpent and rope suggests, however, this is a partial over-simplification. Rama assures his wife Madeleine that "The world is either unreal or real – the serpent or the rope" (p. 335). His own metaphysics always begins from the self as the only reality, and stresses the ultimately illusory nature of everything beyond it; for the Cathars that are the subject of his research, on the other hand, one might suggest that the world was too much with them – their spiritual error deriving from this undue emphasis on the external world.

Even such brief comment suggests that a vast amount of esoteric knowledge is required for a full appreciation of *The Serpent and the Rope*. Referring to his Brahministic formation, Rama recalls reading the *Upanishads* at the age of four (!), although the novel's true inspiration lies in the even earlier Hindu *Vedas*. Sanskrit quotations from these sacred hymns alternate constantly in the narrative with references to the later Indian epics of the *Mahabharata* and *Ramayana*. In anglophone literature beyond India, it is rare to find a text so inseparable from a metaphysical tradition. In the case of the poet Yeats, for example, generations of readers have learned to extract the poetry from the "system"; with *The Serpent and the Rope*, such a process is more difficult. In evaluations of Rao as an *Indian* writer in *English*, therefore, it will normally be the first of these elements that prevails.

R. K. Narayan, the last of the three titans, is perhaps the best known Indian anglophone novelist. He is also so prolific and apparently inexhaustible that it is difficult to propose one novel as more representative than the rest. In other ways, Narayan is less intractable, however, since – like Anand and Rao – he has a clear linguistic profile. Born in Madras, a Tamil-speaking city, he was the son of a headmaster in the old autonomous state of Mysore, now incorporated into modern Kannada-speaking Karnataka. Narayan spent his teens in Mysore, but studied at the University of Madras. His socio-economic background and South Indian, Kannada-speaking, heritage link him with Rao (an acquaintance for many years) rather than to the North Indian (Punjabi- and Hindustani-speaking) artisan origins of Anand.

Narayan is often described as a regionalist, a critical distinction being sometimes made between two kinds of regional novel: one where a stable and clearly defined area becomes a microcosm of the great world beyond, and another in which the chosen environment is under threat from external forces. Normally set in or near the fictional town of Malgudi (based on the city of Mysore), Narayan's "timeless" novels belong typically to the first of these categories.

The author's *oeuvre* is conventionally divided into three periods, the first of which includes the three light and strongly autobiographical novels, *Swami and Friends* (1935), *The Bachelor of Arts* (1937), and *The English Teacher* (1945), together with an uncharacteristically sombre portrait of a Hindu marriage in *The Dark Room* (1938).

Around the 1950s Narayan then produced a sequence of genial novels which many critics regard as his best: *Mr Sampath: The Printer of Malgudi* (1949 / 1955); *The Financial Expert* (1952); *Waiting for the Mahatma* (1955); *The Guide* (1958); and *The Man-Eater of Malgudi* (1961).

The third group of novels, written by a Narayan greatly mellowed but still – in the words of one critic – "in step with a fast-changing world", includes: *The Vendor of Sweets* (1967); *The Painter of Signs* (1976); *A Tiger for Malgudi* (1983); *Talkative Man* (1986); and *The Grandmother's Tale* (1992). The latter is, incidentally, the first work not set in the author's fictional Malgudi. In addition to this already extensive output, Narayan also produced many volumes of short stories, from *Malgudi Days* (1943) to *Under the Banyan Tree and Other Stories* (1985). More specifically, *The Guide* also represents a minor fictional tradition in Indian writing, home or abroad (Naipaul's *The Mystic Masseur* and Cyril Dabydeen's *The Wizard Swami* are other examples), which satirizes the fraudulent *guru* or *pundit* and his gullible audience.

Raju, the novel's protagonist, having recently completed a two-year jail sentence for forgery, takes refuge at a deserted shrine and is promptly adopted as a *swami* by the nearby village. Most of the narrative consists of a night-long account of his past life. Son of a Malgudi shopkeeper, Raju had neglected the family business to work as a tourist guide, later becoming infatuated with Rosie, the neglected wife of a wealthy academic client. Rosie was also an unfulfilled classical dancer, and – in an increasingly fantastic development – Raju had launched his lover on a successful artistic career, before finally being arrested for forging her signature. This long confession fails to shake the faith of his audience, and Raju now begins a career as a very different kind of guide, administering to the spiritual and material needs of an impoverished and drought-stricken rural community. By the end of the novel, his own rather spurious teachings have rebounded on him, as he finds himself committed to a twelve-day fast, together with a programme of ritual bathing, in order to bring rain.

Narayan's novels have a fair sprinkling of words from Indian languages (whose meaning is either glossed or apparent from the context). The English of his dialogues, on the other hand, is clearly not metropolitan, although it often has great *refinement*. The latter term may be understood both in the sense of "delicacy" or "sensitivity", but also in that of a certain "reductiveness" or "minimalism", associated with Narayan's general predilection for irony and understatement. Only occasionally is there a more studied attempt at language representation, as when Raju internally reproaches Rosie's neglectful husband:

"Oh monster, what do you do to her that makes her sulk like this on rising? What a treasure you have in your hand, without realizing its worth – like a monkey picking up a rose garland!"   (p. 69)

Such passages are obvious transcreations of dialogue conceived in an indigenous language. On some occasions, this produces minor linguistic anomalies. The uncle who comes to try and dislodge Rosie from Raju's house thus addresses her "in the singular or something lower" (a syntactic choice hardly available to English), while the young Raju is first sent to school for using bad language (an incomplete "Son of a..."), at which point the literal-minded reader is tempted to ask bad *which* language?

These apparently minor details nevertheless touch on a central paradox of Narayan's writing. It is possible to read many of his novels without finding any indication of an almost four-hundred-year-old British presence in India (*The Guide* has a single reference to the statue of an obscure Englishman), with the sole exception – admittedly a very large one – that the language of expression is English. Elsewhere, however, it is not English alone that provides the linguistic paradox of *The Guide*. The implied language of the text is presumably Tamil, although the fictional Malgudi and its surroundings would be basically Kannada-speaking areas. The ultimate impression of Narayan's fiction, however, is of a world so utterly and undefinably "Indian", conceived in a language which is so idiosyncratically but incontrovertibly English.

Narayan is undoubtedly more popular with the general reader than with the post-colonial theorist; and yet, always within the author's own parameters, *The Guide* will actually support a plausible post-colonial reading. Rosie's (Nalini's) skill as a dancer (when she is no longer repressed by Marco), together with that as an organizer (once she avoids the exploitation of Raju), may be read as an allegory of Empire, with the colonized finally achieving a double independence. It is a suitable final hypothesis for a novel of extreme subtlety, full of ambivalently motivated guidance: Raju the tourist guide, Raju the impresario guide, and – lastly – Raju the spiritual guide. Above each and all of these manifestations, moreover, hovers Narayan himself, a writer whose gentle satire suggests an essentially conservative spirit, but also a final unexpected manifestation of the guide.

Anand, Rao and Narayan were not the only Indian English novelists to have begun writing by the 1930s: K. S. Venkataramani, largely forgotten today, is interesting not just for the early date of his novels of rural life – *Murugan the Tiller* (1927); *Kandan the Patriot* (1932) – but also for the fact that he translated this work into his native Tamil. K. Nagarajan, another Tamil and a close associate of E. M. Forster, published two contrasting novels – the family saga, *Athawar House*, and the provincial tale *Chronicles of Kedaram* – the former as early as 1937.

The period from the late forties to the mid-fifties saw novels by G. V. Desani and Sudhindra Ghose, as well as marking the appearance of three even more significant writers: Bhabani Bhattacharya, Kamala Markandaya and Khushwant Singh.

G. V. Desani occupies a unique position in Indian fiction. An exact contemporary of Anand, Rao, and Narayan, he published only one novel, *All About Mr Hatterr. A Gesture* (1948), republished as *All About H. Hatterr* (1951) and subsequently reissued in several other revised editions. Desani was born in Nairobi, Kenya, and educated privately, before settling in England and eventually arriving in India in 1952. He thus provides an early example of a kind of "double exile" now common among younger writers of Indian origin. In 1968, Desani was appointed professor of philosophy at the University of Texas, Austin. *All About H. Hatterr,* describing the education of an Anglo-Malayan orphan by a succession of Indian wise men, has been widely acclaimed as an *avant-garde* literary text in the parodic, anti-novelistic tradition of Sterne's *Tristram Shandy.*

Born into a Bengali Christian family, Sudhindra Ghose also belongs to an older generation of Indian writers who made a career abroad before returning to India. His more traditional autobiographical fiction, replete with myth, archetype, and allegory, appeared in a sequence of four books: *And Gazelles Leaping* (1949), *Cradle of the Clouds* (1951), *The Vermilion Boat* (1953), and *The Flame of the Forest* (1955). Today, Ghose is even less read than Desani.

Bhabani Bhattacharya is of more interest than either, not least because his earliest published writings (mostly for children) appeared in his mother tongue of Bengali. After graduating with an Indian degree, he spent much of the 1930s at the University of London. International fame arrived with the harrowing *So Many Hungers!* (1947), based on the Bengal famine of 1942–3 when the subcontinent was still under British rule. This was followed by the lighter *Music for Mohini* (1952), on the perennial Indian theme of traditional *versus* modern values, before a return to the realistic mode with *He Who Rides a Tiger* (1954), where attention now turns from incompetent foreign rule to native injustices and corruption. There is a fourth novel with the largely self-explanatory title, *A Goddess Named Gold* (1960), before a very late (and very bad) afterthought, *A Dream in Hawaii* (1978), where an Indian professor turned *yogi* attempts to heal the ills of American society without due awareness of his own imperfections.

The most substantial novelist of this generation, both in the light of a thirty-year writing career and also for some of the novels themselves, is **Kamala Markandaya**. Markandaya worked as a journalist in India, before marrying an Englishman and moving to Britain where she has lived for some forty years. Her first and best-known novel was *Nectar in a Sieve* (1954; see below), followed by a sequence of books which won the novelist respect rather than acclaim. They include *Some Inner Fury* (1955), about an Indian girl and her English lover during the pre-independence years; *A Silence of Desire* (1960), on the rivalry between modern and traditional medicine; *A Handful of Rice* (1966), returning to the rural world of *Nectar in a Sieve; The Coffer Dams* (1969), on the theme of neocolonization in India; *The Nowhere Man* (1972), on an Indian student and freedom-fighter in London; *Two Virgins* (1973), again set in rural India; *The Golden Honeycomb* (1977), on relations between the British and the old Maharajas; and *Pleasure City* (1982), about a multinational company's exploitation of the South Indian coast.

Kamala Markandaya is sometimes regarded as having lost her Indian roots, without having found any alternative literary sustenance, although the writer herself protests that "the eyes I see with are still Indian eyes". Her first novel may be identified with a large group of narratives in English which David Craig (referring to Lewis Grassic Gibbon's *A Scots Quair*) has called the novel of peasant crisis. If the classic realist novel is linked with the rise of the modern bourgeoisie and the advance of industrialism, then it also reflects the simultaneous decline, and even destruction, of traditional rural society. The latter process has many fictional representations, from Thomas Hardy to Claude McKay, from Elechi Amadi to Kamala Markandaya.

Nectar in a Sieve is narrated by Rukmani, wife of the landless South Indian peasant Nathan, and mother of seven children. Rukmani is exceptional in her environment by being literate (in contrast to Raj's female peasant narrator in *Kanthapura*), and at one point even attempts to earn a living as a letter-writer. Her father is also the village headman, and the novel records his gradual eclipse by the local government collector, reflecting the author's characteristic concern with changing social and economic conditions.

As the youngest and plainest daughter of a large family, Rukmani is married without a dowry and begins a life of unspeakable hardship and poverty on land held by an absentee landlord. Her sufferings seem likely to increase when she only produces one daughter in many years, before treatment from an English doctor helps her to produce a succession of six sons. A virtually timeless rural existence is disrupted by the building of a tannery, located symbolically on the *maidan* or open space of the community. Rukmani sees this as the beginning of the process that will destroy the "sweet quiet of village life" (p. 50), which can only "wilt in the blast of the town". The tannery nevertheless brings material prosperity, providing jobs for two of Rukmani's sons until they are dismissed for organizing a strike.

Rukmani's idealization of rural life is surprising in view of the tremendous hardships it involves: an early monsoon that destroys the entire rice crop, a long drought which forces her to relinquish all surplus food and even the family shirts and saris; a traditional Zamindari landlord who eventually sells out to the tannery and drives his ageing tenants from the land. Two of Rukmani's sons emigrate to become tea-workers in Ceylon, and another leaves to work as a servant in the city; she has no further contact with any of them. A fourth son is beaten to death by night-watchmen at the tannery, whilst the youngest dies of malnutrition during yet another crop failure (although the daughter has prostituted herself to provide food for him). Only the fifth son survives to support his now widowed mother and unmarried sister.

Indian fiction, like Indian society itself, is striking for its regular combination of great spirituality and chronic poverty; the sombre *Nectar in a Sieve* contains many examples of such penury. But the ability to be satisfied with so little also has a questionable side, and Markandaya provides a contrasting Western perspective in Kenny, the sympathetic but outspoken doctor who befriends the villagers:

> I work among you when my spirit wills it. ... I go when I am tired of your follies and stupidities, your eternal, shameful poverty. I can only take you people ... in small doses   (p. 74)

There is a recurrent ideological clash between Rukmani's stoic resignation and Kenny's forthright resentment. As the doctor suggests on another occasion. "Never mind what is said or what you have been told. There is no grandeur in want – or in endurance" (p. 115).

In the second half of the novel, inconceivable as it may seem, the trials of Nathan and Rukmani intensify, and the novel's epigraph from Coleridge, "Work without hope draws nectar in a sieve, / And hope without an object cannot live", provides both the initial and the definitive comment on Markandaya's bleak vision.

The same heroism from a simple and humble protagonist characterizes the early fiction of **Khushwant Singh**, a London-trained lawyer with a long journalistic career behind him. Khushwant has published several collections of short stories and three novels. *Train to Pakistan* (1956) is the classic account of Indian Partition in 1947; *I Shall Not Hear the Nightingale* (1959) is the story of a Sikh family, set at the same period; whilst *Delhi* (1989) is a massive historical evocation of the Indian capital through various points in its history.

Events prior to or during partition in 1947 produced a number of fictional accounts, including Attia Hosain's *Sunlight on a Broken Column* (1966), Chaman Nahal's *Azadi* (1975), and Bapsi Sidhwa's *Ice-Candy-Man* (1988), by a Muslim, a Hindu and a Parsi, respectively. Most haunting of all, however, is *Train to Pakistan* by the Sikh Khushwant (perhaps not surprisingly, since the Sikh homeland of the Punjab saw some of the worst bloodshed, and remains divided to this day).

The novel's great achievement is to integrate the microcosm of the small frontier village with the macrocosm of religious and political forces dividing the subcontinent, while obliquely suggesting some possible readings for one of the great tragedies of twentieth-century history. The opening section of the novel thus recreates the frontier village of Mano Majra, inhabited in equal proportion by land-owning Sikhs and their Muslim tenants, together with a single Hindu, Ram Lal the money lender, subsequently butchered by local *dacoits*.

Communal relations in Mano Majra are good until the shadow of sectarian violence falls over the village with the arrival of a "ghost train" from neighbouring Pakistan, full of butchered Sikhs and Hindus. A fragile equilibrium is now destroyed by the arrival of living refugees, intent on physical reprisals. It is at this point that magistrate Hukum Chand, sanctioning a minor injustice in the hope of avoiding a greater one, releases the five *dacoits* arrested for the murder of Ram Lal, letting the villagers assume that this crime had actually been committed by a group of Muslims recently fled to Pakistan. This action increases communal tensions, so that Sikh leaders reluctantly demand the temporary evacuation of Muslim villagers to the nearby refugee camp; the authorities (headed by Hukum Chand) have already anticipated that this will lead to the safer expedient of a permanent move to Pakistan.

Further evidence of massacres in the area appears when the monsoon-swollen river sweeps more butchered Hindu and Sikh corpses past Mano Majra. A group of Sikh commandos arrives to incite the villagers, who eventually agree to ambush a refugee train bound for Pakistan and slaughter its Muslim passengers. A local Sikh thug, who has personal motives for preventing the massacre (his Muslim lover is on the train), intervenes successfully, but loses his own life in the process.

Train to Pakistan is an obvious indictment of religious fanaticism of any kind, whether Hindu, Muslim, or Sikh; but it simultaneously suggests the difficulty of supplementing local loyalties with the broader secular values necessary for social and political stability. Khushwant also offers an indirect critique of male psychology in a narrowly masculinist society. When a Sikh officer remarks ponderously, "One should never touch another's property; one should never look at another's woman" (p. 135), the basic relation between the sexes could not be clearer. The novel does not, however, deal in crude stereotypes, but abounds in the contradictions and paradoxes of character which distinguish the classic realist tradition. Meet Singh, guardian of the Sikh temple and a voice of moderation, is not a saint-like figure, but a work-shy peasant who wanted an easier life; Iqbal, the Western-educated and politically conscious revolutionary, is totally inadequate to the situation; the only heroic gesture comes from Juggut Singh, the designated *budmash* or villain ("All governments put me in jail").

Train to Pakistan is still widely read in India, but difficult to obtain in the West. This is undoubtedly our loss.

The 1950s also saw the debut of two writers who, in their different ways, were both highly alienated from India, although similarities between them end here. Balachandra Rajan was born in Toungoo, Burma (Myanmar) and graduated BA, MA, and PhD from Trinity College Cambridge, before making a career in the Indian Foreign Service and the United Nations. His only two novels, *The Dark Dancer* (1958) and *Too Long in the West* (1961), deal with the eternal Indian theme of cultural conflict between East and West; the title of the second may in fact be read as an ironic comment on the author's own position.

A more fruitful exploitation of the clash between East and West appears in the work of historian and autobiographer, Nirad Chaudhuri. Born in Kishorganj, East Bengal (now Bangladesh), and therefore having Bengali as his first Indian language, Chaudhuri is celebrated for his substantial *Autobiography of an Unknown Indian* (1951) and the shorter but genial *A Passage to England* (1959). His most controversial work, however, is *The Continent of Circe: An*

Essay on the Peoples of India (1966), noted by one critic for its "pathological detestation of everything Indian"; for this reason it is sometimes linked with V. S. Naipaul's travelogues, which similarly offended Indian sensibilities. Not a novelist at all, the caustically eloquent Chaudhuri is undoubtedly the greatest single Indian loss to a "novel-only" survey of this kind. It is less known, however, that Chaudhuri began his writing career with short stories in his native Bengali, and returned at the end of his life to the same form and language.

A third writer who actually made her debut at the end of the 1950s is Nayantara Sahgal. Her chronological position here is in some ways surprising, since she has written fiction over four decades, and is better known for more recent novels. As the niece of Nehru, she had first-hand experience both of the Quit-India movement and of less edifying post-independence politics. Variously labelled a "political" writer (for her concern with the morality of India's ruling elites) and a "feminist" one (for her attention to women's issues), she has written a long series of increasingly sophisticated novels: *A Time to Be Happy* (1958), *This Time of Morning* (1965), *Storm in Chandigarh* (1969), *The Day in Shadow* (1971), *A Situation in New Delhi* (1977), *Rich Like Us* (1985), *Plans for Departure* (1986), and *Mistaken Identity* (1988).

The 1960s, in turn, produced two minor classics (the only novels by their respective authors), and also marked the beginning of three more subtantial literary careers. The minor classics are M. Anantanarayanan's *The Silver Pilgrimage* (1961), an amusing pastiche of travelogue and chronicle, and Ved Mehta's *Delinquent Chacha* (1966), a double-edged satire on the experiences of an Indian in America. The significant literary careers are those of Manohar Malgonkar, Arun Joshi and Anita Desai.

Manohar Malgonkar is another author who is widely read in India, but receives little attention outside. Born into a Marathi-speaking Brahmin family in Bombay, the author was also the grandson of the Dewan in the ruling house of Indore, and spent ten years as an officer in the Indian Army (rising to the rank of Lieutenant Colonel). Malgonkar's inside knowledge of both institutions is openly reflected in his fiction, beginning with *Distant Drums* (1960) on the military life, and continuing with *The Princes* (1963) on the decline of India's many royal houses. His best known novel, however, is *A Bend in the Ganges* (1964), another account of both the Indian Freedom Movement and the tragedy of Partition that succeeded it. Malgonkar subsequently turned his attention to earlier history with a novel on the Indian Rebellion of 1857, entitled *The Devil's Wind* (1972).

Also ranked highly in India, but less read elsewhere, the more innovative Arun Joshi produced five novels before a premature death in his early fifties. *The Foreigner* (1968), a study in alienation, owes a debt to Camus's *L'Étranger* (1942), and perhaps to Colin Wilson's *The Outsider* (1956). His four later novels, more explicitly Indian in theme, include his masterpiece, *The Strange Case of Billy Biswas* (1971), moving between Indian elite society and the tribal world; *The Apprentice* (1974), an experimental narrative in a series of monologues by a civil servant who has become corrupted; *The Last Labyrinth* (1981), plotting the existential crisis of a millionaire industrialist; and *City and the River* (1990), a modern parable of material and spiritual values.

The third author to begin writing in the 1960s, **Anita Desai**, is also – with the possible exception of Kamala Markandaya – India's first important female novelist. Another woman writer sometimes linked with Desai, incidentally, is Ruth Prawer Jhabvala, of whom it is nevertheless legitimate to ask whether she is an Indian writer, at all. Born in Cologne of Jewish parents, she moved to England in 1939 and graduated from London University, before emigrating to India with her Parsi husband in 1951. After a series of (admittedly fine) novels with Indian settings and mainly Indian characters, she moved to the United States in 1976. On the basis of this career, she is discussed at greater length in the epilogue.

Desai is a key example of a novelist who is difficult to place in simple national categories. She has claimed to *feel* about India as an Indian, but *think* about it as an outsider, although it is a superficial Western perspective that harsher Indian critics sometimes find in her fiction. In any event, she must be regarded as more Indian than Jhabvala. Born at Mussoorie (in what is now Northern Uttar Pradesh) of a Bengali father and German mother, she was brought up in the multi-lingual Delhi of pre-partition days. If Hindi and Urdu were the commonest languages around her and German was technically her "mother tongue", Desai has nevertheless written exclusively in English. In her early twenties, the novelist married and moved to another cosmopolitan environment, that of Bombay, the city which provides both title and setting for her most ambitious work to date.

Her early novels, *Cry, the Peacock* (1963) and *Voices in the City* (1965), both follow the lives of orthodox Hindu women trapped under the weight of convention; *Bye-Bye Blackbird* (1968) portrays the ambiguous relationship of two Indians with their mother country. The following novels, *Where Shall We Go This Summer* (1975), *Fire on the Mountain* (1978), and the highly regarded *Clear Light of Day* (1980) all pursue variations on the family-bound woman. These were followed by Desai's first novel to feature a male protagonist, *In Custody* (1984), and the impressive *Baumgartner's Bombay* (1988). It was the latter novel which finally gave Desai the perfect opportunity for exploiting something of her own cultural marginality. The eponymous hero of the novel is a German Jew who manages to escape the Nazi persecutions of the thirties and make his way to India, where, after six years' internment as an enemy alien, he attempts to build a new life.

Baumgartner's constant sense of deracination is reflected primarily through language, and Desai repeatedly emphasizes the kind of linguistic no-man's-land inhabited by her protagonist. The second chapter is thus a long evocation of a Berlin childhood, as the comfortable Jewish bourgeois existence of the Baumgartner family slowly disintegrates. In linguistic terms, the young child's existence is shaped by the menacing associations of German, a Yiddish he barely understands, and the forbidding Hebrew sounds of the *Torah*. Desai's most original touch here is to provide an oblique commentary on Baumgartner's childhood by inserting regular snatches of German nursery rhymes, pointedly left untranslated. For while the rough sense of these verses is mostly clear to the English-speaking reader, such insistence on a foreign language brilliantly recreates for the reader something of Baumgartner's own sense of linguistic alienation in India.

Cultural and linguistic identity are inseparable, as Baumgartner the virtual orphan sets about "building a new language" (p. 92) in his adopted land. And as his mother's old maxim suggested, this process tends to occur on other people's terms: "*Stiefkinder müssen doppelt artig sein*" – Stepchildren must behave doubly well. The attempts of the "orphan" Baumgartner to master the "stepmother tongue", and with it a new environment, are not crowned with success. His most intimate moments of human fellowship are spent with his fellow expatriate, Lotte the dancer, who nevertheless warns him: "Let us face it, *Liebchen*, there is no home for us" (p. 81). His only other regular interlocutor in Bombay is the café proprietor Farrokh, a Gujarati-speaking Parsi, and thus another linguistically and culturally marginal figure. Beyond that, he lives exclusively for the collection of stray cats that fills his apartment.

By a suggestive example of narrative architectonics, Baumgartner meets his nemesis while trying to help the young drop-out Kurt, a fellow German and therefore a product of the very culture that has persecuted him. This gesture of solidarity towards a co-national is based on broad humanitarian urges rather than any nationalistic sentiment, however, for Baumgartner now regards even German as an alien tongue: "the language was slipping away from him, now almost as unfamiliar as the feel and taste of English words or the small vocabulary of bastardised Hindustani that he had picked up over the years" (p. 150).

Baumgartner's individual exile overlaps, finally, with the massive twin exodus of Muslims and Hindus produced by the partition of India in 1947, and Desai's novel thus becomes a moving *requiem* for all displaced persons on the subcontinent (and elsewhere) in the latter half of the twentieth century.

The 1970s were relatively lean years for new talent, but nevertheless marked the debut of two important if totally contrasting novelists, Chaman Nahal and Bharati Mukherjee.

Chaman Nahal, born in Sialkot (now in Pakistan), is already noted as author of the partition novel *Azadi* (1975), where the most traumatic episode of modern Indian history is now narrated from a Hindu perspective; Nahal's second novel, *The English Queens* (1979), provides a satirical exposé of a traditional target, Anglicized Indians. These two works were followed by *The Crown and the Loincloth* (1981), *The Salt of Life* (1990) and *The Triumph of the Tricolour* (1993), a Gandhian trilogy. Mukherjee, on the other hand, is an Indian writer whose links with her native country are increasingly tenuous. Born and educated in Calcutta, she earned an American PhD and has lived most of her adult life in Canada and the United States; discussion of her novels is therefore deferred to the epilogue.

The 1980s, on the other hand, saw a veritable avalanche of fine new Indian English writing. Emerging authors, in order of seniority, include Shashi Deshpande, Salman Rushdie, Boman Desai, I. Allan Sealy, Rohinton Mistry, Shashi Tharoor, Amitav Ghosh, Upamanyu Chatterjee and Firdaus Kanga. Rushdie, whose little-known first novel *Grimus* actually appeared as early as 1975, is the most influential – and arguably the most talented – of all contemporary Indian English writers. *Midnight's Children* was published in 1981. Since Rushdie moved to Britain definitively in 1965, however, he is further discussed in the epilogue with other tellers of "migrants' tales" (the phrase itself is his).

Among the remaining members of the group, Boman Desai (the United States), Sealy (Australia and New Zealand), Mistry (Canada), and Kanga (Britain) may also be regarded as part of the extraordinary modern Indian diaspora. Since all Mistry's fiction to date is emphatically Indian in setting, he is discussed below, together with the other four writers in the list. Such national or regional classifications have an arbitrary element in the case of Mistry, while even Tharoor and Ghosh are hardly rooted to their "native soil". Deshpande and Chatterjee, on the other hand, have a more permanent Indian base, in Bangalore and Delhi, respectively.

Shashi Deshpande was born in Dharwad, in the Southern Indian state of Karnataka. She has written some seventy short stories and six novels, beginning with *The Dark Holds No Terrors* (1980), and followed by *If I Die Today* (1981), *Come Up and Be Dead* (1982), and *Roots and Shadows* (1983). Deshpande achieved full recognition, in India at least, when *That Long Silence* (1988) received the prestigious Sahitya Akademi Award), although *The Binding Vine* (1992) – discussed below – may be an even finer novel.

Like any fiction set in India, the novels of Shashi Deshpande inevitably reflect a complex linguistic reality, and *The Binding Vine* is no exception to the rule. Its main characters are middle-class professionals, competent in Hindi and with varying amounts of English-language education, but working within a predominantly Marathi-speaking environment in Bombay. In addition, Urmila, the young doctor and narrator–protagonist, shares with her husband a South Indian Kannada-speaking background. The range of cultural referents in English is enormous, moving from Humpty-Dumpty, through the *Reader's Digest* to Jane Austen's *Emma*. At work, Urmila may use English to speak above a patient's head, although at home she must switch to Kannada (presumably from English) to prevent her precocious young daughter from understanding. But whereas such code-switching belongs to the background of any anglophone Indian novel, it moves to the foreground of *The Binding Vine* in several striking ways.

The novel begins with the discovery of a hoard of diaries and poetry left by Urmila's mother-in-law, on her death some thirty years previously. The journal entries in English and the poems in Kannada both record the story of a woman unhappy in marriage, particularly its physical aspect. Behind the writer's discreet account, in fact, Urdmila finds strong evidence of some form of marital rape. It is at this point that a destitute young woman,

Kalpana, is brought into hospital suffering severe external injuries but also the victim of a far more violent rape. The girl's distraught mother is less worried by her daughter's physical condition, however, than by her reduced prospects on the marriage market as a result of her "dishonour". The marital rape and the later more savage attack together provide a powerful counterpoint to the theme of male brutality running through the narrative.

In this context, Urmila also comes to understand the great traumatic experience of her own childhood. Once, placed in the charge of an old family servant, she had been discovered in tears by her father. Shocked that his daughter had been left for even a moment "alone with a man", the father had simply dispatched the child, regardless of his wife's pleas, to his own mother in the south of India. As she describes the incident, Inni's face carries once again the look of terror produced by this more subtle but equally cruel form of male coercion.

But whereas the better educated women of *The Binding Vine* possess some insight into the phenomenon of male sexual violence, the socially disadvantaged ones have neither the detachment nor, it seems, even the *language* to comprehend it. When it is discovered that Kalpana had been raped by her own uncle, the aunt sets fire to herself rather than live with what she considers as her personal shame. With the girl's mother, on the other hand, the issue is ultimately reduced to purely linguistic terms: when Urmila tries to explain that her daughter has been raped, she searches in vain for the correct Marathi word and can only suggest that "Someone has wronged her." The mother feels no insult but only indignation ("It's not true, you people are trying to blacken my daughter's name"): the implication is that the daughter alone is responsible for what has happened to her. To add insult to injury, moreover, a Marathi newspaper report puns on the name of Kalpana (which literally means imagination), equating "Kalpana's story" with "an imagined story", in line with police suggestions that the girl was probably a prostitute.

Deshpande is often linked with Western feminist writers, although she herself is not happy with the comparison. Undoubtedly, however, *The Binding Vine* suggests profound forms of female solidarity (the title is a phrase from one of the dead mother's poems, where it refers to the umbilical cord). It also integrates perfectly the external Indian socio-linguistic reality with the internal thematic concerns of the novel.

A Bombay-born novelist moving (geographically at least) in the opposite direction to Rushdie, is **Rohinton Mistry**, who emigrated to Canada in 1975. After *Tales from Firozsha Baag* (1987), short stories featuring the residents of a Bombay apartment block, Mistry produced his first novel, *Such a Long Journey* in 1991. Besides its intrinsic literary qualities, the latter offers shrewd insights into the complexities of linguistic and ethnic identity in India. The main characters in the novel belong to the Parsi community of Bombay, and the implied language of the narrative is therefore Gujarati. The point is emphasized both by a liberal sprinkling of Gujarati terms, and by some more subtle inversions of standard English syntax.

In the first chapter, bank clerk Gustad Noble, listening to the news, is caught between the "clear mellifluence" of Hindi on All-India Radio and the "brashly confident counterpoint" of English on the BBC World Service. Subsequently, Hindi becomes associated with the corruption and political machinations of Indira Gandhi and the Congress Party in Delhi; whilst English is identified with the desperate attempts of the Noble family to better itself through education. Thus the oldest son Sohrab, whose refusal of a place at the prestigious Indian Institute of Technology hurts his father so much, is proudly described as almost fluent in English as a ten-year-old. During his kindergarten interview at the age of three (!), however, he had almost ruined his chances with a comic Gujarati *gaffe*. In the background, on the other hand, looms the sinister presence of the crypto-fascist Shiv Sena movement, with its demands for an ethically cleansed Maharashtra and special status for the Marathi language.

The novel also portrays the complexities of Indian spiritual life, with the subtlest religious subtext (and one of the most memorable images in all Indian fiction) being provided by the pavement artist with degrees in Fine Arts and Comparative Religion. At Gustad's suggestion, this man covers the three-hundred-foot wall outside the Khodadad Building, previously used as public urinal and worse, with religious images of every faith. This promotes religious harmony and civic pride, besides dramatically reducing the number of flies. In a climactic scene, however, the wall is knocked down by a group of bribed municipal workers prior to widening the road: a clear suggestion that India's unique spirituality is never safe from the inroads of crassness and venality.

Such a Long Journey is not a radically experimental text. Behind an obvious surface exoticism for the non-Indian reader lie elements of

Jamesian technique and Dickensian aesthetic. Such parallels should not, however, be taken to Eurocentric critical excess. Mistry is sensitive, even tender, in his portrayal of social groups about which James would have known little and cared less. And if there are Dickensian *avatars* for the eccentric Miss Kutpitia or the unfortunate Tehmul, then such commanding figures as Madhiwalla Bonesetter or Peerbhoy Paanwalla, the self-appointed oral historian, have no obvious models.

Upamanyu Chatterjee, although born at Patna in the state of Bihar, is a Bengali like his rough contemporary Bharati Mukherjee. His first novel, *English, August* (1988), chronicles the year spent by a young Indian Administrative Service trainee in the deep south of India. It serves as a reminder that the concept of cultural clash for an Indian may refer to the North and South of his own country, as well as the more conventional parameters of East and West. Its successor, *The Last Burden* (1993), studies the complex relations within an Indian extended family.

Another Bengali, **Amitav Ghosh** has lived in Calcutta, Dhaka (Bangladesh) and Colombo (Sri Lanka). A graduate of the University of Delhi, he also has an M.Phil. in social anthropology from Oxford. Few novels seem as remote from each other as Ghosh's first two, *The Circle of Reason* (1986) and *The Shadow Lines* (1988). While the former draws on magic realism, fabulation, and traditional oral narrative to describe the progress of Alu the weaver and his fantastic associates from Bengal through Kerala to the Arabian Gulf and, finally, Africa; the latter relies on meticulous detail and an almost obsessive introspection to recover the private histories of a solidly bourgeois Bengali family, scattered between Calcutta, London, and Bangladesh. One clear structural parallel between the two books, however, is the strangely anonymous narrator–potagonist, whilst an even more significant link is the common concern with the very process of memory and its representation.

According to a rather banal critical comment on *The Shadow Lines*, the author had now "found his distinctive voice". In this case, then, he discovered a new authorial persona with his third novel, *In an Antique Land* (1992), a historically inspired reconstruction of the life of an Indian slave in medieval Egypt; and yet another one with his fourth, *The Calcutta Syndrome* (1996), a futuristic tale introducing elements of political thriller and detective story. One can only hope that an author still too little known in the West, but sometimes rated in his native country as the most gifted living Indian English writer, will find many more distinctive voices.

The Shadow Lines is a metafictional work, although for the most part seriously speculative rather than comically subversive: there is no unreliable narrator, but rather an utterly scrupulous one with doubts about the trustworthiness of his own memory. As an only child growing up quietly with his parents and grandmother in Calcutta, the protagonist tends to live vicariously through his more cosmopolitan relatives. Beginning with random recollections of two cousins, he gradually puts together an intimate family chronicle, which moves between Calcutta, Delhi, London, and Dhaka over four generations and almost a century of time. The narrator's patient archeology of conscious and unconscious memory – comparisons with Proust are quite justified – is then challenged in the second half of the novel ("Coming Home") by the increasingly prominent voice of his grandmother. A retired schoolmistress (and a strict disciplinarian), who had moved to Calcutta from Dhaka before partition, she is also a realist horrified by her grandson's "detestable kind of cosmopolitanism". The climactic events of the novel begin with the grandmother's discovery that she has an aged relative still living in Dhaka, and her subsequent decision to go to Bangladesh and rescue him.

The focus now shifts to the old lady's concern about her first ever experience of air travel and, in particular, how she will be able to *see* the new border:

> But if there are aren't any trenches or anything, how are people to know? I mean, where's the difference then? And if there's no difference both sides will be the same; it'll be just like it used to be before, when we used to catch a train in Dhaka and get off in Calcutta the next day without anybody stopping us. What was it all for then – partition and all the killing and everything – if there isn't something in between?   (p. 151)

The nature of this "something in between" is hinted at by the novel's title; for the "shadow lines" are mere political divisions, and therefore far less significant than the contours of individual memory. True identity, then, is personal rather than collective, a cognitive rather than a political concept. The narrator gains his own form of self-knowledge by courageously pursuing his act of recovery to its traumatic climax, where he is nevertheless consoled with the glimpse of a "final redemptive mystery". Ghosh's elegantly metafictional inquiry thus coincides with a profoundly humanistic vision.

The last 1980s debutant discussed here is **Shashi Tharoor**. Born in London, raised in Bombay and Calcutta, educated in India and the United States, Tharoor later worked for the United Nations in Geneva. His two novels are nevertheless both deeply rooted in Indian cultural experiences: *The Great Indian Novel* (1989) is, at its simplest, a veiled account of modern Indian history; *Show Business* (1991) is a satirical glance at the Bombay film industry.

Tharoor prefaces *The Great Indian Novel* with an explanatory note for those who may find the book "neither great, nor authentically Indian, nor even much of a novel". His title (and chief inspiration) are, he explains, provided by the Indian epic of the *Mahabharata*, whose Sanskrit name is the equivalent of "Great India". Tharoor's comment may be one of the great authorial understatements, since – from *Joseph Andrews* to *Ulysses* – there can be no other novel in English which reproduces so comprehensively and ingeniously its ancient epic model.

Reduced to its barest outline, the original *Mahabharata* may be seen as a dynastic struggle between the Pandavas (the five sons of Pandu) and the Kauravas (the hundred sons of Pandu's half-brother Dhritarashtra). In moral terms, it is also traditionally read as a struggle between the forces of good and evil, *dharma* and *adharma*. Fraudulently dispossessed by the Kauravas and forced into exile, the Pandavas later return to reclaim their birthright. The ensuing battle of Kurukshetra, a kind of *Götterdämmerung* and the *Mahabharata*'s climax, is a vindication of the Pandavas, although the cost of victory is so high that there might seem to be no real winners in the contest.

So faithfully does Tharoor's satire translate the events of the *Mahabharata* to modern Indian history, that it may be more useful to consider the significant *differences* between the novel and its epic original, rather than the many *similarities*. Tharoor's Kauravas thus represent the Indian Congress Party; the blind patriarch, Dhritarashtra, is India's first prime minister, Nehru, while the chaste Kaurava *pater familias*, Bhishma (generally referred to as Gangaji), is Gandhi. But rather than a hundred sons, Tharoor's Dhritarashtra fathers a single daughter, Prija Duryodhani (the oldest Kaurava in the *Mahabharata* is called Duryodhana), hailed as the future ruler of all India: an obvious reference to Indira Gandhi. Another important difference lies in the emerging roles of the

Pandavas themselves, as Tharoor moves from "masque" to more direct allegory: Yudishtir symbolizes India's best political traditions, Bhim its loyal armed forces, Arjun an articulate press, Nakul and Sahadev the administrative and diplomatic services, respectively. All five Pandavas are also devoted to their common wife, Draupadi, who in turn personifies the "body politic", or Indian democracy, and wilts visibly with the imposition of Duryodhani's "siege" (a reference to Indira Gandhi's State of Emergency from 1975 to 1977).

The Great Indian Novel is nevertheless no mere *roman à clef*, however entertaining this aspect of the work may be. Tharoor's finest stroke of all may be his choice of narrator, Ved Vyas (with his amanuensis Ganapathi). According to tradition, the *Mahabharata* was compiled by the Sanskrit poet Vyasa, who dictated it to the scribe Ganapathi, at the suggestion of Brahma himself. For those unable to read Sanskrit, knowledge of the epic normally comes through one of the modern "transcreations": Tharoor acknowledges a debt to the English versions of P. Lal and C. R. Rajagopalachari. But Chakravarti Rajagopalachari (or "C.R." as he was popularly known), as a close associate of Gandhi and one of modern India's greatest statesmen, was intimately involved with the events described in the novel. Ganapathi is a Southern Indian like C.R.; and, even more significantly, the fictional Ved Vyas emulates the historical C.R. by becoming the first Indian governor-general of India. Tharoor thus cleverly conflates poet and redactor, ironically authenticating his fantastic narrative by placing this composite figure at its very centre.

The ability to detect literary parallels in the novel is ultimately determined by one's knowledge of the *Mahabharata* and familiarity with Indian history. Pandu (the non-biological father of the Pandavas) becomes Subash Bose, founder of the pro-Japanese Indian National Army; Karna (Kunti Devi's child by the Sun) becomes Muhammad Ali Jinnah, first president of Pakistan etc. There are countless other literary allusions, however, such as those to Paul Scott's novels of the *Raj*, to "Maurice Forster just down from Cambridge" (one of the nastiest colonial administrators is called Ronnie Heaslop), and even to Tharoor's compatriot, Vikram Seth. For once, the familiar review cliché, *tour de force*, seems quite appropriate.

Despite its element of inspired fantasy, however, *The Great Indian Novel* often reflects quite concrete socio-linguistic realities: Gandhi's associates are revealed at one point as having no common language except English; the Pandava Arjun, visiting Kerala, is reduced to sign language. There are also frequent attempts to represent the idiosyncracies of Indian English (a variety also stoutly defended by the narrator). But a major lesson of *The Great Indian Novel* may be directed at those who ignorantly presume that English might be something less in the hands of a Tharoor (or Rushdie or Ghosh). "Stepmother tongue" does not equal "foreign tongue". Or if Tharoor's English is indeed something different, it could well be something *more*, and not *less* than its metropolitan British counterpart. This "something" is derived from the literary tradition on which the author builds; for there can be few other novels that so effortlessly reproduce a particular linguistic medium (English), whilst drawing on an indigenous culture (Indian) so totally extraneous to it.

The 1990s maintained the now customary impetus of Indian English fiction, and once again produced a crop of significant new names: these include Farrukh Dhondy, Meena Alexander, Vikram Seth and Rukun Advani. All except Advani are arguably diasporic writers.

Born in Poona (a three-hour train ride from Bombay) into a Parsi family, Farrukh Dhondy has lived most of his life in Britain; his first novel for adults is the autobiographical *Bombay Duck* (1990). The cosmopolitan Meena Alexander was born in India, spent part of her childhood in Sudan, and now pursues an academic career in the United States; better-known as a poet, she has also written one novel, *Nampally Road* (1991), describing the return home of an Indian woman from Britain. Seth actually made his literary debut in 1986, but became a celebrity with *A Suitable Boy* (1993), his massive document of Indian social life in the early 1950s. The last writer in the group, Advani, is that comparatively rare example of an Indian anglophone novelist who lives in his native country; his *Beethoven Among the Cows* (1994) is an equally rare example of an Indian post-modernist novel. The literary chasm that separates these two works makes them a stimulating choice for the conclusion of this section.

Born in Calcutta, an Oxford graduate and Stanford postgraduate, cosmopolitan in background and an economist by training, Vikram Seth is predictably not an author unduly affected by literary trends. His first novel, *The Golden Gate* (1977), set in California, thus takes its inspiration from Pushkin's *Eugene Onegin* and is written exclusively in 676 sonnet stanzas. His second novel, the most literally monumental achievement of recent Indian English fiction (at almost 1,500 pages), is the extremely readable *A Suitable Boy* (1993). High accessibility does not always impress academic critics, of course, and the book is sometimes dismissed as superior soap opera, an Indian equivalent of, say, *Gone with the Wind*. Whatever the validity of such opinions, it is obvious that *A Suitable Boy* is firmly rooted in a nineteenth-century realist tradition, and its narrative technique can therefore seem an anachronism in the mid-nineties. When the novel is set beside the earlier but more innovative *Midnight's Children* (1981), moreover, it is rather as if Indian fiction found a James Joyce before it had a George Eliot. And the comparison with Eliot is not unjustified: as the meticulous but inspired reconstruction of a historical period, *A Suitable Boy* is certainly superior to *Romola*, and probably more worthy of comparison with *Middlemarch*.

The chronicle of Indian society over a year (1951–2) in the immediate post-Independence era centres on four culturally diverse but socially connected upper-class Indian families: the Mehras (the widow of a senior railway functionary with four children – for one of whom the "suitable boy" of the title must be found); the Kapoors (a government minister, his wife and three children); the Khans (the aristocratic Nawab of Baitar and his three children); and the Chatterjis (a Calcutta high court judge, his wife and five children). Within this frame, Seth skilfully interweaves private and public lives: Minister Mahesh Kapoor's great political legacy, the *Zamindari* land reform bill, for example, will effectively impoverish his great friend, and hereditary landowner, the Nawab of Baitar; the struggle of the self-made Haresh Khanna against patronage in the shoe industry reflects the broader social transformations of an emergent industrial giant.

Seth's panorama, it should be emphasized, is largely restricted to northern India, since the novel's Purva Pradesh obviously corresponds to present-day Uttar Pradesh. The imaginary city of Brahmpur, on the other hand, is clearly based on Allahabad: the fatal stampede during a Hindu festival (*Part 11* in the novel) recalls a historical occurrence in that city during the period, whilst the very name seems to be a cultural and linguistic transcreation (i.e. *Allah/Brahma* and *-abad/-pur/town*). Even within these parameters, however, the cultural range is enormous and, being India, such diversity is inevitably reflected in language.

It would be hard to find a novel, Indian or otherwise, as rich in socio-linguistic observation as *A Suitable Boy*. The complex shifts between Hindi, Urdu, Bengali, and the ubiquitous English are minutely recorded. There is barely a conversation anywhere in the novel, where the precise variety and quality of the language is not specified. Each instance of code-switching is made explicit. Characters know good or bad English (Haresh's strong Midlands accent is a handicap in the marriage stakes); good or bad Hindi (Minister Kapoor cannot read parliamentary records in the Devanagari script); good or bad Urdu (his son Maan is unable to write a letter to his *ghazal*-singing mistress); good or bad Bengali (Justice Chatterji's son, the poet Amit, must justify writing in English rather than in his native tongue). The narrative also subverts facile Western assumptions about the "mother tongue": the heroine, Lata Kapoor, normally addresses her Hindi-speaking mother in English; even little Aparna Chatterji uses English with her mother, reserving Bengali for her *ayah*. On the other hand, the proposed legislation to make Hindi the state language of Purva Pradesh is attacked for its "step-motherly treatment" of Urdu (p. 1105).

The foregoing comment might suggest that *A Suitable Boy* is an indigestible sociological tract, and it is true that after the unexpected emergence of a suitable bridegroom, the remaining strands of the narrative are left curiously dangling, without neat novelistic solutions. But such an impression is utterly misleading, for Seth's narrative has an unwavering lucidity and elegance. It shows an engaging wit and even a certain linguistic virtuosity, so that the only possible rejoinder to the novel's various detractors is that new readers should trust the tale and not the critic.

Rukun Advani's *Beethoven Among the Cows*, on the other hand, is (according to critical judgement) either a skilful blend or a bewildering hotchpotch of contrasting fictional modes. Early sections of the novel, such as "Nehru's Children" (the great leader's death seen through childhood eyes), "Murder in May" (natural disasters in the stifling Indian summer), or "The Othello Complex" (the protagonist's adolescent lust for the young Felicia Blumenthal next door), have an ingenuously autobiographical ring, for all their textual sophistication. Advani then moves into the surreal, however, as the actress Elizabeth Taylor literally steps out from the screen at the Delite Talkies cinema; or into the fantastic, as Mikhail Gorbachev arrives from Moscow with his two pet monkeys, Lenin and Trotsky. But only in the sixth section ("S/he, or A Postmodern Chapter on Gender and Identity") does the narrative finally explode into the full post-modernist parody it has long promised.

The novel's rather pedestrian title invokes the juxtaposition of European and Indian culture. Appropriately to the latter, the book begins and ends with a cow: the first (called Mrs Gupta for its physical resemblance to a neighbour) provides milk for the two young brothers around whom the narrative evolves; the second (found dead on a railway line thirty years later) briefly disrupts the brothers' first trip to the Taj Mahal. It is hardly controversial to see the two incidents as symbolizing, respectively, the sustaining power and the obstructive weight of traditional Indian values. Beethoven, the novel's great Western cultural icon, is treated with similar ironic *élan*: the aesthetic significance of the *Emperor Concerto*, of which Ms Blumenthal owns nineteen versions, is thus eclipsed by childhood obsession with the owner herself; and in later chapters, the composer is reduced to a simple referent for the elder brother's physical appearance (the younger one compares himself more prosaically to E. M. Forster).

European and Indian elements continue to merge and converge relentlessly. The physical setting of the novel is exclusively Indian, but the narrative itself contains an unbroken stream of allusions to anglophone literature, from the initial greeting of *Midnight's Children* to a farewell from *The Waste Land*. Between these, come *Hamlet, Macbeth, Lear, Othello,* and *Cleopatra*; Marvell and Herrick; Sterne, Scott, and Hardy; Blake, Wordsworth, Keats, and Shelley; Browning and Tennyson; Melville, Whitman, and Hemingway; *Pride and Prejudice* and *Treasure Island*; Philip Larkin and *A Fish Called Wanda*, to mention only the most obvious.

Even such density of reference is surpassed in the most patently post-modern section, the account of a literary party held in Delhi. Here there is exuberant satire of the academy, and particularly its feminist establishment, in the person of Lavatri Alltheorie (the name is presumably a composite of Gayatri Spivak and Louis Althusser), known with good reason as the "Tiresias of Gender Studies". The party sequence is followed by the story of one Vincente de Rozio, an approximate college contemporary of the narrator, now stationed with an Indian regiment on the sensitive Indo-Chinese frontier. De Rozio's father had been an army officer in the same zone thirty years earlier during the Chinese invasion of India said to have accelerated the death of Nehru. Advani thus provides a neat return to his opening theme.

There is a narrative *coda* on a more traditional note, evoking the communal violence of the 1990s, as the two brothers make their strongly symbolic trip to the Taj Mahal ("while it is still there"). The title of this chapter, "A Passage through India", ends with a final explicit reference to Forster, an author who has hovered on the edge of the narrative on previous occasions.

OTHER ASIAN FICTION

The sheer range and quality of Indian English fiction over the last fifty years tends to eclipse what has been produced in the rest of Asia. There are nevertheless a number of other countries in the region which should be taken into account, and which for this purpose may be divided into four subgroups: Pakistan and Bangladesh (combined here since they both still formed part of a greater India only half a century ago); Singapore and Malaysia (also linked by obvious historical factors; Sri Lanka (a small, but important special case); and the Philippines (not so small, and extremely complex in linguistic terms).

In Pakistan and Bangladesh, the role of English has been reduced to that of an important foreign language. Pakistan's population of 125 million people already has a *lingua franca* in Urdu, the mother tongue of only 10 million people but spoken fluently as a second language by two-thirds of the population; Bangladesh, on the other hand, has one of Asia's most linguistically homogeneous populations (120 million), the overwhelming majority of which speak Bengali. Beyond purely practical considerations of international communication, then, both countries have a more limited stake in English.

There are nevertheless examples of what might be called Pakistan anglophone fiction, although the pursuit of this claim is a good illustration of the difference between a literature in English and a number of significant writers using the language. Tariq Rahman's useful *History of Pakistani Literature in English* discusses only four novelists at greater length: Ahmed Ali, Zulfikar Ghose, Bapsi Sidhwa and Hanif Kureishi. Ahmed Ali (who incidentally began his career writing in Urdu) produced virtually all his fiction before the creation of Pakistan; Zulfikar Ghose (who spent only two years in Pakistan, before moving to Bombay at the age of seven and England three years later) has now been based for over thirty years in America and set his major trilogy in Brazil; Bapsi Sidhwa (who does actually describe herself as a Pakistani writer) has also lived and worked extensively in the United States; and Hanif Kureishi is often included among the newly fashionable category of "Black British authors".

Of these four writers, the most appropriate in the present context is undoubtedly Sidhwa. Born in pre-partition India, **Bapsi Sidhwa** grew up in Lahore (now Pakistan); she also belongs to the subcontinent's tiny minority of Parsis, the religious group originally driven from Persia by the rise of Islam. Even before life in the United States, then, Sidhwa was situated at the meeting-point of various cultures and languages. On the latter issue, in fact, she is engagingly forthright:

My first language of speech is Gujarati, my second is Urdu, my third is English. But as far as writing and reading goes, I can read and write best in English. I'm a tail-end project of the Raj.[4]

In the same interview, however, she admits to being "fed up" with the language issue and with conferences which spend half their time discussing it. As striking a case of transculturalism as any, Sidhwa is nevertheless quite happy to be considered a Pakistani writer. Her fiction certainly endorses this view. The first published novel, *The Crow Eaters* (1978), is a satirical inside account of Parsi life through the story of Faredoon Junglewallah, an ambitious young businessman who arrives in Lahore from central India at the beginning of the century. *The Bride* (1983), written before *The Crow Eaters* but held back for political reasons, is the harrowing story of a young girl orphaned in the partition riots and married off to a tribesman from Pakistan's northern frontier.

The events of partition are more central to Sidhwa's third novel, *Ice-Candy-Man* (1988), where they are reflected through the eyes of Lenny, a young Parsi girl growing up in a relatively affluent Lahore environment. With much comic gusto and some ribaldry, the naive narrator indirectly provides a penetrating account of mounting ethnic and religious tensions in the undivided Punjab of the 1940s. Lenny becomes traumatically implicated in the escalating violence when she unwittingly betrays her Hindu Ayah to a Muslim mob. *Ice-Candy-Man* is apparently an even-handed version of the atrocities, however, since Sidhwa also incorporates the authentic first-person account of a young Muslim boy literally scalped by a Sikh–Hindu mob, and forced to this day to wear a wig in his new Houston home.

Outside the context of communal violence, Sidhwa is also sensitive to social, cultural and even linguistic variables in a multicultural environment. The emphatic "otherness" of this world for the Anglo-Americo-Australasian reader is emblematically suggested by the epigraph to the first chapter, "Shall I hear the lament of the nightingale...": no reference to a Keatsian ode, but quoted from a lyric by Iqbal, greatest of Urdu poets.

The Parsi community of Lahore is committed to the Raj, although this loyalty is ironically juxtaposed to Lenny's account of her beautiful younger brother: Adi (the "little English baba") is *almost* fair enough to cross the colour line between British and native babies playing in the Lawrence Gardens (Lenny herself being too dark). Skilfully integrated with her experiences of maturation, on the other hand, are Lenny's accounts of adult discussions, whether it is her Ayah's circle of admirers in the park or her parents' dinner guests at home. If the former (in spite of ethnic and sentimental rivalries) are remarkably tolerant, then the latter produce comically grotesque confrontations. In one of these, an unidentified visitor challenges Dr Mody, the family doctor, on Parsi prospectives after partition:

"If we're stuck with the Hindus they'll swipe our businesses from under our noses and sell our grandfathers in the bargain: if we're stuck with the Muslims they'll convert us by the sword! And God help us if we're stuck with the Sikhs!"

"Why? Which mad dog bit the Sikhs? Why are you so against them?" says Dr Mody contentiously.

"I have something against everybody," declares the voice, impartial and very hurt.   (p. 37)

The great architects of modern Indian and Pakistan also appear marginally in Lenny's narrative. Memories of a childhood meeting with Gandhi thus produce a sharp caricature – "this improbable toss-up between a clown and a demon"; Nehru is recalled as both carismatic and charming, particularly to Lady Mountbatten; the ascetic, "pukka-sahib accented" Jinnah (first prime minister of Pakistan), on the other hand, is seen as unable to transcend his natural austerity.

In a narrative poised humorously (even playfully) between different cultural perspectives, Lenny also notes the emergence of her new homeland with ironic detachment: "I am Pakistani. In a snap.

Just like that." A more mature Lenny, and Sidhwa herself (despite the author's cautions against confusing fiction and autobiography), would nevertheless accept this label. By a simple extension, therefore, *Ice-Candy-Man* becomes one of the most significant Pakistani novels in English.

The concept of Bangladeshi English writing is more diffuse. Certain Indian authors, such as Nirad Chaudhuri, were born in what is now Bangladesh; others such as Amitav Ghosh have lived part of their life there; certain Asian writers in Britain can claim a Bangladeshi connection. But that, broadly speaking, is as far as it goes.

Sri Lanka, too, has major novelists who live abroad and (at least in the case of Michael Ondaatje) are hardly regarded any more as Sri Lankan. Ondaatje is now a Canadian citizen, whereas his rough contemporary Yasmine Gooneratne lives in Australia. In addition to these two, Romesh Gunesekera, whose much acclaimed first novel *Reef* (1994) has intertextual links with *The Tempest*, grew up in Sri Lanka and the Philippines, but now lives in London. Shyam Selvadurai, whose *Funny Boy* (1994) chronicles the young Arjie's struggle to come to terms with his homosexuality, is based in Toronto.

English in Sri Lanka nevertheless has a number of interesting socio-cultural dimensions that do not apply to Pakistan or Bangladesh. In a population of 18 million, about 75 per cent speak Sinhalese, while most of the remainder speak Tamil. For ten years after independence (gained in 1948) Sri Lanka was largely ruled by an English-speaking elite, until the government replaced a "Sinhala as official language" policy by a "Sinhala only" law. Much of the country's ethnic conflict dates from this era. English now provides what is vaguely referred to as a "link language", although current "links" between Sinhalese and Tamil separatists are hardly cordial.

But Sri Lanka also has a very small (and once influential) minority of mainly Portuguese or Dutch descent, known as Burghers. The status of the latter has been undermined by both Sinhala and Tamil nationalism, prompting many Burghers to leave the country. Ondaatje and Gooneratne are both connected with this socio-ethnic group. Even in Sri Lanka, then, the concept of an (imposed) "stepmother tongue" is not simple: Gooneratne, who might seem as solidly Sri Lankan as Dickens is English, admitted to me personally that her own Sinhala was "pretty good", thus implying, however, that it was not as "good" as her English – effectively her "mother tongue". To complicate issues further: the old Burghers (as distinct from the English colonial administrators) percolated quite far down the social scale, and were particularly prominent in the railway sector. The inimitable fictional chronicler of this group is Carl Muller, himself a Burgher. Muller's *The Jam Fruit Tree* (1993) and its successor *Yakada Yaka* (1994) – offering "the Continuing Saga of Sonnaboy von Bloss and the Burgher Railwaymen" – are written in a kind of vernacular, featuring some of the most virtuoso speech presentation in the entire range of anglophone fiction.

Among all these figures, **Yasmine Gooneratne** may reasonably be included here, although the decision is based less on the novelist than on a particular novel. A university professor who has lived in Australia since 1972, Gooneratne published a classic immigrant novel, *A Change of Skies* (1991), followed by the brilliantly original post-colonial romance, *The Pleasures of Conquest* (1995).

The latter begins at the New Imperial Hotel in the capital of Amnesia (a thinly disguised Sri Lanka), where attractive American popular novelist Stella Mallinson has arrived to conduct a collaborative writing project. The latter aims at encouraging local literary talent and promoting conservationist causes, without ever missing a photo opportunity for the display of fashionable designer items.

Stella's antithesis is literary scholar and unreconstructed chauvinist Professor Philip Destry, who had been the novelist's colleague (and even briefly her lover) at the fictional Maitland State University, Nevada. New encounters between the two are generated by Destry's growing obsession with his namesake, the enigmatic Sir John D'Esterey, colonial administrator in nineteenth-century Amnesia (and not least, Sir John's relationship to a beautiful young poet, Dona Isabella Cornelia). The likely key to this mystery is provided by the illiterate Mallika, descendant of local tea-pickers, through her access to a local oral tradition now fast disappearing with the introduction of formal English-language education.

Gooneratne's novel is memorable for its insistent equation of older British colonial interests with modern American neo-colonial pressures; and both of these forces, in turn, are consistently depicted as analogous to patriarchal exploitation in contemporary gender relations. Destry is thus forced to admit the powerful auxiliary role played by women in all the historical narratives that interest him. Whether the context is imperialism or patriarchy, Gooneratne refers aptly to "the brazen wheels that had kept the golden hands of empire in motion".

A significant Sri Lankan writer who has not emigrated is James Goonewardene. In both of his early novels, *A Quiet Place* (1968) and *Call of the Kirala* (1971), the protagonist rejects the urban environment in order to return to village life; *Dream Time River* (1984) is an evocation of childhood in colonial Sri Lanka. Far harsher in tone, however, are *An Asian Gambit* (1985), set during the country's Marxist insurgency of 1971, and *One Mad Bid for Freedom* (1990), with its deeply pessimistic view of modern Sri Lankan society. *The Tribal Hangover* (1995) follows the life of the young Harindra, adopted by a German couple, living in Sydney and facing the predictable problems of an Asian boy in a predominantly white community.

By contrast with Sri Lanka, Malaysia and Singapore have a smaller and less significant group of anglophone writers. Formerly under the same British colonial administration and briefly united after independence in the Malay Federation, the two countries subsequently went their own ways. The separation also had linguistic consequences: Malaysia, with an ethnic mix of 53 per cent Malays, 35 per cent Chinese and 10 per cent Indian, has promoted Malay (or Bahasa Malaysia) as the sole national language, causing a corresponding decline in the importance of English; Singapore, where the equivalent ethnic proportions are 15 to 76 to 7, has kept Malay as a national language together with three "offical" languages, English, Mandarin and Tamil. English is not only the main medium of education and cross-cultural communication, but is also often categorized as the language for the expression of national identity – the stepmother, as it were, becoming an integral part of the family.

In spite of the strength of English in Singapore, however, the most significant writers in the region – including Lee Kok Liang, Lloyd Fernando, and K. S. Maniam – are normally categorised as Malaysian. The distinction, it will be seen, is largely academic, since the Malay element is not prominent in any of these three. The culturally cosmopolitan Lee, who studied at the University of Melbourne and at Lincoln's Inn, London, before returning to (the then) Malaya to practise law is primarily Straits-Chinese; Fernando, who was born in Ceylon (now Sri Lanka) and earned two degrees from the University of Malaya (then situated in Singapore), is originally Sinhalese; Maniam, a Tamil who has lived most of his life in Malaya/Malaysia, may be identified with that country's Indian minority.

Lee Kok Liang and Lloyd Fernando have both been concerned with the ethnic mix which characterizes Malaysian and Singapore society, and there is a curious structural analogy between the major works of each writer. Lee's *Flowers in the Sky* (1981) thus comprises *four* related stories, examining the various belief systems present in Malaysia; Fernando's novel *Scorpion God* (1976), set in pre-independence Singapore, is the story of *four* university under-graduates, each representing one of the area's major ethnic communities: Malay, Chinese, Indian and Eurasian.

Less mechanical in structure than either of these works is the fiction of **K. S. Maniam**, who is undoubtedly the finest anglophone novelist the region has yet produced. In addition to three collec-tions of short stories, Maniam has published *The Return* (1981), a powerful *Bildungsroman* and study in cultural alienation, followed by *In a Far Country* (1993), a kind of Malaysian national allegory which transcends the conventional realism of his first novel. *The Return* also acquires added poignancy from its scenario of double exile. Like Jamini in Ismith Khan's *The Jumbie Bird* (or even Anand in V. S. Naipaul's *A House for Mr Biswas*), Maniam's Ravi is a third-generation Indian abroad. His grandmother, the legendary Periathai, had arrived from southern India with nothing but her three sons and one large trunk; she becomes the "Great Mother" in her own lifetime, an honorific which cleverly invokes both the indi-vidual and her country of origin.

Ravi grows up in a faithfully preserved Indian environment, where the observance of such traditional Hindu festivals as *Deepavali* and *Thaipusam* creates what he later recognizes as a "special country" for a population in exile. A new form of cultural displacement begins when Ravi is sent to an English school: as the son of a humble *dhobi* from the "civil lines" now thrown among the more privileged children of the hospital estate, Ravi begins a life of cultural conflict, largely expressed in linguistic terms.

The English school reader thus takes Ravi into the world of Ernie and life on an English farm. Miss Nancy, the teacher, covers the classroom walls with exotically English scenes, including one covered, if not with the proverbial daffodils, then with equally alien buttercups. English, in all its manifestations, comes to dominate Ravi's childhood and adolescence, whether it is the broken lan-guage of boys at play, the constant code-switching between English and Tamil, or exchanges with contemporaries in "rotten English": always, Ravi explains, English "reigned supreme".

English eventually emerges, however, not as mere cultural impo-sition but as a means of escaping an oppressive home environment. Ravi avoids the frustrations of daily life by immersing himself in

English comics; he begins to make Chinese and Malay friends, fills his bookshelves with abridged versions of Dickens, Thackeray and H. G. Wells – and even puts up his own poster of "daffodil land". To the disappointment of his parents, moreover, he gradually withdraws from the family laundry business and, remembering his grandmother's failure to find a true stake in her adopted land, decides to try for a scholarship to England. Ravi's transformation has come far, and Maniam refers in a genial symbolic detail to the old Tamil grammar gathering dust in a corner.

The process of cultural alienation that began with an English-language education is completed by physical dislocation when Ravi reaches Britain: his expectations are largely, if not entirely, fulfilled ("The snow wasn't as white as I had imagined it to be: it muddied the moment the flakes touched the ground"). By the time Ravi returns as a qualified teacher, his professional prospects are bright, but his sense of alienation is now complete: he acknowledges his "failure to earn a home in this land". Ravi's elderly father, who can now only ramble in Tamil or grunt in other garbled languages, can nevertheless underscore the lessons of the novel:

> We can make all the money, get all the learning. But these are useless if our house pillars don't sink into the clay of the land. (pp. 158–9)

Even in his dotage, the old man understands the realities of physical and cultural exile implied by such tags as "their" land and "their" language.

The Philippines, finally, among Asian countries, has a rich tradition of anglophone fiction, quite the equal of Sri Lanka's and second only to that of India. It is even closer to the latter, moreover, in terms of demographic and linguistic complexity.

The national language of the Philippine archipelago (population 70 million) is Filipino (or Pilipino); this is virtually identical to the Tagalog spoken as a native language by about 15 million people in southern Luzon – the northerly island which includes the capital, Manila. Three related Visayan languages, Cebuano (15 million), Hiligaynon (6 million) and Samaran (3 million) are spoken on the middle islands and in the north of Mindanao. Ilocano (6 million) is spoken in northern Luzon, Bikol (4 million) on the Bikol peninsula in the south-east; north-west of Manila there are 2 million speakers of Pampangan. Most Filipinos also speak at least one foreign language, predominantly English, Spanish or Chinese. The value of English as a link language needs no comment. More than 30 million people speak it as a second language, and the country sometimes likes to boast that it has the third largest English-speaking population in the world.

The most obvious distinctive feature of English in the Philippines is that it is of American rather than British origin. With the Philippine–American War (1898–1912), three centuries of Spanish domination was replaced by an American colonial presence. The American administration immediately introduced English-language education (briefly suspended during the Japanese occupation of 1941–4). The Philippines obtained formal independence in 1946, but the United States maintained political and economic control of the country through the presence of several military bases and close relations with the Marcos regime. The bases were dismantled in 1992, at the insistence of Corazón Aquino's government, but the language remains.

In an iconoclastic essay on the Philippines, Isagani Cruz describes the network of dynasties and clan loyalties that dominate Filipino public life:

if you know someone who knows someone, you will always go far up the ladder; if you are related by blood to someone known by everyone, you will be the ladder.[5]

Several novels give disenchanted accounts of the Marcos era; but to the detached observer of Filipino life, it may seem that the so-called "Marcos era" paradoxically began long before the dictator himself and did not end with him. Such considerations are relevant, since the Filipino "masses" who form 75 (perhaps 95) per cent of the population remain outside any of these systems, but are a central concern in such socially-committed writers as F. Sionil José.

There is, and has long been, an extensive literature in the indigenous languages, as well as in Spanish and Chinese. The book sometimes regarded as the Great Filipino Novel, José Rizal's *Noli Me Tangere* (1887), was written in Spanish. The Filipino capacity to absorb new languages and cultures may even surpass that of India, however, and the first novels in English appeared soon after the Americans themselves: Zoilo Galang's heavily sentimental love story *A Child of Sorrow* dates from 1921.

Filipino writers of the last fifty years can be broadly divided into three literary generations, and three representative figures have been chosen from each group.

Carlos Bulosan, N. V. M. Gonzalez and Edilberto Tiempo all began writing in the 1940s or early 1950s. Born into a large peasant family in the poor rural province of Pangasinan province (on Luzon), Carlos Bulosan joined an elder brother in the United States in 1931. He was a migrant worker on the American West Coast and published a disenchanted, quasi-autobiographical narrative entitled *America is in the Heart* (1946); his fiction proper began with the short-story collection *The Laughter of My Father* (1946).

N. V. M. Gonzalez was born on the island of Romblon to a Cebuano-speaking family. At an early age, however, he moved to Mindoro, in the Tagalog-speaking region, and it is this strongly rural environment which provides the background for his early fiction. Gonzalez followed his early novel, *The Winds of April* (1941), with *A Season of Grace* (1954), *The Bamboo Dancers* (1959) and several collections of short stories. He has described the Philippines as "one nation made up of three countries" – Manila, the *barrio* or rural community, and the mountains – and his fiction might be seen as an attempt to record, but also to transcend, these divisions. Gonzalez's regionalism, which has been compared to the Malgudi of Narayan, is evident in the stories of his finest collection, *Look Stranger, on This Island Now* (1954).

Edilberto Tiempo has a writing career spanning more than thirty years. Early works such as *Watch in the Night* (1953) and *More than Conquerors* (1964) were inspired by the Second World War and, above all, by personal participation in Filipino guerrilla activity during the Japanese occupation. Later novels include *To Be Free* (1972) reflecting political changes in the modern Philippines, and *The Standard-Bearer* (1985), returning to the period of Japanese occupation.

A second literary generation would include Bienvenido Santos, Nick Joaquin and F. Sionil José, who all began publishing novels in the 1960s. Santos, born in Tondo, Manila, graduated from the University of the Philippines in 1932, went on to Columbia and Harvard, and had a distinguished academic career (mostly in the United States) before his retirement in 1982. He actually began writing fiction in the 1930s, with socially committed short stories, but his later, better-known story collections typically explore the dreams and frustrations of the Filipino émigré experience: they include *You Lovely People* (1955), *Brother, My Brother* (1960), *The Day the Dancers Came* (1967) and *Scent of Apples* (1979).

Benvenido Santos's first two novels, *The Volcano* and *Villa Magdalena* (both published in 1965), reflect his return to the Philippines after the Second World War and an interest in the effects of the Japanese occupation on Filipino life. *The Praying Man* (serialized in 1971–2, but not published in book form until 1982) gives a disenchanted view of the Marcos era. Later novels, *The Man Who (Thought He) Looked Like Robert Taylor* (1983) and *What the Hell For You Left Your Heart in San Francisco* (1987), return to expatriate themes. The rather cumbersome title of the last novel is a reference to a characteristic Filipino English structure: Santos in the United States, and José at home, are the Filipino novelists who have most consistently explored the socio-linguistic implications of the step-mother tongue, whether on the technical level of language repre-sentation or on the thematic one of cultural identity.

Nick Joaquin, born in Paco, Manila, left school voluntarily after three years of secondary education, supplemented much later by an abortive spell at a Catholic seminary in Hong Kong. He is, there-fore, a largely self-taught writer. A prolific poet, essayist and short-story writer, he has only published two novels, although the first of these, *The Woman Who Had Two Navels* (1961), is widely celebrated. This strongly symbolic work describes the desperate quest of Connie, the protagonist, for some form of stability in the outside world. The title image refers to the double legacy of the Spanish and American pasts. Joaquin's other novel, *Cave and Shadows* (1983) is a mystery thriller written in a more popular idiom.

F. Sionil José, the most internationally acclaimed Filipino writer in English, was born in Rosales, in Pangasinan province on the island of Luzon. After medical studies, he began a career in journal-ism and subsequently published two novellas, eight novels, and four collections of short stories. His reputation nevertheless rests on the "Rosales quintology", consisting of *The Pretenders* (1962), *Tree* (1978), *My Brother, My Executioner* (1979), *Mass* (1982), and *Po-on* (1984). Beginning with contemporary middle-class settings, José's sequence eventually chronicles more than a century of social history in every area of Filipino life. The recent novels, *Ermita* (1988) and *Gagamba* (1991), are also marginally linked to the *Rosales* quintology. Critic Shirley Lim refers, in the context of José, to "the constraints of writing in the English language in a nation where the national language is Pilipino ... and where the present trend is towards writing in the native languages". But José's own popular roots, his identification with the Filipino masses and his sensitivity to their socio-political conditions, help maintain his relation to the stepmother tongue as one of pragmatic adoption rather than incestuous attraction.

Viewed in the broadest terms, these three writers could well be regarded as the most representative figures in Filipino fiction, with Sionil José producing the national (or, at least, Ilcocano) *epic*, Joaquin providing the national *allegory*, and Santos proving the foremost chronicler of the national diaspora.

Significant figures in more recent Filipino English fiction include Ninotchka Rosca, Eric Gamalinda and Jessica Hagedorn, although some reference should be made first to the slightly older figure of Linda Ty-Casper. Born in Malabon on the outskirts of Manila, Ty-Casper is perhaps the most prolific anglophone Filipino author in recent years. Her fictional interests shift between historical reconstructions of the Philippines, such as *Ten-Thousand Seeds* (1987), in which an American honeymooning couple visits the new American colony, and dystopian portraits of the Marcos era in the novels *Fortress in the Plaza* (1985) and *A Small Party in a Garden* (1988).

More experimental than Ty-Casper is Ninotchka Rosca, born in Manila, interned under martial law in 1972, awarded a fellowship to the University of Iowa and later hired by the University of Hawai'i. Her stories in *The Monsoon Collection* (1983), and the novels *State of War* (1988) and *Twice Blessed* (1992), have been compared, for their magic realism, to the fiction of Gabriel García Márquez and Isabel Allende.

Another experimental writer is Manila-born and locally educated Eric Gamalinda, whose novels include *Planet Wars* (1989), *Confessions of a Volcano* (1990) and *The Empire of Memory* (1992). The first of these is a family saga with a strong admixture of the grotesque and fantastic, the second is a story of two Filipinos in Japan, the third yet another chronicle of the Marcos years. Jessica Hagedorn, finally, was born in Manila, but moved to San Francisco at the age of twelve and now lives in New York. Of all the writers in this brief survey, therefore, Hagedorn should perhaps be regarded as Filipino-American rather than simply Filipino. Her first novel, *Dogeaters* (1992) also uses elements of a grotesque but real world to convey the Manila of the Marcos era.

The broadest overview of Filipino English fiction (which is all the present format permits) suggests two points by way of conclusion. The corpus of writing outlined actually seems affected by two distinct forms of colonialism: an internal variety as well as the more obvious external one. It is thus noticeable how many of the major Filipino novelists have a Metro-Manila background, including Santos, Joaquin, and all the younger writers discussed. Bulosan and José have provincial, rural origins (but also on Luzon); only Gonzalez was born on another island (Romblon), although he moved to Luzon at an early age. This suggests a hegemony – even a monopoly – exercised by Manila on Filipino national life. A more obvious form of culturalism, however, is that exercised by America. Six of the ten novelists reviewed (the exceptions being Joaquin, Tiempo, José and Gamalinda) are listed in King-Kok Cheung and Stan Yogi's *Asian American Literature. An Annotated Bibliography* (commissioned by the American Modern Language Association) as "Filipino *American*" writers. It was recently calculated that there are about 120 full-length Filipino English novels published. Whether Filipino or Filipino-American, however, the number condinues to grow, as it does in other Asian countries with an anglophone literary tradition.

NOTES

1. *Journal of Commonwealth Literature* 18, 1 (1983), p. 86.
2. *World Literature Written in English* 14:2 (1975), p. 300.
3. *Interviews with Writers of the Post-Colonial World* (Jackson: University Press of Mississippi, 1992), p. 144.
4. *Interviews with Writers of the Post-Colonial World*, p. 214
5. See the entry for "Philippines" in the Routledge *Encyclopedia of Post-Colonial Literatures* in English.

FURTHER READING

The best single volume survey of the field is still M. K. Naik's *A History of Indian English Literature* (New Delhi, 1982), published by the Sahitya Akademi. This can be supplemented by Nilufer E. Bharucha and Vilas Sarang's collection *Indian-English Fiction 1980-1990. An Assessment* (Delhi: BR Publishing, 1994). G. N. Devy's *In Another Tongue: Essays on Indian English Literature* (New York: Peter Lang, 1993) is particularly relevant to some of the issues raised in this section.

Writers of the Indian Diaspora, edited by Emmanuel S. Nelson (Westport, CT: Greenwood Press, 1993), is a comprehensive "Bio-Bibliographical

Critical Sourcebook", with 58 authoritative essays on authors with Indian antecedents. Also published by the Greenwood Press is Nelson's excellent *Reworlding: The Literature of the Indian Diaspora* (1993), containing 14 critical essays on "representative writers of the diaspora". Meenakshi Mukherjee's *Realism and Reality: The Novel and Society in India* (Oxford University Press: Delhi, 1985) traces two centuries of fiction in the indigenous Indian languages.

The two-part *Penguin History of India* (vol. I by Romila Thapar; vol. II by Percival Spear), originally published in the mid-sixties, has often been reprinted; it is useful for all but most recent decades. C. Rajagopalachari's excellent redactions of the *Mahabharata*, the *Ramayana* and the *Bhagavad Gita* are all available in *Bhavan's Book University* (Bombay). A selection of the *Upanishads*, translated by Juan Mascaró, is published in the Penguin Classics series.

Tariq Rahman's *A History of Pakistani Literature in English* (Lahore: Vanguard Books, 1991) and Wilfred Jayasuriya's *Sri Lanka's Modern English Literature* (Colombo: Lake House Bookshop, 1994) are both helpful, but difficult to obtain outside the Indian sub-continent. Two good general studies of other literatures in the region are Lloyd Fernando's *Cultures in Conflict: Essays on Literature and the English Language in South East Asia* (Singapore: Graham Brash, 1986) and Shirley Geok-lin Lim's *Writing South East Asia in English: Against the Grain* (London: SKOOB Books, 1994). For the Phillipines, see Florentino B. Valeros and Estrelita V.Gruenberg's *Filipino Writers in English* (Quezon City: New Day, 1987).

2
Africa

The anglophone literature of Africa has obvious analogies with that of Asia, even if the period of contact with the English language has in most cases been considerably shorter. On both continents, an alien language and culture were imposed on stable, traditional societies, whilst varying degrees of assimilation were encouraged or enforced. One may therefore refer to English quite literally, in a historical context at least, as a "stepmother tongue".

India has produced Asia's most significant post-colonial literary tradition not least for demographic reasons: through its vast population and sheer size (before independence, of course, the country also encompassed modern Pakistan and Bangladesh); because of its linguistic complexity (which increased the significance of English, as argued in the previous section); and as a result of immigration (whether through the old-time indenture system or the new-style diaspora). Some Asian countries such as Sri Lanka, and – beyond the sphere of British colonial influence – the Philippines, have produced an autonomous anglophone literature; but elsewhere in the region, writers with Indian antecedents (Bapsi Sidhwa in Pakistan, K. S. Maniam in Malaysia, Philip Jeyaretnam in Singapore) are still prominent. According to strict quantitative and qualitative criteria, one might even claim that only India (among Asian countries) has a comprehensive literature in English, whereas the rest have varying numbers of individual anglophone writers.

This paramount position of India in Asia is partly paralleled by that of Nigeria with respect to African anglophone literature. Nigeria shares with India, if to a lesser degree, the elements of size, population, and linguistic complexity. The neatness of the analogy is only challenged by the lack of a truly significant Nigerian diaspora (except to Britain) and the presence of another African country, South Africa, where demography, for quite different reasons, is equally intricate. Bearing these factors in mind, the present sub-section uses a triple division of West, East, and

Southern Africa, rather than a double one (Nigeria and "the rest", as it were) like that already used in the Asian context.

WEST AFRICA

The curve of West Africa from Gambia to Cameroon contains six examples of what are often airily described as anglophone countries: from west to east, these are Gambia, Sierra Leone, Liberia, Ghana, Nigeria and Cameroon. The major contact period between English and West African languages was originally seen as broadly coterminous with the colonial period itself, approximately 1880–1960. After that, the theory goes, the ex-West African colonies, linguistically speaking no less than economically, could go their own way. It is equally well known, however, that the boundaries of the newly independent African nations were originally carved out by the European powers without reference to ethnic or linguistic divisions. With over four hundred indigenous languages, then, modern Nigeria – as far as the retention of English was concerned – initially had very limited options.

In a survey of this nature, two countries may be immediately excluded. In Liberia's population of 3 million, as many as 10 per cent may have English as a first language, but the country lacks a notable literary tradition. Cameroon (13 million) with a minute English-speaking population, although probably the highest proportion of English Pidgin speakers among the six West African countries, also has relatively little anglophone writing. Gambia's few internationally known authors, such as William Conton and Lenrie Peters, often have links with larger Sierra Leone. The latter plus Nigeria and Ghana, then, are the three West African states that require closest consideration here.

Nigeria has a population of almost 100 million, of which roughly a quarter (in the north) speak Hausa, a fifth (in the west) speak Yoruba, and a sixth (in the east) speak Igbo. Yoruba and Igbo belong to the Kwa subgroup of the Niger–Congo language family and so, whatever the ethnic rivalries between the two populations, the linguistic distance between them is not insurmountable. Hausa, on the other hand, is a Chadic language of the Afro-Asiatic family and quite remote from either of Nigeria's other national languages. Since an additional 15 million Nigerians speak Hausa as well as their native tongue, the country's three major languages serve over

75 million of the population. There are still, unfortunately, some 20 million outside these linguistic categories.

Nigerian writers are clearly implicated in the country's linguistic confusion, even as they remain ambivalent towards the English language that is meant to alleviate it. Wole Soyinka, Africa's first Nobel laureate in literature, is a Yoruba and there is an emblematic scene in his autobiographical memoir, *Aké* (1981), where the author, as a child, strays from his parents and gets lost. He is rescued by a white man, who tries to comfort him in rudimentary Yoruba; Soyinka can barely understand the language, and must answer in English. If English is Soyinka's stepmother tongue, then, there is nevertheless some complicity in the relationship, and it is easy to understand feelings of resentment towards Africa's first Nobel laureate among the more nationalistic Nigerian critics. Recently, however, Soyinka himself spoke bitterly of the acculturation process to Adeola James:

> for writers like me, there has always been a resentment, an underlying resentment, that I have to express myself and create in another language, especially a language that belongs to the conqueror.[1]

In the same interview, Soyinka proposes Kiswahili as an African language so that communication with other Africans need no longer "go through the colonial sieve".

Chinua Achebe, Nigeria's most famous novelist, is an Igbo. His views on English have always been moderate and pragmatic, although a character in his novel *No Longer at Ease* (1960) does admit to feeling "ashamed at having to speak to one's countryman in a foreign language". In his own voice, however, Achebe can be equally uncompromising:

> No man can understand another whose language he does not speak (and "language" here does not simply mean words, but a man's entire world view). How many Europeans and Americans know our language?[2]

And finally, a much younger writer – Zaynab Alkali (whose first language is Hausa) – described to Adeola James the sheer mental effort of writing what may be fairly regarded as the "stepmother tongue":

I find writing in English is agonizing, to say the least, especially when it comes to dialogue. My characters "in real life" do not speak in English, and in the act of translation, the native idiom is completely lost, as are the meanings of certain expressions. Naturally I would feel more comfortable writing in my own language but the audience, as you know, would be limited.[3]

Statements like these can be supplemented by the comments of Nigerian authors from smaller linguistic groups. Playwright J. P. Clark (Bekederemo) is an Ijaw speaker from the Niger delta and refers to himself in a poem as the "bastard child" of two cultures. The concept of English as an "alien language" is central to his writing; the autobiographical *America, Their America* (1964) – a title which plays cleverly on Lawrence's *England, My England* – develops this theme. Gabriel Okara, another Ijaw speaker, produced a celebrated novella, *The Voice* (1964), where the whole narrative is transliterated from Ijaw – an example, as the author notes elsewhere, of "African speech...English words". Few African authors have gone as far as Okara, it is true, although such ambivalence towards English is seldom far away in anglophone literature from that continent.

Kole Omotoso, an Arabic scholar who tried writing creatively in that language, began his literary career by transcribing Yoruba folktales; dramatist Ola Rotimi, whose Yoruba father and Ijaw mother shared no common language, actually incorporates several languages in his play "Our Husband Has Gone Mad Again" (1974). But the final word on Yoruba and Igbo (most Nigerian writers are native speakers of one of these languages) in relation to the stepmother tongue may be left with novelist Buchi Emecheta:

unfortunately, I can't write stories in my own language. I can write Yoruba, but not Igbo, so I have to write in English.[4]

Much the same linguistic situation also prevails, if on a smaller scale, in Ghana, with its population of 15 million and almost fifty languages. The two most important among these are the very similar Twi and Fanti, with about 6 million speakers combined, after which come Ewe with one and a half million speakers, and the closely related Ga and Adangbe with about a million speakers each. Ayi Kwei Armah (like poet, Kwesi Brew and dramatist, Efua Sutherland) is a Fante speaker. Kofi Awoonor's native language is

Ewe, Amu Djoleto's is Ga-Adangbe. Novelist Ama Ata Aidoo, another Fante speaker, confesses to Adeola James the same anxieties as her Nigerian colleagues: "here we are, writing in a language that is not even accessible to our people, and one does worry about that, you know".

In Sierra Leone, the situation is slightly attenuated by the fact that 60 per cent of the 4 million population are native speakers of the Niger–Congo languages Mende or Temne; whilst an English creole (called Krio) is also widely spoken throughout the country and now even displacing English. In Gambia, finally, a population of one million speaks only (!) five main indigenous languages.

Beyond the linguistic question, moreover, the West African cultural background (at least, as regards modern fiction from the region) is hardly less complex than that of the Indian subcontinent. Or, more accurately, what suggests less complexity probably reflects a slightly greater cultural homogeneity.

The West African novel, on the other hand, obviously represents a synthesis of Western impulses with a pre-technological traditional culture. The latter was predominantly oral, and writers reproduce this dimension in varying degrees. Like most traditional societies, those of West Africa are hierarchic, occasionally even ossified; their ritualistic and formulaic aspects are particularly evident to outsiders (usually oblivious, in the case of Westerners, to their own rituals and formulae). And if there is a single rhetorical form, moreover, that permeates verbal communication in a traditionally oral culture, then it is the proverb. Achebe catches this point beautifully in the very first chapter of *Things Fall Apart* when Okoye, the musician, goes to visit the protagonist's improvident father to announce his intention of taking a title:

> Having spoken plainly so far, Okoye said the next half a dozen sentences in proverbs. Among the Ibo the art of conversation is regarded very highly, and proverbs are the palm-oil with which words are eaten. Okoye was a great talker and he spoke for a long time, skirting round the subject and then hitting it finally. (p. 5)

In structural terms, on the other hand, some African novels give the Western reader the impression of a kind of minimalism. Compatible with a European mainstream narrative tradition, they maintain a certain formal realism but have little of what has been rather pompously called "solidity of specification". In a very few cases, this apparent thinness can probably be ascribed to linguistic factors, and to the sheer effort of writing in an "alien" tongue. A more likely reason, however, is that the second language is often unable to reproduce cultural experiences rooted in the medium of the vernacular. The best explanation of all, however, involves dropping Eurocentric perspectives and, instead of demanding why African novels have so little detail, asking why many traditional European ones have so much. This kind of question has in fact been regularly posed *within* the European tradition itself, ever since the naive empiricism of eighteenth-century English fiction: with Swift satirizing Defoe, and Fielding ridiculing Richardson. And on the subject of Richardson (whose *Pamela* is an important prototype here), the European bourgeois myth of Romantic love is also largely alien to the African novel.

A final ideological aspect of African fiction concerns the role of the novelist. In societies which stress the values of solidarity and community rather than individualism and self-regard, the didactic potential of literature is not despised. If the European literary archetype for two hundred years has evolved round the rebellious gesture, then its modern African counterpart is the communal act. Achebe is once again exemplary, with a classic early essay significantly entitled "The Novelist as Teacher".

The relevant historical background of West Africa is also less complex than that which pertains for Asia. Novels set in the pre-colonial period (depicting the Atlantic slave trade, for example) are rare, although it should be remembered that Olaudah Equiano, author of the first important slave narrative, was an Ibo. The period of full colonial contact was also far shorter than it was in India or the Caribbean. The order of literary significance assumed by the pre-colonial, colonial and post-colonial periods, then, may be an exact inversion of their chronological one. Independence was achieved fairly peacefully in West Africa, Ghana (1957) being the first British colony on the continent to achieve it, followed rapidly by Nigeria (1960), Sierra Leone (1961) and Gambia (1965). There was no armed struggle, for example, like those that shaped the national consciousness in Kenya and Zimbabwe.

After independence, however, the West African countries faced the same dichotomies – tradition versus innovation, rural versus urban, Western versus indigenous – that confronted most of the post-colonial world. The inevitable processes of adaptation and compromise feature widely in the contemporary fiction of the region. Nowhere was independence painless; in most countries, moreover, it was only nominal. The chaos and confusion of the post-independence period has also generated a series of literary dystopias. In one case, however, mere political squalor was eclipsed by human tragedy on an unprecedented scale: in the Nigerian Civil War (1967–70). The most significant event in the history of independent Nigeria is predictably reflected in the work of almost every contemporary author from that country.

These various cultural and historical elements (with due allowance made for home-grown influences) have been faithfully recorded in a predominantly realistic fictional tradition. Only recently has the West African novel shown much inclination to eschew conventional representation in favour of more radical tendencies. The achievements which contradict such risky generalizations are partly technical (with an increased acceptance of formal experimentation) and partly ideological (as women's voices, in particular, grow increasingly evident).

In the light of these arguments, then, the West African novel is reviewed here under the broad headings of *custom and tradition, post-independence adjustment, post-independence disillusion* – with *civil war* (in Nigeria's case) providing the natural watershed between these two phases – and *new voices*.

Custom and Tradition

A pioneering figure of the modern African novel in English is Amos Tutuola, although he has not proved such a lasting inspiration as Chinua Achebe. A messenger in the Lagos Labour Department with just six years of formal education in missionary primary schools, Tutuola won literary acclaim in the 1950s for a series of novels drawing heavily on traditional Yoruba folklore. The first of these were *The Palm-Wine Drinkard* (1952) and *My Life in the Bush of Ghosts* (1954).

Tutuola's methods changed little over the years. *Simbi and the Satyr of the Dark Jungle* (1955) has numbered chapters and possible European literary influences; *The Brave African Huntress* (1958) and *Ajaiyi and His Inherited Poverty* (1967) use proverbs as chapter headings with stories to illustrate them. *Feather Woman of the Jungle* (1962), Tutuola's best-known work after *The Palm-Wine Drinkard*, is also the most consciously structured, with a seventy-six-year-old

chief providing *Arabian Nights*-style entertainment over ten successive evenings. After *Ajaiyi and His Inherited Poverty*, there is a four-
teen-year gap in Tutuola's output before *The Witch-Herbalist of the
Remote Town* (1981), followed by *The Wild Hunter in the Bush of the
Ghosts* (1982; revised 1989), the author's previously unpublished
first attempt at writing fiction. *Pauper, Brawler, and Slanderer* (1987)
continues patterns which now seem increasingly repetitive, whilst
The Village Witch Doctor and Other Stories (1990) collects miscella-
neous pieces.

An interesting appendix to the fiction is Tutuola's compilation
and translation published as *Yoruba Folktales* (1986). This was
wittily described by Bernth Lindfors as a first exercise in "pure
narrative presentation" in contrast to the "impure narrative
perversion" of Tutuola's own writing. It was also Lindfors
who demonstrated Tutuola's heavy debt to the Yoruba novelist
D. A. Fagunwa. The title alone of Fagunwa's first novel, *Ógbójú ode
nínú igbó irúnmalè* (1938) – translated by Wole Soyinka as *The Forest
of a Thousand Daemons* (1968) – evokes a world that British and
American readers long assumed to be exclusively Tutuola's. After
the excessive praise of early British critics and the horrified
reactions of many educated Nigerians, it has become possible
to form a more balanced view. Tutuola is still interesting for his
skilful transformation of a popular oral (and vernacular) tradition
into a highly characteristic Africanized English idiom. He is not,
however, easily imitated.

Black Africa's most celebrated novelist in English is still **Chinua
Achebe**, whose *Things Fall Apart* (1958) stands in relation to the anglophone African novel much as George Lamming's *In the Castle of
My Skin* does to West Indian fiction. Both works anticipate many of
the techniques and themes central to their respective cultures, such
as the oral tradition, the patterns of village life, and the trauma of
colonial contact.

Achebe has explained how he began writing as a reaction to the
Eurocentric representations of Africa he found as a student of
English. Even such a would-be sympathetic writer as Joyce Cary, in
Mr Johnson (1939), portrayed Nigerians in crude comic stereotypes,
whilst Conrad's Africans in *Heart of Darkness* were mere deperson-
alized extras in the author's private inferno. As Achebe wryly
noted, "if a good writer could make this mess, perhaps we ought to
try our hand". Africa was not, he insists, in a state of mere bar-
barism before the arrival of the Europeans; *Things Fall Apart* is thus

partly an attempt to set the record straight. One way of creating a new African perspective is through a process of "defamiliarization", through which common European phenomena are held at arm's length, as it were, and made to appear strange. The most obvious example of this technique is the description of the first white man, regarded by the villagers as a physical aberration and mistaken for a kind of albino.

The narrative begins with a portrait of Okonkwo, the inflexible and fiercely combative young villager struggling to erase the memory of a weak and feckless father. After the opening chapters, however, psychology gives way to cultural anthropology, as Achebe recreates village life among the Igbo of south-eastern Nigeria at the turn of the century. What emerges from this account is a balanced, hierarchic (if strictly patriarchal) society, in close harmony with the earth that sustains it. Among various rituals, Achebe even-handedly describes the "male" ceremony of *egwugwu*, clan members masked as spirits to provide a court of law, followed by the "female" gathering of the *umuada*, or bride's extended family, before the marriage ceremony.

This leisurely account, which even Achebe considers valid as a historical document, ends abruptly when Okonkwo accidentally shoots and kills a young boy at a funeral ceremony. As a result, he is exiled, with his family, for seven years to the village of his mother's clan. During his absence, Christian missionary activity increases. Villagers regard the preaching of this "lunatic religion" with hilarity, although they are understandably fond of the songs and the pastoral imagery of certain New Testament texts. The only initial converts, however, are the *efulefu* or "worthless, empty men" (p. 101), and the *osu* or tabu-marked tribal outcasts.

But when Okonkwo returns from exile, Christianity is firmly entrenched. The inevitable great clash with traditional values is briefly postponed through the tact of the kindly Mr Brown, participant in a memorable theological debate with Akunna, one of the "great men" of the village. Brown's successor, the Reverend James Smith, is less willing to compromise, however, or as Achebe exquisitely puts it, can only see black and white ("And black was evil"). Smith is also unable to control the fanatics in his congregation such as Enoch, who first kills the sacred python, and then uncovers one of the *egwugwu* maskers.

Increased hostility and escalating violence eventually bring a final confrontation, in which both Okonkwo and his village are the losers. The destruction of tribal life is generally seen as due to lack of solidarity ("we have fallen apart", Okonkwo is made to comment, in a reference to the novel's title). The actual gap between the two cultures is also expressed in *linguistic* terms (literal and metaphorical) when an elder complains of the district commissioner: "he does not even speak our tongue". By the time the novel reaches its tragic climax, Achebe's brilliant revisionist perspective has succeeded where traditional Igbo society has failed. Thus it is now possible to appreciate the irony of the commissioner's efforts to "bring civilization to the different parts of Africa" (p. 147), or his plan for a monograph to be called *The Pacification of the Primitive Tribes of the Lower Niger*.

If *Things Fall Apart* is an important model both for novels of traditional village life and for accounts of colonial contact, then its successor, *No Longer at Ease* (1960), is the classic study of the "been-to", the African who has travelled or studied in Europe. Its protagonist, Obi, privileged possessor of a London University degree, is guaranteed a good job on return to his homeland, but grows increasingly prone to corruption and abuse of office. In the process, he is tragically caught between two cultures, alienated from traditional African life but not fully assimilated into European culture.

Arrow of God (1964; revised 1967), the final part of Achebe's African trilogy, returns to the traditional world of Okonkwo to study shifting power relations in a transitional society. Ezeulu, high priest of Ulu, is jailed by the British colonial government. While he is in prison, two new moons pass, and the sacred yams connected with the natural cycle remain uneaten. After his release, Ezeulu insists on eating the yams in due sequence, and thus delays the harvest, bringing famine on his people. Achebe cleverly portrays Ezeulu's concern to follow custom and tradition (not, of course, unrelated to personal prestige) in the face of social and economic disaster.

The trilogy covers some hundred years of Igbo history. *A Man of the People* (1966) continues the story into the post-colonial era, illustrating a thesis dear to Achebe that Nigeria's (and most of Africa's) fundamental problem is a lack of responsible political leadership. After *A Man of the People*, Achebe published short stories and essays, but no full-length novel for more than twenty years, a gap partly explained by the trauma of the thirty-month Nigerian Civil War in the late 1960s. *The Anthills of the Savannah* (1987), set in a thinly disguised Nigeria called Kangan, is another novel of political disillusionment, closest in character and theme to *A Man of the People*.

Achebe's treatment of traditional village life inspired a number of Nigerian novelists, including Amadi and Munonye. Elechi Amadi is best known for a loosely linked trilogy set in the pre-colonial period: *The Concubine* (1966), *The Great Ponds* (1969) and *The Slave* (1978). The first of these, in particular, has a strong super-natural element skilfully absorbed in a narrative reflecting the apparent simplicity of a traditional oral tale. Amadi also had first-hand experience of the Nigerian Civil War, leading to a fine novelistic memoir, *Sunset in Biafra* (1973), and a fourth novel, *Estrangement* (1986). The latter shows the effect of the war on individual civilians, from the perspective of a young Biafran housewife whose city falls to Federal forces in the course of the conflict.

John Munonye's novels are not calculated to win popularity at home, with their insistence on certain benefits accruing from the colonial experience, and their humorous treatment of the whole process. Munonye supplemented his tragi-comic trilogy of rural life, *The Only Son* (1966), *Obi* (1969), and *Bridge to a Wedding* (1978), with three quite different novels: *The Oil Man of Obange* (1971), *A Wreath for the Maidens* (1973), with its philosophical speculation on the Biafran War, and *A Dancer of Fortune* (1974), sharply satirizing modern Nigerian society.

Largely outside the sphere of Achebe but equally interested in traditional society is Isidore Okpewho, a noted scholar of epic and orature. Okpewho's first novel, *The Victims* (1970), nevertheless recalls *Things Fall Apart* in its use of proverbs and its skilful suggestion in English of African vernacular speech.

Several Ghanaian novels published in the 1960s depict life in the colonial period and immediately afterwards. These include Joseph Abruquah's *The Catechist* (1965) and *The Torrent* (1968), and Amu Djoleto's *The Strange Man* (1967), on the horrors of colonial education. Djoleto also produced *Money Galore* (1975), almost a decade later, depicting corruption in post-independence Ghana. A few years before *The Catechist*, Gambian-born William Conton in Sierra Leone wrote *The African* (1960), about a young boy's rites of passage in a rural community. Gambian poet Lenrie Peters published his only novel, *The Second Round* (1965), set in Sierra Leone and depicting the problems of a young doctor returning home after his training in Britain.

If the early fiction of Amadi is sometimes placed in the category of "village novel", and that of Munonye moves on only a little further to the period of colonial contact, then the later work of both writers tends to move along the thematic continuum sketched above. Achebe, of course, is the key example of these paradigmatic shifts, as his fiction moves successively through the pre-colonial, colonial, and post-colonial phases to his modern Nigerian dystopias; he only stops short of the genuinely radical experimental novel.

Post-Independence Adjustment

The satire of Munonye's last novel is also the province of another pioneer figure, T. M. Aluko, whose *One Man, One Wife* (1959; revised 1967) was the first Nigerian novel to be published by a Nigerian firm. Here, and in its more accomplished successors, *One Man, One Matchet* (1964), *Kinsman and Foreman* (1966), and *Chief the Honourable Minister* (1970), Aluko offers a sardonic vision of Nigerian life. His ironic treatment of local government (*His Worshipful Majesty*, 1973), a creaking legal system (*Wrong Ones in the Dock*, 1982) and regional politics (*A State of Our Own*, 1986) has roused critical indignation over the years. Aluko has continued unrepentant, however, and with the publication of *Conduct Unbecoming* (1993), the output of this often neglected novelist now spans five decades.

Aluko also shifts the perspective to modern urban life, a context that has produced some of the finest West African fiction, including novels by Ekwensi, Soyinka, and the Ghanaian Ayi Kwei Armah.

Although Achebe is widely regarded as the greatest Black African novelist writing in English, he was anticipated and (quantitatively at least) surpassed by his countryman **Cyprian Ekwensi**. In view of the twenty-year silence between *A Man of the People* and *Anthills of the Savannah*, moreover, Ekwensi rather than Achebe is in some ways the key novelist of post-independence Nigeria. A prolific and versatile writer, Ekwensi has produced chapbook-style fiction, children's books, short stories, novellas and ten major novels. The first of the latter, *People of the City* (1954), evolved from a group of thirteen independent stories and established Ekwensi's characteristic mode of social realism in a modern urban setting. After his second and most highly regarded novel, *Jagua Nana* (1961), Ekwensi nevertheless produced the uncharacteristically pastoral *Burning Grass* (1962), based on his experiences among the nomadic Fulani people of Northern Nigeria in the 1940s.

The subsequent fiction is predominantly urban, however, and includes *Beautiful Feathers* (1963), a satire of the pan-African dream, followed by three novels variously anticipating or contemplating the Nigerian Civil War of 1967–70: *Iska* (1966), *Survive the Peace* (1976), and *Divided We Stand* (1980). Two more novels, *For a Roll of Parchment* and *Jagua Nana's Daughter* both appeared in 1986, although the first of these (unique for its English setting) was actually written thirty years earlier. Ekwensi recently produced a tenth novel, *King for Ever!* (1992), in the form of a political allegory on the abuse of power.

There are interesting analogies between Cyprian Ekwensi and the eighteenth-century English novelist Daniel Defoe. Ekwensi's early novelette *When Love Whispers* (1947) was thus the first pamphlet of the so-called Onitsha market literature, and has a literary status roughly equivalent to some of Defoe's popular tracts. More pertinently, *Jagua Nana*, Ekwensi's strongest novel, with his single most sustained character, emerges as a kind of African *Moll Flanders*. Ekwensi also shares with Defoe a familiarity (and fascination) with criminal life, an intimacy with the metropolis (Lagos now rather than London), and even an occasional moral ambivalence towards his characters.

His Jagua Nana is an experienced Lagos "high-lifer" in her mid-forties who has bewitched her young lover, Freddie Namme, a teacher at the Nigerian National College. Jagua's ultimate aim is to finance Freddie's legal studies in England, so that he will return a rich and successful "been-to" to provide for her declining years. Jagua thus also shares Moll's particular blend of hard-headedness and naivety: Freddie does go to England, but first seduces and later marries Nancy Oll, the nineteen-year-old daughter of Jagua's great professional rival.

Jagua's life, like Moll's, is both eventful and mobile, as when she trustingly makes the five-hundred-mile journey by truck from Lagos to her native Igbo region to present herself to Freddie's parents. She finds on arrival that she has been pre-empted by Nancy and her mother, but later receives a serious offer of marriage (together with the correct bride price) from the local chief. Her polite refusal is perhaps influenced by the fact that she would only have been the fourth wife. Back in Lagos, however, Jagua becomes involved in politics through her new protector, "Uncle" Taiwo, eventually inheriting the latter's embezzled campaign funds. She now retires to her home village, happily sponsoring such worthy causes as the completion of the local church, and repaying her bride price. With the substantial remaining sum, she establishes herself as a "merchant princess" in Onitsha. Her new-found prosperity on such morally ambivalent foundations recalls Moll's eventual success in Virginia.

Like Defoe, too, Ekwensi produces enough biographical detail about his protagonist to suggest a highly credible case history. Product of a traditional (read patriarchal) village environment, Jagua has rejected her family, particularly her pastor father, for the greater freedom of Lagos. To an intelligent and independently minded woman, the advantages of this move are obvious; her subsequent career as a prostitute, far from suggesting any kind of moral depravity, merely seems a realistic assessment of limited opportunities in a male-oriented world. The point at which Ekwensi surpasses Defoe, however, is in the feminist implications of his narrative. He thus consistently satirizes male pretensions, whether in the hypocritical Freddie, the unscrupulous Uncle Taiwo, or the many other regulars of the *Tropicana* night club. Jagua, on the other hand, has a firm idea of her own value, certainly considering herself the equal of any of her customers' wives. One of her reasons for refusing to marry Chief Obufara is his foreignness to "the sensation of African woman as equal".

But if Ekwensi emulates *Moll Flanders* with his sympathetic insights into a woman's world, he surpasses it in his range of speech presentation. Jagua and Freddie, although both Ibos, thus speak a Pidgin English together ("to escape clan and custom"), and Ekwensi's skill at reproducing it is justly famous. He in fact represents the whole gamut of Nigerian speech, from the norms of the British Council to the "grammatical English" of the "been-tos" and various degrees of Pidgin, in addition to the Yoruba of the Lagos taxi driver or the Igbo of Jagua's family.

It is fashionable to disparage Ekwensi's writing, and *Jagua Nana* does occasionally contain what seem like stylistic lapses:

> Her complexion glowed livelier than the twinkling lights of the *Tropicana,* her ever-smiling teeth, the ripeness of her lips, charged Freddie with a boundless thirst for her etc.   (p. 16)

Ekwensi's subtle response to language elsewhere nevertheless suggests an indifference here rather than an insensitivity to the requirements of "fine writing". As Ekwensi confessed to Bernth Lindfors: "I don't regard myself as one of the sacred writers, writing for some audience locked up in the higher seats of learning." Nevertheless, *Jagua Nana* will certainly endure for as long as *Moll Flanders*.

Another important novel of the 1960s was **Wole Soyinka's** *The Interpreters* (1965). The title refers to an exchange between two observers at a Christian revivalist meeting, where one comments to his companion on the critical experience the cult leader must have undergone: "If he has chosen to interpret it in a way that would bring some kind of meaning into people's lives, who are you to scoff at it..." (p. 179).

The reference to this scene underlines the narrative's existentialist dimension. Soyinka's group of young Western-educated intellectuals – Egbo the civil servant, Sekoni the engineer, Sagoe the journalist, Kola the artist, Bandele the university lecturer – all face difficult choices in a corrupt society, as they attempt to find meaning for their own lives. The background against which such choices must be made provides ample material for an exposure of Nigeria's post-independence black elite. One of Soyinka's most hilarious scenes (perhaps owing something to Amis's *Lucky Jim*) is the party given by the snobbish Professor Oguazor and his wife, where Sagoe ends by throwing plastic fruit through the window. One of his harshest portraits is that of the homosexual history lecturer, Joe Golder, a fierce attack on *negritude* and all African-Americans racially more white than black, and culturally more American than African.

In broader generic terms, *The Interpreters* is a prototype of the African post-colonial dystopia; Ayi Kwei Armah's *The Beautyful Ones Are Not Yet Born* is another obvious example of the form. Soyinka's juggling of existential quest and satirical invective does not make for easy reading. Also sometimes demanding is the author's meticulous representation of Nigeria's linguistic continuum. Mathias, the office boy at the *Independent Viewpoint*, speaks a barely comprehensible English Pidgin; the rapacious Chief Winsala, when flustered, loses his grasp of English syntax (and even vocabulary), becoming the object of a brilliant parody on the sententious African patriarch ("...it is no matter for rejoicing when a child sees his father naked, *l'ogolonto*. Agba n't'ara. The wise eunuch keeps from women; the hungry clerk dons coat over his narrow belt and who will say his belly is flat?" etc., p. 91). Such crudities contrast with the extreme linguistic facility and enormous cultural range of Soyinka's sophisticated Westernized intellectuals, and, by implication, of the author himself.

Although not as significant in the history of the African novel as the author's drama and poetry in their respective genres, *The Interpreters* is unsurpassed as social and political satire, The precise scope of the latter emerges forcefully in the final chapter, where Sagoe invents a scheme for mass transportation of the city's human waste (by donkey or rail!) to the barren north, thus providing both natural fertilizer and job opportunities. The ease with which the local MP is taken in by the scheme suggests that, in modern Nigeria, the political class represents the problem itself rather than its solution.

The Interpreters is a demanding novel set mainly in the academic communities of Lagos and Ibadan. Soyinka's second attempt at fiction, the more accessible *Season of Anomy* (1973), uses mythological structures to cover many human events and a wide range of moral issues; it was recently reissued together with *Aké: The Years of Childhood* (first published in 1981).

Civil War

Although not explicitly concerned with Nigeria's Civil War, *Season of Anomy* is a powerful meditation on the question of violence in general. Soyinka was imprisoned for two years during the war (1967–9), mainly for a daring mediation attempt in the Biafra conflict, and almost every major Nigerian writer was either directly affected by these tragic events and/or wrote about them in retrospect.

The province of Biafra, which attempted unsuccessfully to secede from Nigeria, corresponds broadly with the Ibo homeland. Chinua Achebe and a number of other Ibo writers campaigned actively at home and abroad on Biafra's behalf. Achebe, who had just published *A Man of the People*, could not write fiction under wartime conditions and produced no new novel for more than twenty years; many of the poems in his collection *Beware Soul Brother* (1971) deal with wartime experiences. Nigeria's greatest poet in English, Christopher Okigbo, was an early victim of the fighting; several prose manuscripts by Gabriel Okara were also destroyed.

Thirty years later, the Civil War had still not lost its hold on the Nigerian imagination. Fictional treatments of it include Kole Omotoso's *The Combat* (1972), John Munonye's *A Wreath for the Maidens* (1973), Flora Nwapa's novella *Never Again* (1975) and collection of short stories *Wives at War* (1980), Isidore Okpewho's *The Last Duty* (1976), Buchi Emecheta's *Destination Biafra* (1982), Ken

Saro-Wiwa's *Sozaboy* (1985), Elechi Amadi's *Estrangement* (1986), Festus Iyayi's *Heroes* (1986) and some of the stories in Ben Okri's *Stars of the New Curfew* (1988).

Post-Independence Disillusion

In the context of *The Interpreters*, it is difficult to decide where "adjustment" ends and "disillusion" begins. In Ghanaian **Ayi Kwei Armah's** *The Beautyful Ones Are Not Yet Born* (1968) – even without the shadow of the war – the divide has definitely been crossed: Ghana had after all gained independence three years before Nigeria. Like Soyinka's novel, Armah's *The Beautyful Ones Are Not Yet Born* is also a two-toned narrative, collating existential fantasy with social realism: it thus combines the personal meditation of its unnamed protagonist (the *man*) in the Ghanaian Railway Administration service with a sweeping indictment of one African society in the years following independence.

In a purely political context, the anonymous "man" registers his distaste for the dishonesty and corruption around him, from the conductor who short-changes him on the municipal bus to "wolf mouth" the timber contractor who comes to the railway office to offer a bribe. Such disenchantment appears nowhere more graphically than in the image reducing man to "something less than the size and meaning of little short-lived flying ants on raining nights" (p. 22). A more general tone of despair emerges, however, in the protagonist's dystopian view of post-independence Ghana, where post-colonial rhetoric is inseparable from post-colonial delusion. According to propaganda, "the sons of the nation were now in charge"; according to the narrator, "how completely the new thing took after the old" (p. 10). For as with Naipaul's "mimic men", the most striking characteristic of the newly independent regime is its insistence on copying its former colonial masters. The narrator protests repeatedly at this process, whether it is against the "black man trying to be the dark ghost of a European" (p. 81) or the "black men with white souls and names trying mightily to be white" (p. 126).

The two elements of the narrative merge neatly in the story of the protagonist's relations with Joseph Koomson, a childhood friend who has prospered dramatically after entering politics, to reach the rank of "Minister Plenipotentiary, Member of the Presidential Commission". Koomson's situation is dramatically reversed, however, by the advent of a political coup (clearly based on

the anti-Nkrumah coup in Ghana in 1966, after nine years of independence). Now a fugitive fleeing for his life, he returns to the
man's house. In a dramatic climax, there is a spectacular convergence of the literal and figurative as the terrified Koomson loses all
control over his physical functions: here, quite literally, is the smell
of corruption and the stench of fear. The novel's *leitmotiv* of waste
and excrement now comes fully into its own as Koomson's only
escape from the soldiers of the new regime (a military *purge*
perhaps) is through the latrine hole of the *man*'s apartment block.

In a neat *coda*, the man takes Koomson to the harbour, where a
cooperative fisherman delivers judgement in what is a clear suggestion of an African vernacular language, before negotiating free
passage in unmistakable Pidgin. As Koomson escapes to sea, his
stench becomes stronger again, whilst the man slips overboard in
an obvious purification ritual, before swimming back to land. On
the beach he witnesses a road-block erected by the new regime, at
which a bus is held up until its driver pays the requisite bribe: *plus
ça change*. As the bus pulls away, however, it reveals the graffiti
giving the novel its title: THE BEAUTYFUL ONES ARE NOT YET BORN, although the reader's reaction might be "How long, Lord, how long."

In addition to their common themes, *The Interpreters* and *The
Beautyful Ones Are Not Yet Born* are even more closely linked by
their parallel emphasis on filth. Realistically, Armah's description
of staff lavatories at the Ghanaian Railway Administration service
recalls conditions at the offices of Soyinka's *Independent Viewpoint*.
And when Sagoe, in *The Interpreters*, walks through the streets of
Lagos at five in the morning, to find an overturned night-cart and
trailer, he inevitably discovers (like Armah) the figurative potential
of so much waste: "Next to death ... shit is the most vernacular atmosphere of our beloved country" (p. 108).

Armah's next two novels, *Fragments* (1970) and *Why Are We So
Blest?* (1972), are essentially variations of the "been-to" narrative,
featuring the clash between African and Western ways. The first
book, more explicitly autobiographical, has its hero return from
America to a family interested only in the material possessions he
may have acquired there; the second, set in a thinly disguised
Algeria during the period of its independence struggle in that
country, follows the revolutionary involvement of a young
Harvard-educated Ghanaian. James Booth described *Why Are We
So Blest?*, with its background of American Black Power politics, as
"a racist fiction about racist fictions" – doubtless referring to

Armah's growing demonization of the "white race". This tendency reaches saturation point in the following novels: *Two Thousand Seasons* (1973), a collective history of African peoples, and *The Healers* (1978), an account of the dissolving Ashanti Empire.

The anger of Armah is most closely matched in Nigerian fiction by Festus Iyayi, whose strong identification with various oppressed groups recalls the attitudes of the Kenyan novelist Ngũgĩ. Iyayi's novels include *Violence* (1979), *The Contract* (1982), and his Civil War novel, *Heroes* (1986), winner of the Commonwealth Writers Prize in 1988.

New Voices

The "new voices" in African fiction, it was suggested above, refers not only to the formal experimentation of a Ben Okri, but also to the increasing body of African women's writing. Among several key figures in the latter context, it may be revealing that the two most interesting, Buchi Emecheta and Ama Ata Aidoo, have long left their native countries.

Women's writing in Nigeria was pioneered by Flora Nwapa, whose work has been described as the "expansion of an African tale". Three of her four full-length novels, *Efuru* (1966), *Idu* (1970), and *One is Enough* (1981), circle rather obsessively around the theme of the childless woman. The fiction of Zaynab Alkali, on the other hand, is unusual both for its author's north Nigerian origins and for its challenge to a male-dominated literary establishment. Her two novels *The Stillborn* (1984) and *The Virtuous Woman* (1985) are thoughtful, if hardly iconoclastic, studies of traditional patriarchal structures.

A more provocative writer is the Ghanaian Ama Ata Aidoo. After two plays and a volume of short stories, *No Sweetness Here* (1970), Aidoo produced the experimental novel *Our Sister Killjoy* (1977), with its mixture of prose, poetry, and epistolary fiction. Better known, however, is her highly accomplished second novel, *Changes: A Love Story* (1991). The latter, with its deceptively Western flavour, dwells on the role conflicts of an educated and career-orientated young woman, although superficial parallels fade from the moment the heroine's husband announces his intention of taking a second wife.

The most significant woman writer from West Africa, however, is **Buchi Emecheta**, whose novels divide naturally into three groups.

In the Ditch (1972) and *Second Class Citizen* (1974) are both largely fictionalized autobiography, although in reversed chronological sequence: the first based on the author's life as a lone parent with five children in a London housing project, the second following the same life through childhood and adolescence to marriage and separation in England. The sequence was later updated by the more explicitly autobiographical *Head Above Water* (1986).

Emecheta's next three novels are set in Nigeria at different periods in the country's recent history, and all of them reflect the injustices perpetrated on women by a reactionary and obscurantist patriarchal system. In *The Bride Price* (1976), set in the 1950s, the young Aku-ana elopes with the village schoolteacher. Their love is doomed, however, since the teacher is a descendant of slaves and cannot therefore marry a free person, whilst Aku-ana's bride price has not been paid. *The Slave Girl* (1977), set several decades earlier and in some ways reminiscent of the "village novels" of Amadi or Munonye, describes the efforts of a young orphan girl to preserve her identity after being sold into slavery by her elder brother. *The Joys of Motherhood* (1979), ranging from the 1930s to Nigerian independence, is nevertheless Emecheta's most ambitious novel to date.

The ironic title refers to the struggles of Nnu Ego to raise a family over almost three decades in pre-independence Nigeria. Born into traditional Ibo society, she marries young, but is rapidly reduced to labourer status on her inability to produce an heir ("if you can't produce sons, at least you can help harvest yams"). Subsequently dispatched to Lagos to marry a man she has never seen, she then produces nine children, with little more than the basic biological contribution from her new husband. The eighteen chapter headings alone (including "A Failed Woman"…"A Man is Never Ugly"…"Sharing a Husband"…"Women Alone") invoke the stations of Nnu Ego's steady progress towards martyrdom, ending fittingly with one entitled "The Canonised Mother". Married to Nnaife, who is successively washerman, grass-cutter, ship's crew and soldier – but habitually drunk or absent whatever his role – Nnu Ego is perpetually dependent on her own resources, reinforced by the solidarity of other women.

In terms of land and language, most of the novel's characters are either rural or urban Igbo (the latter living in a Yoruba-dominated Lagos), with the occasional Hausa from Northern Nigeria providing an exotically inscrutable other. Linguistic relations are clearly specified, with Ibo speakers frequently handicapped or inhibited by their inability to express themselves in Yoruba. Behind both languages, however, English encroaches ever more insistently into Nigerian life, for, as one tribesman is already aware in the 1920s: "This is the age of the white man." But the English language is merely the vehicle of a more total cultural and political hegemony, or in Nnu Ego's words: "Are we not all slaves to the white man, in a way?"

Nnaife does the washing for an English couple, the Meers, but, like the other "boys" lodged in the compound, is reduced to penury on his employers' departure from Nigeria at the outbreak of the Second World War. Later conscripted into the British Army, he spends three years fighting in India and Burma. In addition to these literal encroachments on traditional Ibo life, however, the colonial experience also marks the imposition of a written culture on a traditional oral one. Significant here is the barely literate status of Nnu Ego and Nnaife ("she and her husband were ill-prepared for a life like this, where only pen and not mouth could really talk", p. 179). Necessary as education may be, it is also the ultimate cause of the family's disintegration, as Nnu Ego makes crippling sacrifices for her sons, one of whom leaves for the United States on a scholarship, and – ultimate degradation – marries a white woman.

Emecheta is an eloquent chronicler of Nigeria's transition from traditional rural to modern urban society, an important complement to Achebe, moreover, through her insistence on female perspectives. She is also of enormous interest for her relationship with the English language. She did not begin to study English formally until the age of twelve, and has claimed in an interview to translate most dialogue from her native Igbo. In *The Joys of Motherhood*, not surprisingly then, Emecheta's English achieves a subtle and flexible presentation of Igbo speech. Apart from a liberal sprinkling of Igbo words, glossed, paraphrased, and – just occasionally – untranslated, she also uses praise names, patronymics and other honorific titles in dialogue exchanges. More subtle still, are her syntactic suggestions of an Ibo original: "If you wish to die, why do you want me to be your killer", yells an irate *kia-kia* bus-driver (p. 57); "Nnu Ego, the daughter of Agbadi. Please take that look from your face", begs her childhood friend Ato (p. 74).

Equally characteristic of the narrative, however, is the articulation of the heroine–protagonist's growing self-awareness by modern feminist insights: "it occurred to Nnu Ego that she was a prisoner, imprisoned by her love for her children. ...It was not fair, she felt, the way men cleverly used a woman's sense of responsibility to actually enslave her" (p. 137). Or even more eloquently in her subsequent prayer:

> God, when will you create a woman who will be fulfilled in herself, a full human being, not anybody's appendage?   (p. 186)

Since *The Joys of Motherhood*, Emecheta has produced quite variegated fiction, including a war narrative, *Destination Biafra* (1982), an African campus novel, *Double Yoke* (1983), and a post-colonial allegory, *The Rape of Shavi* (1983). This third group of novels was extended by *Gwendolen* (1989), a grim tale of incest and abuse, unusual in its substitution of a West Indian for the conventional Nigerian protagonist.

Among various kinds of fictional innovation, one may distinguish between the generic, the linguistic, and the conceptual; in Kole Omotoso, Ken Saro-Wiwa and Ben Okri, respectively, the Nigerian novel can supply a fine example of each mode.

Within the context of the stepmother tongue, Kole Omotoso has a special place. Born in Akure, Western Nigeria, he began his literary career transcribing Yoruba folk-tales, and also tried to write creatively in both French and Arabic (he has a doctorate in modern Arabic literature). He has also shown a willingness to experiment in the more marginal fictional genres, such as the detective novel. After *The Edifice* (1971), depicting the strains of a racially mixed marriage in Britain and Nigeria, Omotoso's following seven novels vary widely in range. They include two secret-agent/detective novel hybrids, *Fellah's Choice* (1974) and *The Scales* (1976); a personalized reaction to the Civil War, *The Combat* (1972); and two broad indictments of modern Nigeria, *To Borrow a Wandering Leaf* (1978) and *Memories of Our Recent Boom* (1982). More original than these is *Sacrifice* (1974), the story of a young doctor in a town where his mother still works as a prostitute, the way in which she had paid for her son's education. By far Omotoso's most ambitious work, however, is the long quasi-documentary "faction" (analogous to the New Journalism of Mailer and Capote) of *Just Before Dawn* (1988), spanning Nigerian history from the 1880s to the collapse of the second republic in 1983.

The great linguistic innovator, on the other hand, is Ken Saro-Wiwa. In his attention to popular forms, Saro-Wiwa has affinities with Cyprian Ekwensi; but in his experimentation with non-standard varieties of English, he also invites comparison with Tutuola or Okara. In a colourful and versatile career, Saro-Wiwa held two university posts, became cabinet minister in a civilian government, ran his own publishing business and was probably Nigeria's most popular writer before his execution without due process by the country's military government in 1995. Saro-Wiwa wrote short stories, books for schoolchildren, and numerous scripts for a popular Nigerian television series called "Basi and Company". His most original work, however, is *Sozaboy* (1985), a scathing account of the Nigerian Civil War. Humorously subtitled "A novel in rotten English", *Sozaboy* is the first serious, full-length prose narrative from Nigeria to be written entirely in Pidgin and other popular registers.

The most significant innovator among younger West African novelists in purely conceptual terms is **Ben Okri**. After two essentially autobiographical works, *Flowers and Shadows* (1980) and *The Landscapes Within* (1981), followed by two collections of short stories, Okri produced his massive novel *The Famished Road* (1991). Much of what is most original in the latter derives from the inspired use of an *abiku*, or "spirit child", to chronicle an unspecified (but unmistakable) modern urban Nigeria. Not since Rushdie's thousand and-one children, perhaps, has a novel in English found such a potentially fertile structural device. Azaro's episodic narrative also has a distance or detachment (even a kind of "defamiliarization") towards the human world, features reminiscent of the picaresque and "spy" narratives of eighteenth-century England. At the same time, however, the novel's strong linear thrust, without exhaustive formal realism or complex psychological patterning, seems more obviously African. *The Famished Road* is also saturated with magic and traditional lore, in a manner which (linguistic eccentricities apart) also recalls the novels of Tutuola.

The interpenetration of human and spirit worlds is comprehensive and yet casual, even comic, as in the case of Jeremiah, the local photographer. A constant witness of the misery, squalor, and political violence of urban life, Jeremiah's camera may be read as an allegory of conventional realist techniques; it is a careful recorder of surfaces and, in recognition of the presumed universality of the approach, Jeremiah is even described at one point as the "International Photographer". At the party to celebrate Azaro's homecoming, however, there is an ironic account of the photographer's activity, now acknowledging the worlds that lie beyond it:

> After much prancing and mystery-making, as if he were a magician, the photographer lifted up the camera. He was surrounded by little ghosts and spirits. They had climbed on one another to take a closer look at the instrument. They were so fascinated by the camera that they climbed on him and hung on his arms and stood on his head. He was very drunk and cheerfully took three pictures of the landlord with his flywhisk.   (p. 46)

But just as the *abiku* provides the central narrative structure, so the shifting images of the road produce an (admittedly ambivalent) metaphorical base. The novel's opening image – ("because the road was once a river it was always hungry") – thus seems to contradict a concluding comment – "a road that is open is never hungry". Between these points, moreover, are many other associations. The neighbour's prayer for Azaro ("The road will never swallow you. The river of your destiny will always overcome evil"...) implies a threat. The story told by Azaro's father suggests that danger lies not in the road itself, but in the all-consuming "King of the Road". In the world of spirits, the road can be a path to heaven, where each new material gain or natural disaster destroys what has been carefully built. In the human world, on the other hand, the damage caused by the newly-constructed road suggests, more topically, the environmental cost of material progress.

Another paradoxical element of the narrative is its linguistic medium, in the sense that the latter acquires significance precisely because it is not emphasized. Okri thus excludes most familiar cultural referents without providing any alternative ones of his own (Nigeria is never explicitly named; Yoruba, Hausa, and the town of Ughelli are mentioned once each); there is not even any clear indication of the language his characters would be speaking. Multilingualism in *The Famished Road*, moreover, normally has negative associations: characters swear in several languages; Madame Koto's drunken customers sing "unfamiliar songs in harsh languages"; politicians "make their promises in four languages". And yet, when Azaro's born-again, quixotic father wishes to improve himself, he begins with a comprehensive course of self-study with help from Azaro (featuring Homer's *Odyssey* on one occasion) presumably in English.

An obvious explanation for such ambivalence is the nature of Okri's unconventional narrator, who defies reductive critical approaches. By a simple mental adjustment, moreover, the reader may see these anomalies as a necessary precondition of the narrative, rather than as something to be explained away. *The Famished Road* thus makes concrete allusions to a specific political context (rats are equated with politicians who are in turn equated with colonial authorities – more explicitly British, in fact, than their victims are Nigerian); but at the same time, it offers a more general application to the human condition. The universal does not, however, preclude the historically specific. The clearest identification of Okri's fictional country with Nigeria emerges in his many references to the violence and aggression of political thugs, seen as anticipating the military dictators of a later period. And the final application of the *abiku* image that controls *The Famished Road* is to Azaro's (and Okri's own) fictional Nigeria: the latter is seen as an *abiku* country, in the sense that it is never truly born, but struggles abortively between each fresh attempt at emergence. Okri's novel is thus no mere indulgent formal experiment, but returns to the disillusionment expressed by many of its literary predecessors.

Two other kinds of fictional experiment characterize the work of Kofi Awoonor and Syl Cheney-Coker. Awoonor, a Ghanaian poet and novelist who writes in both English and Ewe, is best known for his synthesis of Ewe oral tradition and modernist techniques. In his allegorical *This Earth, My Brother...* (1972), each chapter of the narrative proper is complemented by a kind of speculative commentary, a division repeated in his mythopeic second novel, *Comes the Voyager At Last (1992)*. Awoonor has also published a survey of African history, culture, and literature, *The Breast of the Earth* (1975), widely regarded as seminal. Cheney-Coker, from Sierra Leone and also originally known as a poet, published a long prose epic with elements of magic realism, entitled *The Last Harmattan of Alusine Dunbar* (1990).

EAST AFRICA

Broad analogies may be drawn between West and East Africa (defined here as Kenya, Uganda and Tanzania), with reference to the importance of oral culture, the sense of community, the strength of traditional patriarchy, and the centrality of the colonial experience. The independence process was nevertheless more traumatic here, particularly in Kenya, scene of bitter fighting between the Land and Freedom Movement (or "Mau Mau") and the British colonial power. This struggle left a profound mark on the national consciousness (much as the *Chimurenga* has done in Zimbabwe), and is often reflected in Kenyan anglophone fiction. In all three countries, moreover, Arab economic and political power were influential – as was German, briefly, in Tanzania (the former Tanganyika). Something of both masters is depicted in Abdulrazak Gurnah's fine historical reconstruction of Tanganyika and the East African interior in *Paradise* (1994). More important still in East Africa, however, was the century-old Indian presence, brutally terminated in Uganda by Idi Amin in the 1970s. The Indian experience is even more closely reflected in fiction, with such novels as V. S. Naipaul's *A Bend in the River* (although actually set in a fictionalized Zaïre) or M. G. Vassanji's *The Gunny Sack*.

In terms of language, however, the situations of East and West Africa to some extent diverge. Kenya is as linguistically polyglot as most African countries: of its population of 28 million, slightly more than half speak one of five Bantu languages, of which Gikuyu (6 million) is the most important; two Nilotic languages, Luo and Kalenjin, have about 3 million speakers each; two Cushitic languages (including Somali) have small numbers of speakers in the east and north-east. But Kenya has a *lingua franca* in Swahili (also belonging to the Bantu family), carrying official status and widely spoken as a second language.

The position of Swahili is even stronger in Tanzania, which has a population of 30 million and 120 other languages, of which one, Sukuma, is used by 4 million people but no other has more than a million speakers. Uganda, with a population of 20 million, has no *lingua franca* – Ganda (or Luganda) is spoken by about 3 million people, including the population of the capital – and the position of English is correspondingly stronger. These linguistic factors in Kenya and Tanzania (in Uganda one would have to substitute political ones) may have conditioned the fact that East Africa does not have a broad literary tradition like that of Nigeria or South Africa.

The region has, on the other hand, produced two of the most remarkable of all African novelists in Ngũgĩ wa Thiong'o and (from neighbouring Somalia) Nuruddin Farah. Besides their unquestioned individual talents, moreover, these two writers also embody diametrically opposed attitudes towards the English language conceived as the stepmother tongue: in Ngũgĩ's case, uncompromising support for African vernacular languages, and the eventual abandonment of English for his native Gikuyu; in Farah's, an apparently almost casual selection of English among the many languages he knew, a choice that he has not subsequently changed. For this reason alone, it is instructive to begin with these authors.

Ngũgĩ wa Thiong'o's first and most autobiographical novel, *Weep not, Child* (1964), is an account of Kenya's armed struggle in the 1950s seen through the eyes of a child. This was succeeded by *The River Between* (published in 1965, although written first) and *A Grain of Wheat* (1966). Ngũgĩ's major work, at least in terms of size, is the massive *Petals of Blood* (1977), after which he progressively abandoned English for Gikuyu. The satirical *Caitaani Mũtharabaini* (1982) was translated by the author as *Devil on the Cross*, while a second novel, *Matigari Ma Njirũũngi* (1986), was translated by another hand as *Matigari* (1979).

A Grain of Wheat scrutinizes the lives of several individuals from the Land and Freedom Movement in the final days before independence in 1963. These include Mugo, solitary orphan and peasant farmer from the Rift Valley; Gikonyo, a carpenter and estranged husband of a wife with a child by another man; and Karanja, assistant at an agricultural research station and now a willing collaborator with the British. All three have suffered for their political activism, and served long periods in various detention centres; all three have also been false to the movement in different ways, one quite specifically by betraying a local freedom fighter to the colonial authorities.

A Grain of Wheat is a complex novel, not least for its constant chronological shifts in the manner of Conrad, as the histories of its three major characters are slowly assembled. But if Ngũgĩ's technique suggests *Nostromo* or *Under Western Eyes* (he is known to have once begun a thesis on Conrad), then his main European character, John Thompson the colonial administrator, recalls the Kurtz of *Heart of Darkness*. Like his Conradian predecessor, Thompson comes to Africa with a "great moral idea" of the benefits offered by enlightened colonial rule. He also records his growing disillusion in a journal that moves from paternalism (endorsing Schweitzer's remark that "The negro is a child, and with children, nothing can be done without the use of authority") to total revulsion: his later call to "eliminate the vermin" is an exact paraphrase of Kurtz's final appeal to "exterminate the brutes". Thompson's notes are intended for a study to be called *Prospero in Africa*, a satirical authorial reference to Shakespeare's own good (white) colonial magician in *The*

Tempest. But there is also an ironic parallel with that other gem of colonial scholarship, *The Pacification of the Primitive Tribes of the Lower Niger*, planned by the District Commissioner in Chinua Achebe's *Things Fall Apart*. The comparison with Achebe is a useful one, moreover, in view of Ngũgĩ's similar account of early colonial history from an African perspective.

By far the most significant literary influence in *A Grain of Wheat*, however, is the Bible. The very title of the novel is explained by its first and last epigraphs, from I Corinthians 15:36–7:

> Thou fool, that which thou sowest is not quickened, except it die. And that which thou sowest, thou sowest not that body that shall be, but bare grain, it may chance of wheat, or of some other grain.

and, even more explicitly, from St John 12:24:

> Verily, verily, I say unto you, Except a corn of wheat fall into the ground and die, it abideth alone; but if it die, it bringeth forth much fruit.

Both quotations may be read as a recognition of the sacrifices (however imperfect) made by members of the Freedom Movement.

Between these verses are the epigraphs from *Exodus*, where the plight of Kenyans under colonial rule is equated with "the children of Israel" captive in Egypt; the comparison is particularly fitting in the context of forced labour by political prisoners in British detention camps. The inspiration of Kihika, the guerrilla leader whose betrayal overshadows the entire novel, is Moses ("Thus saith the Lord, Let my people go"). *Uhuru*, or independence, is seen (however naively) as "the New Jerusalem" or "Canaan's shore". The support of African Christian revivalists for continuing British rule, on the other hand, is compared more shrewdly with relations between Pharisees and Romans in New Testament times. The list of examples could be greatly extended, for the whole narrative is saturated with biblical tropes.

Even more significant in the novel, however, is the hint of Ngũgĩ's changing attitude towards his linguistic medium. *A Grain of Wheat* was followed by one more novel, *Petals of Blood* (1977), written directly in English; Ngũgĩ then switched to his native Gikuyu, believing that the use of an African language was the sole effective means for achieving what he has described as the

"Decolonisation of the Mind". Several stylistic elements in *A Grain of Wheat* even suggest a certain inevitability about this decision. These include the large number of idioms and proverbs left in the original Gikuyu or Swahili; the increasing reliance on traditional oral patterns; the introduction of such essentially African verse forms as the "praise poem"; and the use of a collective village narrator ("We sang song after song about Kihika and Mugo").

After his shift to Gikuyu, Ngũgĩ continued to write what he called "explanatory prose" in English, until the appearance of the four essays collected under the title of *Decolonising the Mind* (1986). Here he announced his "farewell to English" as a vehicle for any kind of writing. Ngũgĩ's justification for his position was, in fact, disarmingly simple: the majority of African people speak African languages, and only a tiny minority of them speak French or English or Portuguese; for these speakers, the ex-colonial language has become the language of "conceptualization", so that African thought has become "imprisoned in foreign languages".

There is naturally some irony in the fact that the last (or latest) version of *Decolonising the Mind* was formulated for the Robb memorial lectures in Auckland, New Zealand. The contents evolved moreover, as Ngũgĩ explains, from papers read and speeches given not only in the author's native Kenya, but also in Zimbabwe, Nigeria, Germany (at the University of Bayreuth) and Britain (at the Commonwealth Institute in London). It is unlikely that Ngũgĩ would have received his many invitations had he not already made an international reputation for himself as an anglophone writer. Far from colonizing Ngũgĩ's mind, therefore, a knowledge of English might be considered to have extended it. Such a principled stand as Ngũgĩ's might incidentally have been more economically damaging for a younger writer who had not yet found an audience; for the same reason, it would also have passed unnoticed among the international literary community.

On a socio-cultural continuum, the Somali novelist **Nuruddin Farah** also occupies a fairly extreme point, but at the opposite end to Ngũgĩ.

Born in Baidoa, the son of the interpreter to the British governor of what is now called the Ogaden, Farah grew up speaking English, Italian, and Arabic, together with Amharic (the official language of Ethiopia) and his native Somali. He received his first formal education in Arabic, and might therefore have been expected to write in that language. He ascribes his choice of English to the simple fact that when he first thought of becoming an author, he only had access to a typewriter with an English keyboard (Somali was beyond consideration since the language had no accepted orthography until 1972). Farah then studied in India for four years, graduating from the University of the Punjab in Chandigarh (by which time, he had already written two novels in English). He admits to feeling closer in many ways to an Indian writer like Rushdie than to his fellow African authors.

Linguistic issues apart, another characteristic of Farah is his concern for an issue raised more obliquely by many African novelists: the links between traditional patriarchy, religious fundamentalism, and political repression. Farah's first novel, *From a Crooked Rib* (1970) – with its sympathetic account of a young Somali girl trying to escape an arranged marriage – was in fact assumed by some readers to have been written by a woman. It was followed by *A Naked Needle* (1976), a study of corrupt and tyrannical patriarchy in both the family and the state. The most thorough analysis of these issues, however, occurs in *Sweet and Sour Milk* (1979), *Sardines* (1981), and *Close Sesame* (1983), the trilogy collectively entitled "Variations on the Theme of an African Dictatorship". *Maps* (1984) continues this process of exploration.

More specifically, *Sardines* is the story of a group of Somali intellectuals (Farah uses the term "privilegentsia") struggling to give their lives meaning in a Mogadiscio held in the tyrannical grip of the "General", a thinly disguised portrait of the real-life dictator Siad Barre. At the centre of the novel is Medina, writer and journalist, with her precocious young daughter, Ubax, and her estranged husband, Sabater, unenthusiastic holder of various portfolios in the General's repressive and nepotistic government.

A careful reading of Farah's fiction suggests that many of the ills of African society may be ascribed less to the colonial legacy than to tribalism, sexism, and traditional hidebound attitudes. There is thus a strong emphasis in *Sardines* on the interdependence of religion, politics, and patriarchy. The general makes Medina think of her own monstrous grandfather; for the latter, too, may be described as "the self-proclaimed protector of tradition and religion, [who] ruled with the iron fist of a dictator" (p. 99). Of this same tradition, the radically feminist Medina has many unpleasant experiences. When she begins a trial separation from her husband, for example, her mother-in-law immediately moves into the family home, bringing a cousin as replacement wife. Elsewhere, Medina ironically notes that the secluded women of her country "lived in the innards of a whale which hardly went ashore" (p. 145). They then required a man to intercede for them with Allah (a woman's own God being her husband), after which they could look forward to the life of a Houri, continuing their earthly existence of serving (and servicing) men.

In *Sardines*, then, the forces of reason, progress, and moderation are invariably Western, and Europe is therefore viewed far less critically than in much contemporary African fiction. Medina, silenced as a journalist, rather naively assumes the monumental task of translating into Somali twenty Western classics from six different languages. Her friend Sagal, the champion swimmer (whose watery environment suggests fluidity, ambivalence, and potential escape – quite appropriately, since she is about to defect at an international meet), speaks several European languages and has a cosmopolitan background. And when Ubax objects to her mother speaking incomprehensible foreign tongues, Medina protests that she is not speaking a foreign tongue, but only Italian.

In spite of its ambitious political scope, however, the novel ends not with the General's downfall, but with Medina – in a presumed reference to Virginia Woolf's famous essay – aspiring more modestly to "a room that she could call her own". The final solution of *Sardines* is thus enacted in terms of individual emancipation rather than national liberation.

The remaining East African novelists relate more easily to Ngũgĩ than to Farah, although they do not have the range or depth of either. Two Kenyan writers roughly contemporary with Ngũgĩ have thus adopted a revisionist approach towards the years of the Emergency; Sam Kahiga in *The Girl from Abroad* (1974) refuses to idealize the guerrillas of the Land and Freedom Movement, whilst Charles Mangua in *A Tail in the Mouth* (1972) actually satirizes them and parodies Ngũgĩ. The early novels of a third Kenyan writer, the versatile and prolific Meja Mwangi, also dealt with the Emergency. These include *Taste of Death* (1975) and *Carcase for Hounds* (1974). The majority of Mwangi's novels are nevertheless set in post-independence Kenya, and some oscillate between the popular and the trivial. More substantial are *Kill Me Quick* (1973) and *Going Down River Road* (1976), with their powerful treatment of young drop-outs in contemporary Nairobi. The more recent *Striving for the Wind* (1990) also has serious literary pretensions.

Some other East African novelists have marginal linguistic links with Ngũgĩ. Grace Ogot moved in exactly the opposite direction to him: before publishing *The Promised Land* (1966), depicting the clash between an African medicine man and a Western-trained doctor, she wrote short stories in two Kenyan languages, Luo and Kiswahili. Ugandan Okot p'Bitek, acclaimed for his satirical poems "Song of Lawino" and "Song of Ocul", also wrote a novel in his native Acoli, *Lak Tar* (1953), which he later translated into English. It appeared posthumously as *White Teeth* (1989).

Like Nigeria, Kenya also produced a large quantity of popular literature in English, the most prolific writer in this area being David Maillu. In the other two East African countries, the anglophone literary tradition is weak: in Tanzania, in fact, it hardly exists at all, although one should mention Ismael Mbise's historical novel, *Blood on our Land* (1974); in Uganda, the tradition is better described as fragmented, as successive coups by Milton Obote (1964) and Idi Amin (1971) drove writers into exile. The highly original, American-educated Taban lo Liyong joined Okot p'Bitek at the University of Nairobi – lo Liyong's collection of short stories, *Fixions* (1969), and the novel *Meditations in Limbo* (1970), represent African fiction at its most idiosyncratic. Peter Nazareth, whose novel *In a Brown Mantle* (1972) provides an insight into the position of Ugandan Asians before the arrival of Amin, was another exile.

SOUTHERN AFRICA

"Southern African Literatures" is the title chosen by Michael Chapman for his magisterial addition to the *Longman Literature in English* series (1996). Under this heading, he includes the eight African states below Zaire or Tanzania where English has some official status, and – rather incongruously – the ex-Portuguese colonies of Angola and Mozambique. The two latter states have obviously been excluded from the present account. Of the eight countries that remain, Lesotho, Swaziland, and Namibia are relatively insignificant in the context of anglophone fiction; Zambia and Malawi have a surprisingly small amount of it; Botswana has, above all, received some distinguished South African exiles and Zimbabwe has fine novelists; but it is South Africa that has recently produced a large crop of remarkable writers under grim social conditions and dauntingly complex linguistic ones.

Until recently, South Africa (population 40 million) had two official languages, Afrikaans and English, with 6 million and 2 million native speakers, respectively. It is worth remembering too that, whatever the historical excesses of the Afrikaner-dominated National Party, roughly half of the country's Afikaans speakers were officially classified as "coloured" (with all the discrimination this involved), whereas virtually all English native speakers are white. After the fall of the *apartheid* regime, nine African languages were also given official status. Of these, the most widely spoken are Zulu and Xhosa, with 8 million speakers each, Tswana (or Western Sotho) with 3 million, and Pedi (or Northern Sotho) with 2.5 million. All five of these languages thus have more native speakers than English; two of them have more than Afrikaans.

The political realities of South Africa under *apartheid* were such as to subvert or invalidate most conventional assumptions about literature and its production. After the catch-all Suppression of Communism Act in 1966, for example, a large number of literary works were banned: to own them or even to quote from them was illegal, so that the idea of a literary tradition hardly applied. With authorities sensitive enough to ban Anna Sewell's *Black Beauty* – presumably on the strength of the title alone – young black South Africans were unlikely to have even seen a novel by Alex La Guma or Esk'ia Mphahlele, let alone be influenced by it. It was also widely believed that, because of the compartmentalization of South African society, no black (or white) writer had the knowledge to create totally convincing characters across the colour line. Some writers (black and white) left South Africa on the notorious one-way "exit visa"; others went into voluntary exile; a certain number remained.

Even the notion of English as the stepmother tongue is partly stood on its head. Mazisi Kunene could regret that "writers who do not write in African languages have come to represent African writing", but many black South Africans actually fought for the right to an English-language education. Esk'ia Mphahlele, for example, lost his teaching post for his opposition to the Bantu Language Act, ostensibly introduced to promote indigenous languages, but widely seen as an attempt to marginalize further the country's black population. In other contexts, too, English was at least seen as a lesser evil than Afrikaans.

Major black South African novelists who left the country voluntarily for long periods, or spent their artistically productive life in exile, include Peter Abrahams, Alex La Guma, Esk'ia Mphahlele, Mazisi Kunene, Bessie Head and Mongane Wally Serote.

Peter Abrahams is harder to place than most of his contemporaries, both for the great length of his literary career but also because he spent fifteen years in England, followed by some forty in Jamaica. Two early novels of urban life, *Song of the City* (1945) and *Mine Boy* (1946), were hardly noticed, moreover, until Abrahams won recognition with his documentary report on South Africa, *Return to Goli* (1953), and his much-acclaimed autobiography, *Tell Freedom* (1954). Abrahams's three following novels are more overtly political: *A Wreath for Udomo* (1956) is set against the independence struggle in West Africa; *A Night of their Own* (1965) deals with the theme of interracial love; *This Island Now* (1966) examines neo-colonialism on a fictional Caribbean island. *The View from Coyaba* (1985), Abrahams's most ambitious work, recreates a hundred and fifty years of Black history in the United States and the Caribbean.

The fiction of Alex La Guma can also be divided between books written before and after exile. Born in the Cape Town coloured ghetto of District Six, Alex La Guma was a Communist and an active member of the ANC, incurring periods of imprisonment and house-arrest before eventual exile. His earlier fiction falls within the parameters of social realism, beginning with the novella *A Walk in the Night* (1962), and continuing with two novels, *And a Threefold Cord* (1964) and *The Stone Country* (1967), where the title supplies an impressive metaphor for South Africa under the *apartheid* system. La Guma also wrote two politically charged novels in exile: *In the Fog of the Season's End* (1972) and *Time of the Butcherbird* (1979).

The life of **Esk'ia Mphahlele** carries a suggestive resonance in the context of the stepmother tongue. Raised in rural Northern Transvaal, Mphahlele spoke Northern Sotho at home, Southern Sotho or Afrikaans in the neighbourhood, and English only at school. He furthermore received no formal education until the age of thirteen, but later became an author who – far from being forced to use English – struggled for the right to do so through his opposition to the Bantu Education Act. A twenty-year exile then took him to Nigeria, France, Kenya, the United States, and Zambia. Mphahlele had begun his literary career with a volume of short stories entitled *Man Must Live* (1946), but – like Peter Abrahams – he achieved fame with an autobiography, *Down Second Avenue* (1959). After a long gap, he produced an autobiographical novel, *The Wanderers* (1971), followed by the better-known *Chirundu* (1979).

Fruit of a political exile in Zambia and based on an authentic trial in that country, *Chirundu* has the formal elegance one associates with Henry James, however incongruous the parallel might seem for such a powerful indictment of post-colonial African power structures. The novel, in any case, repays close formal analysis.

Its three sections are each linked to a day in the bigamy trial of Chimba Chirundu, cabinet minister in an unnamed African country. The first and by far the longest section ("Chirundu") is subdivided into a brief courtroom scene, followed by a long series of flashbacks presented through the perspective of Chimba: early involvement with the National Alliance Party, a spell as a secondary school teacher, marriage by both native law and British ordinance to a nineteen-year-old village girl, a burgeoning political career, ministerial rank in the post-independence era, a second marriage to a sophisticated British-trained secretary in his own ministry. The following section ("Tirenje") is similarly divided into courtroom testimony (now from the "country wife"), followed by the latter's own thoughts and recollections, as well as more recent conversations with Chirundu's sympathetic nephew and his mother. The final section ("Moyo"), after a brief account of the verdict (guilty) and sentence (a year's imprisonment), is filtered through the consciousness of this nephew, himself active in more reputable trade union politics.

Each of the three sections is also preceded by a dialogue between political detainees, which functions as both commentary and chorus on the action of the trial. These passages are neatly linked to the main narrative, moreover, since two of the speakers are languishing in jail for want of an initiative on refugees from Chimba's department, whilst their only prison visitor is the political mentor of the minister's nephew.

The narrative is nevertheless dominated by the ruthlessly arrogant Chimba, an utterly convincing study of political megalomania. Perhaps the most disturbing element here is the abuse of a fine intelligence and genuine talent. Chimba's comments on the imposition of alien customs ("Europeans are trying to revive their own faith by transplanting it onto African soil", p. 29) are shrewd enough; but his arguments exist solely to justify his own bigamous position. Chimba's attitude to language is also enlightened ("I wonder why people would rather speak English badly than speak their mother tongue and let *that* be interpreted", p. 38); but he is only really interested in how far he could personally "spread [him]self on four languages".

Chimba is contested by his quietly dignified first wife, Tirenje, a repository of traditional African (female) virtues. She recalls the words of the young African teacher who had been such a formative influence in her secondary-school years:

> our fathers knew what a woman is worth, where her power lies. But young men of your age, even mine, think that because they call themselves modern, because more women are going to school, more things are open for us to do than there were for our mothers, so more women are also open to men to take and use. (pp. 83–4)

Mphahlele may well be implying a link between patriarchy and political exploitation of the kind that Farah pursues more explicitly in his trilogy, "Variations on the theme of an African Dictatorship". In the context of *Chirundu*, such arbitrary power is brilliantly presented by means of the *nsato* motif. The *nsato*, or sacred python, is used alternatively in the novel as a symbol of sexual and of political power. Of the first aspect, Tirenje jokes with Chimba during their early love-making: "You hold me as if you were never going to let me go, like a python, as if you were going to eat me up alive" (p. 16). On the second, Chimba reassures her: "[*nsato*] is a king. A real king doesn't go about picking fights with small creatures" (p. 17). But it is precisely this kind of power that Chimba abuses when he destroys his marriage, or, in Terenje's poignantly repeated metaphor, burns the house down.

Mphahlele's counterpart to Chimba is the minister's nephew, Mojo, quite obviously a symbol of the author's faith in a better future. Mojo's political idealism and incorruptibility, without any implied loss of traditional values or tribal decorum, speaks volumes.

If Alex La Guma's exile was politically active (he was eventually ANC representative in Cuba), then that of several other writers was predominantly academic. Lewis Nkosi originally left South Africa on a cancelled exit visa and presently teaches in the United States; his novel *The Mating Birds* (1986) is a study of how personal relationships were affected by the political situation. Mazisi Kunene, before his return to South Africa, was a professor of African literature in America for more than thirty years. He is known for his recreations in English of Zulu historical narratives, such as *Emperor Shaka the Great* (1979) and *Anthem of the Decades* (1981).

For some South African writers, exile was nearer home. Bessie Head left South Africa on an exit visa in 1963, and spent most of her short adult life in Botswana. Of her four novels: *When Rain*

Clouds Gather (1969) is a study of expatriation and exile; *Maru* (1971) deals with ethnic conflicts in Botswana; *A Question of Power* (1974) returns more insistently to the theme of personal alienation; and *A Bewitched Crossroad* (1984) is a historical fiction beginning in the late nineteenth century. *Serowe: Village of the Rain Wind* (1981) is an attempt to use popular oral tradition in the recreation of local history, an approach already evident in the short story collection *The Collector of Treasures* (1977).

Poet Mongane Wally Serote also spent a period of (self-imposed) exile in Botswana, although his seminal novel, *To Every Birth Its Blood* (1981), deals with one of the momentous events in modern South African history: the Soweto uprising by black schoolchildren in 1976. Serote's narrative is divided into two sections (almost the equivalent of two distinct novels), with the events of Soweto providing a kind of watershed. There are clear analogies here with the structure of Nadine Gordimer's *Burgher's Daughter* and André Brink's *A Dry White Season*. Serote spoke revealingly of his own linguistic status in Michael Chapman's anthology *Soweto Poetry* (1982):

> I am not English-speaking. I have worked hard at the English language. I didn't complete high school, and of course the English press made me very conscious of the fact that English isn't my home language. There was no way that could stop me from writing. I worked hard. I spent nights at the typewriter writing and re-writing. (p. 503)

Serote is a native speaker of sePedi or Northern Sotho.

An older writer who remained in South Africa is Richard Rive, raised (like La Guma) in Cape Town's District Six, and much influenced (like Abrahams) by Black American writers. After the short stories of *African Songs* (1963), Rive produced *Emergency* (1964), a novel about the Sharpeville massacre of civilians by security forces in 1960, and a fictional account of his own ghetto, entitled *"Buckingham Palace", District Six* (1986).

Two contemporaries of Rive who also survived at home are Sepamla and Tlali. Sipho Sepamla has published four novels: *The Root is One* (1979), *A Ride on the Whirlwind* (1981), *Third Generation* (1986) and *A Scattered Survival* (1989). The most acclaimed of these is the second, celebrating the 1976 Soweto uprising like Serote's *To Every Birth Its Blood*. Sepamla, too, is sensitive to linguistic issues, as

appears from his two-edged comment to Michael Chapman in the
Soweto Poetry anthology:

> I owe nobody an apology for writing in English. Yet inside me is
> this regret that at the moment there is a handicap that mars com-
> plete communication between me and my audience, particularly
> the black audience.   (504)

Soweto-raised Miriam Tlali published *Muriel at Metropolitan*, the
first novel by a black South African woman, in 1975. She followed
this strongly autobiographical narrative of a black accounts typist
working in a Johannesburg store with the novel *Amandla* (1981),
another personal response to the events of Soweto.

Other Southern African Fiction

The remaining states of Southern Africa vary widely in demographic and linguistic terms. At one end of the spectrum, two of
the largest countries in the area, Botswana and Namibia, have
equally small populations (with about one and a half million each).
Botswana, where almost the entire population speaks Tswana, is
the most linguistically homogeneous state in Southern Africa;
Namibia has three main languages, the indigenous oshiWambo,
together with English and Afrikaans. Neither country has a
significant tradition of writing in English, although Joseph Diesco's
Bildungsroman, *Born of the Son* (1988), is the first novel produced by
a native-born Namibian.

With roughly 7 million people each, Malawi (where over half the
population speak Chewa) and Zambia (where the same proportion
speak either Bemba, Tonga, or Nyanja) are also relatively homoge-
nous in linguistic terms. Furthermore, writing in African languages
was encouraged in both countries during the pre-independence
period. More interesting than simple demography, however, are
the contrasting political situations of the two countries, as neatly
summarized by Chapman in his *Southern African Literatures*
(pp. 265–79). It is suggested here that, besides linguistic factors, the
repressive regime of Hastings Banda in Malawi inhibited the
development of a realistic prose tradition in English, whilst in the
more liberal Zambia a certain provinciality of outlook may have
had a similar effect.

In any event, Malawi has produced fine poets such as Steve Chimombo, Jack Mapanje and Felix Mnthali (social protest can perhaps be more elaborately coded in verse), but only two novelists of note: David Rubadiri, whose *No Bride Price* (1967) was banned and who later went into exile; and Legson Kayira, author of four novels and now living in the United States. Zambia fares a little better: Dominic Mulaisho wrote *The Tongue of the Dumb* (1971), dramatizing the eternal conflict between Christian and traditional African values, and followed this with *The Smoke that Thunders* (1979), turning to the political theme of his nation's independence struggle. Gideon Phiri has also written two novels, of which *Ticklish Sensation* (1973) is memorable for its skilful representation (and hilarious send-up) of colloquial Zambian English. Well-known broadcaster Andreya Masiye is also of interest here, for the fact that he has written in both English and Nyanja.

After South Africa, however, the most significant body of anglophone fiction has been produced in Zimbabwe. The most linguistically homogeneous state in Southern Africa (with the exception of Botswana), Zimbabwe is also perhaps the most cosmopolitan and most nationally aware, with an identity forged during the *Chimurenga*, or fifteen-year armed struggle against white minority rule after Ian Smith's Unilateral Declaration of Independence (UDI) in 1965.

The youth and dynamism of the new Zimbabwean novel are well illustrated by the fact that one may already distinguish between two waves of writers, although even the earlier group (with one exception) were only born in the early fifties and published in the late seventies. Their successors are not greatly different in age, but have been active since the late eighties. The two groups are Charles Mungoshi, Stanley Nyamfukudza and Dambudzo Marechera, *versus* Chenjerai Hove, Shimmer Chinodya and Tsitsi Dangarembga.

Charles Mungoshi has written three novels in Shona, but his English fiction includes the stories in *Coming of the Dry Season* (1972) and the novel *Waiting for the Rain* (1975), whose title alludes to spiritual and material drought in the pre-independence period. Stanley Nyamfukudza's *The Non-Believer's Journey* (1980) offers a more sceptical treatment of heroism and patriotic rhetoric. Dambudzo Marechera, the most iconoclastic of the three, wrote *The House of Hunger* (1978), *Black Sunlight* (1980) and – published posthumously – *The Black Insider* (1990), all reflecting the anger of exile during the long interim of Zimbabwean minority rule.

Like Mungoshi, Chenjerai Hove is also noteworthy for his willing-ness to write in both English and Shona. His technically innovative first novel, *Bones* (1988), shows particular sensitivity towards the lives of rural women, whilst its successor, *Shadows* (1991), is a study of generational conflicts. Shimmer Chinodya's *Harvest of Thorns* (1989), a moving "rite of passage" novel about a young man growing up in the war-torn Rhodesia of the 1970s, has obvious analogies with Ngũgĩ's novels of the Kenyan Emergency a decade earlier. In con-temporary Zimbabwean fiction, however, **Tsitsi Dangarembga's** *Nervous Conditions* (1988) may be the finest novel of all.

Set in Zimbabwe (then Rhodesia) in the late sixties and early sev-enties, *Nervous Conditions* is an important example of the African *Bildungsroman* written from a feminine (and feminist) perspective. Narrated by the heroine, Tambudzai – with adult hindsight but a child's vision – the novel emphasizes the double handicap of being African and female ("the poverty of blackness on the one side and the weight of womanhood on the other", p. 16).

Dangarembga's narrative is conventionally realistic, but achieves dramatic examples of defamiliarization by seeing the adult world through the eyes of a child, or the white one through those of an African: the eight-year-old Tambudzai records her initial impres-sions of city life; her grandmother tells stories of how the "evil [white] wizards" cast their spell on her country. The two perspec-tives converge in Tambudzai's sense of revulsion on her first glimpse of elderly white settlers ("papery-skinned Doris and her sallow brown-spotted husband"). Feeling guilty about not being able to love the Europeans as she ought, Tambudzai is at last relieved to discover that "some Whites were as beautiful as we were" (p. 104).

Even more central to the novel than the technique of defamiliar-ization, however, is its thematization of linguistic behaviour. Since about 80 per cent of Zimbabwe's population possess a common lan-guage, Shona, English – in the domestic context at least – lacks the pure convenience value it has, for example, in Nigeria or Ghana. The shift from Shona to English is therefore an important indicator of cultural assimilation, as when Tambudzai's cousins, Nyasha and Chido, return from England unable to speak their native tongue. Tambudzai's brother Nhamo is more than willing to speak broken English with them, however, and after a spell at the local mission school – by a kind of selective amnesia – also forgets Shona as and when it suits him.

Tambudzai satirizes the struggle for Englishness with her account of the ignorant African teacher who confuses the words "peasant" and "pheasant". Her own process of acculturation proceeds relentlessly, however, as she "reincarnates" herself by reading English novels (from the Brontës to Blyton), and eventually wins a place at the prestigious *Young Ladies College of the Sacred Heart* with a faultless recitation of Browning's "Pied Piper of Hamelin"! Cousin Nyasha, the "hybrid child" who eventually becomes Tambudzai's closest friend and something of her psychological antithesis, is more ideologically aware. She regards Tambudzai's transfer to a predominantly white boarding-school as a kind of betrayal: "It's bad enough when a country gets colonised, but when the people do as well! That's the end …" (p. 147). The most conservative (one might also say nativist) attitude is shown by Tambudzai's mother, who never overcomes her bitterness at the quite literal loss of her son to English culture (he had died at the mission school from a complication resulting from mumps): "First you took his tongue so that he could not speak to me and now you have taken everything, taken everything for good" (p. 54). And when Nyasha has a nervous breakdown at the end of the novel, she diagnoses predictably that "It's the Englishness … it'll kill them all if they're not careful" (p. 202).

Dangarembga's title alludes to a comment by Fanon in *The Wretched of the Earth* that "[t]he condition of native is a nervous condition", and the novel itself is an analysis of the cultural schizophrenia this implies. Her novel thus returns to the classic African theme of an alien culture being imposed on a stable indigenous society. The imposition here, moreover, is identified as a primarily linguistic phenomenon. More than almost any other African novel then, *Nervous Conditions*, by virtue of its English-language medium, is paradoxically both a vehicle and an indictment of the stepmother tongue. Dangarembga's subtle representation of this conflict from the doubly marginal perspective of a black woman makes the novel a landmark in African fiction.

NOTES

1. *Talking with African Writers: Interviews with African Poets, Playwrights and Novelists* (London: Heinemann Studies in African Literature, 1992), p. 94.

2. *Morning Yet on Creation Day* (New York: Doubleday, 1975), p. 48.
3. *In their own Voices: African Women Writers Talk* (London: Heinemann Studies in African Literature, 1990), p. 31.
4. Ibid., p. 83.

FURTHER READING

A good overview of the subject is O. R. Dathorne's *African Literature in the Twentieth Century* (Minneapolis: University of Minnesota Press, 1975). More up to date, however, are the *History of Twentieth-Century African Literatures*, edited by Oyekan Owomoyela (Lincoln: University of Nebraska Press, 1993), and G. D. Killam's *Guide to African Literature* (Macmillan, 1997) – with the latter placing greater emphasis on anglophone fiction.

Michael Chapman's *Southern African Literatures* (1998) is a fine addition to the Longman's Literature in English collection. For Nigeria alone, see the two-volume *Perspectives on Nigerian Literature*, edited by Yemi Ogunbiyi (Lagos: Guardian Books, 1988).

A theoretically sophisticated study of the African novel is Abdul JanMohamed's *Manichean Aesthetics: The Politics of Literature in Colonial Africa* (University of Massachusetts Press, 1983); an uncompromisingly "nativist" line is adopted by Chinweizu, Onwuchekwu Jemie and Ihechukwu Madubuike's *Towards the Decolonization of African Literature* (Routledge & Kegan Paul, 1985).

Simon Gikandi's *Reading the African Novel* (London: James Currey, 1987) and Kenneth W. Harrow's *Thresholds of Change in African Literature* (1994), in Heinemann's Studies in African Literature series, deal with both anglophone and francophone writing. The same series (published by Currey in Britain and Heinemann Educational Books in the United States) also includes two useful sets of interviews with African authors: Adeola James's *In their own Voices: African Women Writers Talk* (1990) and Jane Wilkinson's *Talking with African Writers* (1992). Some of the very best interviews with African writers (Ngũgĩ, Farah, Achebe and Emecheta) nevertheless appear in Jussawalla and Dasenbrock's *Interviews with Writers of the Post-Colonial World* (Jackson: University Press of Mississsippi, 1993).

Volumes 117, 125 and 157 of the *Dictionary of Literary Biography* (Detroit: Gale Research, 1992, 1993 and 1995), edited by Bernth Lindfors and Reinhard Sander, cover Black African and Caribbean novelists in English. Hans Zell's *A New Reader's Guide to African Literature* (Heinemann, 1983) is still useful.

3

The South Pacific

Recent indigenous anglophone writing of the South Pacific, although a younger and smaller literary tradition than that of Asia or Africa, could also be logically regarded as "New Literatures" in "Old Worlds": *new* in the sense that a particular linguistic regime was a recent imposition, *old* in the sense that the regime's subjects (however defined) had formed stable, traditional societies. Or, expressed in analogous terms, English was clearly an adjunct of colonial power ("their" language); whilst the territories it inscribed were the home of indigenous populations ("our" land).

Such categorizations may, of course, sound simplistic or even slightly perverse. Whether it is Australia (population 16 million) or Tonga (population 100 thousand), the literary medium of English is now so widespread and so dominant as to suggest an element of cultural complicity in conjunction with externally imposed linguistic hegemony. The South Pacific region has no former British colonies, as in Asia – or even Africa – where English has become culturally subordinate to indigenous languages, although there is now a significant corpus of writing in Maori and Samoan. All writers in the overall category (particularly outside Australia and New Zealand) nevertheless possess (at least in theory) an indigenous language in addition to English. Or if they have had it but lost it, one need not look far to understand why. The sometimes overwhelming economic and cultural pressures to write in the step-mother tongue are nowhere illustrated more poignantly than in the case of Russell Soaba. Recognized as Papua New Guinea's finest novelist, the anglophone Soaba is a native speaker of Anuki, a language with less than three hundred speakers. His literary prospects in this language are clearly limited.

A number of indigenous novelists and short-story writers from the South Pacific region are now internationally known. These include authors of Australian Aborigine background (Mudrooroo Narogin and Archie Weller) or New Zealand Maoris (Witi Ihimaera and Patricia Grace); and to these should be added not only Soaba, but such names as Albert Wendt (Samoa/New Zealand), Epeli Hau'ofa (Tonga) and Subramani (Fiji).

Archie Weller (part-Aborigine and born in Western Australia) explores an urban sub-culture of violence and deprivation in *The Day of the Dog* (1981) and the short stories of *Going Home* (1986). The first black Australian to publish a novel, however, was Colin Johnson (he changed his name to Mudrooroo Narogin as a gesture of protest in the context of his country's bicentennial celebrations).

Of mixed Aborigine and European ancestry, **Mudrooroo** was born (as his name indicates) at Narrogin, 200 kilometres from Perth. He began his writing career with *Wild Cat Falling* (1965), an existential novel of alienation recalling such European precedents as Camus's *L'Étranger* (1942) or Colin Wilson's *The Outsider* (1956). This was followed by *Long Live Sandawara* (1979), a story of urban resistance in the slums of Perth; *Doin Wildcat* (1988), constructed round the filming of his first novel and making extensive use of Aborigine English; and *Master of the Ghost Dreaming* (1990). But Mudrooroo's most impressive novel is *Doctor Wooreddy's Prescription for Enduring the Ending of the World* (1983), tracing the gradual extinction of Tasmania's Aboriginal population – historical events also treated in Robert Drewe's *The Savage Crows* (1976).

The originality of Mudrooroo's novel lies in its consistent adoption of an Aborigine perspective, and in its refashioning of the shadowy historical figure of Wooreddy as a highly intelligent and intensely speculative observer: a philosopher and sage among his own people ("when he wasn't taking theology lessons, he was hunting"). Land and language combine, for the good doctor, to produce a well adjusted cosmogony. Within this world picture, however, the sea is regarded as a carrier of death, for it is the malign spirit of the sea, Ria Warrawah, who sends the white *num*, or "ghosts", to plague Wooreddy's fellow humans. Mudrooroo's subtle techniques of defamiliarization, and the radical conceptual reversals which they bring for the modern non-Aborigine reader, emerge dramatically in an early passage where Wooreddy watches in silent fascination as four *num* rape an Aboriginal woman. After noting with detached curiosity that even the ghosts' penises are white, and that they are greedy for women as they are for everything else, he begins to speculate on the "grammatical structure and idiosyncrasies" of *num* language:

Wooreddy wondered if the ghosts had honorifics and specific forms of address. Perhaps it was not even a real language? – but then each and every species of animal had a language, and so it must be! The kangaroos, possums and even snakes – and though it was not universally accepted, the trees and plants – all had a language.   (pp. 20–21)

The actual "idiosyncrasies" of *num* language appear through a subsequent broadening of the narrative focus beyond Wooreddy's perspectives. Here are the absurdly messianic Mr Robinson (based on the historical figure of the self-appointed saviour of Tasmania's Aborigines) and his wretched neglected wife, Marie. Robinson has a London Cockney accent, in contrast to his wife's more educated middle-class English: as he struggles to acquire an Aborigine language, Robinson also fights to refine his own English speech – particularly in the sounding of his aitches.

The ending of the world referred to in the novel's title simply means the destruction of Aborigine society by the *num*, and its replacement by an alien environment in which "strange animals roamed and even strange grass replaced the old". The true extent of the cataclysm is revealed in one of the movingly elegiac passages filtered through Wooreddy's consciousness:

Hidden in the tangle of ferns and wattle, he sobbed out his loneliness. All that he had known and loved was no more. His country was dead; his people were dead, and his family was no more. Now he was alone until the world ended and nothing existed, not even his loneliness.   (p. 110)

Wooreddy's "prescription" for "enduring" this situation is quite simply compromise with the *num*, although such accommodation should ideally be entered from a position of strength and confidence. The last scenes therefore reinforce the sense of Aborigine identity, first with the tribal dances of the corroboree, and later with increasingly frequent dialogue between Wooreddy and his wife Trugernanna, in the old Bruny Island language "which they had not used for years". Land and language are thus combined in a final image of cultural assertion for the benefit of the contemporary *num* reader.

Ironically enough, the second most famous Aborigine novelist may be Banumbir (or Birumbir) Wongar, later revealed as one Sreten Bozic, a Yugoslav immigrant who had lived many years among Australia's northern tribes. After early collections of stories,

including *The Track to Bralgu* (1978), Wongar published his ecologically insistent *Nuclear Trilogy*, consisting of *Walg* (1983), *Karan*
(1985) and *Gabo Djara* (1987). The discovery of Wongar's true identity by Robert Drewe in 1981 led to a few red faces in the Australian
literary establishment, but did not preclude acceptance by
Aborigine writers. In a recent interview, in fact, Wongar noted astutely that whereas he was a white man writing like an Aborigine,
Mudrooroo's first novel was effectively an Aborigine writing like a
white man.

Maori fiction in New Zealand is now immediately linked by an
international readership, with the name of Keri Hulme. The latter's
plea for a New Zealand culture which does not neglect its Maori
heritage emerges most clearly in her prize-winning novel *The Bone
People* (1984). Hulme's strong identification with New Zealand's
older cultural tradition is apparently based on one-eighth Maori ancestry, not enough to satisfy her countryman C. K. Stead, but generally no obstacle to Maori writers themselves. *The Bone People* is
nevertheless discussed in part three, for its interesting analogies
with other less ambiguous "contact" novels by Australian and New
Zealand novelists.

The Maori writer credited with several literary firsts, however, is
Witi Ihimaera. His *Pounamu, Pounamu* (1972) was the first widely
noticed volume of short stories published by a Maori writer, his
Tangi (1973) the first novel. These were followed by *Whanau* (1974),
a sensitive recreation of Maori village life, and *The New Net Goes
Fishing* (1977), a second volume of short stories. Ihimaera's third
novel, *The Matriarch* (1986), is a more ambitious and experimental
work, while his third volume of short stories, *Dear Miss Mansfield:
A Tribute to Kathleen Mansfield Beauchamp* (1989), was published
for the centenary of Mansfield's birth. The dominant theme of
Ihimaera's fiction, with the exception of *Tangi*, is the clash between
Maori and Pakeha (European) culture. There is almost an inevitability in this, illustrating the truism that whereas a New
Zealand Pakeha writer can, at least in practice, exclude Maori
culture from his writing, a Maori rarely has the reverse option.

This point is equally clear in the fiction of **Patricia Grace**, the
most significant Maori writer. The tension between Maori and
Pakeha life-styles underpins her first collection of short stories,
Waiariki (1975), and first novel, *Mutuwhenua: The Moon Sleeps* (1978).
The 1980s saw the publication of two more collections of stories
and two children's books, but these were largely overshadowed by
Grace's major novel, *Potiki* (1986).

Potiki is the story of Roimata, her husband Hemi, and five children, inhabitants of a twentieth-century Maori coastal community. Two of the younger children are kept out of school and given a traditional education by their mother, her oral tales blending with the school learning acquired by the elder children. It is an appropriate system for a culture where epistemological divisions are evidently distinct from those operating in Pakeha society: Grace thus uses the word "story" to cover many forms of discourse, from myth and legend through chronicle and history to fiction and orature.

The broader drama of *Potiki* is provided by the harsh economic realities of the 1930s, with unemployment in the cities forcing Maoris to return to their traditional homes and resume the market gardening that had earlier gained them a livelihood. Hemi places this process quite explicitly in the wider cultural context of land and language:

> Things were stirring, to the extent of people fighting to hold onto a *language* that was in danger of being lost, and to the extent of people struggling to regain *land* that had gone from them years before.   (p. 60; my emphasis)

Roimata's community must resist pressure from a property company to sell its ancestral land and allow the transfer of the *wharenui*, or traditional meeting-house, to another site. The ultimate saviour of the community, however, is Toko – the *potiki* or "little precious one" – who compensates physical disability with a prescience amounting to psychic gifts. Toko dies from the strain of his efforts, but his effigy is placed on the empty niche, as if preordained for him, in the newly restored *wharenui*.

Potiki, then, contains a quite explicit discourse of land; it is also, with its large admixture of normally untranslated Maori words and phrases, an emphatic reminder of linguistic issues. Grace has spoken of her interest in the technical problems of speech presentation, and her pains to avoid a stereotyped "Maori English" if her characters are actually speaking Maori: standard spoken Maori is naturally encoded as standard written English. She has not published in Maori, however, or shown any undue hostility towards the medium of English. With regard to the large number of Maori expressions used by Maoris speaking English, she merely notes in an interview that these "drop naturally into direct speech", and claims that readers have experienced rather less difficulty than she anticipated. That she was prepared for them to experience at least some, may suggest a hidden but unexceptionable linguistic agenda: if Grace, the Maori writer, has effectively substituted the English of the colonizers for the Maori of the colonized (making "their" language "ours"), then her Pakeha readers must – at least on a symbolic or token level – undergo a similar process with respect to the colonized.

Many additional factors help make *Potiki* a remarkable novel. Certain plot elements, for example, such as the seduction of Roimata's mentally retarded sister-in-law by a Pakeha tramp – leading to the birth of Toko – invite a reading of the novel as colonial allegory, suggesting the fate of Aotearoa (New Zealand) itself at the hands of its first British settlers. The careful re-creation of indigenous culture to correct outside misconceptions, on the other hand, invites comparison with Achebe's *Things Fall Apart* or – nearer home – Albert Wendt's *Leaves of the Banyan Tree*.

Describing the cultural initiatives of the community during a time of particular economic hardship, Grace's narrator also provides a comment that stands as a simple but eloquent epigraph for the author herself as a Maori writer:

> We could not afford books so we made our own. In this way we were able to find ourselves in books. It is rare for us to find ourselves in books, but in our own books we were able to find and define our lives.   (p. 104)

The most internationally acclaimed Polynesian novelist is **Albert Wendt**, born in Western Samoa but educated in New Zealand, where he now lives. Wendt's first novel, *Sons for the Return Home* (1973), is a love-story featuring an unnamed Samoan student and a New Zealand girl. This was followed by a collection of stories, *Flying-Fox in a Freedom Tree* (1974), and the novels *Pouliuli* (1977), a Samoan variant on the King Lear theme, and *Leaves of the Banyan Tree* (1979), an ambitious family saga. Wendt's recent novels have shown a willingness to move away both from the Samoan–New Zealand environment – *Ola* (1991) has an international setting and a female protagonist – and from the classic realist mode – *Black Rainbow* (1992) is an allegorical thriller played out in a post-nuclear New Zealand.

The most substantial (if not the most formally original) novel in Wendt's varied output, however, is *Leaves of the Banyan Tree* (1979), a chronicle of Samoan life constructed round three generations of the *Aiga* [extended family] *Tauilopepe*, from the 1930s to the post-independence period. Wendt has admitted that the motivation to write came partly from inaccurate accounts of his people by explorers and anthropologists such as Margaret Mead, a reaction obviously analogous to that of Achebe in Nigeria.

The first of the novel's three sections follows the intense rivalry between Tauilopepe Mauga and Malo, the local storekeeper, to determine which *aiga* will control the village. Tauilopepe wholeheartedly embraces a debased version of the Protestant work ethic that the *papalagi* [Europeans] have introduced to Samoa, and crowns his triumph with a rousing sermon on "God, Money, and Success", which gives this section its title. The cost of prosperity is high, however, and an increasingly autocratic Tauilo becomes estranged from both wife and children. The second, more experimental, section of the novel, "Flying-Fox in a Freedom Tree" (a revised version of the title piece in Wendt's collection of short stories), is in fact related by the rebellious son, Pepesa (Pepe), dying in hospital from tuberculosis. Relations between father and son never mend, and Tauilopepe transfers his affection to the grandson, Lalolagi, whom he sends away to a *papalagi* school to be groomed as his successor.

In accordance with his aim of avoiding stereotype and cliché, Wendt produces an honest and even-handed portrait of Sapepe village, widely read as an allegory of Samoan society at large. Wealthy and conservative Samoans such as Tauilopepe are thus more than happy with the colonial *status quo* and fear the rising power of the Independence movement.

Relations between colonizer and colonized (which Wendt has defined elsewhere as the central subject of all his fiction) are meticulously recorded in *Leaves of the Banyan Tree* through a wealth of socio-linguistic observation. This is less prominent in the exclusively Samoan-speaking environment of the first section of the novel, where (by a convention akin to that operating in Grace's *Potiki*) what is presumably standard spoken Samoan is simply codified as standard written English. By the time of Pepe's posthumous novella "Flying-Fox in a Freedom Tree", however, codeswitching and *diglossia* are recurrent phenomena. When he begins school, Pepe is thus ridiculed for his own poor English, and frustrated in his efforts to understand either his *afakasi* (part-European) teacher or the New Zealand headmaster. Choice of language assumes an even more central role in the final section of the novel, when Tauilopepe sends his grandson, Lalolagi, away to boarding-school in New Zealand. In a chapter with the wittily ambivalent heading "Correspondence between Worlds" Lalolagi begins writing home in Samoan, before his grandfather urges him to write all his letters in English ("which was the only language worth knowing well"). To Tauilopepe, it is immaterial that he must actually have the letters translated.

Within the text, then, "our" and "their" languages (as metonyms for the respective rival cultures which they embody) are central issues. Wendt declared in his essay "Novelists and Historians" that he could never write a novel from the viewpoint of the Papalagi. He has not, however, expressed any strong alternative desire to write in Samoan: *Leaves of the Banyan Tree* (like the embedded novella produced by Pepe), then, is written in the "stepmother tongue". Wendt's novel also resembles *Potiki* in another respect: a large number of central terms are left in the local language, Samoan, although there is now a fifty-word glossary. Wendt, on the other hand, is the more cosmopolitan novelist. Whereas Grace has only experienced the cultural exile of a Maori in her own country, Wendt worked eight years in Fiji and now lives in New Zealand, where he regards himself as becoming "more and more centred".

It is for the outside anglophone reader, however, that Wendt's fiction may be in need of some domestication. There is a certain novelty, for most anglophone readers, in a text where the great beyond is represented by New Zealand and the immediate image of alterity is a Solomon Islander (the name *sa-moa* apparently means "sacred centre"), but Wendt, like Grace, transcends the superficially exotic. Unlike *Potiki*, however, *Leaves of the Banyan Tree* is a more traditional kind of novel. The epic sweep of Tauilopepe's rise and fall dimly recalls the story of Michael Henchard in Hardy's *The Mayor of Casterbridge*, although Wendt ackowledges a more overt "anxiety of influence" in another European novelist – also linked with Samoa, also frequently patronized as exotic, and also writing in what was in one sense the stepmother tongue: the Scot, Robert Louis Stevenson.

Wendt has also promoted the study of South Pacific writing by editing two large collections: *Lali: A Pacific Anthology* (1980) and *Nuanua: Pacific Writing in English since 1980* (1995). Each of these contains, in Wendt's own words, "a representative selection of prose and poetry in English from the Cook Islands, Fiji, Kiribati, Niue, Papua New Guinea, Vanuatu, Solomon Islands, Tonga and Samoa". Wendt accepts the cultural dominance of English in the region as an irreversible trend, but reacts against so-called post-colonial anthologies that privilege the writing of descendants of European settlers. As he drily observes: "today some writing considered by Pakeha/Papalagi writers to be post-colonial, we consider colonial". Wendt now sees the need for a third anthology, featuring writing in the indigenous Pacific languages. Several of the contributors to *Nuanua* publish in two languages, including poets Ruperake Petaia (English and Samoan) and Kauraka Kauraka (English and Cook Isands Maori).

After Wendt, the most interesting Polynesian novelist may be Tongan Epeli Hau'ofa. Born in Papua New Guinea and educated there, as well as in Tonga, Fiji, Australia, and Canada, he is now professor of sociology at the University of the South Pacific. His published fiction includes *Tales of the Tikongs* (1983), stories based on the "tall tales" of Tongan oral tradition, and the novel *Kisses in the Nederends* (1987), a grotesque satire set on the imaginary South Pacific island of Tipota. The gap between European and South Pacific cultures is nowhere more obvious, however, than in the novels of Papua New Guinea writer **Russell Soaba**, author of *Wanpis* (1977) and the better known *Maiba* (1985).

Maiba, or Yawasa Maibina, is the daughter of the late hereditary chief of Makawana Village, in the Great Anuki region of Papua New Guinea. The longest chapter in the novel portrays village life (*Maiba* is subtitled "A Papuan Novel"), and recalls the anthropological revisionism of Wendt's *Leaves of the Banyan Tree* or even Achebe's *Things Fall Apart*. The stability of the community is later threatened by the attempts of Doboro Thomas, the village orator, to usurp the chieftancy through bribery, fraud and force of arms. The villagers, inspired by the courage of Boas the Church elder, resist these moves and equilibrium is restored.

In the context of land and language, Soaba's novel is an exceptional work. Papua New Guinea has about 750 indigenous languages spoken by a population of 4 million over an area roughly the size of Spain. Soaba's mother tongue, as already noted, is Anuki, a language with about three hundred native speakers, most of whom are illiterate; he writes in English, as he has wrily observed, "out of choicelessness". The novel is nevertheless prefaced with a note explaining that the word "maiba" is "the common form of Anuki communication which expresses truths only through parables and riddles": an explicit example of this technique is the story of a coconut tree with which Boas persuades the villagers to adopt passive resistance rather than violent counter-measures against Doboro and his followers. Anuki language and culture exist covertly, then, in the rhetorical structures of the narrative.

The discourse of land, on the other hand, is most obviously illustrated by a strong sense of place, as in the quasi-mystical evocation of Tubuga Bay in the opening chapter, when the heroine – who in her earliest childhood could never be prevailed on to wear clothes – calmly enters the ocean. In an even more striking passage, land is again identified as place, but now in the physical description of a villager's house:

> It is beautifully architectured; its *bendoro* and *pousarewa* posts stand short but have been carefully hewn and are straight; the ends of the sago-thatched roofings are well-trimmed; the veranda that faces the village square ... appears neat and ventilated to suit any season; and the walls of woven *kipa* and bamboo splits catch the eye with their bright brown and yellow zigzag patterns all around the house. The walls are nailed down by thin timber linings that are painted red, thus giving the whole household the feeling of harmonious colors.   (p. 95)

The house has been built (with his own bare hands) by the father of Christine, the young girl raped by Doboro and his henchmen. As the symbolic representation of a harmonious village world threatened from outside, the description may be read as the central "*maiba*"-type parable of the narrative.

Certain lexical items in the description will baffle all but the local reader, and the passage is also therefore a suitable context in which to mention Soaba's language. *Maiba* is a virtual inventory of devices for the presentation of vernacular speech. Only two Makanawa families (including Maiba's own) actually speak and understand Anuki; the most widely spoken language in the village is Are; knowledge of English, on the other hand, has an important function in the novel's plot. Code-switching between all three languages is constant and clearly indicated, as is the use of non-standard English. Glossing is another common device, although not always helpful: *wagaya* (a kind of green vegetable) is thus defined as "a variety of *chaya*" (p. 44), whilst the song of a familiar bird is represented as "*Idagaboda, idagaboda*", explained in turn as an Anuki word meaning "He, she or it thigh-blocked others' streams" (p. 59)! Soaba thus wittily underlines the assumption among even the best-intentioned *dimdims* that yawning cultural gaps can always be conveniently bridged by mere translation or praraphrase.

With the number of unglossed items in the description of the house, there are parallels between Soaba and a number of South Pacific writers. All clearly feel that their prime responsibility is towards their local readers rather than to an international public. Witi Ihimaera admitted to a certain bemusement at the idea of his novels being read in the United States; Patricia Grace and Keri Hulme place even greater demands on their Pakeha readers. Various contemporary African and Caribbean writers are similarly (and understandably) uncompromising in their more literal examples of the "empire writing back".

A number of other writers who require mention in the context of the South Pacific are Fijian. With its large influx of Indian indentured labourers, Fiji has a cultural history in some ways analogous to that of Trinidad or Mauritius: several of its most prominent writers are of Indian origin. These include Subramani, now a literature professor at the University of the South Pacific, whose collection of short stories, *Fantasy Eaters*, appeared in 1988; and Satendra Nandan, now teaching at the University of Canberra, who published his autobiographical novel *The Wounded Sea* in 1991. And at this point, therefore, the narrative returns again to the remarkably productive Indian (or South Asian) diaspora – a movement, moreover, which no survey of anglophone fiction can ever long avoid. It is reconsidered in the final section of this study.

FURTHER READING

Adam Shoemaker and Mudrooroo Narogin co-edited *Paperbark: A Collection of Black Australian Writings* (St Lucia: University of Queensland Press, 1990). Witi Ihimaera and D. S. Long produced *An Anthology of Maori Writing: Into the World of Light* (Auckland: Heinemann, 1982). Albert Wendt has promoted the study of South Pacific writing by editing two large collections: *Lali: A Pacific Anthology* (1980) and *Nuanua: Pacific Writing in English since 1980* (1995), both published by the University of Auckland Press.

Two invaluable guides are *Writers from the South Pacific: A Bio-Bibliographic Critical Encyclopedia,* edited by Norman Simms (Washington, DC: Three Continents Press, 1991), and *Indigenous Literatures of Oceania: A Survey of Criticism and Interpretation* (Westport, CT: Greenwood Press, 1995) by Nicholas J. Goetzfridt.

Important critical studies are, for Australia: Adam Shoemaker's *Black Words, White Page. Aboriginal Literature, 1929–1988* (St Lucia: University of Queensland Press, 1989) and Mudrooroo Narogin's *Writing from the Fringe: A Study of Modern Aboriginal Literature in Australia* (Melbourne: Hyland House, 1990); for New Zealand, Peter Beatson's *The Healing Tongue: Themes in Contemporary Maori Literature* (Palmerston North: Massie University, 1989); and for the remaining South Pacific, Subramani's *South Pacific Literature: From Myth to Fabulation* (Suva: University of the South Pacific Press, 1985). Subramani has also edited *The Indo-Fijian Experience* (St Lucia: University of Queensland Press, 1979), an interesting combination of critical essays and literary anthology, and *After Narrative: The Pursuit of Reality and Fiction* (Suva: University of the South Pacific Press, 1990), with critical essays on writers of the region.

Part II
New Literatures in
New Worlds

4

Afro-America

What has hitherto been little more than a regional division of anglophone fiction, partly modified by the trope of the "stepmother tongue", clearly assumes new dimensions with the above heading. Unlike Asia, Africa, or the South Pacific, Afro-America does not exist as a geographical entity on any map; and as to its possible status as a region of the mind, the burden of proof still rests with the critic. Furthermore, the inclusion of Afro-American fiction under any heading and its classification with Caribbean writing are not self-evident procedures. Black American writing is not conventionally regarded as post-colonial literature, and is even remoter from the British Commonwealth. Either Africa or "mainstream" America itself might seem logically closer entities with which to link it – they do, after all, provide the constituent elements for the label itself – and some justification of the present policy is therefore required.

One strong argument is provided by the significant ties of many Caribbean writers with African American literature,[1] beginning with Claude McKay, the Jamaican-born poet and novelist who became prominent in the Harlem Renaissance. More recent examples of such cultural crossovers include the Antigua-born Jamaica Kincaid or the Grenada-linked Audre Lorde. An interesting case, too, is the ex-Barbadian but Toronto-based Austin Clarke, a novelist not normally associated with African *American* literature. But as an adoptive Canadian, Clarke should also surely be regarded as an "American" writer: the restriction of a broad geographical term to citizens of the United States (at the expense of those other Americans who happen to hold a Canadian passport) is a terminological anomaly comparable to that already noted in the word "English" itself.

Among Afro-American writers linked with the Caribbean, on the other hand, the classic case is that of Zora Neale Hurston, whose interest in Black folklore took her beyond her native Florida to the West Indies in the 1930s and to Belize (then British Honduras) in the following decade. *Tell My Horse* (1938) was based on ethnographic material collected in Jamaica; *Their Eyes Were Watching God* (1937) was written in seven weeks during a stay in Haiti. Contemporary African American novels where Caribbean culture and setting are intrinsic include Toni Morrison's *Tar Baby* (1981) and Paule Marshall's *Praise Song for the Widow* (1983).

Other novelists, finally, such as Trinidad-born Frank Hercules or Jamaica-raised Michelle Cliff, are simply difficult to place in either category, and implicitly question our compulsion to do so. The multiculturalism of such writers is neatly suggested in *Soul Clap Hands and Sing* (1961), Paule Marshall's group of novellas celebrating the African presence in the New World. Herself the daughter of Barbadian immigrants in New York, Marshall entitles the four units of her book "Barbados", "Brooklyn", "British Guiana", and "Brazil".

These exchanges are nevertheless merely individual examples of more pervasive historical ties between Afro-American and *Afro-*Caribbean culture produced by the exile and diaspora of slavery. The most compelling testament to the latter occurs in the slave narratives of the eighteenth and early nineteenth centuries, which simultaneously provide the earliest examples of Black anglophone literature. The finest of these accounts, before the *Narrative of the Life of Frederick Douglass* (1845), is undoubtedly the *Life of Olaudah Equiano*, first published in 1789.

Olaudah Equiano may be fairly considered the father of anglophone (West) African, Afro-American, or even Black British literature. An Ibo from the kingdom of Benin, in what is today Nigeria, Equiano spent most of his adult life in England, the West Indies, and the American colonies – or on the high seas between these points. Land and language are integral issues in an autobiographical narrative which, although it does not strictly qualify as fiction, shows the rhetorical skill and artistic self-awareness of the greatest novels. The significance of ("our") land emerges in the author's myth of origin, a poignant evocation of the Vale of Essaka in his native Africa. Beside this, England can never be more than a surrogate home. Predictably, Equiano shows no great tenderness, either, towards any of the fifteen Caribbean islands he knows, and far less to Virginia and Georgia, although he describes more enlightened, Quaker-dominated Philadelphia as his "favourite old town".

The question of language, on the other hand, is less clear. Equiano refers to a childhood knowledge of "various African languages" (perhaps dialects of Ibo, as his modern editor suggests), and to his gradual acquisition of English. When shipped to Virginia as a child, he is "not able to talk much English", although, by the time of his transfer to England shortly afterwards (1759), he claims to "speak English tolerably well" and feel "almost an Englishman". There are no other direct allusions to personal linguistic competence, and nothing (beyond the above references) even to suggest that the *Life* was not written by a native speaker. In a practical sense, then, there seems little distinction between "our" and "their" language; English for Equiano has apparently become a cultural given, although, from his traumatic experiences among its speakers, it is difficult to regard it as anything but a stepmother tongue.

Like many prototypes, Equiano's *Life* is also fascinating for its anticipation of numerous themes and motifs found in its literary successors: in this case, black colonial and post-colonial writing. Here, for example, are the ironic reversals and defamiliarization techniques earlier associated with travel narratives, including the classic cannibal *topos*, when it is Equiano and his African countrymen who more than once expect to be eaten by their red-faced European assailants. Equiano is also a valid historical source, confirming the segregation of slaves along linguistic lines, but providing important evidence for the preservation of African culture. He thus records the Sunday gatherings in Kingston, Jamaica, where "each different nation of Africa meet and dance [sic] after the manner of their own country": the scene could almost be Carriacou's Big Drum, as portrayed in Paule Marshall's *Praisesong for the Widow*.

Olaudah Equiano's autobiography is also a good introduction to some of the pitfalls that await attempts to integrate such potentially disparate categories as Afro-American and anglophone Caribbean narrative. The problems involved may be broadly classified as historical, generic or demographic, and are here briefly discussed in that order.

Most obviously, African American literature has an uninterrupted literary tradition from Equiano through the nineteenth century to the Harlem renaissance and beyond. Besides the *Narrative of the Life of Frederick Douglass* (1845), acknowledged as the last and finest of the great slave autobiographies, there is a fictional tradition beginning with William Wells Brown's *Clotel* (1853) and Harriet Wilson's *Our Nig* (1859), admittedly flawed works, but nevertheless anticipating the more impressive novels and stories of

Charles Chesnutt and Paul Dunbar at the turn of the century. The 1920s brought fiction by Jean Toomer and Nella Larsen; the 1930s added novels by James Weldon Johnson, Langston Hughes, Zora Neale Hurston (three) and Arna Bontemps (three). From Equiano to George Lamming in the Caribbean, however, there is – with the exception of a few honourable precursors – correspondingly little.

The generic problem centres around narrative forms. A study of Caribbean prose narrative limited to the novel would exclude such seminal autobiographies as C. L. R. James's *Beyond a Boundary* (1963) and Austin Clarke's *Growing up Stupid under the Union Jack* (1980), or discriminate against such a fine short-story writer as Olive Senior; but the corresponding wealth of full-length West Indian fiction partly atones for these omissions. A chronological study of Afro-American fiction, on the other hand, would be – relatively speaking – far poorer. The autobiographical tradition has always been strong among Black writers, and, until some (debatable) point in the twentieth century, was actually predominant. No nineteenth-century Afro-American novel captured the public imagination (black or white) as dramatically as Douglass's *Narrative* or even Booker T. Washington's *Up from Slavery* (1901). And even today, the autobiographical sequence begun by Maya Angelou with *I Know Why the Caged Bird Sings* (1971) has a reputation comparable to that of any modern Black fictional *oeuvre*.

The issue, however, is also often one of generic distinctions. Harriet Jacobs's *Incidents in the Life of a Slave Girl* (1861) seems to straddle the divide between autobiography and novel. James Weldon Johnson's *The Autobiography of an Ex-Colored Man*, published anonymously in 1912, is now recognized as a novel of the so-called "colour line"; the same author's *Along this Way* (1933) was his true autobiography. Most notoriously of all, Jean Toomer's remarkable *Cane* (1923), frequently considered a novel, virtually defies classification with its unique mix of stories, sketches, poems, personal chronicle, and the novella "Kabnis".

In demographic terms, the obvious difference is the fact that Afro-Americans constitute a clear minority in the United States, whereas Afro-Caribbeans form an overwhelming majority in the anglophone Caribbean, with the exceptions of Trinidad and Guyana; in both of these countries, however, the other large ethnic group is of East Indian origin, and whites are, here too, comparatively rare. At various points since Emancipation, Black Americans as a whole (and individual writers) have seen themselves as essentially "American" (in the early twentieth-century "integrationist" view, for example) or primarily Black (as with the more radical currents of the 1960s). Caribbean writers may reject (or transcend) their origins like Naipaul, pursue a nativist aesthetic like Kamau Brathwaite, or advocate multi-culturalism like Wilson Harris; the demographic realities of the Caribbean nevertheless remain distinct from those of the United States.

The present study does not claim to provide a comprehensive view of Afro-American fiction, even for the last half of the twentieth century. Its interest in the themes of "land" and "language" will nevertheless require the consideration of a wide range of novels.

Olaudah Equiano's *Life* is the point of departure for two seminal studies of Black American narrative: Houston A. Baker's *Blues, Ideology, and Afro-American Literature* (1984) and Henry Louis Gates's *The Signifying Monkey* (1988). Baker offers "blues" – broadly defined as a synthesis of "work songs, group seculars, field hollers, sacred harmonies, proverbial wisdom, folk philosophy, political commentary, ribald humor, elegiac lament, and much more" (p. 5) – as a *matrix* of African American culture. Besides the two most substantial slave narratives (those of Equiano and Douglass), his series of illustrative readings also features Paul Laurence Dunbar's *The Sport of the Gods*, Hurston's *Their Eyes Were Watching God*, various texts by Richard Wright, and the "Trueblood" episode of Ellison's *Invisible Man*.

The first half of Gates's *The Signifying Monkey*, subtitled "A Theory of African-American Literary Criticism", is an extended essay in cultural anthropology, tracing links between the African divine trickster figure of *Esu* and his New World counterparts in Brazil, the Caribbean, and the American South. In the latter setting, Esu has been transformed into the traditional figure of the "signifying monkey". Here Gates draws on a characteristic Black usage of the word "signify", to denote parody, mimicry, or ridicule. "Signifyin(g)", as Gates calls it – in deference to vernacular phonology – is seen then as the privileged trope of African American oral culture, and, by extension, of its literary tradition. The individual texts analysed by Gates are thus a sequence, with each one "signifyin(g)" on its predecessor(s): from the slave narratives to Zora Neale Hurston's *Their Eyes Were Watching God*; from Hurston to Ishmael Reed's *Mumbo Jumbo*; and from Hurston and Reed to Alice Walker's *The Color Purple*. Gates's theory is by no means exclusive to Black culture, however. His definition of Afro-American narrative as a tradition of "grounded repetition and difference" characterized by "its urge to start over, to begin again, but always to begin on a well-structured foundation" seems equally applicable to European or Euro-American authors. Gates himself admits that sig-nifyin(g) also describes Cervantes's relation to the novels of chivalry, or Fielding's to Richardson's *Pamela*.

Such passionately argued, but theoretically sophisticated, holistic readings of an entire newer literary tradition, in the manner of Baker or Gates, are not common outside the field of Afro-American writing (although Abdul JanMohamed's study of African literature, *Manichean Aesthetics* (1983), is a notable exception); and this is reason enough for their inclusion here in the main body of the text, rather than in the appendix to this section. Particularly interesting in both critics, moreover, is the emphasis placed on vernacular speech. *Blues, Ideology, and Afro-American Literature* is subtitled "A Vernacular Theory"; and *The Signifying Monkey* begins with William Labov's famous 1985 hypothesis that Black English is be-coming increasingly distinct from standard American, in fact "going its own way". A fuller treatment of Black Englishes in the New World is deferred to the introductory note on the Caribbean, where such issues have even greater significance. Here it is enough to recall that purely academic accounts of vernacular – convention-ally defined as the indigenous language or dialect of a community – are haunted by half-forgotten etymologies: the Latin word *verna* denoted a "home-born *slave*", whilst the adjective *vernacular*, by ex-tension, meant "born on his/her *master*'s estate". In historical retro-spect, the term Black English *Vernacular* is ironically appropriate.

The relevance of the above preamble should now be clear. The general scheme of this study argues that Afro-American, as well as Afro-Caribbean, writers in English are also effectively using a "stepmother" tongue. The term here has a broadly metaphorical sense, since it is patently absurd to suggest that, for Toni Morrison or Gloria Naylor, English is in any literal sense a second language, as it is for Chinua Achebe or Ngũgĩ wa Thiong'o. Jamaica Kincaid nevertheless alludes suggestively in *Lucy* to the cruel irony by which African American (or Caribbean) writers are reduced to ex-pressing themselves in (what was once) the language of the master.

Not quite, of course: this is to forget the legacy of *vernacular* itself, the "language of the *slave*". Many Afro-American writers incorpo-rate the vernacular voice into their narratives. Although Black critics have been pronouncing the "dialect novel" dead ever since the Harlem Renaissance of the 1920s, their predictions have been confounded by Zora Neale Hurston and, more recently, by Alice

Walker; all the other works analysed by Baker and Gates are also essentially vernacular texts. It is significant, of course, that both critics totally ignore Toni Morrison, a writer not associated in the 1970s with Black Vernacular, although she subsequently produced *Tar Baby* (1982) and *Jazz* (1993), whose very titles proclaim their cultural affinities with Afro-American popular culture. Few Black writers have been as radical as Walker in *The Color Purple* (1982), more than half of which is in a very broad vernacular, although virtually all of them have incorporated the language in variously attenuated forms, whether in dialogue or even straight narrative. In this way, they have imperceptibly (or sometimes quite provocatively) tempered the exclusivity of "their" language (standard English) with "our" language (Black English Vernacular).

To some extent, it is possible to find a similarly subversive process in the context of *land*. For many Afro-Americans, it could be argued, America is (at least symbolically) not "our" but "their" land. It is a place to which few went of their own accord, and where many remain alienated even today, although – by a strange quirk of history – the first group of African Americans actually arrived in America a year before the Pilgrim Fathers (they were of course intended as slaves for the Virginia colony). America, the painful sojourn, and Africa, the lost home, are subsequently among the commonest tropes in African American writing, religious or secular. In fiction they appear, for example, in Milkman Dead's obsession with flying away in Morrison's *Song of Solomon* (1977), or the myth of Ibo's Landing in Marshall's *Praisesong for the Widow*, where a group of slaves walk off over the water: the destination in both cases is the lost African home.

Alternatively, Black writers have created enclaves of "our land" in the New World. Hurston thus immortalizes her home town of Eatonville, Florida (America's first exclusively Black incorporated township), in *Their Eyes Were Watching God*; whilst it is enough to recall the symbolic position of Ibo's landing (in *Praisesong for the Widow*) on the South Carolina coast, near the "sea islands" where African American roots are deepest, and where Gullah, the linguistic descendant of Plantation Creole, is still spoken. Perhaps the most extraordinary novel of all in this context is Gloria Naylor's *Mama Day*. Naylor's main setting is a fictional island between South Carolina and Georgia, but belonging to neither. Since, moreover, the island's exclusively Black population is both completely autonomous and entirely self-sufficient, as well as being in the capable hands of a matriarchy headed by Mama Day herself, one might speak in more than one sense of a cultural no-*man*'s-land. Here, by a development analogous to that operating for language, the realities of a socially and politically alien White America are also erased in the processes through which "their" land becomes "ours".

The broadest overview of modern African American fiction would note a significant gender shift in successive generations: three powerful male novelists, Richard Wright, James Baldwin, and Ralph Ellison (together with a number of lesser known female figures) are followed by a wave of remarkable women writers who, in turn, tend to overshadow the men. The possible causes of this reversal, both within the Black community and in American society at large, would be issues significant enough for a separate study. They are, in any case, beyond the scope of this one.

In practical terms, in fact, a large number of Afro-American writers may be located on a broad continuum based on their relation to the symbolic issues of land and language, and it is these factors that have determined the texts discussed at greater length here. Claude McKay's *Banana Bottom*, an early treatment of cultural alienation, thus combines important geographical and linguistic perspectives. Ralph Ellison's *Invisible Man* remains the monument of Black fiction; there may be no candidate for the "great (Euro)-American novel" as strong as *Invisible Man* for its Afro-American equivalent. For all its significance as a vernacular text, however, it is paradoxically as much a European (or Euro-American) as an Afro-American novel. Zora Neale Hurston's *Their Eyes Were Watching God* and Alice Walker's *The Color Purple* conversely represent the most radical vernacular impulses. With Gloria Naylor's *Mama Day* or Ernest J. Gaines's *The Autobiography of Miss Jane Pittman*, on the other hand, the symbolism of land is as important as that of language. In Toni Morrison's *Tar Baby* and Paule Marshall's *Praisesong for the Widow*, the parameters of *both* land and language are fundamental, although the two dimensions have now been extended to embrace the Caribbean. Ishmael Reed's *Flight to Canada*, finally, is an irreverent satire on the traditional slave narrative, an irreverence which nevertheless presumes and confirms the strong presence of the literary tradition it parodies. These, then, are the nine novels considered in greater detail below.

Claude McKay was born in Jamaica, but emigrated to the United States at the age of twenty-two. After *Home to Harlem* (1928), describing a black soldier's return from France, and *Banjo* (1929), an account of life on the Marseilles waterfront, his third novel, *Banana Bottom* (1933), has a Caribbean setting. It follows the return of Bita Plant to her native Jamaican village after seven years of mission-ary-sponsored education in England.

The "return of the native" motif inevitably recalls Thomas Hardy's novel of the same name – a useful association, since there are numerous parallels with the English writer: the common em-phasis on proverbs and folklore, the frequent quotation of ballads and folksong, the close links of the narrative to the natural cycle, and the *patois*/dialect-speaking peasant chorus. More specifically, *Banana Bottom*'s "Big Picnic at Tabletop" echoes the Midsummer dance that opens *Tess of the D'Urbervilles*, whilst the village "tea meetings" resemble the barn dance in the same novel; even the vil-lagers' reliance on Wumba the Obeah Man is comparable to Henchard's visit to the soothsayer in *The Mayor of Casterbridge*; the blossoming relationship between Bita and the unlettered Jabban, finally, recalls that of Grace Melbury and Giles Winterbourne in *The Woodlanders* (although without Hardy's tragic resolution). Such parallels emphasize the common concern of McKay and of Hardy, fifty years before him, to record the confrontation between a traditional peasant (essentially pagan) culture and the demands of a new bourgeois respectability underwritten by Christian morality.

The conflict between a puritanical Christianity and more relaxed local custom dominates the novel, and it is easy to see where the author's sympathies lie. When her missionary sponsors try to marry her off to theological student Harald Newton, Bita is only saved when her fiancé causes sexual scandal just before his farewell sermon to Banana Bottom. In a fairly crude illustration of McKay's thesis of the sexual repression inherent in Christianity, Harald is caught "defiling himself with a nanny goat": the exquisite pun on this incident ("from the dizzy heights of holiness to the bottom of the beast") may be unintended.

After Bita, the most significant character in the novel is the Englishman Squire Gensir, a kind of amateur anthropologist who has abandoned the material comforts of England to live a simple life in Jamaica. At one point, Gensir and Bita provide a kind of cultural *chiasmus*, with the cultivated Englishman who has turned his back on "civilization" pitted against the simple village girl who has later been moulded by this same metropolitan culture. As the narrative unfolds, however, McKay's sympathy for indigenous values, against the claims of the various Christian Churches, becomes more insistent. Besides the narrow, repressed nature of both Anglicanism and the Free Churches, McKay also emphasizes the racism, hypocrisy, and social prejudice rife among the various Christian groups.

At the centre of the book, however, is the issue of sexuality, and here McKay could hardly differ more radically from Hardy, although comparisons are still useful. When the pubescent Bita is raped by the eccentric Crazy Bow, her innocently provocative behaviour is reminiscent of the unconscious sexuality of Hardy's Tess. Tragic as the incident is, however, Bita is – to all appearances – neither permanently traumatized nor tragically doomed by the loss of virginity, as would have been the case in the bourgeois novel from Richardson onwards. More significant in *Banana Bottom* is Bita's growing tenderness for her father's drayman, despite a social and cultural gap of the kind that normally proves insurmountable in Hardy. In successive scenes that are difficult to avoid reading emblematically, Jubban rescues Bita both from the religious flagellants of the *Big Revival* and from the sexual advances of a marauding planter. During the preparations for Bita's marriage to Jubban, the bride is conspicuously pregnant, although it is made clear (in a final stab at bourgeois Christian convention) that this is an entirely private matter.

An Afro-Caribbean in the United States, McKay was sociologically (and perhaps psychologically) a double exile. His tender celebration of Jamaica (where the novel is predictably popular) affirms a sense of belonging, an attempt perhaps to convert "their" land into "ours". *Banana Bottom* is not, however, linguistically radical, in spite of a lengthy concluding speech in praise of marriage – delivered entirely in creole. McKay actually wrote dialect poems, although his characteristic poetic idiom is a late Victorian diction that sounds a little incongruous in the new flowering of Black culture in the 1920s known as the Harlem Renaissance.

Black American fiction really achieved full international recognition with a trio of novelists: Wright, Ellison and Baldwin. Richard Wright may well illustrate the generic ambivalence common to Black writing, in that his two most celebrated works are a novel, *Native Son* (1940), and an autobiography, *Black Boy* (1945). The story of a black ghetto dweller, Bigger Thomas, who accidentally kills the daughter of his rich white employers, is illuminated by Wright's comment in *Black Boy*: "All my life has shaped me for the realism, the naturalism of the modern novel."

The major novels of James Baldwin have the same powerful autobiographical impulse. *Go Tell It on the Mountain* (1953) thus represents a settling of scores with his stepfather and religious upbringing (as a boy, Baldwin was a teenage preacher). *Another Country* (1962), set in Harlem, suggests the restorative power of Afro-American blues culture; but his second novel, *Giovanni's Room* (1956) – where the author comes to terms with his homosexuality – portrays an American's affair with a young Italian in Paris. As in the second novel by Ann Petry, *Country Place* (1947), the protagonists are explicitly white. Clearly, critical judgements on Baldwin and his relation to the Black vernacular tradition are conditioned by the particular texts one chooses to emphasize.

In contrast, vernacular culture has a clear significance in the only novel of **Ralph Ellison**, *Invisible Man* (1952), a text that reproduces the motifs of land and language, even as it revisits the concept of the stepmother tongue. A massive work that shifts between naturalism, expressionism, and surrealism, Ellison's novel also reflects fruitful encounters with both American and European literary tradition: Dreiser, Faulkner and Melville are regularly advanced as literary predecessors, whilst the title follows H. G. Wells's *The Invisible Man*, and the final image of the anonymous protagonist in a subterranean refuge evokes Dostoevsky's *Notes from the Underground*. Among Afro-American precursors, on the other hand, Ellison acknowledges Langston Hughes and Richard Wright (a short story by the latter is entitled *The Man Who Lived Underground*), whilst the inspiration of blues and Black vernacular culture is always apparent.

The nameless hero's frustrated search for identity during a picaresque-like Odyssey from the American South to New York City locates the novel in a tradition of Negro protest fiction, but also recalls conceptually (if not technically) the fiction of Kafka. The synthesis of so many elements produces a major existential novel whose universality ultimately invalidates distinctions of black and white, and transforms Afro-American to all-American once again.

If the blues aesthetic is not as central to *Invisible Man* as Houston Baker might like, there are nevertheless numerous occasions on which Ellison privileges the form, together with other aspects of vernacular culture: the protagonist himself notes that, whereas he may start with a church song, he always "ends up singin' the blues"; Trueblood, the sharecropper who is the indirect cause of the hero's expulsion from college, is a noted blues singer; the refuse collector in New York pushing a cartload of rejected blueprints, and Mary Rambo, the good-hearted landlady, also sing the blues. The old man from South Carolina selling yams speaks with the hero at length in Black Vernacular, reaffirming his Black Southern roots with the pun, "I yam what I am."

The central quest for identity encounters a number of false gospels, purveyed by variously benighted characters: the Reverend Homer A. Barber, who preaches the Founder's Day sermon, is – like his Greek namesake – literally blind; the hypocritical college president, Dr Bledsoe, merely turns a blind eye to racism and other injustice; Brother Jack, the Communist ideologue has a glass eye (causing the narrator to reflect ironically on which eye is the blind one). Mr Norton (comically confused by drunken veterans with Thomas Jefferson) and the Emersons (where the cultural association is onomastically explicit) are also ridiculed. Only the ambivalent Rinehart, the last new character – in fact, a non-character, a mask or cipher – can teach the hero anything: i.e. the fact of his own invisibility.

The latter point requires some comment here, since conventional exegesis of the trope (equating it simply with White obliviousness of Black people) is highly questionable. In the immediate context, the significance of invisibility is twofold: after buying a white hat and large pair of sunglasses, the hero manages to pass unrecognized even among his own acquaintances; or alternatively, when the protagonist later falls down a manhole whilst fleeing the accomplices of Ras the Exhorter, he becomes quite literally invisible to both whites *and* blacks.

In general terms, then, *Invisible Man* undergoes a gradual but insistent transition from Negro protest novel to broader existentialist quest in the turmoil of mid-twentieth-century America. A clear indication of this shift appears in the phrase "We are Americans all of us" from one of the hero's last political speeches, a claim that should probably be taken at face value. A discourse of complicity, even mutuality, between Black and White is also implied in the Epilogue with the reference to "whites busy escaping blackness and becoming blacker every day, and the blacks striving towards whiteness, becoming dull and grey". In this largely unexplained process, there is only one land: America, with a single common language.

The trope of the stepmother tongue nevertheless literally fits the novel's two great (and false) ideologues: Ras the Exhorter admits to speaking "bahd English" ("Hell, it ain't ma tongue, mahn"), while the furious Brother Jack – when accused of racist bias – begins "spluttering and lapsing into a foreign tongue". These characters may literally be struggling with the language, but are treated satirically, without poignancy or pathos.

In defiance of much Afro-American critical praxis, then, Ellison could also be regarded as an American writer *tout court*, who owes as much to Euro- as to Afro-American tradition. Similarly, other novelists such as Chester Himes in *If He Hollers Let Him Go* (1945) and Ann Petry in *The Street* (1946) used the European-imported naturalism of Wright to describe the grim post-war realities of American life. For an Afro-American novel more closely implicated in the dichotomies of land and language, one must turn to a long neglected woman writer of the previous generation, Zora Neale Hurston.

A pupil at Columbia University of the great American anthropologist Frank Boas, **Zora Neale Hurston** did extensive fieldwork in Jamaica, Haiti, and the American South, producing two studies of popular culture, *Of Mules and Men* (1935) and *Tell My Horse* (1938). Her expertise with this type of material appears in *Their Eyes Were Watching God*, for example, at the ritualistic "dragging-out" of Matt Bonner's mule in Chapter 6.

In the present context, however, the most striking element of Hurston's novel is its language. The frame narrative, itself strongly colloquial, includes the heroine's extensive supposedly oral account, delivered entirely in Black English Vernacular. At a time when many critics regarded the so-called "dialect novel" as obsolete, Hurston used vernacular not merely for comic purposes, but to express an entire range of emotions. And yet land acquires almost comparable significance, both in the novel and beyond: born in Eatonville, Florida, the first incorporated all-black town in America, Hurston fictionally recreates her childhood home. Simply expressed, then, it might be claimed that Hurston's replacement of standard English with vernacular is the equivalent of replacing "their" with "our" language, whilst her then unfashionable cultural separatism may be seen, in turn, as a struggle for "our" over "their" land.

But such arguments ignore the importance of *Their Eyes Were Watching God* as a feminist text. Married at the age of sixteen to a local sharecropper, Janie Crawford escapes a life of drudgery by running away with Jody Starks, who becomes the leading light of the black town of Eatonville, only to stifle Janie as effectively as her first husband had done. Left a widow after twenty years, a still attractive Janie finds love, happiness and self-fulfilment with itinerant labourer and inveterate gambler Tea Cake Woods, before the latter's untimely death.

In this liberating process, the narrative supplies new dimensions to the concepts of land and language, portraying the latter as female *voice* and the former as female *space*. In the first sense, Janie – although recognized as a "born orator" – is initially excluded from the "speechmaking" and entire oral tradition associated with the front porch; when she tries to defend the woman's position, Jody warns her about "getting too moufy". With Tea Cake, on the other hand, Janie feels she is learning "de maiden language all over"; and when she leaves with her third husband for a tough but rewarding life in the Everglades, she is now able to participate fully in social interaction and tell "big stories" herself.

Land, in the new feminist perspective, also undergoes a similar metaphorical shift. No longer mere physical territory, it becomes a broader existential space, whether this is denoted explicitly by porches or bedrooms, or more figuratively by pedestals and horizons. The original appeal of Eatonville to Jody Sparks was that of "makin' a town all outa colored folks", although it is soon clear that this intrinsically worthy gesture is a strictly gendered enterprise: while Janie unpacks in the bedroom, Joe holds forth on the porch about the need for the "*menfolks*" to assemble and form a committee. When Tea Cake takes Janie away to the Everglades, the novel's other major physical setting, the true significance of space continues to be existential rather than merely geographical. The move is also of mutual benefit, since the relationship with Janie offers a grateful Tea Cake what he memorably describes as the "keys of the kingdom".

As already noted, *Their Eyes Were Watching God* is a key text for both Baker and Gates in their respective vernacular-based models of African American narrative. And yet, *Their Eyes* is paradoxically both the most and the least African American of texts analysed by these two critics. As a love story or tragic romance, Hurston's novel thus follows a pattern less typically Afro- than Euro-American (or even European). If the prototypical Black fictional heroine, in Harriet Jacobs's *Incidents in the Life of a Slave Girl*, reluctantly accepts concubinage with a white neighbour rather than abuse from her master, then her white bourgeois counterparts, since Richardson's *Pamela* (1740), typically find true love and marriage in similar contexts. The intertextuality of *Their Eyes Were Watching God* may ultimately, however, implicate *Pamela* more strongly than *Incidents in the Life of a Slave Girl*. For Hurston clearly "signifies" (consciously or not) on Richardson's archetypal romance of hypergamy, as she lets her own heroine find happiness by marrying *down*.

Much of the credit for the belated recognition of *Their Eyes Were Watching God* goes to **Alice Walker**, who published a long tribute to Hurston ("Looking for Zora") in her essay collection *In Search of Our Mothers' Gardens* (1983). For more than twenty years, however, Walker herself has proved a powerful and provocative novelist on a wide variety of themes. These range from three generations of sharecroppers (*The Third Life of Grange Copeland*, 1970) and civil-rights activists (*Meridian*, 1976) to scenes of Black history (*The Temple of My Familiar*, 1989) and female circumcision or clitoridectomy (*Possessing the Secret of Joy*, 1992). Her most celebrated work nevertheless remains the strikingly original letter fiction *The Color Purple* (1982).

In one sense, of course, the novel's correspondence begun between two sisters from rural Georgia at the beginning of the century proves abortive. The letters of the semi-literate and much abused Celie are originally written to God – for want of another addressee – and predictably remain unanswered; while those of the younger and better-educated Nettie, now a missionary in Liberia, are long concealed by Celie's vindictive husband. The true force of the novel, then, is not in the psychological interactions between the two correspondents, but in their shrewd and often humorous independent comments.

Much of *The Color Purple's* appeal lies in Celie's triumphant attempt to overcome a legacy of racism, poverty, and abuse ("You black, you poor, you ugly, you a woman", her husband sneers on one occasion), and acquire a new human dignity. The novel's full scope, on the other hand, is derived from sending Nettie to Africa, thus giving Walker easier access to African history in its pre-, post-, and neo-colonial phases. But Walker's novel is also remarkable for its radical reversal of literary convention, by which Nettie's standard English acquires a structurally subordinate role to Celie's Black Vernacular. The latter therefore regularly assumes the status of central textual authority. Celie's authoritative insights normally occur by a process of direct (or indirect) satire. Her narrative is a legitimization of her own folk idiom: issues of race, gender, and class are now defined by reference to a *black, female,* and *vernacular* voice. It is this dimension of the text which links *A Color Purple* with the similarly demotic *Their Eyes Were Watching God* by Walker's frequently acknowledged literary predecessor.

Walker's technique (with all its humour and irony) is nicely illus- trated by Celie's hazy recollections from first grade of the "discov- ery" of America ("Columbus come here in boats call the Neater, the Peter, and the Santomareater. Indians so nice to him he force a bunch of 'em back home with him to wait on the queen", p. 19). These gems of colonial history are incidentally offered to God, who, from his position at the apex of the patriarchal system, might be thought to have possessed them already. As her real education pro- gresses, however, Celie eventually comes to terms with the system itself. Identifying the God she has been praying to as a *man*, and therefore presumably "trifling, forgitful and lowdown" like the rest, she insists that "if he ever listened to poor colored women the world would be a different place". She regenders God as "it", and continues writing to Nettie instead.

At a certain point in the narrative, a well-meaning Memphis friend tries to teach the now prosperous Celie "correct" English. After early efforts, however, Celie eventually abandons her new textbooks ("White folks all over them, talking bout apples and dogs", p. 193), producing the unassailable argument that "only a fool would want you to talk in a way that feel peculiar to your mind" (p. 194). The episode is clearly an oblique comment on the whole process of involuntary acculturation. Many African American (and Caribbean) authors write from an awareness of the "stepmother tongue" in its broader figurative sense as a metonym for Anglo-American cultural hegemony: the book "bout apples and dogs" is presumably the same reading primer that torments the wretched protagonist of Toni Morrison's *The Bluest Eye*. Some nov- elists, like Walker (and Hurston), have gone further and experi- mentally abandoned either literary English, or – in the case of Ngũgĩ wa Thiong'o and Mazisi Kunene – any form of English whatsoever.

In the fiction of **Gloria Naylor**, on the other hand, *land* effectively surpasses *language*, for the symbolic significance of setting can hardly be exaggerated. The early collection of stories, *The Women of Brewster Place* (1982), thus follows the lives of seven black women living on a condemned street in small-town America; the title of the first novel, *Linden Hills* (1985), refers to the private residential estate where physical elevation reflects the upward mobility of ambitious young Blacks striving to emulate the material success of the white middle classes. *Mama Day* (1988), finally, is set on the offshore island of Willow Springs, on the border between Georgia and South Carolina, but officially part of neither. The exclusively black population of the island has been both self-regulatory and self-sufficient since the 1820s when the legendary Sapphira Bascome had persuaded her master to bequeath the island to his ex-slaves.

The narrative is split between three perspectives: Ophelia (Cocoa) Day, the young woman from Willow Springs who has lived and worked for seven years in New York; her lover (and subsequently husband) George Andrews, product of the Staten Island shelter for boys, and now a successful hydraulic engineer; and – most interestingly, from a technical point of view – the garrulous, quasi-Faulknerian *vernacular* voice of an anonymous Willow Springs inhabitant.

Speech presentation (or *mis*representation) and linguistic register, whether treated with humour or seriousness, are thus prominent aspects of the narrative from the very first page. In lighter tone, the folklore student who comes to the island announces his extensive "field work", a phrase with quite different connotations for a rural black population; George, the affluent *engineer*, is rumoured to own a train, although, for the inhabitants of Willow Springs, the term normally refers to the person who drives one. On a more complex level, however, socio-linguistic observation in *Mama Day* is precise, as Ophelia works to hide her Southern accent, or her grandmother "straightens up" to use her "best English" on George's arrival. In giving the main narrator a much attenuated (if still conspicuous) form of vernacular, on the other hand, Naylor may actually be "signifyin(g) on" Hurston's *Their Eyes Were Watching God*. The precise quality of this voice is well illustrated by a lyrical evocation of the passing seasons:

> Living in a place like Willow Springs, it's sorta easy to forget about time. Guess 'cause the biggest thing it does is to bring about change and nothing much changes here but the seasons. And if we get a warm spring, a slow fall, and a light winter it don't seem like even the seasons change much at all.   (p. 160)

But if the use of the vernacular voice is significant, then the physical specificity of the island is even more important. Emphatically not part of white mainstream America, Willow Springs maintains its own customs and folklore. Christmas is overshadowed by the traditional ceremony of Candle Walk night (Ophelia had not known what a Christmas tree was before she started college in Atlanta at the age of eighteen); the "standing-forth" (or burial) service for a small child strikes George as a pre-Christian (i.e. African pagan) ritual. The cultural heritage, then, like the land on which it is experienced, also seems more effectively "ours" than "theirs". This double reaction to the legacy of exile and diaspora is, in turn, typical of a tradition in African American fiction that can be traced through such seminal novels as Marshall's *Praisesong for the Widow* or Morrison's *Tar Baby*, discussed below.

The tutelary genius in this Afro-American New World enclave is Miranda (Mama) Day, great-granddaughter of the legendary Sapphira. Midwife, herbalist, or simply "the greatest conjure woman on earth", Mama Day has magic powers that she occasionally invokes for the benefit of the community. More than mere guardian, however, Mama Day is also historian and oral chronicler, additional roles underlined by a series of puns on "the Days I will live to see" – or the symbolic activity of sewing a magnificent double-ring quilt for Ophelia's wedding present; various critics have emphasized the Greek etymology of "text" as something woven (texture and textile are obvious cognates), and a reminiscing Mama Day literally weaves history into the quilt.

Gloria Naylor is merely one of a number of remarkable African American women writers of recent decades. A precursor here is poet Gwendolyn Brooks, whose *Maud Martha* (1953) is a "coming-of-age" narrative of a kind often met among Caribbean women novelists of the following generation. Brooks has lived most of her life in Chicago, and another, younger novelist who initially used big city environments is New Yorker Toni Cade Bambara. Her first collection of short stories, *Gorilla, My Love* (1972), is notable, among other things, for its representation of young black urban speech; her second, *The Sea Birds Are Still Alive* (1977), shows the influence of a Caribbean trip, but to Cuba. Her novel *The Salt Eaters* (1980) has a thematic link with Naylor's *Mama Day*, in its portrait of an elderly black woman with extra-sensory gifts.

The most significant contemporary African American writer, however, is **Toni Morrison**, whose profile was certainly further enhanced when, in 1993, she became the first Black American Nobel laureate.

Morrison's fiction begins from the rivalry and conflict between competing cultural identities (in the crudest terms: "black" *versus* "white"); it continues in her two most substantial novels, *Song of Solomon* (1977) and *Beloved* (1987), with the attempt to fill the gaps and silences of African American history. Current cultural divisions are also reflected quite literally in a clash of tongues. Morrison's first novel, *The Bluest Eye* (1970), thus deals explicitly with the issue of language. The story of a physical obsession which eventually leads a young black girl to madness is structured around a traditional school reader (Dick, Jane, with parents and dog), reflecting the cultural (and linguistic) ideals of white middle-class America. But the heroine's cultural transformation in response to this model is no more likely than the physical one she seeks through the acquisition of blue eyes. Language maintains its particular significance in *Jazz* (1992), Morrison's re-creation of Harlem in the 1920s. For among the many benefits enjoyed by Blacks moving north is a new linguistic freedom experienced among "hundreds of others who moved the way they did, and who, when they spoke, regardless of the accent, treated language like the same intricate, malleable toy designed for their play" (pp. 32–3).

At a rough half-way point between these novels, *Tar Baby* (1981) also places a special emphasis on language by filtering the narrative through several culturally marginalized figures. The discursive norm is initially provided by the sophisticated Valerian Street, a retired candy magnate who has constructed his magnificent mansion on an almost deserted Caribbean island. But the title of the novel, referring to the traditional decoy of Afro-American folklore set to capture the intruder on forbidden territory, hints at two more voices on the island: the rebellious black stowaway, Son (the intruder), and Valerian's not-so-black and highly Europeanized protégée, Jadine (the decoy). In the course of the novel, moreover, other linguistic registers (or cultural norms) jostle for space, and as Valerian's island idyll disintegrates, his patrician Philadelphian speech is also eclipsed – by the black demotic of Sydney and Ondine Childs, his long-serving butler and cook; or by the speech of the two native Dominique islanders, Gideon and Thérèse (the latter's "crumbling English" eventually dissolving into the local French *patois*).

Language in *Tar Baby*, then, may once again be regarded as a metonym for an entire cultural heritage, a heritage that Son and Jadine respectively ridicule or betray, with Morrison even-handedly allowing each to deconstruct the other's position: Jadine thus rejects Son as a "cultural throwback" with his "white-folks–black-folks primitivism"; while Son brands Jadine as a "tar baby side-of-the-road whore trap", but also suggests more astutely that it was not Valerian but the poor Blacks working for him who had put her through college. Almost inevitably, the two become locked in an explosive but finally destructive relationship.

Morrison summarizes the cultural conflict between Son and Jadine when she succinctly contrasts "mama-spoiled black man" with "culture-bearing black woman", hinting at her serious reservations about both groups. Beyond these categories, however, lies another more powerful and positive type, represented in the novel by a succession of "nurturing" rather than "culture-bearing" black women. One reason why Valerian had reacted so mildly on the discovery of a black stowaway in his wife's closet is related to a traumatic childhood experience: left alone and neglected on his father's death, Valerian's only consolation had come from the family's old black washerwoman. And when (as is later discovered) Valerian's wife Margaret had abused her own child, only Ondine the black housekeeper ("I love anything small that needs it") had intervened. This capacity for nurturing assumes symbolic, even mythological, stature in Thérèse the Dominique islander, whose "magical breasts" had been one factor in luring Gideon back from New York to his native island.

With its account of a powerful white man on a Caribbean island, *Tar Baby* is unlikely to escape the current enthusiasm for parallels with Shakepeare's *The Tempest*. But Valerian's world, where the bees have no sting but no honey either, suggests sterility rather than creative potential; and in a boldly suggestive touch, the cyclamen plant in Valerian's hothouse does not bloom until the vitally energetic Son gives it a shake. A contrastingly negative detail in the case of Jadine is the luxurious but ecologically outrageous baby-sealskin jacket with which she returns to Europe at the end of the novel.

In recent years, Morrison seems to have been a catalyst for a number of Black women writers. Gayl Jones's oral narratives of psychotic women, such as *Corregidora* (1975) or *Eva's Man* (1976), were actually published through Morrison's initiative; Marita Golden's chronicle of the deep friendship between three women, *A Woman's Place* (1986), carries echoes of Morrison's second novel, *Sula* (1973); while J. California Cooper's reconstruction of the atrocities of slavery, *Family* (1991), seems inspired by *Beloved*.

Another novelist – remoter from Morrison – who has used Caribbean settings more frequently, is **Paule Marshall**, herself the daughter of immigrants from Barbados. Almost twenty-five years after her first novel, *Brown Girl, Brownstones* (1959), depicting the

life of a young immigrant in New York, Marshall turned her attention more comprehensively in *Praisesong for the Widow* (1983) to the
search for roots and the recuperation of history. In this process, she
combines elements of African, Afro-American, and Afro-Caribbean
culture. The "praisesong" is thus the exemplary poetic form of sub-
Saharan Africa, whilst the entire novel is a homage to an elderly
African-American woman who dramatically rediscovers her *African*
heritage in the course of a *Caribbean* cruise.

The first section of the narrative ("Runagate") suggestively
borrows the obsolete form of "renegade", once used to describe
escaped slaves: for "run" is precisely what Avey Johnson does, as
she impulsively leaves the *Bianca Pride* (or "White Pride") at
Grenada, with the intention of returning to New York by plane.
Her action is a response to growing feelings of physical and mental
distress, culminating in the disturbing dream in which her great-
aunt Cuney tries to drag her back to her Southern childhood home.
The latter is situated at Tatem in the South Carolina Tidewater
country, near the mysterious Ibo Landing, where, according to
legend, a group of African slaves had once escaped by walking
back across the water to Africa. Avery's own initial escape does not
take her beyond a five-star hotel, ominously reminiscent of the
cruise ship she has fled.

The second part of the novel ("Sleeper's Wake") consists of
Avey's recollections of family life with her husband, Jay. These
trace the almost inhuman efforts of the couple to better themselves,
as they move from Harlem to a tenement building on Halsey Street,
and finally, to their own home in the suburb of North White Plains.
But material prosperity brings spiritual impoverishment, reflected
for example in the neglect of the jazz and blues records which had
brought both release and solace to their early married life. Avey's
memories end with both a *requiem* – as she mourns her husband
properly for the first time – and a *litany* – ritualistically repeating
the phrase "too much", in reference to the excessive emotional cost
of material advancement.

In the following section ("Lavé Tête"), Avey leaves the hotel and
finds her way to the elderly Lebert Joseph's rum shop, where she
learns of the annual celebrations on the neighbouring island of
Carriacou. Lebert explains the relation of these ceremonies to
African tradition, expressing his sympathy for "People who can't
[re]call their nation": it is an obvious, if unintentional, pointer to
Avey, who later postpones her return to New York and travels to

Carriacou. On a purely physical level, the crossing from Grenada is traumatic and Avey is violently sick. In symbolic terms, however, it is clearly another kind of passage, as Avey acquires a new sensitivity to common echoes in the African, Afro-American, and Afro-Caribbean experience. Most pointedly, the trip to Carriacou on a crowded boat recalls the annual excursions up the Hudson River with her husband and friends, as well as the New Yam festival she had once witnessed in Ghana. The old Carriacou ladies on board, on the other hand, remind her of the Baptist Church elders in Tatem. She even associates the island *patois* with the Black Gullah language of her Tidewater childhood.

After the horrors of the crossing, the final section ("The Beg Pardon") begins with the symbolic bathing and annointing of the shattered Avey, who then agrees to attend the main nocturnal festivity of the "Big Drum", where she notes further cultural parallels. The ceremony itself then begins with the older African nation dances, as elderly islanders dimly "call their nation", followed by the more lively Creole dances of the younger generation. Avey finally joins the celebrations in the "Carriacou tramp", which proves virtually identical to the "Ring Shout" of her own childhood, thus implying ever closer bonds between the Afro-Caribbeans of Carriacou and the Afro-Americans of Tatem. On the basis of her dance, moreover, Lebert is even able to identify Avey's African nation. From her experiences on Carriacou, Avey acquires a renewed awareness of her cultural heritage, and returns to America with the intention of selling her New York home and returning to her roots in Tatem.

Between *Brown Girl, Brownstones* and *Praisesong for the Widow*, Marshall produced another novel with a Caribbean setting, *The Chosen Place, The Timeless People* (1969), as well as a collection of novellas – "Barbados", "Brooklyn", "British Guiana" and "Brazil" – under the collective title of *Soul Clap Hands and Sing* (1961). *Praisesong for the Widow* nevertheless remains Marshall's most successful attempt, and perhaps the most remarkable in all Black American fiction, to come to terms with a pan-African heritage.

The extraordinary flowering of Black women writers in recent decades has sometimes drawn attention from their male counterparts. These would include such figures as Amiri Baraka (formerly LeRoi Jones) and Ernest Gaines. Poet, dramatist and black political activist, Amiri Baraka published an important autobiographical novel (adapted from one of his plays) entitled *The System of Dante's*

Hell (1965). In contrast to Baraka, who is from Newark, New Jersey, **Ernest J. Gaines** was born and raised in rural Louisiana, before moving to California in his teens. Much of his fiction is regionalist, typically set in a fictional Bayonne County, and exploring the folkways of Louisiana Cajuns and Creoles.

Gaines is a novelist who may paradoxically be said to have found his voice by losing it: after several unpublished novels, he shifted to a first-person vernacular narrator in *Of Love and Dust* (1967). He maintained this perspective in his most celebrated novel, *The Autobiography of Miss Jane Pittman* (1971), the oral account – by a one-hundred-and-ten-year-old woman – of Black history from the end of the Civil War to the civil-rights movement of the 1960s.

Presented by a pseudo-editor, Gaines's novel is divided into four books: "The War Years", "Reconstruction", "The Plantation" and "The Quarters". In a symbolic opening scene at the end of the war, the heroine is given the name of Jane Brown (her slave name had been Ticey) by a passing Yankee corporal. This does little good, since Jane is beaten by her mistress as soon as the Northern soldiers leave, and sent to work in the fields. After the Emancipation Proclamation of 1862, however, all of Jane's ex-slave companions assume new names, the younger ones moving north and the older people staying in the area. Jane leaves with a group bound for Ohio, but they are attacked by "Patrollers" (poor whites and ex-confederacy soldiers) and their natural leader, Big Laura, is killed.

Jane then proceeds, with Laura's infant son Ned, on a picaresque-like journey through the war-ravaged South, before she finds paid work on a plantation. There is now a long ellipsis, after which an adult Ned returns as a qualified schoolteacher. Jane marries the widower Joe Pittman, and leaves for the Louisiana–Texas border, where her husband finds work breaking horses; Jane works as a housemaid. After another chronological break, Joe is killed by a horse and Jane eventually moves away with her second husband. She later returns to the Bayonne area and works for another white family, although much of the final part of the narrative deals with the hopeless love of her employer's son for a Creole schoolteacher, an indication that the underlying racial tensions and prejudices remain strong.

The discussion of language in the context of the *Autobiography* veers automatically towards Gaines's clever re-creation of a fictional oral history in a consistent but fairly attenuated form of vernacular. Figuratively speaking, however, "language" is also a trope for the Black *voice* or the Black *identity* in general, in the face of continuous efforts to stifle it. In the Frederick Douglass–Booker Washington debate, for example, Jane's son Ned is an uncompromising supporter of the former in his demands for immediate integration of black people into American society. It is precisely for these convictions that he is murdered. The question of land, on the other hand, devolves on the two quasi-mythical goals beckoning to African Americans after Emancipation: a fabulous Ohio, to be reached by following the North Star, or the chimerical "Luzana", of whose precise whereabouts Jane is often equally unclear. She abandons her journey to the first, while her life in the second brings her almost unrelieved pain and hardship. As emblems for the alternatives facing Black Americans from the Southern states even today, Ohio and "Luzana" still retain a certain force.

The most significant Black male contemporary novelist may, however, be **Ishmael Reed**. In the Afro-American tradition, Reed's fiction is generally closer to the fantastic mode of Ellison's *Invisible Man* than to the social realism of Wright or Baldwin. A predilection for satire is already apparent in an early story entitled "Something Pure", where Christ returns as an advertising agent, whilst the first two full-length novels, *The Free-Lance Pallbearers* (1967) and *Yellow Back Radio Broke-Down* (1969), parody the confessional mode and the Western, respectively. The complex (and occasionally cryptic) *Mumbo Jumbo* (1972) is a post-modernist and highly self-referential text about writing itself. *Flight to Canada* (1976) returns to Reed's predominantly satirical method, with its parody of the traditional slave narrative.

The phrase "Flight to Canada" refers both to Raven Quickskill's escape from the Swille plantation in Virginia, and also to his poem celebrating this escape. In Reed's parody, moreover, "flight" acquires a new dimension (since it is made in a Jumbo Jet rather than by the light of the Pole Star), whilst the poem itself reveals Quickskill's whereabouts to his pursuers, thus generating most of the narrative's subsequent action. The projection of Reed's twentieth-century fantasy on nineteenth-century history is also the chief source of the novel's surrealist humour, as when the bounty hunters let their bloodhounds sniff Xerox copies of Quickskill's poem, or Ryan's [Slave] Mart in Charleston is treated much like a Seven-to-Eleven store.

A more significant, but equally amusing, element is provided by Reed's extensions or revisions of history. There is thus a long

meeting between Swille and Abraham Lincoln, where the former
(now revealed as a major international financier) offers the Union a
large loan. To the president, on the other hand, the importance of
the slavery issue only comes as an afterthought, although he soon
understands the media potential ("Phone the networks") of his
Emancipation Proclamation

Beyond the comedy of anachronism and historical revisionism,
however, Reed also highlights the ideological struggle between
competing narratives, both historical and modern. The ante-bellum
South is thus identified with the Camelot of Tennyson's *Idylls of the
King*; Swille, whose first name is significantly Arthur, dreams of as-
suming the Confederate Crown, and (in a kind of "devil's temptation" scene) offers Lincoln any title or position he wishes under the
new dispensation. The president remains unimpressed. Besides
broad farce, however, the narrative includes shrewd commentary
on the post-emancipation period, when Quickskill warns that
"what Camelot can't win on the battlefield it'll continue in poetry",
in a form of cultural nostalgia from Poe to *Gone With The Wind*. By
the late twentieth century, moreover, when Native rather than
African Americans are "the exotics of the new feudalism", Camelot
itself will become a mere symbol for the commercialization or
commodification of such regressive longings.

Never a writer to pull his punches, Reed also offers a scathing
indictment of the kind of Christianity that could condone the slave-
based society of the old South. When Swille dies, "Castle" and
plantation are unexpectedly inherited by the trusted slave Robin,
an Uncle Tom-like figure who proves less accommodating than his
literary forebear; for he has altered his master's will. Robin now
also decides that Christianity will have to "stop being so bossy"
and make way for some of the livelier "fun" cults. Besides his ideological thrusts, moreover, Reed is also a fine exponent of generic
parody. He plays hilariously with the props of American Gothic,
and produces subtle verbal distortions of Southern atmosphere
("The whipperwills were *chirping* outside. In the distance a negro
harmonica could be heard *twanging* dreamily", p. 170).

And finally, Reed shows a remarkable sensitivity to shifts in linguistic code and register over more than a century. Swille, at one
point, refuses to speak anything but French; his wife is compelled
by the fierce Mammy-talking Barracuda to resume her Southern
drawl; the fictional Lincoln's idioms and proverbs are a travesty of
frontier speech. Even more significant are the linguistic efforts of

Reed's ethnically marginalized figures. Uncle Robin, who "never did understand good Anglish", finds it takes "even an effort to read the Bible good". When he becomes the new master, Cato the Overseer tries – ironically, without success – to change his "'low" to "allow". Quaw Quaw the "tame Indian", on the other hand, speaks in a travesty of "Anglicized sentences". In the examples of Quaw Quaw and Robin, above all, Reed shows his awareness of the changing relations between mainstream language and other registers.

Reed's thematization of land in *Flight to Canada* should thus be interpreted in some broader sense as the whole demographic history of Afro-Americans, whilst language, in turn, must be taken as referring to the sum of texts with which they have inscribed this experience. Reed plays over both fields with a relentlessly (sometimes even caustically) satirical eye. Like the best and strongest satire, however, Reed's own fiction fails to demolish its targets, but paradoxically reaffirms their very substantiality. As a Black American himself, Reed could surely have wanted nothing more.

This brief review of an older, but related, fictional tradition, hopefully, provides a suitable introduction for a survey of anglophone Caribbean fiction. One valid reason for concluding such a survey with Ishmael Reed, moreover, is to avoid accusations of special pleading, for Reed is one prominent example of an Afro-American author for whom it is difficult to find a Caribbean equivalent.

NOTE

1. The use of this term interchangeably with "Afro-American" may seem inconsistent, but is in fact an attempt at terminological compromise. "African American" (without a hyphen) is now the preferred usage, but "Afro-American" has useful formal analogies with "Afro-Caribbean" (or even "Euro-American") and is therefore occasionally retained.

FURTHER READING

The major theoretical models are those discussed above: Henry Louis Gates's *The Signifying Monkey* (New York: Oxford University Press, 1988) and Houston Baker's *Blues, Ideology, and Afro-American Literature* (Chicago:

Chicago University Press, 1984). A good overview of Black fiction is Bernard W. Bell's *The Afro-American Novel and its Tradition* (Amherst: University of Massachusetts Press, 1987). A more general idea of Black literature (with only editorial headnotes) can be obtained from the second and enlarged edition of Richard Long and Eugenia Collier's *Afro-American Writing. An Anthology of Prose and Poetry* (University Park: Pennsylvania State University Press, 1993).

The Dictionary of Literary Biography series includes *Afro-American Fiction Writers after 1955* (vol. 33, 1984), edited by Thadious M. Davies and Trudier Harris, and *Afro-American Writers, 1940–1955* (vol. 76, 1988), edited by Harris alone. *Black Women Writers, 1950–1980*, edited by Mari Evans (London: Pluto, 1985) has both interviews and critical evaluations. A recent more specialised study is Eva Lennox Birch's *Black American Women's Writing* (London: Harvester Wheatsheaf, 1994).

John O'Brien's *Interviews with Black Writers* (New York: Liveright, 1973), although slightly dated, features 17 African American writers, including Ellison, Gaines, Reed and a very young Alice Walker.

The great linguistic authority in this context is J. L. Dillard, all of whose work, but particularly *Black English: Its History and Usage in the United States* (New York: Random House, 1972), is most helpful.

5

The Caribbean

By way of introduction, the concept of the anglophone Caribbean should be clarified. As demographic accounts of the area are often tendentious and sometimes simply misleading, moreover, mere statistics are not enough, without some indication of how the latter have been compiled.

The most significant, if often forgotten, point is that roughly two-thirds of the Caribbean is actually *Spanish*-speaking. Even French, according to some calculations, is more commonly spoken than English, whereas Spanish speakers outnumber English ones by about four to one. Estimates of this kind are sometimes used (with some justification) to jolt British cultural pretensions, and are typically produced by adding together the populations of all the political units claiming a particular official language. It is a very crude method. In the present case, it first assumes (fairly unexceptionably) a Spanish-speaking group of about 23 million – the combined populations of Cuba, the Dominican Republic and Puerto Rico; it then (more questionably) regards 3.6 million Puerto Ricans as Spanish monoglots, and ends (quite absurdly) by counting 6.5 million Haitians as francophone – few linguists would consider Haitian Creole a simple "variety" of French, and large numbers of a destitute and illiterate peasantry speak nothing else.

At the bottom of this linguistic hierarchy is English, although it is not really necessary to inflate the significance of French in order to reduce that of English. By the above methods, for example, the number of English-speakers in the anglophone Caribbean would reach five and a half or six million. The use of the term "anglophone" nevertheless fails to note that for most of these people, English – although an official language – cannot be regarded as a "mother tongue". In Jamaica, Guyana, and Belize (the two latter countries are often considered Caribbean for cultural and historical reasons) most of the population speak an indigenous creole barely intelligible to an English speaker. The small qualification is only necessary since these varieties are not widely standardized, but exist on a kind of continuum, where linguists distinguish between a *basilect* (the "broadest" creole), a *mesolect* (more attenuated forms), and an *agrolect* (corresponding to standard English): the closer a creole gets to the agrolect, of course, the easier it is for the mainstream anglophone to understand.

On another group of islands, including Barbados, the Bahamas and Trinidad and Tobago, one may legitimately speak of a dialect or variety of English, rather than a creole; opinion differs as to whether the form now spoken has become "decreolized" or whether no true creole ever existed. Most inhabitants of the other so-called "anglophone" islands normally use an English creole, roughly equidistant – in terms of comprehension – between these two groups. Two important exceptions, however, are St Lucia and Dominica, where English is not even a "second" language, but literally a *foreign* one, since most of the population speaks a *French*-based creole. The latter (and not an English creole or some lost African tongue) is incidentally the referent of J. Edward Chamberlin's evocatively titled study of West Indian poetry: *Come Back to Me My Language* (1983). The phrase is taken from the St Lucian poet Derek Walcott. Since much anglophone fiction of the Caribbean is highly representational, moreover, it faithfully reflects these socio-linguistic realities, regardless of their relation to the creole continuum. The results are not always easy for an outside reader.

Whatever the relative strength of English beside Spanish or French, however, the anglophone Caribbean is remarkable in terms of political evolution. Cuba, the Dominican Republic, and Haiti coexist with no less than *twelve* formally independent states where English is the sole *official* language. These include Jamaica (in the Greater Antilles); Antigua and Barbuda, and St Kitts and Nevis (in the Leeward Islands); Dominica, St Lucia, St Vincent, and Grenada (in the Windward Islands); Barbados, and Trinidad and Tobago. To these may be added Guyana, Belize, and – more remotely – the Bahamas. There are literary traditions of varying strength in all of these countries. Demographically speaking, however, most of the twelve are extremely small, with Jamaica and Trinidad accounting for 60 per cent (or, together with Guyana, 75 per cent) of their combined population. Barbados and the Bahamas have slightly more (Belize rather less) than a quarter of a million inhabitants each, whilst, of the remaining nations, only St Lucia has even half this number. In spite of these dimensions, however, cultural and physical differences are enormous.

Besides the purely linguistic aspect already discussed, Trinidad and Guyana are exceptional for large populations of Asian origin (roughly 50 per cent in each case), chiefly a legacy of Indian indentured labour introduced by the British in the nineteenth and early twentieth centuries; Belize (like Guyana) has a sizeable Amerindian minority. Physically, the twelve countries range from highly developed Barbados, often known (if hardly flatteringly) as "Little England", to the barely charted Guyana, whose immense rain forests situated just beyond a narrow coastal strip affect the national psyche as profoundly as do the Canadian wilderness or the Australian bush in other contexts.

It may also come as a surprise that writers and scholars in the region, indifferent to the errors of an obsolete European geography, still habitually speak of the "West Indies" rather than of the anglophone Caribbean. Politically, the former name never denoted more than an ill-fated and short-lived federation (1959–62), severed by the withdrawal of Jamaica, which feared that the smaller islands would become an economic burden (ironically, the GNP *per capita* of Jamaica today is a third of Trinidad's and barely a fifth that of Barbados or Antigua). In concrete terms, the concept of the West Indies now hardly exists beyond a university and (together with Guyana) a cricket team. The term nevertheless remains a viable critical and cultural label; the university itself, with campuses in Jamaica, Barbados, and Trinidad, and extensions on most of the other islands, has proved a magnet to literary talent which might otherwise have been lost to London, New York or Toronto.

The trope of the stepmother tongue is applicable to the region. No African languages are spoken anywhere in the West Indies, but Caribbean creoles are considered to be lexically English (or French in the case of St Lucia and Dominica) and syntactically (although the precise degree is disputed) often African. The fictional writing of these various traditions is in English, although the discourse of dialect, vernacular, Creole, *patois* ("patwa") or "nation language" is never far away. Whether writers regard their linguistic loss as referring to an ancestral African language, or to a local vernacular, the notion of standard English as "their" language is in almost every case justified. The poet Edward Kamau Brathwaite noted provocatively:

It was in language that the slave was perhaps most successfully imprisoned by his master, and it was in his (mis-)use of it that he perhaps most effectively rebelled.[1]

The twin concepts of "new literatures" (a reasonably objective evaluation by most criteria) in "new worlds" (an ironic gesture to the ethnocentricity of the region's European "discoverers") also seem fairly unexceptionable.

PRECURSORS

Most of the important precursors of modern Caribbean fiction in English were linked with the literary magazines that have flourished intermittently in the region since the 1920s: examples are: in Jamaica, *Planters' Punch* (edited by H. G. de Lisser, 1920–45), followed by *Focus*; in Trinidad, the review *Trinidad* (Alfred Mendes and C. L. R. James, 1929–30), followed by *The Beacon* (Albert Gomes, 1931–3, 1939); in Barbados, *Bim* (Frank Collymore, from 1942); and in Guyana, *Kyk-over-al* (edited by poet A. J. Seymour, 1945–61).

Although (with the possible exception of Erna Brodber) Jamaica has no contemporary novelist with the stature of V. S. Naipaul or Wilson Harris, it produced some of the earliest native West Indian fiction through such writers as Redcam, de Lisser and McKay. Tom Redcam (pseudonym of *Jamaica Times* editor Thomas Henry MacDermot) wrote two rather wooden novels, *Becka's Buckra Baby* (1903) and *One Brown Girl and* – (1909). Less dated and more prolific was H. G. de Lisser, who published *Jane: A Story of Jamaica* (also known as *Jane's Career*) in 1933. His tale of a young black girl who leaves the countryside in a quest for self-improvement still reads well, although the author's most popular work today is the historical romance *The White Witch of Rosehall* (1929). Claude McKay, sometimes regarded as Jamaica's unofficial national poet, was discussed in the context of Afro-American fiction.

A group of Trinidad novelists included the three more radical figures of Mendes, James and de Boissiere. Alfred Mendes produced *Pitch Lake* (1934), a harsh attack on the Trinidad middle classes – particularly the Portuguese community to which he belonged; C. L. R. James, better known as a historian and autobiographer, wrote *Minty Alley* (1936) in the tradition of the working-class "yard" novel; Ralph de Boissiere's *Rum and Coca Cola* (1956) depicts Trinidad's social unrest in the 1930s and the American occupation of the island in the Second World War.

Guyana's first important novelist is Edgar Mittelholzer, who produced over twenty novels between *Corentyne Thunder* (1941) and

The Pilkington Drama (1965), as he moved from what was predominantly social realism to a highly personal brand of comic-erotic
fantasy. At the mid-point of his writing career, he also produced a
substantial saga of Guyanese family life over three and a half centuries, known collectively as the *Kaywana* novels. Of particular interest in the present context, is Mittelholzer's second novel, *A
Morning at the Office* (1950), often praised for its detailed study of
race, class, and economics in an urban Trinidad environment. It
offers comic (or almost tragi-comic) vignettes of forced cultural assimilation, as in the portrait of the chief clerk's typist:

> Together with her negro, East Indian, Portuguese, Spanish, and
> coloured school companions, she had grown up with the *Royal
> Reader*, *Gentle Jesus Meek and Mild*, Sir Walter Scott, and *Drink to
> me only with thy eyes*.   (p. 208)

The typist happens to be a "creole Chinese", but her case is not exceptional: Mr Jagabir, the East Indian assistant accountant, had
once been made to recite Tennyson's *Charge of the Light Brigade* and
Young Lochinvar!

But the 1950s also marked the emergence of a more influential
novelist than any of those mentioned so far: **George Lamming**, a
writer whose fiction covers virtually the entire range of colonial
and post-colonial themes. Lamming's working-class upbringing on
a former Barbados sugar estate, his experiences as a scholarship
boy, and subsequent departure for Trinidad at the age of eighteen,
provide the material for *In the Castle of My Skin* (1953), the classic
Caribbean *Bildungsroman*. *The Emigrants* (1954) examines the
phenomenon of West Indian immigration at first hand: Lamming
incidentally left for England in 1950 on the same ship as the
Trinidadian novelist Samuel Selvon. Extensive travel in the
Caribbean, particularly in Guyana, provided material for the politically charged *Of Age and Innocence* (1958), where the imaginary
island of "San Cristobal" is a synthesis of all aspiring Caribbean
nations. *Season of Adventure* (1960) returns to San Cristobal to
examine the competing cultural claims of Europe and Africa in the
newly independent Caribbean state.

Lamming wrote no new fiction in the next decade, although the
essay collection *The Pleasures of Exile* (1960) contains his seminal discussion of Shakespeare's *The Tempest*. His reworking of the Caliban
myth also provides the frame for his return to fiction in *Water with*

Berries (1971). His last novel, *Natives of My Person* (1972), is a historical reconstruction of one of the voyages of exploration and conquest which preceded the whole Caribbean tragedy.

Although exactly contemporary with James Baldwin's *Go Tell It
on the Mountain* (1953), Lamming's *In the Castle of My Skin* might be
more fruitfully compared with Achebe's *Things Fall Apart* (1958).
Neither novel is quite literally a first in its region, but each is the
true fountain-head of a rich and flourishing tradition. Admittedly,
Achebe's irony and understatement are not obviously present in
what one critic calls Lamming's "encyclopedic impulse" (his novel
is nearly twice the length of Achebe's); both writers nevertheless
probe beyond the life of their protagonist to provide the spiritual
biography of a whole community; both also record the break-up of
traditional village life (whether through initial colonial contact or
more recent socio-economic change); both pay careful attention to
popular oral tradition; both show skill in speech presentation
(whether Caribbean *patois* or indigenous African languages). All of
these elements are common to subsequent Caribbean and African
fiction, and the pioneer status of Lamming's novel is only the final
and most obvious analogy with Achebe.

Lamming's densely referential account of the young G's childhood and adolescence on a Barabados estate defies brief summary.
Three of the fourteen chapters nevertheless account for exactly half
of the novel, and therefore carry particular weight within its overall
structure. Each of them also introduces a virtually distinct narrative tradition in the West Indian novel.

The third chapter thus features a classic *topos* of early Caribbean
writing: Empire Day celebrations. Lamming's version of events
anticipates the fictional account in V. S. Naipaul's *A House for
Mr Biswas* (1961) or the more explicitly autobiographical version in
Austin Clarke's *Growing Up Stupid Under the Union Jack* (1980). The
conventional presentation of Barbados as an idyllic Little England
is then undermined and later demolished in the course of the
chapter. The official celebrations nevertheless stimulate an act of
collective memory, by means of which G and his friends (drawing
on the community's oral tradition) are able to generate a more
authentic account of the past. Recent fuller attempts at such historical recuperation include the novels of Caryl Phillips and Fred
D'Aguiar.

In the long sixth chapter set on the beach, G and his friends Bob,
Boy Blue and Trumper also use reminiscence, anecdote, and speculation to reconstruct a personal narrative of Barbadian life. Here,

Lamming's technique alternates between conventional narrative and straight dramatic format, while his perspective recalls both Mark Twain's *ingénus* and Thomas Hardy's chorus. The resulting narrative is secret ("We wouldn't dare tell anybody what we had talked about"), but the child's vision for Lamming is both privileged and justified. The rich legacy of this kind of writing extends through Michael Anthony to Olive Senior, to mention only the most obvious examples.

In the final chapter of the novel, the eighteen-year-old G prepares to leave his mother and his native island for a teaching appointment in Trinidad, according to the now familiar pattern of the hero's departure for broader horizons. (There is a passing dig here at traditional expectations and institutionalized prejudices when G's mother regrets her son is not *light* enough to get a job in Barclay's Bank.) More interesting, however, is the neat counterpoint provided by the return of G's friend Trumper from New York, with a new sense of racial pride. The competing claims of education and ideology, with the emotional conflict before such choices as emigration or repatriation, will absorb many future Caribbean novels in the autobiographical mode.

The classic status and continued appeal of Lamming's novel may rest on two distinct elements. On the one hand, a realism of representation co-exists harmoniously with experimental techniques: the social and political realities of Barbados are actually conveyed in a striking blend of monologue, dialogue, pseudo-orature, and other more conventional forms. Such virtuosity has not lost its power. Secondly, Lamming has a natural propensity for merging realistic observation with powerful figurative language. The nine-year-old G's disillusion at a ruined birthday party is thus synthesized with the great flood of the opening chapter, so that the disconsolate G waits "for the weather to rehearse [his] wishes". Or, in an even stronger instance, a more mature protagonist comments:

> Once there was a wood where we walked, thick and cool in the afternoon. The trees blinded you to everything beyond the landlord's house. Now there wasn't a tree left. The space was open, bare, and black.   (pp. 282–3)

Originating in a quite naturalistic account of deforestation on Barbados by an exploitative colonial economy, the description can also stand as a *requiem* for the lost security of an island childhood.

For these reasons not least, then, Lamming's *In the Castle of My Skin* remains a landmark in the history of the West Indian novel.

HOME AND AWAY

One could make a very crude division in Caribbean fiction between "home" and "away": a large number of novels are set in the region, and portray an indigenous culture or reflect the socio-political realities of the day; another smaller, but still substantial, group are placed outside the Caribbean, the immigrant novel being only the most obvious example of this tendency. It is not, however, a question of where an author lives. Austin Clarke, based in Toronto, deals primarily with Barbadian immigrants in Canada; Roy Heath, in London, writes almost obsessively of his native Guyana. It is not, in fact, a classification of *novelists* at all, but one of *novels*. An older writer's *oeuvre* will often follow a classic itinerary, from colonial childhood to immigration and beyond: Lamming is once again the prototype. There are understandably few Caribbean writers whose books are *all* set outside their home region, but many shift regularly between "home" and "abroad" (Selvon was the obvious example), and there are now, happily, an increasing number of authors who write essentially from and about the Caribbean – "happily", because the implication is that many writers can now create an economically viable existence without the need to emigrate.

"Home" or "away" becomes conspicuously home *and* away in one of the region's most distinguished novelists: V. S. Naipaul, an author who transcends simple national identities just as his writing defies rigid academic classification. Unity among such diversity appears only in a recurrent concern with human displacement and a growing sense of aloofness and disenchantment. The grandson of high-caste Indians who emigrated to Trinidad under the indenture system, Naipaul won a scholarship to Oxford in 1950 and, despite a lifetime of travel, Britain has remained the writer's base ever since. Naipaul's early fiction, set in Trinidad, includes *The Mystic Masseur* (1957), a comic account of the rise of a self-proclaimed Hindu *guru*, and *The Suffrage of Elvira* (1958), a similarly satirical treatment of political opportunism, based on the Trinidad elections of 1950. The seventeen humorous stories of *Miguel Street* (published in 1959, although written before the two novels) are united by the common physical setting of the title. The early Trinidad cycle ends with

Naipaul's first undisputed masterpiece, *A House for Mr Biswas* (1961). Based on the struggle of the author's journalist father for an individual identity outside the Indian extended family, the novel links this hard-won independence with the symbolic acquisition of a house.

A House for Mr Biswas was followed by *Mr Stone and the Knights Companion* (1964), an attempt at an entirely English setting. This novella-length study of spiritual and artistic renewal not only ends the author's early involvement with Trinidadian material, but also cancels a more obvious debt to the comic realism of Dickens and H. G. Wells. Naipaul's next novel, *The Mimic Men* (1967), both in its emphasis on the theme of displacement and in its fragmented chronological mode, suggests a new sensitivity towards the fiction of Joseph Conrad.

Over the following three decades, Naipaul's fiction became more sporadic, whilst the structure of individual volumes also showed increasing discontinuity. *A Flag on the Island* (1967) thus consists of the title novella, in which an American narrator revisits the island where he had been stationed during the Second World War, and three short stories from an earlier period. *In a Free State* (1971) also combines a novella, in which two Englishmen travel though an unnamed East African country, with several shorter pieces, although the various elements of the book now have a certain unity in their common concern with cultural displacement in the post-colonial world.

If Naipaul's next novel, *Guerrillas* (1975), the portrait of a self-proclaimed black "radical" in Trinidad, is Conradian in its political scepticism, then its successor, *A Bend in the River* (1979), in which a young Indian trader leaves his people on the East African coast to run a store in the interior, offers a kind of post-colonial *Heart of Darkness*. The increasingly lengthy gaps between Naipaul's novels are filled with substantial travelogues. Prominent in this field are three books on India and as many on Trinidad and the Caribbean, as well as reports on the Congo, the world of Islam, and the American Deep South. Fiction and journalism tended to elide in Naipaul's first new novel (if it is that) for eight years, the outwardly autobiographical but densely allegorical *The Enigma of Arrival* (1987), set on a slowly decaying Victorian or Edwardian estate that evokes the imperial swansong. In the characteristically fragmented *A Way in the World* (1994), subtitled "A Sequence", the fictional impulse is again reinforced by explicitly autobiographical and historical elements.

Regarded by many critics and some fellow writers as politically offensive, Naipaul nevertheless has few rivals in Caribbean fiction, whether "home" or "away". The same cultural split which this writer so admirably illustrates occurs on a lesser scale with such writers as Salkey, Carew or Dathorne.

Andrew Salkey left his native Jamaica in 1952 to study in Britain, and is thus linked to the important Caribbean expatriate group which included Lamming, Selvon, V. S. Naipaul, and Hearne. Although his first novel, *A Quality of Violence* (1959), deals with Christian and African rituals in a rural Jamaica, its better-known successor, *Escape to an Autumn Pavement* (1960), is a classic expatriate novel about a young middle-class Jamaican in London. After a number of books for children and writings about his native island, Salkey produced *The Late Emancipation of Jerry Stover* (1968), a study of social frustration among Kingston middle-class intellectuals, and *The Adventures of Catullus Kelly* (1969), the erotically charged account of a young Afro-Caribbean man adrift in London. "Home" and "away" would thus seem finely balanced. *Come Home, Malcolm Heartland* (1976), which marked Salkey's physical return to Jamaica and confirmed his commitment to the adult novel, expresses increasing disillusion with Caribbean society.

The fiction of Jan Carew seems less successful, the further it moves from the writer's native Guyana. *Black Midas* (1958) and *The Wild Coast* (1959) have a sometimes superficial primitivism; *The Last Barbarian* (1961), set in Harlem, and *Moscow is Not My Mecca* (1964), a Soviet dystopia, both reflect political disillusion. Carew's most controversial work may yet be his part in Sylvia Wynter's *The Hills of Hebron* (1962), a story of Jamaican revivalism; according to an interview with Daryl Cumber Dance in *New World Adams*, this contribution amounted to half, or even more.

More satirical in approach than either Salkey or Carew is O. R. Dathorne, now better known as a scholar of African literature, but also a versatile novelist. His *Dumplings in the Soup* (1963), another account of black student life in London, was followed by *The Scholar Man* (1964), a post-independence satire of Northern Nigeria where the author taught for some years, and *Dele's Child* (1987), set in the author's native Guyana.

After Naipaul, however, the most significant novelist among those whose fiction shifts between "home" and "away" is probably Samuel Selvon. Son of an Indian father and a part-Indian/part-Scottish mother, Selvon described himself as a "creolized West Indian". After working briefly as a wartime wireless operator in the

Royal Navy Reserve and for five years as a journalist on the *Trinidad Guardian*, he sailed for England in 1950. In 1978 he moved on to Canada.

Although Selvon is best-known for his classic account of West Indian ex-patriates in *The Lonely Londoners* (1956), the narrow majority of his novels are actually set in his native Trinidad. The earliest book, *A Brighter Son* (1952), is an example of the Caribbean *Bildungsroman*, although Selvon follows his young protagonist further than Lamming, through an arranged marriage and departure from his native village. *A Brighter Son* had a fictional sequel, *Turn Again Tiger* (1958), whilst two other more distantly related novels of Trinidad peasant life are *The Plains of Caroni* (1970) and *Those Who Eat the Cascadura* (1972). All four books are generally more highly regarded than two other early Trinidad novels, *An Island Is a World* (1955) and *I Hear Thunder* (1963). *The Housing Lark* (1965) is a superficial sequel to *The Lonely Londoners*, although the latter's true sequels are *Moses Ascending* (1975) and *Moses Migrating* (1983). In the first of these, the situation of Moses in London has acquired a certain stability without any great material improvement, whilst in the second, Moses actually returns to his native Trinidad, permitting ironic reversals of the conventional migration pattern. It is on the so-called London trilogy that Selvon's future reputation may eventually rest.

The Lonely Londoners is the classic West Indian novel of immigration. It is also important as a rare early example of a novel written entirely in a vernacular mode, as may be seen from the first paragraph:

> One grim winter evening, when it had a kind of unrealness about London, with a fog sleeping restlessly over the city and the lights showing in the blur as if it is not London at all but some strange place on another planet, Moses Aloetta hop on a number 46 bus at the corner of Chepstow Road and Westbourne Grove to go to Waterloo to meet a fellar who was coming from Trinidad on the boat-train.   (p. 23)

Selvon's account of West Indian expatriates in London in the early fifties is celebrated for the way in which it draws on oral literature, the narrator sometimes being seen as a kind of calypsonian figure. In the opening passage, Moses-the-prophet or Aloetta-the-lark (a sequel to the novel was to be suggestively named *Moses Ascending*), goes to lead one more of his tribe to the promised land. The latter, of course, is no "land of milk and honey", but only an inhospitable, wintry London. And here, surely, Selvon's narrator remembers the opening chapter of *Hard Times*, which he can later gloss with his own image of "your hand plying space like a blind man's stick in the yellow fog" (p. 138).

At Waterloo station, Moses meets Henry Oliver, or "Sir Galahad", who is impervious to the English cold, and, in keeping with his name, prepared to romanticize London and its familiar landmarks. Moses becomes Sir Galahad's guide to this winter purgatory, helping him negotiate the public transport system on the way to the employment exchange. The novel thus becomes a wryly humorous relation of the perennial search for work, food, accommodation, and – once such basic needs are satisfied – encounters with the ever-present white women. The pattern of this account, as shared between Moses and Selvon's anonymous narrator, seems randomly episodic, even anecdotal, as it follows the escapades of London's West Indians and their African allies in the working man's hostel and beyond. It nevertheless returns insistently to the related issues of race and language.

At the employment exchange, Moses explains unconcernedly how colour prejudice is institutionalized ("you will see mark on top in red ink. J—A , Col. That mean you from Jamaica and you black."). At Picadilly tube station, Galahad bends down to pat the head of a white child, who promptly bursts into tears. At his girlfriend's house, light-skinned Bart tries to pass as a Latin American, but his prospective father-in-law throws him out rather than risk "curly-hair" children in the family. On one occasion, Galahad vents his frustration with a tragi-comic apostrophe to his own hand: "Colour, is you that causing all this, you know. Why the hell you can't be blue, or red or green, if you can't be white?" (p. 88).

The other factor is language. When Daisy admits to Galahad her difficulty in understanding West Indian speech, he exclaims indignantly: "What wrong with it.... Is English we speaking". The Nigerian student known as Cap has "the sort of voice that would melt butter, and he does speak like a gentleman", although his West Indian friends soon succeed in correcting this. Galahad, too, can "put on the old English accent" although it is not enough to re-assure the weeping child at the tube station. Most spectacular of all is Harris, with his impersonation of a city gent, down to bowler, umbrella, and *The Times* protruding from his pocket. His language is also exemplary ("when Harris start to spout English for you, you realise that you don't really know the language"); but as the narrator ironically reminds us in his own vernacular: "Only thing, Harris face black" (p. 111).

The Lonely Londoners is appealing in its humorously philosophical account of an inhospitable post-war England; arresting in its bold representation of Caribbean vernacular; disquieting in its portrayal of cultural alienation among unskilled black migrants; and, alas, disturbing for West Indian attitudes towards women which are often as crudely exploitative as those of whites towards blacks. The abiding impression of the narrative, however, is of a humour and wisdom which do not preclude pathos, as when Moses notes the passing of time:

> Sometimes I look back on all the years I spend in Brit'n ... and I surprise that so many years gone by. Looking at things in general life really hard for the boys in London. This is a lonely, miserable city, if it was that we didn't get together now and then to talk about things back home, we would suffer like hell.   (p. 130)

The novelist most closely associated with the North American, as opposed to the British, immigrant experience is Austin Clarke. The best known Barbadian author after Lamming, Clarke is also – on the basis of some forty years in Toronto – widely regarded as Canada's most prominent Black writer.

Born the son of an artist and a hotel maid, Clarke emulated Lamming's progress as a scholarship boy, before leaving Barbados definitively for Canada and the University of Toronto at the age of twenty-one. His first two novels, *The Survivors of the Crossing* (1964) and *Among Thistles and Thorns* (1965), are angry accounts of exploited workers on Barbados sugar plantations. Clarke then, however, turned his attention to the lives of Barbados immigrants in Canada, producing his so-called Toronto trilogy: *The Meeting Point* (1967), *Storm of Fortune* (1973), and *The Bigger Light* (1975). In addition to two rancorous novels about post-independence Barbados politics, Clarke has also published the volume of memoirs suggestively titled *Growing Up Stupid under the Union Jack* (1980), voicing a sentiment which runs like a *leitmotiv* throughout this section. The latter is in many respects a more explicitly autobiographical equivalent of Lamming's *In the Castle of My Skin*.

In both quantitative and qualitative terms, however, Clarke is an "away" novelist. Other notable writers in the latter category would include David Dabydeen and Jamaica Kincaid, based in Britain and the United States, respectively.

David Dabydeen left Guyana for London in his early teens. His first novel, *The Intended* (1991), plots the experiences of four Asian schoolboys (including the Indo-Guyanese protagonist) growing up in England; it invites comparison with Hanif Kureishi's *The Buddha of Suburbia*. Its successor, *Disappearance* (1993), is a richly allegorical account of a Guyanese engineer working on a project to prevent a Sussex cliff-top village from subsiding into the sea. Jamaica Kincaid (born Elaine Potter Richardson) emigrated from her native Antigua to the United States in 1966, and has remained there ever since. She could well be considered an African American writer. After *Annie John* (1985), with its bitter conflict between a Caribbean mother and daughter, Kincaid's meticulous and sometimes minimalist fiction has tended to deal with the American immigrant experience, as in *Lucy* (1990).

In quantitative terms at least, however, "homes" seem increasingly to prevail over "aways" in West Indian fiction of the last fifty years. Significant examples of the former category are Roger Mais, Orlando Patterson, and Sylvia Wynter (Jamaica), Roy Heath (Guyana), Garth St Omer (St Lucia) and, most prominently of all, Earl Lovelace (Trinidad).

Born into a family of middle-class, Kingston land-owners, Roger Mais was particularly sensitive to anomalies of cultural background in pre-independence Jamaica; Kamau Brathwaite sees Mais as committed to the search for a "nativist aesthetic". The first novel, *The Hills Were Joyful Together* (1953), is a classic "yard" narrative, set among the "harsh realities of shack, cesspool, and poverty" in the Kingston of the time; Mais's tough social realism recalls the even grimmer circumstances of Patterson's *The Children of Sisyphus* (1965). *Brother Man* (1954) is a study of the Rastafarian cult, in the person of John Power the shoemaker, while *Black Lightning* (1955) is less typical of Mais, in terms of its rural setting.

Guyanan novelist Roy Heath has lived in London since 1951, but his eight novels show an overwhelming concern with the yards and poorer housing complexes of his native Georgetown. Most acclaimed among this *oeuvre* (although even here, critical attention has been grudging) is the Armstrong family saga, *From the Heat of the Day* (1979), *One Generation* (1981), and *Genetha* (1981), also called "the Guyana trilogy". Heath's studies of family discord may also be read allegorically with reference to the conflicts of post-independence Guyana. A more recent novel is *The Shadow Bride*

(1988), an impressive study of acculturation from the perspective of an Indian woman sent to Guyana.

The fiction of St Lucian expatriate Garth St Omer, has a scrupulous realism that has been compared to Joyce's *Dubliners*. Thematically, too, the mental paralysis of St Omer's native Castries is analogous to that of Dublin, with the Catholic Church bearing partial responsibility in both processes. The novels incidentally present minor problems of ordering and continuity: *The Lights on the Hill* (1968), an existentialist novella set at University College, Mona (Kingston), and *Another Place Another Time* were eventually published as *Shades of Grey* (1968). St Omer's other novels are *A Room on the Hill* (1968), *Nor Any Country* (1969), and *J– Black Bam and the Masqueraders* (1972). *A Room on the Hill* is a specifically St Lucian story of unconsummated love (it actually contains a fishing-boat with the name "In God We Trust", later immortalized in Derek Walcott's *Omeros*); *Nor Any Country* is a "been-to" novel of two brothers, one of whom is recently returned from England. Further details are almost superfluous, however, since all of the novels share the same obsessive sense of *Angst* and alienation.

St Omer's best potential escape from such characteristic solipsism might have lain through his acute awareness of socio-linguistic realities on his native island. In *J–, Black Bam and the Masqueraders*, for instance, the protagonist Peter makes an astonishing reflection on the speech of his wife Phyllis, a barely literate islander:

> Her language was the language of a child, or of a slave to whom language had not been taught. When she spoke patois, she used English words; and the English she used was little more than transliterations of words and phrases from patois. More than a century after Emancipation her language was still a makeshift one used not so much to express as to indicate.   (p. 63)

Here, and in the fine but little-known vernacular novella "Syrop", St Omer enters quite literally into the complexities of land and language.

The major "home" novelist of the anglophone Caribbean, however, is probably **Earl Lovelace**. Born in Toco, Trinidad, Lovelace grew up in Tobago, studied (and taught) briefly in the United States, and then returned to his native island. His first novel, *While Gods Are Falling* (1966), reflects the decline of traditional community values in an urbanized Port of Spain. This was followed by *The Schoolmaster* (1968), where the rural idyll of

Kumaca is threatened by the imminent arrival of a new road. The historically and thematically interesting *The Wine of Astonishment* (1982) chronicles the persecution of a group of Trinidad Spiritual Baptists in the early years of the twentieth century. Noteworthy here is the virtuoso re-creation of vernacular speech in the voice of an elderly peasant woman, a technique recalling Raja Rao's saga of Indian village life, *Kanthapura* (1938).

Lovelace's major novel, however, is *The Dragon Can't Dance* (1979). His study of Port of Spain's underclass in the late 1960s borrows forms and themes central to Trinidadian culture. It thus belongs to the fictional sub-genre known as the "yard novel", being the chronicle of a small, close-knit community living around a yard (here, in the slum of Calvary Hill); it is also the classic novel of Carnival, the island's spectacular pre-Lenten processions with music, dancing, and masquerade; finally, it draws on the unique musical forms of Carnival: "pan", or the indigenous steel-drum bands, and "calypso", the island's witty, abrasive, and often politically subversive tradition of popular song. Lovelace's "Prologue", subtitled "The Hill", "Carnival", and "Calypso", sharply establishes each of these elements. His achievement is to recreate within this frame a full panorama of the social tensions and political unrest that characterized Trinidad in the 1960s.

The first five sections of the novel have an almost Faulknerian density as the major characters are successively introduced: Cleothilda ("Queen of the Band"), self-appointed mascot of the local steelband, together with Philo, her eternally rejected suitor; Sylvia ("Princess"), the beautiful seventeen-year-old with few prospects beyond a career in prostitution; Aldrick ("The Dragon"), the man without ties, totally absorbed in sewing his Carnival costume; Fisheye ("The Bad John"), the aggressive rebel seeking an identity in the "warriorhood of the steelband"; and Pariag ("The Spectator"), the lonely young Indian fleeing family dependence and the grind of rural life.

The subsequent narrrative faithfully records the personal and collective transformations produced by several years of life on Calvary Hill. In the broadest socio-economic terms, there is a gradual shift from a negative philosophy of pure survival to a more positive one of self-improvement and advancement. Pariag first buys a bicycle to carry his *channa* and peanuts, before eventually acquiring a small corner-shop; Philo abandons his socially critical calypsos for more commercial themes, and becomes an international star. In the context of Carnival itself, finally, Aldrick sets aside his dragon costume – long the yard's most spectacular if also its most harmlessly ritualized gesture of rebellion – and becomes unwilling to dance. Only Fisheye opposes the new tendencies. In a final unplanned and ultimately futile political gesture, he joins other marginalized elements (including Aldrick), who then drive round Port of Spain in a hijacked police car, proclaiming themselves the People's Liberation Army. After prison sentences have been served for this escapade, Aldrick attains greater maturity and a new political awareness. He becomes the novel's most positive focus for other reasons, too, with the final hint that Sylvia will avoid a soulless marriage with Guy, the cynical rent collector, to seek greater self-fulfilment with him.

Lovelace always retains a sharp eye for subtle local distinctions of colour and class. Cleothilda the "mulatto woman" assumes social superiority on the basis of her colour; Philo ("black as he is") is not good enough for her; Sylvia pursues European aesthetic norms by having her hair straightened *every* week; Fisheye objects to the new respectability of pan, with the arrival of "white" bands. Regardless of such chromatic niceties, however, the old colonial masters are still in charge, through their domination of banks and major businesses. With such social divisions as these, there is little substance in the island's facile (and vernacular) political slogan of "All o' we is one".

The novel's socio-economic pyramid also translates neatly into linguistic terms; as Fisheye points out, "the radio still spoke with a British voice" (p. 80). The dramatic confrontation of the novel's trial scene pits the black, London-trained, smooth-talking, radical defence lawyer with the equally black, but rigidly establishment, local judge. The inarticulate Fisheye is impressed, and concedes that both men are way above him: for judge and counsel speak a master-language, a simple synonym for what in other contexts has been called the stepmother-tongue. The trial is ironically paralleled to a cricket match at the local Queen's Park Oval; in court, however, as opposed to what normally happens on the cricket field, England defeats the West Indies; Fisheye and his associates receive lengthy prison terms.

It is instructive, finally, to compare *The Dragon Can't Dance* with V. S. Naipaul's *Guerrillas* (1977), also set in Trinidad during the same period of unrest and violence. The contrast between Naipaul's fastidiously detached account of his psychopathic political activist, Jimmy Ahmed, and Lovelace's more sympathetic portrait of the pathetically inadequate Fisheye speaks volumes for the temperamental differences between the two writers. Such a comparison may also provide a final reflection on "home" and "away" in terms of positive or negative emotional involvement with the Caribbean.

POLITICS AND HISTORY

The reference to Naipaul's *Guerrillas* is a suitable point at which to turn to the significant amount of Caribbean political fiction. However carefully the settings are disguised, these novels characteristically depict recognizable modern dystopias in the *post* or simply *neo*-colonial era. They also tend to be limited to one (or at most two) isolated novels in a writer's *oeuvre*. The prototype again is George Lamming, whose extensive experience of pre-independence Guyana, fictionalized as San Cristobal, inspired *Of Age and Innocence* (1958) and *Season of Adventure* (1960). Later examples include *The Prime Minister*, Austin Clarke's harsh, even vindictive, account of political corruption on Barbados; *This Island Now* (1966, revised and slightly enlarged 1985), by the South African Peter Abrahams, who moved to Jamaica in the 1950s; and *A Hot Country* (1983; reissued in 1984 as *Love and Death in a Hot Country*) by **Shiva Naipaul**.

The younger of the Naipaul brothers, Shiva wrote several fine novels before his untimely death in 1990: *Fireflies* (1970) and *The Chip-Chip Gatherers* (1973) deal with the theme of East Indian exile and identity crisis in the Caribbean; *A Hot Country* uses the familiar device of a fictional country to reconsider many of the same issues. But the latter novel is also a fairly representative example of the post-colonial political dystopia. The novel is set in Charleston, Cuyama (thinly disguised versions of Georgetown, Guyana), against a background of political turmoil. There is to be a plebiscite on the suspension of the Constitution, which will effectively give the president a life-mandate (these events, too, have their historical equivalent in the politicking of Forbes Burnham and his People's National Congress in the late 1970s). Also as in Guyana, Cuyaman political parties are formed on ethnic lines, and the campaign rings with such crude racial slogans as "Black Men Have Nothing To Lose But Their Chains".

Naipaul's two chief characters are Aubrey St Pierre, scion of an old Creole family that had fled Haiti in the eighteenth century, now owner of an unprofitable bookshop; and his wife Dina, *née*

Mallingham, a name which reflects her father's attempts to conceal the family's Indian origins. The sense of sterility and savagery is consistently emphasized, from the narrator's initial reference to "the wilderness that lay behind their backs" to Aubrey's damning judgement that "Nothing worthwhile had ever been created on this sterile pitch of earth perched on the edge of a cruel continent."

A Hot Country inevitably invites comparison with *A Bend in the River*, published only four years earlier and set in a fictional Zaïre. The analogies are both ideological and technical. Here, for example, is an apparently clinical eye for detail, reminiscent of the older Naipaul but perhaps ultimately originating in Graham Greene; here, too, is that literary sleight of hand according to which these metonymies are projected as detached and objective – whereas they are, of course, primarily elements of the novelist's imagination. A fairly blatant example of the Naipaul method (V.S. or Shiva, as it happens) is the description of St Pierre's Afro-Guyanese protégée, the resentful Selma:

> She was dressed in her Sunday best: mauve, pleated skirt reaching to her knees (he recognized it as one of Diana's – it had disappeared some weeks before), blunt shoes of mock patent leather. Pendent earrings glinted. Her face was ghostly with powder. A small, imitation snakeskin handbag dangled from her wrist. She reeked of some cheap scent.   (p. 131)

Here is a female equivalent of V. S. Naipaul's mimic man. In the final chapter, even Dina suggests a form of cultural regression as she goes to visit a *clairvoyante* in the squalid down-town area (a setting based on a disenchanted view of Georgetown's Starbroek market); Pierre, on the other hand, is – like his creator – a novelist, who is hoping to atone by his writing for two centuries of injustice and oppression.

But, ultimately, political dystopia is as prominent as personal alienation in *A Hot Country*. When Aubrey eventually sells the family house and donates a collection of prints to the National Museum, the pictures are sold for personal gain by the minister involved. As Aubrey himself comments more generally, "we've done nothing worthy of interest – the seeds of our humanity lie unfertilised".

If there is a single West Indian writer who may be regarded as a political novelist, however, it may be John Hearne. Hearne, who was born in Montreal but returned to Jamaica as a small child, wrote novels expressing deep concern about Caribbean society, although from a Westernized and largely middle-class perspective. After *Voices Under the Window* (1955), tracing the growing political awareness of a young "brown" lawyer, Hearne produced four politically charged novels set in a thinly disguised Jamaica renamed Cayuna: *Stranger at the Gate* (1956), *The Faces of Love* (1957), *The Autumn Equinox* (1959), and *Land of the Living* (1961). There is always an arbitrary element to classifications of this kind, and Hearne himself liked to describe Cayuna as "my own Yoknapatawpha". The political urgency of his middle novels nevertheless suggests an explicitly political writer rather than a more explicitly "home" or regional one like Faulkner.

Hearne's last – and some would argue his finest – work, *The Sure Salvation* (1981), is set on an illegal nineteenth-century slave-ship, and thus exemplifies a natural corollary to Caribbean political fiction of time present: the historical novel in time past. The earliest approximations to the latter mode, according to date of publication, are the romances of de Lisser (*The White Witch of Rosehall*, 1929) and Mittelholzer (*Corentyne Thunder*, 1941; and the *Kaywana* saga, 1952–8). But here, romance clearly prevails over history, just as European takes precedence over Afro-Caribbean, until the more discriminating contact narrative of Lamming's *Natives of My Person* (1972). One of the earliest historical reconstructions in terms of narrative chronology, on the other hand, is the astonishing "New Clothes" section of V. S. Naipaul's *A Way in the World* (1994), where an Amazonian tribe preserves an Elizabethan doublet from Tudor times.

Authentic Caribbean historical novels are generally more recent, however, both in publication date and in fictional context. They might be read as a collective reaction to the seminal passage in Jane Austen's *Mansfield Park* (famously scrutinized in Edward Said's *Culture and Imperialism*), where *pater familias* Sir Thomas Bertram is inexplicably detained on his Antigua estate. No reason is ever given for the delay, although some insight can be gleaned from the narrative of another canonic novelist, Matthew "Monk" Lewis's *Journal of a West Indian Proprietor* (1834); even more is available from *The Life of Olaudah Equiano* (1789), the first of the classic slave narratives. The majority of Caribbean historical novels follow Equiano in their attempts to fill the gaps and silences of Afro-Caribbean history, and thus begin from the eighteenth century or later.

Black Albino (1961), by Jamaican artist Namba Roy, is about the eighteenth-century Maroons (or escaped slaves) in the island's impenetrable "Cockpit" country; *Abeng* (1984) by fellow Jamaican Michelle Cliff – the *abeng* was a kind of conch used to assemble slaves on a plantation – shifts between the eighteenth century and the 1950s. *The Longest Memory* (1994), a fine slave narrative by Guyanan poet Fred D'Aguiar – although more poeticized than historicized – also evokes the days before Emancipation. It is to this group that John Hearne's re-creation of a clandestine slave voyage obviously belongs.

The post-Emancipation period has produced two broad historical panoramas in V. S. Reid's *New Day* (1949) and Peter Abrahams's *The View from Coyaba* (1985). Reid provides a chronicle of Jamaican history for the period 1865–1944, from the Morant Bay rebellion until the year in which the island was granted a limited degree of self-rule by Britain; Abrahams's massive *montage* selects significant episodes from 150 years of Black history in Africa, the Caribbean, and the American South. Both novels are seminal, but neither author makes easy reading: Reid for his pioneering attempt to write the people's history in the people's vernacular, Abrahams for his uncompromisingly didactic approach. The cross-cultural concerns of Abrahams are more accessible, however, in the recent fiction of **Caryl Phillips**.

If length of residence in the region were the sole criterion, Phillips would hardly be considered a Caribbean author. Born on St Kitts, he moved to England at the age of one, and his subsequent links with his native island have been limited to periodic visits; Phillips's relations with the Caribbean are nevertheless significant and profound. His first novel, *The Final Passage* (1985), works the familiar theme of deracination in the case of a couple equally disillusioned by Britain and the Caribbean, but his subsequent fiction has greater power and originality. Three novels, *Higher Ground* (1989), *Cambridge* (1991), and *Crossing the River* (1993), all have a certain family resemblance in their effective use of multiple voices in re-creating scenes of Black history, be it African, American, or Caribbean. In *Crossing the River*, Phillips thus perfects the technique developed in *Cambridge* of using a polyphony of voices. The scope is more ambitious here, however, as Phillips now inserts (between Prologue and Epilogue) not two but four narrative sections, each re-creating scenes from two and a half centuries of African and African American history.

The prologue of the novel reproduces the voice of a desperate African father selling two children to the captain of an English slave ship. His agonizing lament is punctuated by short, prosaic extracts from the captain's private journal. The narrative proper ("The Pagan Coast") begins with the account of Edward Williams, an enlightened Virginia planter who sends Nash Williams, one of his most promising ex-"bondsmen", to the recently founded colony of Liberia. Nash's experiences in his new home are recorded in a series of letters to his old master, although these are in fact long concealed by Edward's mad wife. Hearing no news, Edward decides to go and visit his protégé, who by this time has become first acclimatized and eventually (re-)assimilated to native African culture.

From initially cautious praise of the country's potential, Nash has undergone a gradual process of indigenization among his new countrymen, "even speaking a little of their crude dialect". He consequently becomes estranged from his fellow colonists, both black and white, on account of his "*native* style of living". In the last letter Edward ever receives, Nash speaks of polygamy, and refers to assiduous study of what is no longer a "crude dialect", but "the African language". In a final rejection of his ex-master's values, he has even adopted (or reverted to) traditional African religion. Edward had always intended to take Nash's children home with him to America, and when he sees the squalor of their existence, he astonishes onlookers by involuntarily bursting into a hymn. In an ironic challenge to conventional expectations, however, Phillips has a native African spectator wonder "what evil spirits had populated this man's soul and dragged him down to such a level of abasement". Edward's mission predictably ends in failure.

The shorter and (as it initially appears) autonomous second section of the narrative ("The West") follows the experiences of another ex-slave, Martha, sold from her Virginia plantation on the death of her master, and cruelly separated from her husband and child. At the beginning of the section, Martha is dying of cold and exhaustion on the street in a Colorado winter. Before this, however, it emerges from a series of flashbacks that she has successfully run a restaurant in Dodge City, before joining a group of coloured pioneers in Leavenworth as cook and laundress.

The third section of the novel ("Crossing the River") is a meticulous historical reconstruction from the captain's log on the *Duke of York*, as he accumulates a load of slaves from the West African coast for the "middle passage" over the Atlantic. The long final section ("Somewhere in England"), amounting to almost half of the book, is divided into two parts – both set in Britain, at various points during the Second World War and in 1963, respectively. A young Englishwoman, Joyce Kitson, has an affair with a black soldier stationed with the American forces in England. When her lover is killed in action, Joyce allows their son to be taken from her for adoption. In 1963, the furthest point forward in the narrative, the son returns from the United States to find his mother, now remarried with a new family.

The narrative then ends with an Epilogue in which the voice of the disconsolate father returns from the Prologue to assume a choric dimension and lament men and women of colour throughout the world, and throughout history. The various figures from the narrative are now revealed as at least symbolically, if not literally, related. *Crossing the River* is a movingly transparent text, whose pathos and lucidity hardly require exhaustive analysis. It also quite explicitly thematizes the concepts of land and language, most conspicuously in the person of Nash, who tries to re-embrace both through a return to his ancestral home.

FICTIONAL AUTOBIOGRAPHIES

The more or less fictional autobiography, and its close relation the *Bildungsroman*, are common models in Caribbean writing. The earliest variations on these forms reflect conditions in pre-independence societies, and their spirit is collectively invoked by Austin Clarke's memoir of a Barbados childhood.

The child's perspective as a structuring principle is associated above all with the Trinidad writer Michael Anthony, whose sensitive portraits of adolescence include *The Year in San Fernando* (1965) and *Green Days by the River* (1967). These were followed by the more radically innovative *Crick Crack, Monkey* (1970), the only novel of Anthony's countrywoman Merle Hodge. The latter is memorable both for its hilarious view of middle-class pretensions from a child's perspective and for its virtuoso presentation of vernacular speech.

In the next generation, novels of childhood proliferate (often transcending the autobiographical), and with the further difference that the protagonist is now typically female. Jamaican Olive Senior, although not a novelist, should be mentioned here for her many fine evocations of children's voices in *Summer Lightning and Other Stories* (1986). To these may be added longer narratives by Grenadian Merle Collins and two Guyanan writers, Grace Nichols and Janice Shinebourne.

Merle Collins's *Angel* (1987), described as a "coming-of-age-chronicle", has a strongly "nativist" element in its wide use of *patois* ("patwa" is her preferred term) or creole. Grace Nichols's *Whole of a Morning Sky* (1986), another semi-autobiographical first novel, de-cribes a Georgetown childhood during a period of social unrest in the 1960s. Janice Shinebourne's *Timepiece* (1986) begins roughly from the time where Nichols's novel ends; more ambitious, however, is Shinebourne's second novel, *The Last English Plantation* (1988), with its broader canvas of ethno-religious interaction and conflict in the Guyana of the 1950s and 1960s. The continuing vital-ity of the autobiographical mode is also confirmed by recent novels from Tobagan Marlene Nourbese Philip and Trinidadian Lakshmi Persaud. Philip's *Harriet's Daughter* (1988) – the title is a reference to legendary abolitionist Harriet Tubman – is a study of upwardly mobile Jamaicans in Toronto and a homesick Tobagan girl; Persaud's *Butterfly in the Wind* (1990) describes the childhood of a young East Indian girl in a Port of Spain suburb.

Among novels of childhood, **Zee Edgell**'s *Beka Lamb* has a special place not merely for its unusual Belizean setting, but also as a rep-resentative genre example with a feminine (and feminist) perspec-tive. Beka's account admittedly follows barely a year in her own life and that of her unfortunate friend, Toycie, who dies after an unplanned pregnancy. The relatively short timespan and frequent chronological shifts (less typical of the genre) do not, however, detract from the intrinsic interest of the narrative.

Beka Lamb is also responsive to the parameters of land and lan-guage. On the first count, there is an evocative moment when Beka and Toycie sense that they are being pursued by the ghosts of long-dead slaves; historical interaction between Carib and Creole is often recalled, moreover, whether in the official classroom versions of St Cecilia's Convent School or in the oral traditions of Beka's grand-mother. Latter-day descendants of both groups in Belize City nev-ertheless occupy a lowly position on a carefully segregated hierarchy headed by *bakras*, *panias* (here, those of British and of Spanish American "stock", respectively) and expatriates.

In terms of identity, Belizeans are caught between the two dom-inant colonial cultures, British and Spanish: a fact brought home emblematically when Beka and Toycie procure a guitar, but note with dismay the "made in Spain label" inside. After some deliberation, the two friends scratch this out, and replace it not by "made in England" but with the name of Belize. Political awareness (naturally oppositional) is also fostered by such crudely jingoistic occasions as the Battle of St George's Caye Day, an event reminiscent of Empire Day celebrations in half a dozen Caribbean novels. As the children are herded off to Government House for a glimpse of Sir John and Lady Radison amid wild cheering, the more subversive elements sing a jingle under their breath: "Dog di walk, and puss di talk and rabbit and rabbit deh behind, O!" – the syntax is significant, for it reproduces the indigenous Belizean creole, of which Edgell provides such a convincing representation. It is this language which offers the strongest and most explicit expression of local identity.

Both Edgell and her heroine in fact show great sensitivity towards the language question, with Beka providing amusing parodies of Lady Radison's diction or schoolmaster Trudell's articulation. Creole, on the other hand, has a vital harmonizing function in Belizean life. As a mature Beka notes of her native Belize City:

> It was a relatively tolerant town where at least six races with their roots in other districts of the country, in Africa, the West Indies, Central America, Europe, North America, Asia, and other places, lived in a kind of harmony. In three centuries, miscegenation, like logwood, had produced all shades of black and brown, not grey or purple or violet, but certainly there were a few people in town known as red ibos. Creole, regarded as a language to be proud of by most people in the country, served as a means of communication amongst the races.   (pp. 11–12)

Language is, of course, only one means of enforced assimilation; institutionalized religion is another, and, to obtain even a rudimentary education, Beka and her companions are forced to attend a Catholic school. There is an ironic episode here when Beka, who normally prays to the Holy Ghost as the member of the Trinity most reminiscent of the *obeahman*, confesses her agnosticism and is immediately sent home to reconsider her position. There is further irony, too, in the next chapter when Toycie becomes pregnant by a good Catholic boy, Emilio, who nevertheless refuses to marry her because it would both interfere with his studies and upset his mother. The same kind of cultural conditioning, and eventual escape – in this case from the British cultural strangle-hold – appears more whimsically in the case of Beka's mother, Lilla, who is obsessed at the beginning of the narrative with planting English roses, against all her husband's advice that she should be concentrating on bougainvillea, crotons, and hibiscus. This more obvious cultural symbolism is continued in a later chapter when a reformed and enthusiastic Lilla takes it upon herself to master all the *cuisines* of Belize's various ethnic groups.

It is common to regard the individual story of the young Caribbean man or woman as an allegory for the destiny of an entire nation, and *Beka Lamb* is also responsive to this kind of reading: most explicitly, the heroine describes herself on one occasion as feeling "bruk down just like my own country" (115). But the novel is also a psychological portrait of a young girl with a compulsion for lying during a particularly traumatic phase of her life. When an understanding mother provides a notebook to record these "lies", a subsequent source for Beka's own narrative, the colonial allegory is complemented by a metafictional one. This particular combination, together with a sensitivity to the parameters of land and language, make *Beka Lamb* a rewarding example of Caribbean fictional autobiography.

In many modern Caribbean coming-of-age chronicles, however, one may legitimately regard gender as more significant than age. Even *Beka Lamb*, in spite of frequent shifts to a child's perspective, is narrated by an adult (and female) protagonist. One major contemporary writer who unmistakably privileges the woman over the child, on the other hand, is Jamaican **Erna Brodber**.

Brodber's *Jane and Louisa Will Soon Come Home* (1980) is a difficult work even for many West Indian readers, and becomes increasingly so, the further the reader is placed, culturally or geographically, from the anglophone Caribbean. *Jane and Louisa* nevertheless remains a seminal example of both the new vernacular writing and the woman's text. Here as in few novels, moreover, the author's extra-textual comments are invaluable. Brodber is a trained sociologist who has produced several authoritative studies of working-class Jamaican life. She regards fiction as an extension of her sociological work, and began writing it as a reaction to the conventional "objectivity" of scientific methodology; the immediate results were brief speculations on her informants, in contexts that questionnaires never touch, in a kind of "twinning of fiction and science". The form of *Jane and Louisa* is fragmentary and impressionistic; its chronological leaps and startling shifts in linguistic register are closer to the radical innovations of Joyce's *Portrait of the Artist as a Young Man* than to traditional West Indian chronicles of childhood and adolescence.

Brodber emphasizes the relationship between individual history, tradition, and "personal defense mechanisms", seeing *Jane and Louisa* as a kind of "heuristic device". Its telling becomes a form of regression therapy, with beneficial effects for the female narrator. It is useful to know here (although Brodber never mentions a point so familiar to the Caribbean reader) that "Jane and Louisa Will Soon Come Home" is the first line of a popular Jamaican nursery rhyme. Performed as a ring dance, the song contains a fluctuating corpus of verses, many of which may be read as veiled sexual allegory. The final line of the title verse ("Into This Beautiful Garden") also suggests the promise of a psychic healing offered by the narrative process.

Quite divorced from any conventional sociological method, then, Brodber moves between history, chronicle, autobiography, and prose poem. *Jane and Louisa* re-creates the conflicts and traumas of Nellie Richmond's childhood and adolescence. The formative influences on her life are initially those of the isolated Jamaican village, in a community with strong religious principles. These are most clearly reflected in a harshly repressive attitude towards sexuality (exacerbated by a constant fear of seduction and unwanted pregnancy – above all, by a lover with too dark a skin). The first section ("My Dear Will You Allow Me") depicts an outwardly idyllic childhood, physically destroyed when a neighbour cuts down the surrounding protection of cedar trees. Psychically, however, childhood is desecrated by the onset of puberty and menstruation, or as Nellie wittily comments: "Period. End of sentence. I presume I am dismissed" (p. 23). There are now flashbacks to earlier childhood memories, as well as portraits of Nellie's father and grandfather, together with jumps forward to a period spent studying in the United States, and a subsequent immersion in Black political activism.

In the following section ("To Waltz with You"), Nellie – now a young adult – lives and works in a Jamaican government "yard-house" for the destitute, where she loses her boyfriend in a tragic fire. She finds solace through an old childhood friend, the Rastafarian Baba, who first encourages Nellie to express her grief, and then nurses her in his own apartment. This is followed by "Into

This Beautiful Garden", a sequence presented as a more conventional family chronicle (although Brodber can make even genealogy tough reading), before the unfolding of the final section, whose heading is the same as the novel's title. The family chronicle now leaps back as far as "great-grandfather Will" – the legendary wise (and white) patriarch – as well as developing the novel's recurrent "kumbla" motif. The latter term (literally a *calabash*, but also denoting "protection" or "camouflage") is reviewed here in all its metaphorical extensions, whether "beach-ball", "eggshell" or "parachute". As Nellie leaves the last "kumbla" of her now sterile and meaningless communal life, the recuperative process is complete. The title of the novel may thus be read, in conjunction with other connotations, as an expression of the new psychic equilibrium that Nellie achieves at such cost.

Jane and Louisa Will Soon Come Home was followed by the equally challenging *Myal* (1988), built around the Afro-Caribbean religious cult of Myalism, and *Louisiana* (1994), about a young African American anthropologist with Caribbean connections, in the American deep South of the 1930s. Like *Jane and Louisa*, both of these novels continue to explore what Toni Morrison has called "ways of knowing beyond the five senses".

Such concerns also provide a key as to how one might apply language categories to Bodber's fiction. Most obviously, the author is notable for a tendency to move further than most (in dialogue or narrative) along the continuum from standard English to broad creole: a linguistic reversal that now privileges the vernacular and marginalizes the stepmother tongue. At another level, however, Brodber interrogates and subverts a colonial discourse (white, European, male – and, above all, positivist) with another idiom (black, Afro-Caribbean / Afro-American or simply African, female – and transcendentalist): a confrontation which, in the cultural shorthand occasionally proposed in this study, also opposes "our" to "their" language.

EXPERIMENTALIST NOVELISTS

Such a strikingly innovative writer as Brodber could well be included under the heading of "experimental novelists" (not to mention other sub-categories). She would be a welcome addition, moreover, capable of softening a paradox at the heart of modern

Caribbean fiction: for although the latter is sometimes superficially (even patronizingly) regarded as "exotic", it is generally representational in mode. Often strikingly original in linguistic or sociocultural terms, it is nevertheless characterized by what the Guyanan novelist Wilson Harris has called the "realist fallacy". Once again, however, the great innovator is Lamming, whose first novel, the autobiographical *In the Castle of My Skin*, often transcends the classic realism with which it is generally associated.

One of the few genuine formal experimenters in Caribbean fiction is the Guyanan Denis Williams, whose *Other Leopards* (1963) and *The Third Temptation* (1968) reveal the influence of the French *nouveau roman*. The key example, however, is **Wilson Harris** himself, a writer not merely the equal of a Naipaul or Selvon, but perhaps the most profoundly original novelist yet to emerge from the anglophone Caribbean. Of mixed ancestry (African, European, and Amerindian), Harris was educated in Guyana and worked for sixteen years as a government surveyor (making a number of expeditions into the Guyanan interior) before emigrating to London in 1959. His first novel was *Palace of the Peacock* (1960), later combined with three other novella-length fictions, *The Far Journey of Oudin* (1961), *The Whole Armour* (1962), and *The Secret Ladder* (1963), to form the "Guyana Quartet".

Harris's fiction draws on a wide knowledge of literature, history, and myth; his techniques range from traditional realism to metafictional experiment. The evocation of a fantastic river journey in *Palace of the Peacock* provides a counterpoint to the three, more realistic, narratives that follow, and a technically closer sequel, therefore, is Harris's next book, *Heartland* (1964), which also resurrects characters from his first novel.

Also typical of the fiction is a gradual fragmentation of human identity and time, prominent features of both *The Eye of the Scarecrow* (1965) and *The Waiting Room* (1967); these two narratives are also united by a strongly self-reflexive element, provided by the fictive editor and diary form. Harris's next novels, *Tumatumari* (1968), *Ascent to Omai* (1970), *The Sleepers of Roraima* (1970) and *The Age of the Rainmakers* (1971), are marked by an increased interest in Guyanan history and its corollary of Amerindian mythology; the following books, *The Black Marsden* (1972), *Companions of the Day and Night* (1975), *Da Silva da Silva's Cultivated Wilderness* (1977) – with its continuation *The Tree of the Sun* (1978) – and *The Angel at the Gate* (1982), nevertheless move outside Guyana to locales as varied as Scotland, Mexico, and London.

In 1983, Harris published *The Womb of Space: The Cross-Cultural Imagination*, an ambitious study of literature, metaphysics, and comparative mythology that also offers useful insights into the novels. Harris's emphasis on the anthropological traces that link historically disparate periods co-exists with a belief in the redemptive powers of love. Both of these dimensions are prominent in the serene optimism of *Carnival* (1985), the childhood evocations of *The Infinite Rehearsal* (1987), and the metaphorical landscapes of *The Four Banks of the River of Space* (1990). The latter three novels together form the "Carnival Trilogy", among the latest fruits of a talent that is unique to Caribbean fiction and rarely equalled elsewhere.

Palace of the Peacock (1969) is the independent first volume of what is now usually found packaged as the "Guyana Quartet". It opens with an up-river expedition (led by the rapacious Donne, brother – or perhaps simply *alter ego* – of the anonymous narrator) to an Indian mission in the middle of the jungle. The journey is structured by three apparently naturalistic events: the shooting of Donne by an enraged mistress prior to departure, the narrator's shocked discovery of a "skeletal foot-fall and image" in the forest, and the boat's impalement on a snag in the river. The most significant element of the opening section, however, is the revelation that the names of Donne's companions match, to a man, those of a famous crew that had previously perished in the rapids.

The inhabitants of the mission understandably vanish into the jungle rather than confront the occupants of a ghost vessel, but Donne decides to pursue the Indians. Under the guidance of an old Arawak woman, there now begins a hazardous, but mythologically resonant, seven-day journey beyond the falls into unknown territory. Recorded fragments of the past lives of crew members alternate with scenes of violent quarrels and fatal accidents in present time. The status of these episodes is undermined, however, by clear hints that they are either no more than fantasies by a single survivor (together with his Indian guide) of an earlier navigational disaster, or else reminiscences of the ghost crew members before their previous deaths. At the conclusion of the voyage on the seventh day, the survivors are reunited with those already dead on the high savannah, underneath the deep blue canopy of stars which gives the novel its title.

Palace of the Peacock is a complex and highly suggestive work, although the most obvious key to its elusive allegory lies in its allusions to the colonial experience. Undoubtedly central to the narrative here is the cruel figure of Donne, who has consistently abused his native mistress, just as he attempts to coerce her people into working on his plantation. Donne's offences towards one individual are homologous to those committed against the indigenous people, which are in turn equivalent to the more general affront towards nature in the *El Dorado* of four centuries of European exploitation. It would nevertheless be wrong to restrict the novel's allegory to post-colonial paradigms. The trip up river from the Mariella mission is full of references to other places and other times, in accordance with Harris's characteristic polymythic and cross-cultural vision. The journey may even be seen as a kind of trial and expiation, reminiscent, at certain points, of the voyage of Coleridge's Ancient Mariner.

Harris uses physical landscape as metaphor, even allegory, in the other volumes of the "Guyana Quartet", and throughout a long and prolific career. A number of passages from *The Womb of Space* provide suggestive comments on the fiction. Moving over a wide range of texts (from Faulkner and Poe to Ralph Ellison and Jean Rhys), but also drawing on Jung and his own multi-cultural background, Harris finds in the apparent unity of literary texts:

> a cloak for, and a dialogue with, eclipses of live "otherness" that seek to break through in a new light and tone expressive of layers of reality.   (p. xvii)

It is ultimately this quasi-mystical vision which provides a unifying element in a prolific and versatile *oeuvre*.

OTHER VOICES

It would be a grave mistake to regard the anglophone Caribbean as a culturally homogeneous zone. Ethnic diversity is most obvious in Trinidad and Guyana, in both of which, roughly half of the population is of East Indian origin, usually the descendants of indentured labourers imported by the British in the nineteenth and early twentieth centuries. Writers with partially or exclusively Indian background include V. S. Naipaul, Shiva Naipaul, Samuel Selvon, Ismith Khan, Neil Bissoondath and Lakshmi Persaud (Trinidad); David Dabydeen, Cyril Dabydeen, and Janice Shinebourne (Guyana).

Among the several fine novels of Shiva Naipaul, *Fireflies* (1970) and *The Chip-Chip Gatherers* (1973) deal with the theme of East Indian exile and identity crisis in the Caribbean; *A Hot Country* (1983) used the familiar device of a fictional country to reconsider many of the same issues. The themes of alienation and exile also characterize two novels by Neil Bissoondath, a nephew of the Naipauls, who emigrated to Canada in 1978. *A Casual Brutality* (1988) thus records the traumatic experiences of a doctor from the Caribbean who returns home briefly with his Canadian wife; more originally, *The Innocence of Age* (1992) describes the alienation of a white Canadian in his native Toronto. Of the three Guyanans, Cyril Dabydeen – the one not previously discussed – emigrated to Canada in his mid-twenties. He has written two novels with a Guyanese setting: *The Wizard Swami* (1985), a caustic account of religious chicanery, and *Dark Swirl* (1989), a work reminiscent of Harris in its use of Amerindian folklore and myth.

The East Indian origins of certain novelists should not, however, be exaggerated. Obviously important in the early fiction of V. S. Naipaul, for example, or even in such later novels as *The Mimic Man* and *A Bend in the River*, it is sometimes correspondingly marginal to the fiction of Selvon. Selvon's mother was the daughter of a Scotsman and a Hindi-speaking woman; his father was a Tamil (although never heard, on the son's evidence, to speak anything but English). But in spite of the writer's predominantly Indian background, the immigrants in *The Lonely Londoners* are obviously Afro-Caribbean.

With Ismith Khan, on the other hand, the Indian heritage is more significant. Khan was born in Port of Spain, the grandson of a Muslim Pathan who had moved to Trinidad not as an indentured labourer but as a free immigrant. After attending various island schools and working briefly on the *Trinidad Guardian*, Khan obtained his higher education in the United States, where he has lived for over forty years, holding a variety of university posts. His best-known novel is *The Jumbie Bird* (1961), an autobiographical account of three generations of Pathan immigrants in their slow and painful adjustment to their new home. Khan's other two novels, *The Obeah Man* (1964), examining the potential of traditional African religion for confronting alienation, and *The Crucifixion* (1987), a more critical study of religious revivalism, are not as conspicuously successful as *The Jumbie Bird*. All of Khan's fiction is nevertheless remarkable for its particular skill in representing colloquial Trinidad speech. This is particularly noticeable in *The Crucifixion*, with its dual narrative of which roughly a third (appropriately italicized) is written in broad creole. The themes of land and language assume an added dimension with these writers of the Indian diaspora, who – in the case of British or North American immigrants – have undergone a process of double physical displacement (to end in "their" land with a vengeance), as well as some form, literal or figurative, of linguistic exile.

A second smaller, and correspondingly more marginal, group in anglophone Caribbean literature is formed by authors of European origin. These white novelists include Allfrey (Dominica), Drayton (Barbados), McDonald (Guyana) and Scott (Trinidad and Tobago). Phyllis Shand Allfrey's *The Orchid House* (1953) chronicles the resistance of three sisters to the stifling atmosphere of their childhood home; Geoffrey Drayton's *Christopher* (1959) and *Zahara* (1961) recall the fiction of Michael Anthony in their portrayal of adult impact on a childhood world; Ian McDonald's *The Humming-Bird Tree* (1969) studies the effect of race and class on a group of young Trinidad children; Lawrence Scott's *Witchbroom* (1992) has been received as a Caribbean example of *magic realism*. These novels have received little acclaim from indigenous West Indian critics, a state of affairs which does not apply, however, to what is by far the most acclaimed novel in this group: **Jean Rhys's** *Wide Sargasso Sea* (1966).

Rhys's imaginative re-creation of the early life of *Jane Eyre*'s first Mrs Rochester provides an interesting challenge to literary classification. The daughter of a Welsh father and a Dominican white Creole mother, Rhys might be considered a product of "settler" culture, a kind of footnote to the white writing of Australia, New Zealand, Canada, or South Africa. Her background suggests a literary genealogy shared by Doris Lessing or Pauline Smith; her early fiction is almost contemporary with Katherine Mansfield's. Rhys's last and best-known novel is nevertheless a record of alienation from metropolitan English culture, an alienation quite as profound and as disconcerting, moreover, as anything triggered by the Canadian prairie or the Australian outback.

The Jamaican adolescence of Antoinette (Bertha) Cosway coincides with the Emancipation Act of 1830. Tensions between ex-slaves and their former masters slowly increase, until Colibri, the Cosway plantation house, is eventually attacked and fired by an angry mob. But antagonism towards white Creoles like herself, Antoinette realizes, is almost as strong in Britain: "I've heard

English women call us white niggers. So between you and me I often wonder who I am and where is my country and where do I belong and why was I ever born at all" (p. 35). If *Wide Sargasso Sea* has an underlying thesis, however, it must be the extent to which marginalization and oppression are gender-specific as much as ethnically related; and when Antoinette's Martinique maid Christophine remarks bitterly, "All women, all colours, nothing but fools" (p. 91), the equation between colonialism and patriarchy is made explicit. It is largely for this analogy, identifying woman with the colonized subject, that *Wide Sargasso Sea* is recognized as an important post-colonial text.

At a concrete level, identities and affinities in the novel are constantly underlined in purely linguistic terms. In Antoinette's narrative, Christophine is said to speak "good English if she wanted to, and French as well as patois" (p. 18). Baptiste, in turn, "spoke good English" and was more than willing to do so. Antoinette herself is obviously a native speaker of English, but there are various objects in the island environment (a kind of crab, for example) for which she knows no English name. Language repeatedly suggests her sense of solidarity (even identity) with the house servants, as well as her links with the other islanders.

When Antoinette's husband (not directly named) takes over the narrator's role, however, he seems irritated or even threatened by the same linguistic phenomena. He remarks suspiciously that Christophine "couldn't speak English, or said she couldn't", and dislikes Baptiste's "mutter[ing] in patois" (p. 117). He reacts angrily to Antoinette "imitating a negro voice, singing and insolent". When he finally quits the West Indies, his decision to leave a bitterly disappointed young boy behind is largely linguistic: Antoinette protests that the child has "tried very hard to learn English", to which her husband replies brusquely: "He hasn't learned any English that I can understand."

For the unprepared reader, it is only in the brief final section of the novel that Antoinette's identity becomes clear. Now known as Bertha, she is placed under the guard of Grace Poole in the cold attic of a "cardboard house". The priggish Rochester, who had married Antoinette for her fortune but later experienced a brief passion for his young wife, has long been devoured by unmotivated suspicions and unarticulated fears. There is surely a pathological element (and perhaps even a displaced sexual one) in his final rejection of Dominica and the West Indies: "I hated its beauty and its magic and the secret I would never know." For Antoinette, however, imbibing the fragrances of her old red dress, "The smell of vetivert and frangipanni, of cinammon and dust and lime trees when they are flowering" (p. 151), there is only a sense of irreparable loss.

It may be appropriate to place Rhys at the end of this section, in view of her literary links with white exiled writers of the "settler" colonies proper, for these figures provide a substantial element in the following section.

NOTE

1. Quoted in Laurence Breiner's essay on Brathwaite in the *Dictionary of Literary Biography*, vol. 125, p. 11.

FURTHER READING

The best literary history is the *Introduction to West Indian Literature*, 2nd edn (Macmillan, 1996), edited by Bruce King, which may be supplemented by David Dabydeen and Nana Wilson-Tagoe's *A Reader's Guide to West Indian and Black British Literature* (Kingston-upon-Thames: Rutherford Press, 1987).

Michael Gilkes's *The West Indian Novel* (Boston, MA: Twayne, 1981) and Kenneth Ramchand's *The West Indian Novel and its Background*, 2nd edn (London: Heinemann, 1983) are helpful. Selwyn Cudjoe's *Resistance and Caribbean Literature* (Athens: Ohio University Press, 1980) is an important thematic study; more recent is Glyne A. Griffith's challenging *Deconstruction, Imperialism and the West Indian Novel* (Kingston: Press University of the West Indies, 1996).

Frontiers of Caribbean Literature in English, edited by Frank Birbalsingh (Macmillan/Warwick Centre for Caribbean Studies, 1996), consists primarily of interviews with writers from the region. Two fine collections compiled by Daryl Cumber Dance are: *Fifty Caribbean Writers: A Bio-Bibliographical Critical Sourcebook* (Westport, CT: Greenwood Press, 1986) and *New World Adams: Conversations with Contemporary West Indian Writers* (Leeds: Peepal Tree, 1992).

Among other titles in the Warwick Caribbean Studies series, Renu Juneja's *Caribbean Transactions: West Indian Culture in Literature* (1996) deserves attention. The comprehensive *Out of the Kumbla: Caribbean Women and Literature*, edited by Carole Boyce Davies and Elaine Savory Fido (Trenton, NJ: Africa World Press, 1990), is a good example of the gendered approach to writing from the region.

Volumes 117, 125 and 157 of the *Dictionary of Literary Biography* (Detroit: Gale Research, 1992, 1993 and 1995), edited by Bernth Lindfors and Reinhard Sander, cover Black African and Caribbean novelists in English. Routledge has published a large *Reader in Caribbean Literature* (1996), compiled by Alison Donnell and Sarah Lawson Welsh.

J. Edward Chamberlin's *Come Back to Me My Language* (Urbana: University of Illinois Press, 1993) deals with Caribbean poetry, but its arguments are relevant to the present study, while the book itself is inspiring.

The *Short History of the West Indies*, 4th edn, by J. H. Parry, Philip Sherlock and Anthony Maingot (Macmillan, 1987) is helpful.

Part III
Old Literatures in New Worlds

Introduction

Apart from the mainstream traditions of Britain and the United States, the "white" writing of Australia, New Zealand, South Africa and Canada is most obviously "what's left" at this point. It is an awkward category, not least because it lacks a suitable name: talk of "former dominions" or "old settler colonies" seems anachronistic by the end of the twentieth century. One may then ask whether (outside their common colonial history) the four countries can be linked at all; and, if so, whether there is any suitable term to denote four countries with such discrete literary traditions spanning three continents. And finally, after (or perhaps *before*) these issues are resolved, one could question whether this literature has any place in a discourse of the stepmother tongue. The three issues are obviously linked.

The Introduction to this survey sketched broad parallels between Australia and New Zealand, and (more tentatively) between South Africa and Canada. The first pair are similar in their geographical situation, their large English-speaking majorities of European origin, their now correspondingly small indigenous populations, and their history of European settlement in the nineteenth and twentieth centuries. South Africa and Canada were regarded as less comparable (most obviously for the large black majority in the former), although each contains, in addition to an English-speaking group, another substantial population, speaking an Indo-European language and claiming a colonial history considerably longer than their anglophone neighbours.

But even if these two sets of analogies carry any weight, the great majority of ("white") anglophone writers in these four countries surely possess English literally as a "mother tongue" (if such an ultimately figurative expression can have a literal meaning), although, particularly in Canada, there are fascinating anomalies. For most writers of European origin in all four countries it was then argued, however, that the possible significance of the stepmother tongue rested in the fact that English was in some sense an alien language *not* to those who used it, but rather to the *new environment on which it was imposed*. The "stepmother tongue" thus became an epistemological rather than a purely linguistic notion. The classic

199

example of linguistic alienation in this context is that of the nightingale: sub-Keatsian romantic effusions being misplaced in countries – like Australia or New Zealand – where the bird is unknown. More pertinently, Canadian novelist Robert Kroetsch has described the experience of inhabiting a "mandarin language" that lacks roots in the New World landscape, or quite simply of "writing a new country in an old language". This kind of awareness naturally informs the rubrick *Old Literatures in New Worlds* (chosen with ironic awareness of European ethnocentricity) which heads the present section.

Now it happens that South Africa, often the most problematic member of the group in terms of general classification, is exemplary here. Its poetic tradition in English is considered to have begun with the six-year stay in the country of the minor Scottish Romantic poet Thomas Pringle (1789–1834). A careful reading of Pringle's poems written in or about South Africa reveals quite explicitly the epistemological gap between Anglo-Scottish Romanticism and the South African physical reality. And in his acclaimed study of South African culture and society, novelist John Coetzee redefined *white writing* as "white only insofar as it is generated by the concerns of a people no longer European, not yet African". Coetzee sees African landscape writing from the beginning of the nineteenth century to the middle of the twentieth as the search for a language "to fit Africa". Unable to learn one of the many indigenous African languages from the inside, the English-language writer falls prey to a crisis of cultural identity:

English carries echoes of a very different natural world – a world of downs and fells, oaks and daffodils, robins and badgers – partly because English makes no claims (as Afrikaans does) to being native to Africa ...[1]

It is, of course, the very point made with respect to their own countries by the Canadian novelists Robert Kroetsch and Rudy Wiebe, or the Australians Thomas Keneally and David Malouf.

If the concept of "stepmother tongue" is given an additional figurative twist, then, the fiction of Australia, New Zealand, South Africa and Canada can also be incorporated into the present paradigm. There is a related point here, incidentally, of whether such novelists as Martin Boyd, C. K. Stead and Morley Callaghan can – in the same sense as Erna Brodber, Shimmer Chinodya or Wally

Serote – be regarded as *post-colonial* writers; whether, that is, the socio-cultural formation and historical legacy of affluent white middle-class authors in Australia, New Zealand or Canada are genuinely comparable to those of local writers in Malawi, Bangladesh or Guyana. The fact that these equations *are* so frequently made may reflect more on the self-interest of professional academics (particularly in the first-named countries) than on any more objective basis. As Albert Wendt, the Samoan novelist, noted bluntly in his introduction to the anthology *Nuanua*:

> Colonial literature created a whole mythology about us. This is still being perpetuated in some of the supposedly post-colonial anthologies and in writing by the descendants of the Papalagi/ Pakeha settlers. Today some writing considered by Pakeha/ Papalagi writers to be post-colonial, we consider colonial. (p. 2)

Here quite emphatically, to borrow the now famous catch-phrase, the Empire is writing back. The present study is fortunately not required to decide whether (or how much) a particular writer is post-, neo- or just plain *palaeo*-colonial; it merely has to consider in the first instance whether a text is written in English.

And so to the question of a name to cover these four literary traditions. One possible alternative, with at least the virtue of originality, is the acronym *ansac* – or, even better, *anz/sac*. In the first, typographically simpler, form, the name would combine the initial letters of *A*ustralia, *N*ew [*Z*ealand], *S*outh *A*frica and *C*anada. The alternative version would manage to include the Z of Zealand, as well as suggesting both Zuid Afrika and South Africa, the English and Afrikaans names for the country. More subtly still, the Z/S digraph also inverts the title of a celebrated study by Roland Barthes. In Barthes's exhaustive analysis of Balzac's short story "Sarrasine", the digraph S/Z was the master symbol for textual polyvalence (or even textual indeterminacy); in *anz/sac*, by analogy, the same symbol could be taken to signify the *cultural* polyvalence (rather than the *cultural* indeterminacy!) now privileged in all four of these countries, but particularly in South Africa itself. The double reference to Zuid Afrika/South Africa may be insufficient, however, since nine more languages have recently been given official status in that country; but if South Africa's black majority ever replaces the name South Africa with the alternative Azania, then only the smallest of adjustments will be necessary in a future edition of this study. The change to *anzac* would merely give new life and an alternative meaning to an acronym (denoting Australia and New Zealand Army Corps) slowly losing its emotional force in Australian and New Zealand life, but to which this whole exercise has of course been an indirect homage.

PIONEERS

In the present context of definitions and parameters, the position of the United States is also ambivalent, both with regard to the step-mother tongue and in relation to post-colonial literature. In linguistic terms, the seventeenth-century English colonists also imposed their tongue on an alien environment; that they managed to naturalize the language so well emerges from any history of the English language (*robins* or *creeks*, to quote two classic examples, will never have the same reference again in Britain and the United States). In literary terms, on the other hand, Ashcroft, Griffiths and Tiffin's study of post-colonial literature *The Empire Writes Back* (1989) suggests that "the literature of the USA should also be placed in this category" (p. 2), but does not seriously consider this proposal. This might be the moment to do so.

In terms of an heroic struggle with an alien environment (but also the dispossession and/or extermination of local populations), the American experience seems closest to that of Australia and New Zealand – producers of what in current terminology are called post-colonial literatures. In terms of dynamism and self-belief (but also several decades of arrogant hegemony, reinforced by the eclipse of the only other global power), the American experience seems more similar to that of early industrial Britain – producer of what may be called a metropolitan (or colonial) literature. The resolution of this ambiguity would require another book, one moreover in which the concept of modern anglophone fiction would itself be largely eclipsed. At the root of the business, too, there is certainly a historical perspective, or – more crudely – a simple time factor: as generations and even centuries pass, it is surely difficult to remember who was mother and who was stepmother (as in the fairy-tales, they are finally inseparable), or that one's ancestors once lived somewhere else. Like *The Empire Writes Back*, however, the present study must also ultimately skirt round the issue, or, at best, limit itself to concrete examples by glancing at two classic American writers in the context of land and language.

In his critical biography of Hawthorne, the novelist Henry James lamented his country's lack of "High Civilisation":

> No sovereign, no court, no personal loyalty, no aristocracy, no church, no clergy, no army, no diplomatic service, no country gentlemen, no palaces, no castles, nor manors, nor old country houses, no parsonages, nor thatched cottages, nor ivied ruins; no great universities, nor public schools – no Oxford, nor Eton, nor Harrow; no literature, no novels, no museums, no pictures, no political society, no sporting class – no Epsom, nor Ascot.[2]

In response to James's anguished query as to what remained, novelist and critic William Dean Howells could reply: "simply the whole of human life". And James's inventory also seems a remarkably prescient account of what is *not* normally depicted in the postcolonial novel, which might also claim to cover the whole (or most) of human life. Grandson of a poor Ulster immigrant, James ultimately found (or recovered) his "High Civilisation" in England, providing an early unorthodox example of the "Empire writing back" – or perhaps just the "Empire coming home".

James never wrote anything about *language* as revealing as the above remarks about *land*. At the turn of the century, however, he visited New York's multi-ethnic Lower East Side, and commented on what he heard there: "whatever we shall know it for ... we shall not know it for English". Without a transcript of what he did hear, it is difficult to form an independent judgement on this point, but in James's own case, there is all the material one could wish for. Consider the following lines from *The Ambassadors*:

> She was in no position not to appear to expect that Chad should treat her handsomely; yet she struck our friend as privately stiffening a little each time she missed the chance of making the great nuance. The great nuance was in brief that of course her brother must treat her handsomely – she should like to see him not; but that treating her handsomely, none the less, was not all – treating her handsomely buttered no parsnips.   (Book X, ch. 1)

The passage is a fairly representative sample of James's later style, and one might well turn the novelist's own words against him:

"whatever we shall know [this] for ... we shall not know it for English". A "stepmother tongue" that supplanted such linguistic atrophy would, like Suniti Namjoshi's Wicked Stepmother, bring new blood to the succession. James's mannerisms, moreover, seem as remote from normative patterns of English as many a Caribbean basilect. What, indeed, is "our" language and what is "theirs"?

James's friend Howells divided nineteenth-century American authors into "redskins" and "palefaces" according to their degree of earthy familiarity with their own country: in this sense, no-one was paler than James, and no-one perhaps redder than his great contemporary, Mark Twain. Twain's first major work, *Innocents Abroad* (1869), satirizes the exaggerated admiration of a group of Americans in Europe for anything old – in Jamesian terms, in fact, for "High Civilisation". Howells's trope of "redskins" and "palefaces" does not score high on political correctness today, but there is a particular appropriateness in thinking of Twain as a "redskin", in view of his intimate identification – like the Native American's – with the land (or, allowing for minor psychic displacement, the river).

In language, too, Twain is no less a pioneer. Alistair Cooke has tried to convey the effect produced on the American literary establishment by the opening lines of *Huckleberry Finn*; perhaps the dismay caused in Nigeria by Tutuola's *The Palm-Wine Drinkard* is a modern equivalent. Before the beginning of his most famous narrative, Twain also inserts his celebrated boast about speech presentation:

> In this book a number of dialects are used, to wit: the Missouri Negro dialect; the extremest form of the backwoods South-Western dialect; the ordinary "Pike-Country" dialect; and four modified varieties of this last. The shadings have not been done in a haphazard fashion, or by guesswork; but painstakingly, and with the trustworthy guidance and support of personal familiarity with these several forms of speech.

There may be wilful exaggeration here – Twain is never the man to undersell himself – but *Huckleberry Finn* still remains the first great vernacular novel in English. Whatever the validity of the author's claims, moreover, the symbolic significance of Twain's gesture is unmistakable. Without a literal alternative tongue at his disposal, Twain follows the example of those who turned "their" land (an English colony) into *ours* (the United States) a century earlier: he now converts "their" language (the mandarin tongue of England – and latterly *New* England) into something just as indisputably *ours*.

The aptness of Mark Twain in the present context lies in the fact that each of the *anz/sac* constituents also produced a pioneering vernacular writer in the first half of the twentieth century. The authors in question are Henry Lawson, Frank Sargeson, Stephen Leacock and H. C. Bosman.

Australia's Henry Lawson was born on the New South Wales goldfields. He later led a rough and variegated existence, reflected in a large body of short stories which are essentially regarded as an authentic portrait of the outback, Australia's own equivalent of "frontier life", at the end of the nineteenth century. Lawson's first prose collection was *While the Billy Boils* (1896), followed by *On the Track* and *Over the Sliprails* (both from 1900), *Joe Wilson and His Mates* (1901), *The Country I Came From* (incorporating previous work; from 1901) and *Children of the Bush* (1902); his later work never recaptured the brusque humour of the first stories. The opening lines of "Stiffner and Jim (Thirdly, Bill)", an early story written between 1893 and 1894, are a good example of Lawson's lively if fairly attenuated vernacular mode:

> We were tramping down in Canterbury, Maoriland, at the time, swagging it – me and Bill – looking for work on the new railway line. Well, one afternoon, after a long, hot tramp, we comes to Stiffner's Hotel – between Chistchurch and that other place – I forget the name of it – with throats on us like sun-struck bones, and not the price of a stick of tobacco.
>
> We had to have a drink, anyway, so we chanced it. We walked right into the bar, handed over our swags, put up four drinks, and tried to look as if we'd just drawn our cheques and didn't care a curse for any man. (p. 148)

In terms of character and setting, this is some way from *Huckleberry Finn*, but Lawson's admiration for Twain is on record, and even a high level of familiarity with his writing is implied by an obscure reference in "A Fragment of an Autobiography": "Does anybody remember the second pilot that Mark Twain worked under in *Life on the Mississippi* (not the Mississippi pilot)?" (p. 58).

In the "Fragment", Lawson also speaks of the problem of identity faced by the Australian writer of his day: he himself was described on various occasions as the Australian Burns, the Australian Bret

Harte or the Australian Kipling. The same ethnocentricity lives on gloriously in those critics who see R. K. Narayan as some kind of Indian Jane Austen! Such patronizing comments by British readers may even have encouraged Lawson to broaden the vernacular in a story such as "Brighten's Sister-in-law":

> Jim was born on Gulgong, New South Wales. We used to say "on" Gulgong – and old diggers still talked of being "on th' Gulgong" – though the goldfields there had been worked out for years, and the place was only a dusty little pastoral town in the scrubs. Gulgong was about the last of the great alluvial "rushes" of the "roaring days" – and dreary and dismal enough it looked when I was there... .
>
> We lived in an old weather-board shanty that had been a sly-grog-shop, and the Lord knows what else! in the palmy days of Gulgong; and I did a bit of digging ("fossicking", rather), a bit of shearing, a bit of fencing, a bit of Bush-carpentering, tank-sinking, – anything, just to keep the billy boiling.   (p. 278)

But here already, are signs of a literary self-consciousness (the fixation with minor details, the glossing of one word with something even more obscure for many readers) which sometimes mars Lawson's later work.

The New Zealand writer closest to Twain and Lawson is Frank Sargeson (born Norris Frank Davey), son of a local government official and his wife – both staunch Methodists. Sargeson's first collection, *Conversation with My Uncle and Other Sketches* (1936), with *A Man and His Wife* (1940) and *That Summer and Other Stories* (1946), all use a characteristically colloquial style; the two stories "I've lost my pal" (1938) and "A Pair of Socks" (1936/1940) go a stage beyond this, and may be regarded as genuine vernacular.

"The Making of a New Zealander" (1939/1940) describes an encounter with two Dalmatian immigrants, although Sargeson's dialogue barely suggests that they might be anything other than English native speakers. His true linguistic originality functions more as a reaction to the notion of "colonial literature", conditioned by metropolitan English tastes. This emerges effectively in the naively garrulous narrator of "The Making of a New Zealander":

> Now I'm running on ahead so I'd better break off again, because this isn't just a no-account story about how I began to get cheeky

and put wisecracks across Mrs Crump. It's not about Mrs Crump, she only comes into it. I'm not saying I haven't got a story about her too, but it's another one I'll be round to another time.   (p. 100)

Here, the echoes of Huck Finn's voice are unmistakable. Once again, it is obviously absurd to suggest that English for Sargeson was a stepmother tongue in the more literal sense which can be applied to Achebe or Soyinka, but his stories are a consistent attempt to naturalize the English he possesses, in conformity with New Zealand sensibilities. In this context, a recent collection of Sargeson's stories was given the particularly appropriate title of "Speaking for Ourselves".

The Canadian representative of the present group, Stephen Leacock, is certainly the weakest link in the thesis; many would consider Thomas Haliburton to be Canada's first great demotic writer. Unfortunately, Haliburton died in 1865, the year in which Twain published his first work, making him a possible precursor but an unlikely disciple. Leacock himself was born in Hampshire, England, and lived briefly in South Africa (where his father failed as a farmer), before the family emigrated to Canada in 1876. After such impeccable colonial credentials, Leacock graduated from the University of Toronto and completed a doctorate under Torsten Veblen at the University of Chicago; he became professor of political economy at McGill University, Montreal.

An alternative writing career began with *Literary Lapses* (1910) and *Nonsense Novels* (1911), but reached its high point with *Sunshine Sketches of a Little Town* (1912), gently satirizing the pretensions of provincial Ontario society. Leacock's sketches or extended anecdotes have the savour of orality, but it would be an exaggeration to call them vernacular. In his edition of the stories, Robertson Davies calls Leacock's idiom "the language of common speech, for it moves easily and frightens nobody", but describes his humour as that of the classical mind. Leacock actually ends his light-hearted meditation on growing old, "Three Score and Ten", with a veiled reference to his own literary legacy: *non omnis moriar*, glossed for the peasantry as "I shall not altogether die". It is difficult to imagine Lawson or Sargeson quoting Latin!

But Leacock also published a popular study of Mark Twain (with the same title) in 1932 – not a powerfully original work, but one with many useful insights. Twain is thus compared favourably with Longfellow, for whom "the form of his language and his thought was the same as that of his English contemporaries" (p. 91). Leacock suggests more provocatively that "there is as yet no Canadian literature, though many books have been written in Canada, including some very bad ones". *Sunshine Sketches of a Little Town* is certainly not one of these, but neither (apart from its provincial Ontario setting) is it, in the final reckoning, particularly Canadian. Leacock's writing is popular rather than populist, and its style – if not actually patrician – is informal rather than demotic.

The South African Herman Charles Bosman is quite another proposition. His relative obscurity outside his native country is regrettable, since he is in many ways the most interesting of the entire group, including Twain himself. Although Afrikaans was his home language, Bosman was educated at English-language institutions. In 1926 he spent six months as a schoolteacher for a rural Afrikaner community in the Groot Marico District of the Western Transvaal, and his experiences here provided the basis for his most famous work, the collection of stories published as *Mafeking Road* (1947). Other collections include *Unto Dust* (1963); *A Bekkersdal Marathon* (1971); and *Jurie Steyn's Post Office* (1971), consisting of so-called *voorkamer* ["front room"] conversation pieces published in *The Forum* (a weekly newspaper of liberal sympathies). *Jacaranda in the Night* (1947) and the posthumous *Willemsdorp* (1977) are novels, whilst *Cold Stone Jug* (1949) is a memoir of prison, where Bosman spent four years for the slaying of his stepbrother after a quarrel in 1926.

The Groot Marico district (near Zwingli) was the source for all but half a dozen of Bosman's 150 short stories. A few of these were originally written in Afrikaans and later translated into English; others were once English stories, now published in Afrikaans versions. The posthumous collection *Unto Dust* (1963) actually contains two stories for which no complete English version survived, and these were therefore translated by critic Lionel Abrahams. Bosman could be said, therefore, to have surrendered to the stepmother tongue, although he was certainly aware of the choice that faced the South African writer: to see him/herself as a European, contributing to European literature, or to say: "I have European origins but am committed to Africa ...". His genial, but ultimately ironic, portraits of the South African *dorp* in the early decades of the century firmly embrace the second alternative. The point is well illustrated by a glance at the hermetic world of the 21 *Mafeking Road* stories.

In "The Rooinek", for example, the Englishman Webber buys a farm in the Groot Marico; he speaks Afrikaans tolerably well and even joins his neighbours on an unsuccessful *trek* across the Kalahari, but is still regarded as the *uitlander*. Local girl Grieta in "Willem Prinsloo's Peach Brandy", on the other hand, goes as far as finishing school in Zeerust "to learn English manners and dictation and other high-class subjects". The father of narrator Oom Schalk Lourens does actually speak Sechuana, but there is no indication that he or any of his fellow settlers know a word of English. The provinciality of the *dorp* is nicely suggested in the character of Dirk Snyman ("The Music Makers"), who knows from his history books about the exploits of Vasco da Gama at the Cape, but is more struck by his own experiences there: "the last time he went down to the Cape a kafir came and sat down right next to him on a tram" – and people seemed to *think nothing of it*.

Bosman's irony can also be considerably harsher, as in the opening lines of "Makapan's Caves", where Lourens expresses what he doubtless regards as moderate views on some of South Africa's non-European populations:

"Kafirs? (said Oom Schalk Lourens), Yes I know them. And they're all the same. I fear the Almighty, and I respect His works, but I could never understand why He made the Kafir and the rinderpest ...".   (*Mafeking Road* (1947/1991), p. 54)

Bosman's radical attitude towards English might be seen very broadly as a struggle to convert "their" language into "ours"; the process is illustrated most clearly by the Afrikanerisms of "The Music-Maker" (only a longer quotation can do justice to the story's inimitable *ambience*):

No bushdance was complete without Manie Kruger's concertina. When he played a vastrap you couldn't keep your feet still. But after he decided to become the sort of musician that gets into history books, it was strange the way that Manie Kruger altered. For one thing, he said, he would never again play at a dance. We all felt sad about that. It was not easy to think of the Bushveld dances of the future. There would be the peach-brandy in the kitchen; in the voorkamer the feet of the dancers would go through the steps of the schottische and the polka and the waltz and the mazurka, but on the rempies bench in the corner where the musicians sat, there would be no Manie Kruger. And they would play "Die Val Hare en die Blou Oge" and "Vat Jou Goed en Trek, Ferreira" but it would be another's fingers that swept on the concertina's keys. And when, with the dancing and the peach-brandy, the young men called out "Dagbreek toe" it would not be Manie Kruger's head that bowed down to the applause.   (*Mafeking Road*, pp. 32–3)

Writers to whom Bosman paid tribute include Leacock and – most significantly – in a piece called "Innocents Abroad", Twain. Where the linguistic revolution of *Huckleberry Finn* is syntactic, however, that of *Mafeking Road* is primarily lexical, as Bosman embarks on his personal process of naturalizing the tongue.

Lawson, Sargeson and Bosman, then, may be seen as pioneers of Australian, New Zealand and South African narrative, respectively, even if Leacock is admittedly more of a literary appendix in the Canadian context.

The introductory model also emphasized, however, that all of the *anz/sac* countries have major indigenous writers for whom English was therefore in some sense "their" (i.e. a foreign) language, just as the country was once quite literally "our" land: these may be Aborigines, Maoris, Native Canadians or simply black South Africans. It is therefore easy to regard the *anz/sac* literature of "contact" – with the land or, more crucially, with the peoples already inhabiting it – as somehow particularly central to the respective literary traditions of these countries; it is the approach adopted unreservedly here. The list of writers who have revealed this double awareness is impressive. The rest of Part III therefore deals with the *anz/sac* countries individually for ease of reference, but the above criteria have partly determined the amount of coverage given to a specific author.

NOTES

1. *White Writing: On the Culture of Letters in South Africa* (New Haven, CT: Yale University Press, 1988), p. 8.
2. Quoted in the Introduction to Walter Allen's *Tradition and Dream* (1964), pp. 14–15.

6

Australia and New Zealand

Some early twentieth-century Australian fiction has fairly tenuous links with the country itself; novels, and even novelists themselves, were culturally or geographically remote from the Australian scene. These factors naturally have no intrinsic bearing on literary value or interest, although they may throw light on the significance of traditional national canons.

Henry Handel Richardson, for example, left her native Melbourne at the age of eighteen and returned only once, very briefly, in 1912. After studying music at Leipzig, she moved permanently to England in 1903. Her first novel, *Maurice Guest* (1908), is a study of the destructive effect of romantic love; her second, *The Getting of Wisdom* (1910), is a *Bildungsroman* or "novel of development"; both works are recognizably European in subject and mode. *The Fortunes of Richard Mahony* (1930) – consisting of *Australia Felix* (1917), *The Way Home* (1925) and *Ultima Thule* (1929) – is admittedly mostly set in Australia, and it is on this trilogy that the author's reputation now rests. Richardson nevertheless saw even this work as her major claim to a place in the *English* literary pantheon.

Martin Boyd, born in Lucerne, Switzerland, and brought up in Melbourne, spent his early adult life in Europe and served as an officer in the British Army during the First World War. An early work, *The Montforts* (1928), is a meticulous chronicle of upper-class Anglo-Australian life, much like *Lucinda Brayford* (1946) and *Such Pleasure* (1949). The four succeeding novels, *The Cardboard Crown* (1952), *A Difficult Young Man* (1995), *Outbreak of Love* (1957) and *When Blackbirds Sing* (1962) – known collectively as the Langton tetralogy – continue to combine what one critic genially describes as the nostalgia of Waugh and the pedestrianism of Galsworthy. For all its merit, then, Boyd's fiction has even closer ties to the old order of an Australia culturally dependent on England.

A generation before Richardson, however, there was a writer who described himself as "of Temper democratic, bias offensively Australian". This was Joseph Furphy, who led a rambling life before working for twenty years in his brother's foundry, and producing the massive *Such is Life: Being Certain Extracts from the Diary of Tom Collins* in 1903 – two offshoots from the original were published as *Rigby's Romance* (1946) and *The Buln-Buln and the Brolga* (1948). But however interesting its metafictional explorations in the tradition of Cervantes, Fielding, and Sterne, *Such is Life* is still ultimately a satire on *English* pastoral and *English* colonial romance. It is unnecessary to ask, moreover, for *whom* Furphy's Australian bias might have been offensive. England again becomes the object of the Australian novelist's "anxiety of influence".

A more genuinely innovative author from the first half of the century is Xavier Herbert, who left school at the age of fourteen, visited England in 1930, and eventually managed to find a publisher for his *Capricornia* in 1938. Herbert would later boast that this novel "did in Australia what *Uncle Tom's Cabin* did in the United States". With its scathing account of relations between whites and Aborigines, and its ironic treatment of miscegenation, here at last was a work Australian enough for anyone, and too Australian for many. And since Herbert's literary career spanned almost forty years, he may also be regarded as a contemporary writer: the novella *Seven Emus* (1959) revisits some of the issues of *Capricornia*; *Soldiers' Women* (1961) deals with the after-effects of the Second World War on a group of city dwellers; the sprawling *Poor Fellow My Country* (1975) – unkindly reviewed by one critic as "Poor Bugger My Novel" – is an Edenic epic of a pre-European Australia.

The distance of Furphy and Herbert from Richardson and Boyd reflects a divide in Australian letters between "populist" and "elitist" tendencies. This distinction is neatly encapsulated in the title of G. A. Wilkes's study *The Stockyard and the Croquet Lawn*. In a country where "mateship" is institutionalized, moreover, the populist tendency clearly prevailed. The stories of Lawson, and even the fiction of the "bush poet" A. B. "Banjo" Paterson, have a secure place in the national heritage. The historical novels of Brian Penton, who consciously emulated Richardson, are only a literary footnote.

In social background, Australia's major twentieth-century novelist **Patrick White** might have seemed destined for the croquet lawn rather than the stockyard. Born in London and educated partly in

Australia, but also at Winchester College and Cambridge, White lived in England, served as an RAF intelligence officer, and did not return to Australia until 1948. His ability to absorb and then transcend the great Australian cultural divide must in large part be ascribed to his almost mystical identity with the land. White's first book, *Happy Valley* (1939), is the study of a small community on New South Wales; its successor, the England-based novel of manners *The Living and the Dead* (1941), is the only novel set entirely outside Australia. The early *Tree of Man* (1955), with its chronicle of Australian life from pioneer settlement to modern urbanization, draws on the traditional historical novel, but is also an attempt to find the soul of the country. The same dual purpose is even more apparent in *Voss* (1957), inspired by the journals of the nineteenth-century explorers Leichhardt and Eyre, offering nothing less than an epic and a myth of Australia. *Riders in the Chariot* (1961) and *The Solid Mandala* (1966), despite their predominantly suburban settings, consolidate this process. *The Vivisector* (1970) and *The Eye of the Storm* (1973) both emphasize art and the creative process, but *A Fringe of Leaves* (1976) is White's closest approach to the explicit "contact novel".

By a curious coincidence, Patrick White's tally of twelve full-length novels – completed by *The Aunt's Story* (1948), *The Twyborn Affair* (1979) and *Memoirs of Many in One* (1986) – exactly equals that of Dickens; for White, however, Australia is not simply a vaguely ominous other, experienced by a Magwitch or a Micawber, but a massive physical reality. As such, it conditions every kind of destiny, whether European, Euro-Australian, or Aborigine. Aborigine figures are in fact prominent in several of White's most Australian novels, including Dugald and Jackie, who join the explorers' party in *Voss* (1957), and Alf Dubbo, the artist of *Riders in the Chariot* (1961) who paints the chariot of fire that gives the work its title. *A Fringe of Leaves* (1976), part "contact novel", part "captivity narrative", and – with the introduction of Jack Chance – part "convict story", is nevertheless White's most significant exploration of European–Aborigine relations.

White is often cited as a major force in subverting the predominant mode of social realism in Australian fiction, but the opening chapters of *A Fringe of Leaves* in fact often recall the nineteenth-century comedy of manners, from Austen to Trollope. The novel depicts the journey of elderly valetudinarian Austin Roxburgh (with his young Cornish wife, Ellen) to his older brother in Van

Diemen's Land. On the return voyage to England, the ship hits a reef off the Queensland coast. The sole survivors of the subsequent ordeal are the second mate, Pilcher, and Ellen herself who, after being abducted by an Aborigine tribe and treated as a kind of slave-nurse, is helped to escape and led to safety by an escaped convict, Jack Chance. After taking Ellen within sight of a Queensland farmhouse, however, Chance flees for fear of colonial justice. Ellen, on completion of at least a physical recovery, returns to England a widow.

It is Ellen Roxburgh's experiences that lie at the heart of the novel. Raised on a Cornish farm, she is carried away – on the death of her parents – by the much older and socially superior Austin Roxburgh, to be refashioned for Regency society through a well-meaning mother-in-law during a period of *purdah* in Gloucestershire. Caught in the process between two "incompatible worlds", in an operation from which she will never entirely recover, Ellen effectively loses both "land" and "language", although she will never be as close to either again as during her time in the Australian bush. In linguistic terms, as a native of Cornwall (that *remote* county, as one Sydney spinster is ironically made to describe it), she is incidentally linked with a language – Cornish – which was becoming extinct just as she was born. The Roxburghs, in turn, extirpate her Cornish dialect of English, which later only returns in moments of great tenderness or stress: with Oswald Dignam, the adoring cabin boy swept out to sea while attempting to gather shellfish; with the nameless Aboriginal children that the tribe entrusts to her; and, most obviously, with Jack Chance, the escaped convict who responds in his own Cockney vernacular.

But the land, too, is denied her. In common with most natives of Cornwall, Ellen regards England as a foreign country, and having once crossed the River Tamar, she will never see her native land again. She regularly draws analogies between the Australian bush and her home county (in some ways, no more clement), while certain Aborigine customs even bring back memories of her childhood on a Cornish farm. Austin Roxburgh, on the other hand, experiences his closest contact with rural life through an intimacy with Virgil's *Georgics* (horticulture appeals to him principally for its "Latin names" and "dead specimens"), but recoils fastidiously on a real farm from the smell of pig dung.

Much of White's power as a novelist derives from his bold attempts to construct a mythology of Australia, sometimes trans-

forming it into a country of the mind. The land thus becomes a projection of the unconscious itself. For the timid Austin Roxburgh, it
represents the abyss, whilst for Delaney, the happy Irish *emancipist*,
or Oakes, the affable ex-sergeant of the Moreton Bay settlement, it
suggests a potential site of peace and harmony. For Ellen, trapped
between two worlds, the associations of Australia are more ambivalent, as she finds herself caught between Victorian prudery and
a sensual affirmation of life. Her more romantic or impulsive responses predictably generate strong guilt feelings, hardly relieved
by a crude seduction at the hands of her brother-in-law, Garnet.
With the convict Jack Chance in the Australian outback, however,
she enters what is certainly the most intense, and perhaps the most
meaningful, relationship of her short life, before Chance flees to
avoid reprisals. The world he fears, the dehumanizing one of
convict labour, is unequivocally regarded by Ellen as more "bar-
baric" than anything found in Aborigine society; she in fact asks at
one point during her ordeal (with that peculiar lucidity common to
madness) whether the whites will kill Chance as the Aborigines
murdered her husband (although only, incidentally, in response to
European violence).

In view of the country's traumatic past, it is understandable that
many novelists have attempted to come to terms with Australian
history. Eleanor Dark, born in Sydney and living most of her life in
the Blue Mountains town of Katoomba, is best known in this
context. Her trilogy of *The Timeless Land* (1941), *Storm of Time* (1948),
and *No Barrier* (1953) is a meticulous reconstruction of Australian
history from the first settlement to the crossing of the Blue
Mountains in 1813.

Katharine Prichard achieved notoriety in her day with *Coonardoo*
(1929), for its frank treatment of miscegenation between Europeans
and Aborigines. She later, however produced a meticulously re-
searched historical trilogy – *The Roaring Nineties* (1946), *Golden Miles*
(1948), and *Winged Seeds* (1950) – about life in the West Australian
goldfields. In a far more innovative mode more than thirty years
later, Brian Castro returned to the gold-rushes with *Birds of Passage*
(1983), alternating between the perspectives of a nineteenth-century
Chinese immigrant and of his modern mixed-race descendant.

Jessica Anderson also wrote a historical novel, *The Commandant*
(1975), set in the Moreton Bay penal colony of the 1830s. *The Tilted
Cross* (1961), the most successful novel of Hal Porter, depicts colonial Hobart Town. More popular fictionalized history appears in

the novels of Ruth Park, such as *The Harp in the South* – the story of an Irish working-class family in Australia – later expanded by *Poor Man's Orange* (1949) and *Missus* (1986) to become the *Harp in the South* trilogy. More sensational material is characteristic of Barbara Hanrahan, whether the setting is nineteenth-century Adelaide in *The Peach Groves* (1979), or London during the same period in *The Albatross Muff* (1977).

In the work of **Peter Carey**, however, history is transformed rather than merely dramatized. A science graduate and former advertising copy-writer, Carey was first attracted to fiction by the literary experiments of Robbe-Grillet and the *nouveau roman*. His collection of stories *The Fat Man in History* (1974) was followed by a first novel, *Bliss* (1981), a satirical view of the advertising world and the Americanization of Australian culture. *Illywhacker* (1985), the confessions of a 139-year-old confidence trickster, is a uniquely Australian example of the picaresque; *The Tax Inspector* (1991) is a black comedy describing the audit of a Sydney car firm in the late eighties; *The Fat Man in History* was combined with a second volume of short stories, *War Crimes* (1979), and published as *Exotic Pleasures* in 1980; *The Unusual Life of Tristan Smith* (1994) is a broad post-colonial allegory in the fantastic mode. Carey's unique (if largely indirect) contribution to historical fiction, however, is the massive *Oscar and Lucinda* (1988), which gradually abandons classic realism as it moves from nineteenth-century European drawing-rooms to the twentieth-century Australian bush. In this process, it treats fictional conventions with the playfulness of Rushdie, and revisits the Victorian novel with the hindsight of John Fowles.

The novel's enigmatic narrator (just once obliquely referred to as Bob) traces the lives of two highly original and utterly engaging characters: the Reverend Oscar Hopkins, his great-grandfather, and Miss Lucinda Leplastrier, who – against readerly expectations – does *not* become his great-grandmother. If one life-story brings rich insights into the theological turbulence and moral hypocrisy of Victorian religion, then the other opens new perspectives on the social history of nineteenth-century Australia. Oscar, son of a Plymouth Brethren minister but later ordained an Anglican priest, defies everlasting hellfire and chronic hydrophobia "to bring the word of Christ to New South Wales". Lucinda, orphaned daughter of a gentleman farmer and an unfulfilled visionary mother, uses her inheritance to purchase the Prince Rupert glassworks in Sydney. Her own struggles are conditioned by society's ingrained prejudice against the independent woman, as well as by the venality and censoriousness that characterize Australian colonial society.

The two protagonists are brought together by their addiction to gambling, a common passion that acquires increasing metaphysical and psychological implications. Oscar, for example, gambles reluctantly to finance his studies at Oxford and then the voyage to Australia (only committing himself to the latter by the toss of a coin), but never uses his talents for personal gain. In between original speculation about God's possible views on the matter, he also quotes Pascal's famous analogy of the greatest gamble of all, where Christian faith is the stake and Heaven the prize.

With Lucinda, on the other hand, gambling ultimately means a compulsion to lose, an attitude generated by feelings of guilt about the sources of her own wealth. And since the theme of gambling is all-pervasive, it is tempting to speculate on a third dimension to Carey's novel. One of Oscar's earliest impressions of Australia is that its chief industry seems to be gambling; here, perhaps, is a forerunner of the comic stereotype according to which Australians will happily bet on two flies crawling up a window pane. More seriously, of course, the passion might be linked with some residual sense of the risk (with its related elements of courage, enterprise, or sheer desperation) involved in any emigration, not least to nineteenth-century Australia.

Such speculation apart, the climax of *Oscar and Lucinda* involves the construction of a glass church (at Lucinda's factory) and its transportation overland (on Oscar's insistence) to the remote settlement of Boat River. In this respect, *Oscar and Lucinda* may seem remote from the concept of the "stepmother tongue", or the discourse of land and language. "Their land" becomes an increasingly pivotal issue, however, even without the author's ideologically loaded reference to the "white invasion of Australia". For, like White's *Voss* or Stow's *To the Islands*, *Oscar and Lucinda* is also in part a "novel of contact". Most of the characters can be defined by their attitude towards Australia's indigenous population. As a small child, Lucinda tries to give her blond English doll black features; as an adult, she feels mounting guilt at the source of her own prosperity ("The money was stolen from the land. The land was stolen from the blacks", p. 126). Most of her Sydney acquaintances, on the other hand, have a pathological hatred of Aborigines; Oscar's superior, Bishop Dancer, shows a cynical indifference ("mission work was a waste of time. The blacks were dying off like flies", p. 276). Mr Borrodaile, the entrepreneur from Ultimo, has a personal construction of blacks which assumes a "total absence of religious beliefs" (p. 235). Only Oscar himself is constantly aware of the ghosts of slaughtered individuals.

In a poignant climax to the novel, the perspective actually shifts to the oral narrative of the old Aborigine, Kumbaingiri Billy. This describes the assembly of the church, where thick grease "made the white chaps into blackfellows" (p. 487), and the conversion of Billy's Aunt: "When she saw this glass church built she became a Christian" (p. 488). Both images can only begin to suggest the rich symbolic associations of a gleaming, transparent glass church floating down the Benninger River.

Some of the most remarkable Australian novels have predictably been concerned with the traumatic relations between settlers and the indigenous population. Two other important examples of these "contact narratives" are provided by Drewe and Keneally.

In *The Savage Crows* (1976), **Robert Drewe** reconstructs the fate of the last Aborigines in Tasmania. His method is to alternate fictional extracts from a journal of the historical George Augustus Robinson with the life of broadcaster Stephen Crisp, ex-member of the Commission for Aborigine Affairs and now engaged on research in the field. Analogies between the tragic fate of Tasmania's indigenous population and Stephen's own somewhat aimless existence become increasingly apparent with each section. "Travels with Anna" thus relates Robinson's first contacts with Aborigines on Bruny Island to Stephen's own exploration (with a girlfriend) of Papua New Guinea; "Mortality Reports" juxtaposes Robinson's notice of Aborigine deaths from pneumonia with Stephen's memory of a childhood friend drowned while surfing. More subtle (even humorous) linguistic parallels ("Ameliorating the Natives") link Robinson's first addresses to the aborigines in their own tongue with Stephen's adjustment of his accent for the white natives of Northern Queensland.

Robinson is initially a sympathetic figure, as he attempts to construct friendly relations with the Toogee tribe – he had, after all, run a "building and joinery business" in early nineteenth-century London. Ultimately more builder than joiner, however, he becomes obsessed with his "new site for our civilization", and grows increasingly autocratic with both Aborigines and settlers. Now a builder of empires rather than houses, moreover, he condemns "any encouragement to seduce [the Aborigines] away from dependence on me", and reassures a weeping Woody Island woman: "I am Mr Robinson, the Father. ... You are going to a happy place" (p. 194). Such grotesque religious parody clearly reflects the writer's sense of the Christian Church's long history of complicity in the colonial enterprise. But no complicity is possible without prior communication, and language has both formal and thematic significance in Drewe's novel. Robinson's travelogue is thus called *The Savage Crows*, subtitled "My Adventures Among the Natives of Van Diemen's Land": the term "savage crows" was originally applied to Aborigines by white Tasmanian settlers, a blatant example of a verbal reconstruction which dehumanized the subject and made the subsequent process of extermination more comfortable.

Linguistic misunderstandings are rife, and when the few remaining Aborigines are finally assembled on Flinders Island, the inability of isolated members of different tribes to communicate with each other seems to have accelerated the general apathy which leads to the demise of the settlement. The process may in fact be seen as a grotesque inversion of that earlier and far more extensive uprooting, the Atlantic slave trade: the new colonizers now forcibly unite those who spoke different languages, whereas their predecessors had forcibly segregated those who spoke the same one.

There are a number of Aborigine words and phrases in *The Savage Crows*, all of them carefully glossed. Transcending mere local colour, these sometimes genuinely reflect an Aborigine viewpoint and undermine an ethnocentric colonial one, as when Truganini remarks with presumably unconscious irony that "there are plenty of *Parlerwar* [natives] in England". Fuller communication on Aborigine terms is nevertheless always precluded. There is a poignantly emblematic moment in this context when Robinson describes the oral performances of his travelling companion Umarrah, some of them lasting upwards of an hour "in the manner of the Eastern storytellers". Umarrah's voice is, of course, never heard.

Drewe pursued simultaneous careers as novelist and journalist. His second novel, *A Cry in the Jungle Bar* (1979), is the story of an Australian agricultural consultant in South Asia, an "ugly Australian" as culturally out of place as Graham Greene's "quiet American". The more recent *Fortune* (1986) and *Our Sunshine* (1991) – the latter narrated by the outlaw Ned Kelly – have been compared to the "New Journalism" of the American writer Tom Wolfe, and effectively unite Drewe's two careers.

Thomas Keneally is a difficult novelist to classify or even to assess: he enjoys great popularity, but is widely disparaged by academics and castigated by feminists. His most famous work, *Schindler's Ark* (1982) – reissued as *Schindler's List* after the success of Spielberg's film adaptation – has little connection with Australia, and none at all with current post-colonial parameters: it seems, moreover, to have been originally conceived as pure investigative journalism.

Keneally's other novels are remarkable for their wide range of narrative voices and physical settings. Three early examples, *The Place at Whitton* (1964), *The Fear* (1965), and *Three Cheers for the Paraclete* (1968), have a strong Catholic bias, unsurprising in a writer who trained for the priesthood before becoming a schoolteacher. Another larger group shows a preoccupation with war and violence, past and present, and is generally ignored by critics; the series includes *Blood Red, Sister Rose* (1974), *Gossip from the Forest* (1975), *Season in Purgatory* (1976), *Confederates* (1979), *The Cut-Rate Kingdom* (1980), *A Family Madness* (1985), *Towards Asmara* (1988), and *Flying Hero Class* (1989). In the present context, Keneally's most interesting novels are those with characteristically Australian themes or settings: *Bring Larks and Heroes* (1967), about convict society; *A Dutiful Daughter* (1971), about bush life; and *The Playmaker* (1987), a fictional reconstruction of the first-ever theatrical production on Australian soil. Keneally's own "contact narrative", *The Chant of Jimmie Blacksmith* (1972), also clearly belongs to this group.

Set in the years immediately before Federation and based on a historical event, the novel portrays the clash between Aborigine and white settler cultures. "Half-breed Jimmie" is rescued from jail by Mr Neville, the Methodist minister, and started on a life of spiritual uplift and material acquisition. For Jimmie, moreover, as for many of his co-religionists, the two discourses rapidly merge after his insight that "property was the key" and that "possession was a holy state" (p. 15). But attainment of these goals is not easy. Robbed and abused by the settlers he works for, cheated into marriage by a white servant girl pregnant with another man's child, Jimmie nevertheless resists until the moment when an employer denies him his rightful food rations. Then, after calmly chopping up his employer's wife (the first in a series of killings), Jimmie takes to the bush, retraces his steps, and begins to settle old scores.

The hero's sufferings arise largely from the fact that he is caught between two alien and mutually antagonistic cultures; or, as

Keneally memorably expresses it, "lost beyond repair between the Lord God of Hosts and the shrunken cosmogony of his people" (p. 148). The cultural gap is not insurmountable, however, and the author often suggests that white settlers on the verge of nationhood might have found more in common with the Blacksmith brothers than with their old colonial masters. Without the bogey of race, in fact, the country's formative social divide might have had a quite different expression, simply ranging all Australian colonizers against all Australians colonized.

If the status of Keneally's Aborigines is distressingly obvious, then the situation of his white Australians is pointedly ambivalent. The years preceding Federation were also those before the Boer War, and analogies with South Africa are often used to create a broader colonial perspective. All but one of Jimmie's pursuers are "Britannically minded" and regard the manhunt as a "novitiate for the war in South Africa" (p. 106). The exception is Toban, grandson of an Irish evictee, who identifies Australia's white settlers with the Boers rather than with the British. The war itself is Britain's private affair, even a cause for grim hilarity in view of the greater number of casualties from enteric fever than from Boer guns ("the British Empire versus gut-ache"). Toban's "Irish catechisms" are humorously tolerated but ironically cheered by friends who score higher on *mateship* than on political awareness.

Back on Australian soil, however, the element that both unites and divides Keneally's characters is language. It is striking that such an action-packed narrative still pays close attention to linguistic issues. It is thus noted on several occasions that the Aborigines speak a kind of Cockney English, suggesting a relationship as close to the British proletariat as to the Australian fauna. "Code-switching" or alternation between languages is also common. Great emphasis is thus placed on what can be said in English and what must be left in Mungindi: in "the old language", for example, there is no word for a regular *job*.

Jimmie invariably also shows great sensitivity to language: when he goes to Verona Blacks Camp, he drops his aitches in tactful deference to the speech habits of the residents. When Sergeant Farrell interrogates his suspect in a kind of pseudo-Pidgin, Jimmie relates this to the white man's concept of how the native spoke English. During their subsequent flight, the Blacksmith brothers use English together until the emblematic point at which they switch to Mungindi "for greater force". The emphasis on a special link between Aborigine language and the land of Australia itself is consistently maintained throughout Keneally's novel. Schoolmaster McCreadie's beloved *Palgrave* (the classic Victorian poetry anthology) hints ironically, on the other hand, at the status of metropolitan English as a stepmother tongue bearing an increasingly alien culture.

A more overtly speculative contact narrative is **David Malouf**'s *Remembering Babylon* (1993). Son of a Lebanese father and English mother, Malouf is from Brisbane and was educated at the University of Queensland, but spent most of the 1960s in Europe before returning to Australia in 1968. With his access to elements of Arab and francophone culture, Malouf in Australia might seem to qualify as a transnational writer, although little of this ambivalence is apparent in the semi-autobiographical *Johnno* (1975), a fine evocation of the novelist's Brisbane childhood. *An Imaginary Life* (1978), on the other hand, is a brief synthesis of convict myths of exile and imprisonment with the story of Ovid's banishment from Rome.

The short fictions *Fly Away Peter* (1982) and *The Great World* (1990) both juxtapose secure and peaceful Australia with the horrors of the First World War. The title novella of the collection *Child's Play* (1981) is a metafictional experiment, in which a terrorist kills a famous author, who has already anticipated and therefore manipulates the course of events. *Harland's Half Acre* (1984) is a more realistic representation of the artist theme. Malouf's most significant novel in terms of the "stepmother tongue", however, is his extraordinary parable of exile, identity, and language loss in *Remembering Babylon*.

The novel's complex shifts in chronology and focus yield a dramatically simple story. A white man emerges naked from the North Queensland bush in the middle of the nineteenth century, and gives himself up to three young children playing in a paddock. Cast overboard from an English ship at the age of thirteen, Gemmy Fairley had survived to join an Aborigine tribe, with whom he spent the next sixteen years. He is subsequently adopted by Jock and Ellen McIvor, parents of the children who discovered him, and lives in harmony with them until the suspicions and fears of other settlers make his life unbearable. He then moves to an eccentric old lady outside the settlement, at which point the exact details of his life become obscure. Gemmy may have taken up a position as Customs Officer, before eventually returning to his adopted tribe. He may finally have been one of the nine fatal casualties in a notorious "dispersal" raid carried out by settlers in the region some years later.

The eventual marginalization of Gemmy's story results from the fact that it is merely one more element in a many-faceted parable of alienation and assimilation, developed through an extended meditation on language and identity. For *Remembering Babylon* is nothing less than a study of colonization (only in the first instance Australian) through the prism of language. It embraces language mutation and language loss. Among the Aborigines, Gemmy has lost his own language and acquired a new one; the immediate motive for seeking the white man is for "the connection that would put the words back in his mouth". The subsequent novel is a microcosm of all linguistic adaptation and change.

Ironically, the McIvor family who adopt him are from Scotland, and do not really speak English either, but Scots; for them, too, there is a gradual language loss, and particularly their adopted son Lachlan (and the latest arrival) is fond of "slipping into the old tongue". George Abbot the schoolmaster, coarsened in his own estimate by life in the bush, valiantly teaches Shelley's "To a Skylark" (as near to Keats's nightingale as one could imagine) to his ragged barefoot pupils, and increases their vocabulary with such useful items as "mettlesome", "benign", and "decorum" (p. 45).

The most original member of the settlement, however, is the visionary minister, Mr Frazer, who also befriends Gemmy and takes him out on "botanizing" expeditions. Gemmy watches in fascination as Frazer records data on local flora: "*Small creeping leguminous plant that runs in and out of the grass, Kardolo in the native tongue*" (p. 128). The clumsiness of Frazer's paraphrases merely underlines a point which Gemmy has long before understood:

> a good deal of what they were after he could not have told, even if he had wanted to, for the simple reason that there were no words for it in their tongue; yet when, as sometimes happened, he fell back on the native word, the only one that could express it, their eyes went hard, as if the mere existence of a language they did not know was a provocation, a way of making them helpless. (p. 65)

Gemmy comes to pass on his almost mystical view of the oneness of language and environment to Frazer, a sentiment embodied in his idea that "there was no way of existing in this land, or of

making your way through it, unless you took it into yourself, discovered on your breath, the sounds that linked up all the various
parts of it and made them one" (p. 65). Words, like objects, are also
sacred, and Frazer's clumsy attempts to repeat native names transcend the merely comic to approach the blasphemous.

The inability to adapt linguistically is matched by a similar failure
to adjust culturally. This point is subtly underlined by twin references to the English southern counties: Frazer's note on the exotic
flora he finds is recorded in a copperplate "as straight and orderly
as a row of cabbages in a Berkshire field" (p. 121). Mr Herbert the
state premier, on the other hand, has established a Horatian retreat
resembling "fifty acres of Cambridgeshire". The comic absurdity of
distant England as a point of reference could not be plainer. Frazer's
proposal, on the other hand, that "if the land will not present itself
to us in terms that we know", then it is we that must change rather
than the land, will obviously stand as a motto for a modern
autonomous Australian literature.

Another writer for whom the contact narrative is of central
significance is **Randolph Stow**. Like his mentor White, Stow has
been sufficiently gripped by Australia's own "grand theme" to
return to it at different points in his career. *To the Islands*, his study
of a remote West Australian Aborigine mission, was published in
1958 (when the author was barely twenty-two), but reissued in a
revised edition in 1982. Possibly Stow's most remarkable attempt in
the genre, however, is *Visitants* (1979), where the clash between
European and indigenous cultures takes place not in Australia, but
in Papua New Guinea. The originality of the novel lies in its dual
perspective. The main events occur against a background of
unidentified flying objects (UFOs) seen over the country in 1959;
but to the islanders of Wayouyo, the local Australian administrators (or "Dimdims") are as strange as these other "visitants".

The narrative ends in a violent uprising provoked by a local religious cult, inspired in turn by a legend explaining the much envied
European technological superiority. On the sudden appearance of
UFOs, the same legend is exploited by a vicious elderly chief who
wants his clan to perish with him. The islanders are promised that
if they destroy their villages and even the white man's home, then
the star-people will bring new material wealth (the idea is clearly
related to the "cargo cults" widely recorded in this region).

Throughout *Visitants*, Stow maintains an emphasis on cultural
diversity with constant shifts of focus (in short clearly labelled

sections) between his major characters: Cawdor, the Patrol Officer; Dalwood, his young trainee assistant; Osana, the government interpreter; MacDonnell, a local white planter; Saliba, a domestic in his household; Benoni, heir to the local chief; and, occasionally, Browne, the Assistant District Officer, heading the inquiry into the uprising. All of these characters reflect different stages of alienation and acculturation with respect to colonial and indigenous society. MacDonnell, long the only European on the island of Kailuana, is nevertheless content with this situation – "White men are more trouble than they're worth"; Cawdor, one of the few officials to speak the local language, has a strong empathy for Papuans – "Misa Kodo is one of us. Some people say that he is a black man truly"; Osana, mission-educated and contemptuous of island customs, resents the loss of prestige caused by having a boss who rarely needs him. Dalwood, Cawdor's successor, is less culturally ambivalent and therefore more dependent on the grateful Osana. Saliba, who sleeps once with Dalwood mainly out of curiosity, and then gravitates towards Benoni, also comes to represent the forces of continuity.

The exact forms of these cultural relations are elaborated with a precise but humorous regard for linguistic detail. Although often linked thematically with both *The Tempest* and *Heart of Darkness*, then, *Visitants* is more explicitly realistic than the one and less gloomily portentous than the other. Linguistic authority is highlighted by the fact that three of the narrators are using an unspecified local language (it is worth remembering that many of the groups in this area do not even have a specific name for their own language). Cawdor is a fluent speaker of "the language", while Dalwood (as Osana contemptuously observes) has only five words of it. MacDonnell often goes for weeks without using a word of English.

Like Malouf's *Remembering Babylon*, *Visitants* is a disturbing study of cultural and linguistic assimilation. It reflects the writer's originality, but hardly his breadth, the latter resulting partly no doubt from a variegated life. As a young man, Stow worked on an Aboriginal mission and later in Papua New Guinea; he subsequently lectured in Britain, Canada, and Australia, and travelled widely in the United States, before settling in Suffolk, England, in 1966. His most popular work, *The Merry-Go-Round in the Sea* (1965), is a nostalgic evocation of a West Australian childhood; *Tourmaline* (1963) is a philosophical novel contrasting Taoist and Christian ideas; *The Girl Green as Elderflower* (1980) links the Suffolk of the 1960s with medieval myth.

A lesser-known writer who explores the myths of Australian experience like White and Stow is Peter Mathers, born in England but taken to Australia as a child. Of his three novels, *Trap* (1966), *The Wort Papers* (1972), and *A Change for the Better* (1984), the first is the most interesting, with its history of black–white relations in Australia *via* the part-Aborigine protagonist, Jack Trap.

In spite of its natural prominence in the present paradigm, however, it would be grossly reductive to see the contact narrative as an exclusive master trope of Australian fiction. Modern urban life is the thematic core, for example, of three such highly disparate if equally original writers as David Ireland, Helen Garner and Kate Grenville.

David Ireland suffers more than most novelists from attempts to fit him into narrow literary categories. His novels feature a wide range of narrative voices, whilst never losing their high political awareness: *The Chantic Bird* (1968) is thus a straight naturalistic text with a teenage narrator, reminiscent of Salinger's *The Catcher in the Rye*; *The Unknown Industrial Prisoner* (1971) explores worker exploitation by a multinational company – a subject revisited in *The Flesheater* (1972). *The Glass Canoe* (1976) examines gender roles in a male-dominated sub-culture; the futuristic *City of Women* (1981) imagines a Sydney without men. Between these two novels, Ireland published *A Woman of the Future* (1979), where the heroine is transformed into a leopard. The animal protagonist is maintained in *Archimedes and the Seagle* (1984), which is narrated by a red setter. The ambitious and demanding *Bloodfather* (1987) maintains Ireland's idiosyncratic approach.

Helen Garner, originally a schoolteacher by profession, is noted for her fragmentary post-modernist manner and knowledge of "contemporary Australian lifestyles". Both elements are prominent in her first novel, *Monkey Grip* (1977), a chronicle of urban counter culture in the 1970s. *The Children's Bach* (1984) is interesting for its use of music as a structuring principle, whilst *Postcards for Surfers* (1985) is a collection of characteristic short stories. Garner's most highly regarded work, *Cosmo, Cosmolino* (1992) – often classified as a novel, but effectively a novella preceded by a group of short stories – returns to the settings of *Monkey Grip* a generation on.

In the fiction of Kate Grenville, finally, the urban dimension is subordinated to a powerful feminist discourse. *Lilian's Story* (1985) allegorizes the relationship of England and newly independent Australia in terms of a father–daughter conflict (the father is significantly called Albion); *Dreamhouse* (1986) depicts a woman suffering in a one-sided relationship; *Joan Makes History* (1988) is a comic revision of Australian history.

Australians are generally numbered among the world's great travellers, and if the stereotype has any objective basis, it would be surprising not to find it reflected in their fiction. A case in point, then, is Murray Bail. After spending two years in India (1968–70), and four more in Europe (1970–4), Bail returned home and published his first novel, *Homesickness* (1980). This grotesque account of an Australian package-tour to Europe was nevertheless followed by the home-grown *Holden's Performance* (1987), the comic epic of a young man's path through Australian society.

Even more travelled than Bail is ex-professional broadcaster C. J. Koch. After *The Boys in the Island* (1958; revised 1974), an account of childhood and adolescence, Koch treated the theme of Australians abroad more seriously in *Across the Sea Wall* (1965; much revised 1982), and – above all – *The Year of Living Dangerously* (1978). Set in a violent and dangerous Jakarta just prior to the fall of Sukarno in 1965, the latter is a classic account of overlapping private and public lives. Koch's fiction also points to a broader category of ex-patriate writing. Several of these Australian novelists, from Christina Stead through Shirley Hazzard to Janette Turner Hospital, are discussed in the context of transnational writers.

A final writer difficult to place is Jessica Anderson. Born in Brisbane, she spent a few years in London, but has lived most of her life in Sydney. Her reputation rests primarily on *The Impersonators* (1980) and – above all – *Tirra Lirra by the River* (1978), both depicting the attempt of an older ex-patriate woman to rediscover Australia.

NEW ZEALAND

Seen from a broad external perspective, certain of the patterns and themes of Australian fiction recur in the New Zealand tradition. The strong bias towards a traditional realistic mode is thus maintained, whether it is refracted through a colonial or a post-colonial prism. Novels of urban or provincial childhood and adolescence abound; some of these are susceptible to allegorical readings, according to which the growth of the young protagonist parallels the emergence of the new nation, although the classic example of this technique remains *Lilian's Story* (1985) by Australian novelist Kate Grenville. New Zealand – like Australia – also has a strong feminist presence, but is less conspicuous in the field of experimental fiction.

However significant in themselves, these various literary trends are less interesting in the present context than the trope of the step-mother tongue. New Zealand's so-called "ethnic" writing, the work of authors in a European tradition (or a European language) from outside the British Isles, is admittedly thin; far stronger, in contrast, is the work of Maori authors. It is difficult to find three novelists of the stature of Patricia Grace, Witi Ihimaera and (more controversially) Keri Hulme among indigenous writers in either Australia or Canada. More central to the present argument, however, are certain historical novels, few in number but often of great literary interest. The latter in turn, given the strength and prominence of the country's pre-European culture, are almost inevitably "contact narratives" of some kind. These, then, complement New Zealand fiction's current "grand theme" of Maori–Pakeha interaction in contemporary society.

A classic paradigm of the New Zealand colonial writer is provided by James Courage. Courage left his native country to read English at Oxford at the age of twenty, visited New Zealand in 1927 and 1934, but lived the rest of his life in England. Most productive in the 1950s, Courage produced a series of novels, including *Desire without Consent* (1950) and *Fires in the Distance* (1952), characteristically depicting a genteel Canterbury of sheep stations and private schools of the pre-war years. More urgent social realism, but the same geographical displacement, characterizes Dan Davin, who studied at the University of Otago before winning a Rhodes scholarship to Oxford in the mid-1930s. After distinguished war service in Europe, Davin returned to Oxford and remained in England for the rest of his life, only returning to New Zealand for occasional visits. The subjects of his seven novels range between an Irish Catholic (New Zealand) childhood in *Cliffs of Fall* (1945), wartime experiences in *For the Rest of Our Lives* (1947) and the situation of New Zealand expatriates in post-war London in *The Sullen Bell* (1956).

Moving in the opposite direction, M. K. Joseph was born in Essex, England, but lived for two-thirds of his life in New Zealand.

Two of his six novels are also set in the Second World War, including *A Soldier's Tale* (1976); *The Hole in the Zero* (1967), on the other hand, is an early example of science fiction. The mainstream realist tradition is further evident in the work of two writers roughly contemporary with Joseph, who confined themselves to local settings: Ronald Morrieson was a wild chronicler of small-town New Zealand life in *The Scarecrow* (1963) and *Came a Hot Friday* (1964); Bill Pearson attacked New Zealand provincial apathy in *Coal Flat* (1963). Marilyn Duckworth produced an imaginative study of alienation in London in *A Gap in the Spectrum* (1959), and a speculative fable on language and identity in *A Barbarous Tongue* (1963), before returning to a more conventional realistic mode in the 1980s with *Disorderly Conduct* (1984) and *Married Alive* (1985).

At the core of New Zealand realism, however, looms the substantial figure of Maurice Gee. A graduate of the University of Wellington, Gee published his first novels – *The Big Season* (1962), *A Special Flower* (1965) and *In My Father's Den* (1972) – while still working as a teacher and librarian. He then established his reputation with *Plumb* (1978), later expanded into a trilogy with the addition of *Meg* (1981) and *Sole Survivor* (1983). The *Plumb Trilogy* depicts three generations of a twentieth-century New Zealand family from alternative perspectives; the use of an interlinked trilogy to obtain a broad social panorama recalls Robertson Davies; the contrasting perspectives of the three books are reminiscent of Joyce Cary; the overriding theme of the *Plumb trilogy*, the effect of New Zealand's Puritan inheritance on public and private life, is nevertheless Gee's own, and recognizable throughout his fiction. The trilogy is a substantial achievement by any standards, and the New Zealand critic who could only describe it as "up there with E. M. Forster and Graham Greene" may even have undersold his author.

The most favoured subjects of New Zealand realism include childhood, adolescence, the *Bildungsroman* and – a variant of the latter – the *Künstlerroman* or "portrait of the artist". Two minor classics in the first category were produced by Ian Cross: *The God Boy* (1957), providing an eleven-year-old child's account of a family break-up; and *The Backward Sex* (1960), depicting the painful sexual initiation of its seventeen-year-old narrator. A more ambitious novel by Cross is *After Anzac Day* (1961), a panoramic view of modern New Zealand society through the perspectives of the four central characters – aiming to achieve in one volume something of what Gee produced in three. *The Backward Sex* is thematically linked to *Sydney Bridge Upside Down* (1968) by David Ballantyne, the story of an emotionally disturbed juvenile protagonist. C. K. Stead's *All Visitors Ashore* (1984) may also be read in part as a reaction to the traditional *Bildungsroman*.

New Zealand has a number of significant feminist writers. The novels of Fiona Kidman, *A Breed of Women* (1979), *Mandarin Summer* (1981), *Paddy's Puzzle* (1983; republished as *In the Clear Light* in 1985), and *The Book of Secrets* (1987), belong to an international feminist tradition, with their female protagonist struggling against various forms of patriarchy, puritanism and provincialism. Rachel McAlpine's fiction includes *The Limits of Green* (1985), with its important ecological dimension, the autobiographical *Running Away from Home* (1987), and the historical *Farewell Speech* (1990), studying the Christchurch suffragette movement. Jean Watson wrote several shorter novels before producing the highly speculative *Address to a King* (1986).

On the other hand, New Zealand has few novelists with a non-anglophone but European background, the best-known example being Yvonne du Fresne. Born and raised in a Danish–French Huguenot community on Munawatu Plains, Du Fresne therefore has a more literal claim to writing in the stepmother tongue. Her novels, *The Book of Ester* (1982) and *Frédérique* (1987), both draw on her multi-cultural background.

Among New Zealand writers who are experimental, or have at least questioned the tenets of orthodox realism, the most significant is **Janet Frame**, widely regarded as the country's greatest living novelist. As Patrick Evans comments in his *Penguin History of New Zealand Literature*: "No one has based her writing on such a thoroughgoing rejection of the daily life of her own country as Frame, or written with such determination to remain free of other people's prescriptions as she writes" (pp. 195–6). Frame's artistic autonomy and versatility often recall the position of J. M. Coetzee in South African literature. *Owls Do Cry* (1957), *Faces in the Water* (1961) and *The Edge of the Alphabet* (1962) form a loose trilogy which tend to ignore outer reality and reflect a fantastic inner world expressed in lyrical prose. To this already uncompromising base, Frame adds metafictional experiment in *Daughter Buffalo* (1972), *Living in the Maniototo* (1979) and *The Carpathians* (1988). Where the latter novel is concerned, however, Evans's comment is not entirely valid: for all its magic realism, *The Carpathians* is also deeply rooted in the everyday reality of New Zealand provincial life. Set in the small coastal town of Puamahara (named after the Maori legend of a "Memory Flower"), it is the story of Mattina Brecon, globe-trotting New York philanthropist and wife of writer Jake Brecon. Mattina rents a house on peaceful Kowhai Street in downtown Puamahara and begins to study her neighbours.

For a novel that is unabashedly metafictional, moreover, *The Carpathians* pays remarkable attention to linguistic codes and registers. Mattina thus learns the metaphors of sport (cricket, horse-racing and football) which permeate New Zealand life; she similarly recreates the perspective of murdered Madge McMurtrie with her colonial vocabulary of "creeks" and "paddocks", words now replaced by "streams" and "fields". But language is rooted in a landscape, and the novel also highlights the differences between settlers and tourists (however discriminating, like Mattina herself) and the "people of the land".

Land and language are potentially reconcilable in the Maori family of Hene Hanuere, who runs the corner shop, although – to Mattina's surprise – Hene is unable to speak Maori. Mattina comes to view cultural loss in terms of physical separation:

> It's strange, you know. Like someone you turned out of your house years ago, and now they've come home and you're shy, and ashamed of having turned them out and you have to get to know them all over again.... (p. 26)

Hene later invites Mattina to the family's second home on the traditional *marae* a hundred miles upriver from Puamahara. She eagerly accepts in the hope of learning more about the legend of the Memory Flower among the "people of the land", who presumably retain a source of memory which the European "latecomers" are only just beginning to understand.

Frame's naturalistic, almost sociological, stance towards land and language is, however, only the starting-point for a more searching allegorical treatment of the same issues. In the final cataclysm, the people of Kowhai Street lose their language and simply disappear, with an official conspiracy of silence refusing to ascribe this to anything beyond conventional migratory movement. Mattina has nevertheless felt the haunting presence (a "disorder of time and space") and heard the wordless screams of her neighbours, before they are all discreetly removed in coffins.

If the Memory Flower promises the preservation of the past, then the newly discovered "Gravity Star" ("a galaxy that appears to be both retroactively close and seven billion light years away") threatens to annihilate all memory and perspective, doing for the rest of the world what has already been accomplished for Kowhai Street. The only comfort that Frame offers is the force of her own story, or the complexities of the very narrative act. A central purpose of Mattina's life had been to provide her writer-husband with material for his long-awaited second novel. In the end, however, it is John Henry Brecon, the couple's son, who emerges as author of the freely indicted account of his parents' experiences. The recuperative gesture has an obvious sense of "fragments I have shored against my ruins", as the son becomes – in an image quite as striking as Eliot's, and originally intended for the novel's title – one of the *Housekeepers of Ancient Springtime*.

Another novelist to have varied realism with fable, allegory and even metafiction is C. K. Stead. Born in Auckland, Stead travelled widely, completed a Ph.D at Bristol University, and reveals a heavy debt to European literary tradition. After an early poetic career broken only by the anti-totalitarian political fable *Smith's Dream* (1971), Stead concentrated more seriously on fiction from the 1980s. His most acclaimed novel is his second, *All Visitors Ashore* (1984), which – in addition to satirizing the traditional *Bildungsroman* – depicts the Waterfront dispute, New Zealand's major industrial conflict of the post-war period. *The Death of the Body* (1986) and *Sister Hollywood* (1989) are about cultural shifts between Europe and New Zealand, whilst *The End of the Century at the End of the World* (1992) shows an increasing interest in metafiction. Stead nevertheless remains the paragon of the cosmopolitan intellectual, sceptical towards his country's new multiculturalism, and apparently oblivious to the figurative potential of the land and language tropes.

A more uncompromisingly experimental novelist than Stead is Ian Wedde, who was educated at Auckland University but spent much of his early life abroad. His novels, such as *Dick Seddon's Great Dive* (1976), have been compared to the surrealistic fantasies of the American Thomas Pynchon; the fanciful re-creation of nineteenth-century New Zealand history in *Symmes Hole* (1986) nevertheless seems more reminiscent of Peter Carey. *Survival Arts* (1988) is a lighter, comic novel.

The creative historicism of *Symmes Hole* is a natural point of entry to other historical novels, almost inevitably – in the New Zealand context – variations on the contact narrative. The major Pakeha novelist here is **Maurice Shadbolt**. Journalist and scriptwriter as well as novelist, Shadbolt graduated from short stories, and the *Bildungsroman, Among the Cinders* (1965), to a long series of *Künstlerromanen*, where the writer–protagonist tries to come to terms with the social environment of modern New Zealand: Ben Blackwood in *This Summer's Dolphin* (1969), Frank Firth in *An Ear of the Dragon* (1971) and Ian Freeman in *Strangers and Journeys* (1972). He then used a realistic historical mode in *Strangers and Journeys* (1972) to cover the Depression and the Waterfront dispute of 1951, before producing *The Lovelock Version* (1980), a New Zealand epic of magic realism that is inevitably compared with García Márquez's *One Hundred Years of Solitude*.

Shadbolt's future reputation may, however, rest on a recently completed historical trilogy of the British–Maori Wars in the nineteenth century: *Season of the Jew* (1986), on the Te Kooti uprising of the 1860s; *Monday's Warriors* (1990) on the contemporaneous campaign of Titokowaru on the other side of North Island; and *House of Strife* (1993), on events from the mid-1840s around the Bay of Islands. The trilogy is more a private mythology, laced with pageant, than history in any conventional sense. Shadbolt does not provide the imaginative participation in pre-European culture achieved by White or Wiebe. His interest lies more in debunking traditional "white" pieties, rather than replacing them with new orthodoxies. An indifference to plausible speech presentation, for example, is evident from the epigrammatic (almost *hip*) idiom consistently accorded to Maori, Pakeha and anonymous narrator alike. A random (if necessarily extended) example of this is the exchange between army deserter Kimball Bent and his Maori captor, Long Beard:

> "Riding beside us", Long Beard said, "are men anxious to dispatch you. More so if you think to take a direction other than ours. You understand?"
> "Ample," Kimble said.
> "Mercy is not to be seen as weakness," Long Beard explained.
> "It never crossed my mind," Kimball said truthfully.
> "We are just a little at sixes and sevens."

"Like how?"
"Some chiefs think to continue warring; others think peace."
"You?" Kimball asked.
"I act mad," the Maori said. "I am not crazy."

(p. 30)

Not surprisingly, Kimball is struck by the "splendid mission English" of Long Beard. And Kimball's subsequent adoption by Titoto or Titokowaru, the major historical figure in the narrative, is strongly influenced by the old chief's hopes of acquiring "new fluency in the English tongue"!

If language is handled in cavalier fashion, however, then the treatment of land is more serious. In New Zealand history, the colonists' quarrel with Titokowaru had begun over disputed land sales in the Mount Taranaki region. By focalising the narrative through Kimball Bent, a Maine Yankee who has ended up incongruously in the British Army, Shadbolt proposes thematic links between Maori aspirations in New Zealand and the American War of Independence. When formal hostilities cease and the inevitable compromises are made, however, an unreconciled Kimball and his companion, Big, begin an outlaw existence together. But the narrative has already conveyed Maori sentiments in a series of metaphors more effective than any painstaking speech representation. Titoko thus explains to his men the close links between Pakeha religion and Pakeha territorial occupation ("Christians came to tame the Maori horse... . Colonists came to ride it") and later suggests the absurdity of collaboration or appeasement (a Maori "steering the British canoe").

Shadbolt ends his own historical note to *Monday's Children* with a reference to the modern oil-wells and gas bores on the old battle sites, but he also evokes Mount Taranaki itself, a volcano silent for two centuries, but which nevertheless "still rises coolly from a green wreath of rain forest". If the wreath suggests funeral or *requiem*, then the reference to the dormant volcano itself hints that the repressed will return: an appropriate image, perhaps, in the light of multi-cultural awareness in today's New Zealand.

There are other more subtle, if less comprehensive, contact narratives than those of Shadbolt. Sylvia Ashton-Warner draws on Maori myth in her fourth novel proper, *Greenstone* (1964); James McNeish, whose *Mackenzie* (1970) apparently attempts to emulate Patrick White's great Australian epic, *Voss*, set his sixth novel in New

Caledonia with an Englishwoman among indigenous Caldoches and Kanaks. But the most memorable novels about contemporary relations between Maori and Pakeha are, with one key exception discussed below, the fiction of Noel Hilliard. Over almost twenty years, Hilliard published the Netta Samuel–Paul Bennett tetralogy – consisting of *Maori Girl* (1960), *Power of Joy* (1965), *Maori Woman* (1974) and *The Glory and the Dream* (1978) – at the centre of which is the cross-cultural relationship of his two chief characters. Hilliard is also sensitive to the socio- (and even psycho-) linguistic distinctions between English and Maori. There is thus a significant exchange at the beginning of *The Glory and the Dream*, where Netta (the Maori) uses the expression "Sparrow-*te*" to Paul (the Pakeha):

> "Sparrow fart is the expression."
> "I know," she said. "You've got your way of saying it. I've got mine. Your way, it doesn't sound polite to me."
> "What about your way? Means the same thing."
> "But it's not swearing. We don't have rude words. We have names for things and that's all. You say *te* in Maori, that's exactly what it means. But you say it in pakeha, it means a lot of other things as well. Lot of pakeha words like that. Not names but rude."
>
> (p. 5)

Such ideas are not, of course, romantic Pakeha projections, but correspond to authentic Maori beliefs about the sacredness of the word. Witi Ihimaera discussed this point in some detail with Feroza Jussawalla and Reed Dasenbrook, emphasizing that – for the Maori writer – the English language was fortunately "profane":

> It is profane enough to do whatever I want with it. But Maori, you cannot do whatever you want with it. It is a tapu language. It is the language of the people, it is a sacred language.[3]

In the context of Hilliard's complete tetralogy, a casual exchange like that between Netta and Paul has far broader implications. The contamination and debasement of *language* may be seen as parallel to the contamination and debasement of *land* that occurred through colonial appropriation. The kind of reparation, both linguistic and territorial, that the Pakeha might make is implicit in a number of Maori novels. The vision of a new synthesis of Maori and Pakeha spirituality which might thus emerge lies at the centre of the last novel to be discussed here.

Among writers who feel a particular empathy with Maori culture, perhaps the most famous (and certainly the most controversial) is **Keri Hulme**, winner of Britain's prestigious Booker Prize in 1985 with *The Bone People* (1983). Hulme's close identity with New Zealand's minority population has provoked scepticism in some circles, although never apparently among Maoris themselves.

Hulme's novel began in the mid-sixties as a short story entitled "Simon Peter's Shell", and even the final version fifteen years later retains counter-cultural elements consistent with that decade. In its present form, however, *The Bone People* has become the densely uncompromising narrative of three isolated and variously alienated individuals: Kerewen (Kere) Holmes, painter and recluse in a remote South Island location; James (Joe) Piripi Tainui, local factory worker and lonely widower; and Joe's adopted son Simon – of unknown age and origin – the sole survivor of a recent shipwreck. Kere and Joe are united by their interest in this deeply disturbed child, who has lost the ability to speak. The developing friendship is nevertheless threatened by Kere's realization that Joe, for all his loving care and patience, has been physically abusing Simon. A tragic climax is reached when Joe beats Simon so badly that the child is taken into hospital, whilst the adoptive father loses custody and is sentenced to a month's imprisonment.

In the fourth and final section of the novel, each of the three characters undergoes a period of physical and emotional purgatory leading to spiritual renewal: Joe, on release from prison, breaks an arm in the outback and is cured by an old Maori *kaumatua* (or wise man); Simon makes a virtual recovery from his injuries, resists every attempt at placement with foster-parents, and only wishes to return to Joe and Kere; Kere herself survives a severe illness (possibly stomach cancer) on little more than alternative medicine and personal determination. At the end of the novel, the three are reunited.

The Bone People may be read as thinly disguised autobiography: the name of the protagonist and the setting of Moerangi (a thinly disguised version of Hulme's native Moeraki) are fairly explicit. More significant however is the novel's allegorical dimension, as it emerges from a glance at the other two main characters: Joe (with a single *Pakeha* grandparent), a Maori forced to assimilate to European culture; and young Simon, the European castaway of apparently Irish origin, who has learned to understand Maori through his adoptive father. The voluntary adherent to Maori culture, the enforced assimilator to Pakeha culture, and the symbolic survivor of the "Old World" are united in a new solidarity for which Kere, the narrator–protagonist, is guarantor and catalyst. Such bold symbolism is underwritten by Hulme's uncompromising attitude to language. The novel contains words, phrases, and even short dialogues in Maori – amounting to several hundred linguistic items – translated in an appendix on a page-to-page basis rather than in alphabetical order. Since each word is normally only translated once, moreover, certain demands are placed (presumably quite intentionally) on the energy and good will of the Pakeha reader.

In a recent interview, Hulme unwittingly echoes a concern common to many writers of the old "settler colonies", from Kroetsch and Wiebe to Malouf and Brink: that of expressing a new landscape in an old language. *The Bone People* is characterized by occasional opacity and by the sometimes excruciating self-consciousness of its author–narrator–protagonist; it nevertheless remains a powerfully original study of land and language, seen as metonyms for physical and cultural identity.

NOTES

1. *Interviews with Writers of the Post-Colonial World*, p. 231.

FURTHER READING

The Penguin New Literary History of Australia (Ringwood: Penguin, 1988), edited by L. Hergenhan, contains specialist essays by various scholars. Ken Goodwin's *A History of Australian Literature* (Macmillan, 1986) is a lucid survey by a single hand. An interesting thematic study, in the light of arguments advanced in this section, is G. A. Wilkes's *The Stockyard and the Croquet Lawn* (Melbourne: Arnold, 1981).

Ray Willbanks's *Australian Voices* (Austin: University of Texas, 1991) is an excellent set of interviews with 16 major Australian novelists; it supplements Candida Baker's *Yacker: Australian Writers Talk about their Work*, 3 vols (Sydney: Pan Books, 1986, 1987 and 1989).

For New Zealand fiction, the obvious guides are Patrick Evans's (sometimes idiosyncratic) *Penguin History of New Zealand Literature* and *The Oxford History of New Zealand Literature in English*, edited by Terry Sturm (Auckland, 1991).

Elizabeth Alley and Mark Williams's *In the Same Room: Conversations with New Zealand Writers* (1988) and Williams's own *Six Contemporary New Zealand Novelists* (1990) – both published by the University of Auckland Press – also contain interviews with Maori writers.

Two good collections on relevant linguistic issues are *Language in Australia* (Cambridge: Cambridge University Press, 1991), edited by Suzanne Romaine, and *Dirty Silence: Aspects of Language and Literature in New Zealand* (Auckland: Oxford University Press, 1991), edited by Graham McGregor and Mark Williams. Linguistic issues also emerge frequently in the excellent set of essays edited by Werner Senn and Giovanna Capone as *The Making of a Pluralist Australia, 1950–1990* (Bern: Peter Lang, 1992).

7

South Africa and Canada

SOUTH AFRICA

The "Other Language"

The themes of land and language have a special resonance in the case of South Africa, where a second tongue of European origins is also spoken. The qualifier "European origins" (rather than simply European) is required here because, although its major source is Dutch (of which it was long considered a mere dialect), Afrikaans is not – and never was – spoken outside Africa. Culturally if not philologically, then, it might even be considered an "African" language, rather as Afrikaners can regard themselves as the "white African tribe"; both assumptions are in fact common in Afrikaner constructions of national identity, with their emphasis on the indivisibility of the *volk* (people), *eie taal* (a language of one's own), and the *land* (the African "homeland"): all of which concepts dramatically pre-empt any dicussion of land and language restricted to comparisons with the mainstream fiction of England or the United States.

The close association of Afrikaans with almost half a century of *apartheid* (the Afrikaner National Party held uninterrupted power from 1948 to 1994) conceals a number of historical paradoxes. Contemporary Afrikaner oppression of other ethnic groups often simply mirrors earlier British treatment of Afrikaners. As regards enforced *anglicization*, moreover, the various edicts of the early British administration in South Africa (1823–1837) bear an uncanny resemblance to traditional English attitudes towards Wales; whilst renewed pressure on Afrikaans after the Anglo–Boer War (1899–1902), with a clear element of reprisal, has certain parallels with attempts to extirpate Scots Gaelic following the Jacobite rebellions. Whatever its effect on Welsh or Gaelic, however, British heavy-handedness in South Africa seems only to have strengthened Afrikaner resistance.

There is further irony in the context of linguistic origins. Afrikaans began as a vernacular tongue used by early Dutch settlers and, amongst others, their slaves (the etymological link of "vernacular" with the word "chains" is thus once again appropriate). With its Dutch base (plus various African increments), together with its role as contact language, Afrikaans could also suggest an evolution analogous to that of Plantation Creole (and its successor, Gullah, on the United States south-eastern seaboard) in relation to English. The relative dissemination and prestige of Gullah and modern Afrikaans, of course, are hardly (or perhaps not yet) comparable! Afrikaans won official recognition as an independent language in 1925, fifteen years after the creation of the Union of South Africa. Under the National Party, the language was invested with almost mystical status, although Nazi-inspired doctrines of racial and linguistic purity are particularly incongruous here, since about half of today's Afrikaans native-speakers are actually non-white. On the other hand, South Africa's great classic writer, H. C. Bosman, like one of the country's leading contemporary novelists, J. M. Coetzee, was bilingual in English and Afrikaans – but the ancestry of both men was predominantly Afrikaner. Another major modern author, André Brink, publishes regularly in both languages, although he is more unequivocally an Afrikaans-speaker by origin. As anglophone writers, then, all three might be perversely regarded as culturally diasporic authors writing in an "alien" tongue, together with Lovelace and Lamming; or even – in deference to Afrikaner mythology – as indigenous writers in the same situation as Achebe or Mudrooroo. Other more pragmatic considerations have nevertheless prevailed here.

Anglophone South African Fiction

South African fiction in English has modest beginnings. Stephen Gray, doubtless remembering F. R. Leavis, speaks of a "Little Tradition" consisting of Olive Schreiner's *The Story of an African Farm* (1883), Pauline Smith's *The Beadle* (1926), and Alan Paton's *Cry, the Beloved Country* (1948). In terms of readership, however, none of these works could match such popular South African-based colonial romances as H. Rider Haggard's *King Solomon's Mines* (1885) or John Buchan's *Prester John* (1910). To the former "Little Tradition", one might add William Plomer, noted in his day for a sympathetic treatment of miscegenation in *Turbott Wolfe* (1926); and the more technically accomplished novelist, Sarah Millin, noted in ours for her demonization of the same issue in *God's Step-Children* (1924): with regard to the latter writer, Coetzee has written perceptively of a "poetics of blood".

Personally, however, Plomer had no wish to identify himself with a South African tradition, and there is a curious disclaimer to this effect in his autobiography *Double Lives*:

> Since nobody, if a cat happens to have kittens in an oven, regards them as biscuits, I should be no more justified in pretending to be a South African than in declaring myself a Bantu.   (p. 9)

But since the author took pains to conceal his South African connections from English acquaintances, his main concern seems to have been less that of being a kitten or a biscuit, than the fact of having been born in an oven – an early case, perhaps, of cultural cringe.

The fiction of Pauline Smith, also including the short stories of *The Little Karoo* (1925), is too early for the scope of this study, although the author's representation of Afrikaner speech habits provides interesting examples of what Coetzee calls linguistic "transfer". Smith's connection with South Africa was also tenuous, however, and her *physical* transfer was early: she left the country at the age of twelve and lived mainly outside it for the next forty years. Artistically, too, her links were weak, since her friend and literary mentor for fifteen formative years was the British Edwardian novelist Arnold Bennett.

Alan Paton may well be the first unambiguously South African writer in English, although he is sometimes remembered more for his political activism than for his fiction. He may be most South African in the former role. *Cry, the Beloved Country* (1948) has been defined as a cross between *The Grapes of Wrath* and *Uncle Tom's Cabin*, whilst its author has been placed in an English Puritan tradition from Bunyan through George Eliot to Lawrence. Two other Paton novels are nevertheless South African enough in theme: *Too Late the Phalarope* (1953) revisits the miscegenation taboo, while *Ah, But Your Land Is Beautiful* (1981) depicts the early years of the country's liberal party.

Doris Lessing, who arrived in Rhodesia (now Zimbabwe) at the age of six and moved to England definitively in 1949 (publishing her first novel in the following year), is hardly a South African writer by any reckoning; she belongs, if anywhere, to the final section of transnational writers. But three other white writers of English-speaking rather than Afrikaner (or mixed) background, all unambiguously South African, began publishing in the 1950s: Cope, Jacobson and Gordimer.

Jack Cope is the author of eight novels and more than a hundred short stories, throughout which the predominant theme is the destruction of black culture in South Africa by the white man. His first full-length novel, *The Fair House*, was published in 1955, a year that also marked the fictional debut of Dan Jacobson with *The Trap*. Jacobson had recently spent two years on an Israeli *kibbutz* (1949–51) before returning briefly to South Africa (1951–4), but was by this date in England, where he has been based ever since. *The Trap* and its successor, *A Dance in the Sun* (1956), both depict life on a South African farm, whilst *The Price of Diamonds* (1957) is linked with the Kimberley diamond mines. *The Evidence of Love* (1960) returns to the theme of miscegenation, whilst *The Beginners* (1966) – the last of Jacobson's novels to be set in South Africa – is also his most autobiographical work. The more idiosyncratic later fiction includes *The Rape of Tamar* (1970), retelling an Old Testament story, *The Wonder-Worker* (1973), and *The Confessions of Joseph Baisz* (1977), set in England and a fantasy country, respectively.

Nadine Gordimer's autobiographical *Bildungsroman, The Lying Days*, was published in 1953, although her first collection of short stories, *Face to Face* (1949), had appeared four years earlier. Gordimer's early fiction has often been compared to that of Lessing, both for its study of racism and the colonial mentality, and for the effect of these phenomena on individual lives. It includes *A World for Strangers* (1958), *Occasion for Loving* (1963), and *The Late Bourgeois World* (1966). After a series of novels focusing on the Black experience in South Africa, however, the long and complex *A Guest of Honour* (1970) – set in a thinly disguised Zambia – considers the political predicament of the independent Black African states. Its successor, *The Conservationist* (1974), is a political fable hinting at loss and recovery of the land by its black population. *Burgher's Daughter* (1979) portrays a family of Afrikaner Marxists, *July's People* (1981) the story of an English-speaking family sheltered by their "houseboy" during an insurrection. *A Sport of Nature* (1987) deals with radical Black politics, *My Son's Story* (1990) with emotional relationships across races.

Widely considered Gordimer's finest work, *The Conservationist* is also the novel most sensitive to the parameters of land and language. Its protagonist, Mehring, a wealthy Johannesburg industrialist, owns a four-hundred-acre farm on the high veld, run during the week by the herdsman Jacobus, together with a group of "boys" who live permanently in the compound. Despite his material success, however, Mehring becomes increasingly isolated during the course of the narrative: his ex-wife now lives in the United States; his mistress, a fashionably radical English-speaker, flees South Africa for England; his teenage son later rejoins the mother in New York, with the express intention – to the father's disgust – of avoiding South African military service.

Mehring's concern for the farm and its environment seems in one sense genuine. In an early scene, for example, he deplores the fact that the local children have removed guinea fowl eggs to play with: his comment that they "don't understand the language" might refer quite literally to English or more figuratively to some "country code". But Gordimer consistently undermines Mehring's position, whether in the subtle juxtaposition of his mile-long willow drive with the over-crowded local township, or in the more obvious irony of his complaints about blacks with "no bloody feeling for animals". His own raptures ("What more could you ask? Four hundred acres of arable land. Perpetually-flowing water" etc., p. 160) certainly transcend mere ecological chic, and may hint at older pastoral myths among South Africa's white land-owning elite.

Unsurprisingly, in an author so closely linked with a European realist tradition, language in *The Conservationist* is recorded as meticulously as other socio-cultural elements, in all its multicultural variety. The English-speaking Mehring thus normally switches to Afrikaans ("the white man's other language") when dealing with officialdom or with his farming neighbours. The latter, in the case of the De Beers, generally defer to Mehring by speaking English, but code-switch regularly among themselves. Bismillah, the local storekeeper, and his family are Gujarati-speakers, but can manage Pidgin Afrikaans or English with their mainly black customers from the local township. Lower in the racial hierarchy, Jacobus speaks English with some difficulty, although he is still able to vary his register for an Indian or white interlocutor. The men under Jacobus can barely communicate at all outside their unspecified African language.

Even as a painstaking record of social reality in the South Africa of the seventies, *The Conservationist* would command respect. There are nevertheless enough hints that the novel can also be read as a kind of colonial allegory. The very first section thus records the discovery on Mehring's property of an unidentified dead African, later simply buried on the spot. When the current four or five-year drought is finally relieved by torrential rain, however, the corpse is uncovered, with a resulting stench that pervades the whole farm. In purely meteorological terms, the rain is produced by a cyclone from the Mozambique Channel, although a figurative reading is certainly encouraged by the fact that the Frelimo uprising in Mozambique began the year before the publication of Gordimer's novel.

Mehring meets his nemesis – in a slightly ambivalent conclusion – when he offers a lift to a coloured prostitute, and is about to be either robbed, or arrested by the vice squad. At this point, however, the narrative shifts to the re-emergence of the partly decomposed corpse on the farm, now given a decent burial in a makeshift coffin; reliable confirmation of Mehring's own death hardly seems necessary to stress Gordimer's veiled allusions to days of reckoning or the return of the repressed. In an obvious echo of the original colonial allegory, moreover, Mehring's appropriation of the land is mirrored in his exploitative attitude towards women – his former mistress, a Portuguese girl on a night flight from Europe, the teenage daughter of a friend, and now, the young woman in his car. In this context, the flight to America of Mehring's son Terry may acquire added significance. The boy's indifference to both the farm and the female sex suggests a rejection of colonial conquest and possession, whether on the land or in the bedroom.

Gordimer is unique in being a white, exclusively anglophone author who has remained in South Africa, writing (almost) always about that country, and in a classic representational mode. Neither of South Africa's other most internationally acclaimed novelists, Brink and Coetzee, meet all of these criteria.

A native-speaker of Afrikaans, **André Brink** admits to doing "more and more writing in English" from the 1980s; his transfer in 1991 from Rhodes University (where he had taught Afrikaans literature for thirty years) to the English Department of the University of Cape Town seems almost an emblematic move. An early novel from 1958 (*Die Meul Teen Die Hang*) remains untranslated, but from the 1970s Brink produced a series of novels written and published in both languages: the English titles include *Looking on Darkness* (1974), *An Instant in the Wind* (1976), *Rumours of Rain* (1978), *A Dry White Season* (1979), *A Chain of Voices* (1982), *States of Emergency* (1988), *An Act of Terror* (1991), *The First Life of Adamastor* (1993) and

On the Contrary (1993). On the basis of these, he is unchallenged in his skilful and authoritative presentation of Afrikaner history, psychology and morality.

Language in *A Dry White Season* (1979), a contemporary and (until recently) even topical novel, has both formal and thematic significance. It follows the story of history teacher Ben Du Toit, who becomes involved in the fate of the Xhosa school caretaker and his son, both detained by the South African Special Branch. Du Toit's explicit Afrikaner identity has particular significance, since white English-speaking liberals were often suspected by the *apartheid* regime of divided loyalties; the fact, therefore, that even a conventional, "apolitical", middle-class *Afrikaner* pursues private inquiries suggests the perceived excesses of the police authorities. Logically, however, the medium of the entire narrative is also Afrikaans, the native language of the white characters (at least), despite the English translation. The latter point is clear by inference (Ben teaches history at an exclusive Afrikaans school in Johannesburg), but also emerges from various narrative markers, such as forms of address ("Oom [Uncle] Ben"; "My Baas"; "Dominee" [Priest]), and other examples of speech presentation.

Land and language both, moreover, acquire a powerful figurative dimension within the novel. Ben, who at one point registers the "incomprehensible comments" of a Radio Bantu announcer, later feels a total *foreigner* to the scene on his visit to Soweto, and then feels equally "foreign" when he returns to his own middle-class home. The talk of his ambitious, and later estranged, wife comes to sound like a "different language" to him. The metaphors of land and language are also reflected in Ben's sensation, after the search of his house by the Special Branch, that this is a "frontier crossed"; whilst, with the overturning of his cosy middle-class world, it is as if he is "learning a wholly new language". In his trek to the Magaliesburg, finally, Ben now has the sense of an older Africa, where "man hasn't really taken root ... yet" and which is "still unclaimed territory". This land, in turn, may perhaps be read figuratively as the promise of a new South Africa, within reach of men and women of all races who share the protagonist's faith and integrity.

If André Brink can experience English quite literally as a stepmother tongue, then **J. M. Coetzee** (who has produced critical work but not fiction in Afrikaans) is less directly implicated in such claims.

Coetzee's combination of realism and allegory is matched by a similar duality in his roles as South African and "international" novelist. Such a divide was already clear from the first novel, *Dusklands* (1974), juxtaposing narratives of American involvement in Vietnam and an eighteenth-century Dutch expedition in Southern Africa. This was followed by *In the Heart of the Country* (1977), the monologue of an elderly Afrikaner spinster. More openly allegorical are *Waiting for the Barbarians* (1980), the portrait of a kindly magistrate on an unnamed imperial frontier; *Foe* (1986), a retelling of Defoe's *Robinson Crusoe*; and *Age of Iron* (1990), narrated by a woman dying of cancer. Coetzee's recent *The Master of Petersburg* (1994), with its powerful Dostoevskian subtext, has tenuous links with South Africa, but the earlier *Life and Times of Michael K* (1983) – widely regarded as his finest novel – is unequivocal in this respect.

The latter work, following the odyssey of its frail but indestructible protagonist in a war-torn, futuristic South Africa, is also intriguingly poised between realistic novel and fictive allegory. As Michael leaves Cape Town with his invalid mother, and later survives both his solitary existence on an abandoned farm and the rigours of a government resettlement camp, the precisely representational nature of the text is enough to suggest a realistic narrative. Coetzee has nevertheless indicated his preference for "fictitiousness" over "realism", and the novel also suggests significant reworkings of earlier texts. The fusion of realism and allegory thus creates the effect of a novel by Kafka out of *Robinson Crusoe*. It is worth recalling here, moreover, that *Foe* (1986), the post-modernist allegory more explicitly linked with Defoe, was chronologically Coetzee's following novel.

The echoes of *Robinson Crusoe* are clearest in *Michael K* when the protagonist is living on the Visagies family farm in the Karoo and begins his life as a cultivator: the farm is actually described as "one of those islands without an owner"; the figure of Michael, "a wild man all skin and bone and rags", has a Crusoe-like aspect; the well-stocked farmhouse recalls Crusoe's wreck; and both novels prominently feature a herd of goats.

Language in *Michael K* has a fairly subsidiary role, although cultural marginality is regularly suggested when Michael hears languages he does not understand. Land, on the other hand, is a far more immediate concern. In his search for a place to stay, Michael comments on the miles of silence and isolation on now abandoned farms where every inch of land is nevertheless claimed. The land, and who it might belong to, subsequently become increasingly significant issues. Michael thus describes himself as "an ant that does not know where its hole is". Such termites form an overwhelming majority, however, and – in an unambiguous indictment of South Africa's old regime – Coetzee has Michael ask:

> What if the hosts were far outnumbered by the parasites, the parasites of idleness and the other secret parasites in the army and the police force and the schools and factories and offices, the parasites of the heart? Could the parasites then still be called parasites?   (p. 159)

The logic of Michael's suggestion is counterpointed by the wry comment of Noel, the relatively enlightened camp superintendent: "We are fighting this war ... so that minorities will have a say in their destinies" – heavily ironical in its implication that *only* minorities would have that say, with the majorities perhaps interned in resettlement camps. But as the novel progresses, and Michael resists each attempt to control or contain him, he assumes a kind of mystical power in connection with the land that sustains him. In this process, he becomes a figure for all objects that resist indiscriminate incorporation into the narratives of others. And in accordance with Coetzee's double technique, Michael's position may be read both in literal/realistic and figurative/metafictional terms.

It is always stimulating to negotiate the versatility of Coetzee, who is variously described as "post-modernist", "experimental", "non-realist", "anti-realist", or "anti-illusionist" (presumably according to which novel(s) the critic knows best). In its profound meditation on South Africa (as well as its sharp interrogation of land and language), *Life and Times of Michael K* may reconcile – or even transcend – such theoretical divisions.

The best-known white South African ex-patriate writer may be **Christopher Hope**. Based in London since 1975, Hope mounted satirical attacks on the myths and mystique of Afikanerdom in a series of novels beginning with *A Separate Development* (1980). These were followed by the better-known *Kruger's Alp* (1984), *The Hottentot Room* (1986), and the novella *Black Swan* (1987). Hope's semi-autobiographical *White Boy Running* (1988) was then followed by two more satirical novels, *My Chocolate Redeemer* (1989) and *Serenity House* (1992).

Kruger's Alp is unusual for its recourse (by an anonymous narrator) to a kind of Bunyanesque dream allegory. It follows the pilgrimage of Father Theodore Blanchaille (expelled by reactionary parishioners) to the last refuge of Paul Kruger in Switzerland, and his parallel quest for the ex-president's legendary personal fortune. In the process, Blanchaille moves from his Merrievale home to South African exile and expatriate circles in London and Geneva. The allegory is consistent, as the priest searches for his "shining city on a hill", but invariably eclipsed by Hope's satire. Like Bunyan's Christian, South Africa's white minority regime asks "what shall we do to be saved", although the cynical response is usually "shoot to kill".

Hope's narrative ranges stylistically from the traditional prose satire of Smollett or Waugh to the dystopias of Swift, Wells, and Orwell. The more surrealistic episodes of the government campaigns for sterilizing blacks or increasing the white birth-rate (under the slogan of "breed or bleed") are close to the techniques of Heller; certain rapid thematic shifts between political ambivalence (in the mining magnate, Himmelfarber), government complicity (with Russia over gold), and national paranoia (Afrikaner scenarios of destruction) are reminiscent of Pynchon. And when satire fails, Hope can resort to ridicule (a regime described as "ready to die for the sacred right to segregated lavatories") or pure invective (Afrikaners seen as "a gang of wooden headed, rock-brained farmers terrified that their grandfathers might have slept with their cooks").

Like most satire, *Kruger's Alp* has the virtues and defects of topicality, now joined to the occasional notoriety of a *roman à clef*. Even without onomastic associations, the casual reader will thus recognize the "powerful dignified bearing" of the imprisoned nationalist leader Horatio Vilikaze, although suggestions of his eclipse by younger forces proved premature; the vignette of the writer Labush Labuschagne and his Eskimo wife, on the other hand, presumably represents Afrikaner poet and novelist Breyten Breytenbach. Other references will doubtless become increasingly obscure with the passing of time.

Land and language (*een land, eie taal*) are clearly fundamental elements of Afrikaner mythology, and if language is critically examined in the more realistic fiction of Gordimer and Brink, then Hope's satire tends to concentrate on the element of land. He thus targets the traditional *laager* mentality (a pre-condition of any Afrikaner homeland would be a stretch of sea, for fighting with one's back to in a last-ditch defence), or more recent paranoid tendencies (the four scenarios of destruction in a nuclear age). The novel's military manoeuvres, known graphically as the "Total

Onslaught", actually anticipate these, although the term would do equally well for Hope's own satirical barrage.

The Hottentot Room is in some ways a complement to *Kruger's Alp*. The title refers to a legendary Earl's Court club for African expatriates, run by the exotic Frau Katie, a self-confessed Zionist who had managed to thrive in Nazi Germany. Such ideological contradictions were, of course, the essence of *Kruger's Alp*, although satire is now directed chiefly at the self-indulgent nostalgia of various radical South Africans in exile, as well as at the ignorance and hypocrisy of some English sympathizers. There is more political ambivalence, too, in a kind of complicity (even Hope himself may be guilty) by which South Africans occasionally feel closer to their internal opponents than to their external supporters. It suggests the jealous possessiveness of an invalid towards his own illness, although the latter may be terminal cancer.

As the final metaphor suggests, both novels could date quickly. After recent historical events, Hope – like a number of South African authors, black and white – risks becoming a writer without a subject. Hope's first post-*apartheid* fiction, *Darkest England* (1996), thus comically inverts a historical theme by sending his African "explorer" to Britain.

CANADA

"Multi-Ethnicity"

If South Africa's ethnic and linguistic mosaic places the concept of a stepmother tongue under some strain, then the literature of Canada (the term seems more neutral than "Canadian literature") looks set to explode it entirely. It has thus been crudely suggested that Canada in recent times has less a national literary tradition than a liberal immigration policy; and the cosmopolitan range of the fiction produced in the country over the last fifty years is certainly impressive. More constructively, however, it could be argued that Canada illustrates in microcosm all four variants of the broad constellations tentatively proposed in the introduction – "our land/their language", "their land/their language", "their land/our language" and (just conceivably) "our land/our language" – at which point, the validity of what were admittedly never more than very rough distinctions is further undermined.

There are thus Canadian Native writers, from Basil Johnston to Thomas King, for whom "America" – in the broadest geographical or historical sense – is "ours", just as English is figuratively (or even quite literally) "theirs". An example of the latter category is contemporary dramatist Tomson Highway, perhaps the most celebrated case of a Native Canadian writer who literally learned English as a foreign language (after compulsory enrolment in a government residential school). There is, incidentally, a slight terminological anomaly in the case of such writers: Canadian Native (and Native American) are today's politically correct terms for yesterday's Indians; but although "Indian" is a cultural and geographical misnomer, it at least avoids defining the original inhabitants of North America in relation to two recently imposed political units. The name "Indian", after all, only suggests European ignorance rather than European cultural and political hegemony. Native North American writers (a term that should logically serve for both Canada and the United States) are therefore treated together, but in the following section.

Canadian literature has, on the other hand, also been enriched by immigrants from Asia, Africa and the Caribbean. Significant arrivals from Asia included Sri Lankan-born Michael Ondaatje, who had already spent ten years in Britain when he landed in Canada in 1962; Bengali-speaking Bharati Mukherjee, who arrived in 1966 via the United States, and eventually returned there in 1980; and Rohinton Mistry, who exchanged Bombay for Toronto in 1975. From Africa, on the other hand, came M. G. Vassanji, born in Kenya of Indian parents and raised in Tanzania, but who has been living in Canada since the 1980s. The earliest important example in the last category is Barbadian Austin Clarke, who has lived in Canada almost uninterruptedly since the mid-1950s. From neighbouring Trinidad came Harry Sonny Ladoo in 1968 and Neil Bissoondath in 1973. Some of these writers have already been mentioned elsewhere; others are left for the *extro*duction at the end of the survey. All of them have undergone a double physical exile; all (with the possible exception of Ondaatje, from Sri Lanka's traditionally English-speaking *Burgher* class) have experienced a similar linguistic exile: in brief, they might, not too fancifully, be linked with the double tags of "their land / their language" as representatives of "New Literatures" in "New Worlds".

In the four countries of the *anz/sac* group, moreover, Canada undoubtedly has the most major novelists of European background who were not technically native speakers of English. An important example here is Frederick Grove. Born Felix Greve in Germany, this novelist did not arrive in Canada until 1911, after a two-year stay in the United States. He assumed a new identity, after apparently staging a fake suicide in Europe, and also adopted a new language, his "mother tongue" having been German. Of particular interest in the new identity he constructed was the desire to pass as a Swede rather than a German, and the protagonist of his first novel is similarly a Swedish rather than a German immigrant. Grove's reputation rests on four "Western novels", or his fiction of the Canadian prairie: *Settlers of the Marsh* (1925); *Our Daily Bread* (1928); *The Yoke of Life* (1930); and *Fruits of the Earth* (1933). The first major realist in Canadian literature, Grove is also (together with Wiebe), then, the most notable example of a Canadian novelist whose mother tongue is not English, but another European language.

In the same year as Grove's *Settlers on the Marsh*, there appeared another now neglected classic of prairie realism, *Wild Geese* (republished in the same year as *The Passionate Flight*) by Norwegian-born Martha Ostenso. Unlike her compatriot, Ole Rolvaag, who continued to work in Norwegian, Ostenso only wrote in English, although it is clear from her biography that her first language was Norwegian. Canada's earliest "ethnic" writer, however, was Laura Goodman Salverson, whose Icelandic parents emigrated to Canada in 1887. Salverson only began to learn English when she started school, which – for health reasons – was at the late age of ten; her novel *The Viking Heart* (1923) was one of several she wrote about the Icelandic immigrant experience.

A. M. Klein, who emigrated from the Ukraine to Montreal with his family in 1910, represents a more recent cultural hybrid: his single novel, *The Second Scroll* (1951), is a personal response to the Holocaust, as it depicts the search for a European uncle who survived it. More directly affected by Nazi persecution was Vienna-born Henry Kreisel, who escaped to England and only arrived in Canada as an adult in 1941. Kreisel's celebrated essay "The Prairie: A State of Mind" (1968) is a remarkable attempt by an outsider to understand a Canadian landscape and a Canadian mentality. An admirer of Conrad's "mastery of English" (after his similarly late introduction to the language), Kreisel wrote two novels overshadowed by the Holocaust: *The Rich Man* (1948) and *The Betrayal* (1964).

Jewish writers born in Canada, on the other hand, include Wiseman and Richler. Adele Wiseman's two major novels, *The*

Sacrifice (1956) and *Crackpot* (1974), both deal with the immigrant experience in Winnipeg in the first half of the twentieth century. Mordecai Richler grew up in Montreal, but spent the 1950s and 1960s in London, before returning definitively to his home city in 1972. After the early apprentice novels, *The Acrobats* (1954), *Son of a Smaller Hero* (1955), and *A Choice of Enemies* (1957), he achieved fame with *The Apprenticeship of Duddy Kravitz* (1959), where the protagonist is the archetypal Montreal Jew. This was followed by satires on Canadian nationalism in *The Incomparable Atuk* (1963), and on London of the swinging sixties in *Cocksure* (1968). Richler's most ambitious novel is *St Urbain's Horseman* (1971), which – like the subsequent *Joshua Then and Now* (1980) and *Solomon Gurky was Here* (1989) – consolidates his position as the chronicler of Jewish-Canadian life. For double exile, Richler effectively substitutes double marginalization with his famous comment that "to be a Canadian and a Jew is to emerge from the ghetto twice".

The concept of the stepmother tongue is admittedly attenuated in the case of a Wiseman or a Richler, but acquires renewed centrality with Rudy Wiebe and Robert Kroetsch, both discussed in greater detail below. Wiebe was the son of Russian Mennonites, and spoke Low German until he began school; Kroetsch (like the American novelist Henry Miller) was also raised in a German-speaking environment.

The idea of an immigrant writer assumes quite different dimensions in the case of Japanese-Canadian Joy (Nozomi) Kogawa. Like other Japanese Canadians, Kogawa was interned with her family in 1942, an experience which provides the background for both her poetry and her fiction. After the publication of her first novel, *Obasan* ["Aunt"] (1981), Kogawa became increasingly involved in the "redress movement" (crowned by a historic settlement in 1988); her second novel, *Itsuka* [roughly translatable as "Someday"] (1992), describes the narrator's participation in this cause.

Some reference should be made, finally, to Canadian writers who continued to write in a European language other than English or French after emigrating to Canada. These include Josef Škvorecký (Czech), Walter Bauer (German) and George Faludy (Hungarian). Unlike the post-war immigrants from non-European countries, none of these Euro-Canadians have any obvious place in the survey outside this section, even if they also tend to undermine the implications of "*their* land / *our* language", which might otherwise seem the most appropriate blanket terms for anglophone Canadian novelists.

The major writers who best fit the latter category (one might have assumed it to be the predominant one in the Canadian context) divide most logically into two major groups: an Ontario tradition (whether metropolitan or provincial), featuring such names as Hugh MacLennan, Robertson Davies, Timothy Findley, Alice Munro and Margaret Atwood; and the prairie tradition, including Sinclair Ross, W. O. Mitchell, Margaret Laurence and Robert Kroetsch.

Hugh MacLennan was born in Glace Bay, Nova Scotia, but pursued undergraduate studies at Dalhousie University and Oxford, followed by a PhD at Princeton. In 1935 he returned to Canada and taught at Lower Canada College, finishing his career as Professor of English at McGill University in Montreal. His conservative, didactic approach – in the tradition of nineteenth-century realism – is evident in *Barometer Rising* (1941), about Canadian decolonization, *Each Man's Son* (1951), on the destructive effects of Calvinism, and *Voices in Time* (1980), a documentary history of the present from a post-nuclear holocaust future. MacLennan's most significant novel, however, may be *Two Solitudes* (1945), where the title phrase from Rilke ("love consists of this, that *two solitudes* protect, and touch, and greet each other") is used to denote the cultural divide between anglophone and francophone Canada.

Robertson Davies, born in Thamesville, Ontario, and educated at Upper Canada College, Queen's University, and Oxford, has an almost patrician colonial background. After his return to Canada in 1940, Davies's eclectic interests included the theories of Freud and Jung; his elegant formal style was nevertheless once quantified by Robert Cluett's computer analysis and labelled "the Tory Mode". Davies's writing career began with the Marchbanks trilogy in 1943, revised as *The Papers of Samuel Marchbanks* in 1985. His international reputation nevertheless rests on two fictional *tours de force*: the *Deptford Trilogy* and the *Cornish Trilogy*, including the much acclaimed *What's Bred in the Bone* (1985) – perhaps his most celebrated single work. Strong anglophile sympathies and an emphasis on the European roots of Canada's national heritage incidentally make this writer an unfashionable subject among post-colonial critics.

Davies's novels also underline the prominence of the provincial Ontario setting in much modern Canadian fiction. This factor links Davies with such an otherwise disparate figure as Alice Munro. Exclusively an author of short stories and a self-confessed "regional writer" bound to her native Ontario, Munro has seven collections to her name, including the "linked stories" in *Who Do You Think You Are?* (1978), and the quasi-novel of *Lives of Girls and Women* (1971). The domestication of Ontario – with Munro's Jubilee, Robertson Davies's Deptford, Sarah Duncan's Elgin and Stephen Leacock's Mariposa – can sometimes make the province seem a Canadian version of the quaintly named English "Home Counties" surrounding London.

More versatile than Munro is Timothy Findley, born into an affluent Toronto family, and author of two apprentice novels, *The Last of the Crazy* People (1967) and *The Butterfly Plague* (1969), before establishing his reputation with *The Wars* (1977), about a Canadian soldier's experiences in the First World War. This was followed by the historical "prose kinema" of *Famous Last Words* (1981) – the words themselves belonging to Pound's poetic "hero" Hugh Selwyn Mauberley; *Not Wanted on the Voyage* (1984), a comic rewriting of the story of the Flood; and *The Telling of Lies* (1986), built round the rise of European fascism. Findley's esoteric subjects, together with his wide-ranging experimental techniques, conspire to produce a writer with little that is specifically Canadian. Despite Findley's gifts as a novelist, however, a presumably off-the-cuff comment reveals fairly muddled views about linguistic status:

> The one thing you do write in is you definitely write in your own language and therefore that's the one definite thing you can put around me – "he writes in the English language. He thinks in that language, that is what is at his disposal when he sits down to work".[1]

Whatever his own position, Findley clearly has little idea of what the concept "your own language" might mean to Achebe, Rao, or virtually any African or Asian writer in English.

Margaret Atwood is more sensitive to such issues. Born in Ottawa and raised in Toronto, she has held a succession of academic posts at various Canadian universities, between periods of travel or longer residence in England, the United States, and Australia. The profile of a white, feminist author in a wealthy, industrialized society does not immediately encourage post-colonial paradigms applicable to, say, Erna Brodber or Miriam Tlali, whilst the issue of the stepmother tongue in Atwood's case is surely irrelevant. Her early poetry and her controversial *Survival: A Thematic Guide to Canadian Literature* nevertheless throw new light on both questions.

Atwood's fourth book of verse, *The Journals of Susanna Moodie* (Canada's nineteenth-century literary pioneer), thus describes the *land* as vast and alien, and suggests that *all* Canadians are like immigrants; her fictional Moodie also complains significantly that she lacks the *language* to describe her new environment.

Atwood's first novel, *The Edible Woman* (1969), studies the restrictions on women in a male-oriented consumer society, whilst its successor, *Surfacing* (1972), is an existential fable about spiritual renewal. Her third novel, the gothic *Lady Oracle* (1976), parodies both of its forerunners, whilst the three following novels, *Life Before Man* (1979), *Bodily Harm* (1981), and the futuristic fantasy *The Handmaid's Tale* (1985), all reveal an important feminist dimension. The childhood theme of *Cat's Eye* (1989), on the other hand, is more explicitly autobiographical.

Of these novels, it is *Surfacing* that commands a special place in Atwood's fiction for its implicit interrogation of both the *land* and *language* issues. The novel describes a trip by two young couples (David and Anna, Joe and the anonymous narrator) to the wilderness of Northern Quebec. The most emotionally involved of the group is the protagonist–heroine, who has come to search for her mysteriously vanished father, but simultaneously relives (in a series of flashbacks) much of her previous life: childhood in the wilds with her naturalist father and now dead mother, the painful break with the family, a rootless urban existence, training as a graphic artist, an affair with her professor ending in pregnacy and abortion, marriage with another man ending in divorce and lost custody of the only child.

But the novel is also a bitter attack on consumerism: its very first sentence refers to the white birches dying by the lake, and "the disease is spreading up from the south". Pollution, in turn, is as much cultural as environmental, and a gas station displays three stuffed moose, dressed in human clothes and wired to stand on their hind legs. The journey ends, on the other hand, with a glimpse of graffiti on a cliff: THÉ SALADA, BLUE MOON COTTAGES 1/2 MILE, QUÉBEC LIBRE, FUCK YOU, BUVEZ COCA COLA GLACÉ, JESUS SAVES, a "mélange of demands and languages" that encapsulates the social history of the region.

None of these components are forgotten in this tightly controlled narrative, and the protagonist's three companions are all contaminated in varying degrees. Language is the most significant element in this process, for – as the narrator remarks – "language is everything you do" (p. 123). Worst affected, perhaps, is David, reduced in moments of excitement to making the "Yuk, Yuk" sounds of Disney's Goofy, the kind of anthropomorphic *kitsch* already exemplified by the stuffed moose; in his more irritated moments, too, as when the protagonist refuses him sex, he sinks into a debased American slang: "Second-hand American was spreading over him in patches like mange or lichen" – an image that recalls the dying trees of the opening paragraph; whilst beyond the graffiti of advertisements and political slogans, finally, lies another more evocative kind of hieroglyph: the indigenous rock carvings discovered by the narrator's father.

The chief source of both environmental and cultural pollution is obvious, although the novel's virulent anti-Americanism is not reflected in dispassionate argument as much as refracted through the distorted focus of a neurotic and traumatized narrator. The attitudes of David are even more extreme, although his constant references to the "Bloody fascist pig Yanks" evoke a fantastic parody scenario of Revolution, with Nationalist guerrillas living off the land – and all from a superannuated hippie who would clearly not survive the first cold snap of a Canadian winter.

Beside this absurd figure – or the unfortunate Anna (whose main concern in the Quebec wilderness is that her lover should not see her without makeup), or even the semi-articulate Joe – the narrator appears increasingly sane. She seems close to an emblematic truth, for example, when she finds she has forgotten her childhood knowledge of plant names, or notes elsewhere that "the English words seemed imported, foreign". The true inheritors of the land are the fauna of the wilderness (birdsong marking territory is seen as a kind of "rudimentary language"), and the indigenous peoples, whose past presence is always felt. In contrast, David's culturo-linguistic slumming as he slips into his imitation "yokel dialect" is only the grossest of travesties. The heroine–protagonist later remains alone on the island, gradually regressing to a more genuine state of nature: and by the time local villagers rescue her, she has become so detached that she hears the English they speak to her as the "other language".

Surfacing, then, is the fictional (re)creation of an existential crisis rather than a measured indictment of consumerism. Behind the narrator's paranoia, however, lie disturbing truths about a powerful nation that had squandered its chances and "turned against the gods". Its subsequent fall is reflected in linguistic terms – both literally and figuratively – throughout the course of the novel.

According to the criteria applied in this section (which in no sense denote a value judgement) and the chosen trope of the step-mother tongue, the Ontario novelists – even when they are as sub-stantial as MacLennan and Davies – are inevitably (if regrettably) marginalized; only Atwood emerges strongly from this group. Writers in the prairie tradition, on the other hand, may be geo-graphically more provincial but are clearly more thematically central in terms of land and language.

Canadian regional novelists include a small but significant group linked with British Columbia, although the term is more obviously associated with writers from the prairie provinces. Ethel Wilson, born in Port Elizabeth, South Africa, moved to England at the age of two, and to Vancouver at the turn of the century. She insists that her locale "has to be" British Columbia, and this is the setting of *Hetty Dorval* (1947), *The Innocent Traveller* (1949), *Love and Salt Water* (1956) and her most acclaimed work, *Swamp Angel* (1954). British Columbia is also the backdrop for the fiction of Jack Hodgins. Born to a family of loggers on Vancouver Island, Hodgins thus repre-sents quite literally the Far (or "Farthest") West of Canada. He has published two collections of short stories, *Spit Delaney's Island* (1976) and *The Barclay Family Theatre* (1981), as well as the novels *The Invention of the World* (1977), *The Resurrection of Joseph Bourne* (1979), *The Honorary Patron* (1987), and *Innocent Cities* (1990). Another native of British Columbia is Sheila Watson, whose much acclaimed experimental and "anti-regional" novella, *The Double Hook* (1959), was nevertheless inspired by two years in a remote area of the province.

The major impetus of the Canadian regional novel nevertheless comes from the prairies. After Frederick Grove, an acknowledged pioneer of the prairie school is Sinclair Ross, who was born in Saskatchewan, and worked for the Union Bank of Canada in various small prairie towns, before moving to Winnipeg. He is better known as a short-story writer, although his 1941 novel *As for Me and My House* is a minor classic of "prairie realism". Other novels in the same genre are *The Well* (1958), *Whir of Gold* (1970), and *Sawbones Memorial* (1974).

W. O. Mitchell, another native of Saskatchewan, was an early example of the writer in residence at several Canadian universities. His first novels, *Who Has Seen the Wind* (1947) and *Jake and the Kid* (1961), brought national recognition as a chronicler of small-town prairie life. These were followed by *The Kite* (1962) and *The*

Vanishing Point (1973), the latter directly concerned with the treatment of Western Canada's native peoples. More recently still, *Since
Daisy Creek* (1984) and *Ladybug, Ladybug* (1988) are, respectively,
comic and more serious treatments of university life.

The Vanishing Point depicts the experiences of Carlyle Sinclair as
teacher (later, government agent) on the Stony Indian Reserve in
the ironically named Paradise Valley, Saskatchewan. The initial
impetus of the narrative is provided by Sinclair's search for Victoria
Rider, his most promising ex-pupil, who has disappeared while
working as a trainee nurse in the city general hospital. Mitchell
then satirizes the attempts of various government officials to "civi-
lize" the Stony: the ludicrous Rev. G. Bob Dingle has incongruously
taught his flock several hymns in Cree, and learned in turn what he
assumes to be the Stony word for *thankyou* (although the phrase actually means *bullshit*); Regional Director for Indian Affairs Ian Fyfe
has given the Stony the Fyfe Minimal Subsistence cooky, a granite-
like oatmeal substance that would have been uneatable even in the
director's native Scotland. Fyfe is, incidentally, the proud owner (in
Regina, Saskatchewan!) of a conservatory of orchids, which he
force-breeds in a rigorously controlled environment, an activity
that provokes a significant exchange with the visiting Sinclair:

> "You're trying to – for something that hasn't got anything to do
> with what the orchid wants."
> "Orchid wants ..."
> "Impertinent."
> "To what?"

(p. 89)

As an allegory of government intervention in Indian affairs, the
passage hardly needs further comment.

For all his good intentions, moreover, Sinclair also remains an intruder on Stony land; or as he himself admits, "After all these years
he was still outlander to this valley" (p. 13). The more general en-
croachment on a pristine rural environment obviously lacks even
the saving grace of good intentions. On his drive into Regina,
Sinclair notes, among the hamburger and root beer stands, only the
offers to exterminate, excavate, level or crush in the process of
urban expansion. It is worth noting that *The Vanishing Point* was
published the year after Atwood's *Surfacing* (1972), with which it
shares a number of ecological concerns.

The narrative is even more explicit on issues of language. The children in Paradise Valley regularly refuse to speak English, whilst Sinclair cannot contemplate learning Stony. English is moreover inseparable from the teachings of Christianity. The variant of Mary carrying Jesus in a moss-packed *yo-kay-bo* as they flee the Bethlehem wizard (in Ezra Powderface's redaction) admittedly has a certain charm; but the propagation of Christian dogma inevitably entails the rejection of Stony cosmogony and the demonization of their gods. Language (culture) thus joins land (livelihood) in Powderface's subsequent stocktaking of what has been lost:

> Before white people come to this country Indian had a good livin' – never hungry for himself – for his horse. Been huntin' in the fall – put up for dry meat and put up for dry berries too. We lost all that now; we lost the Indian good life. Those days we had buffalo-hide wigwam that was wind-proof – cold-proof. Now we haven't. The Indian child get sick out of it. There is why my people suffer in their heart.   (pp. 408–9)

The "vanishing point" of the title refers initially to the line where earth and sky meet, or to lessons in perspective from Sinclair's school art class. The phrase later becomes a *leitmotiv* in the narrative, however, suggesting the demographic threat hanging over all of Canada's first peoples.

In this dimension, *The Vanishing Point* falls short of another (historical) contact narrative from the same year, Peter Such's *Riverrun* (1973). More lyrically but less conventionally, Such depicts the literal extinction of the Beothuk Indians of Newfoundland at the beginning of the nineteenth century. *The Vanishing Point* ends with an image of hope, as Rod Wildman finally retrieves his broken-down truck from the river. Satire and humour apart, however, it is not an encouraging tale.

Margaret Laurence is an anomalous figure in Canadian literature, since much of her adult life was spent outside Canada. Born in the small prairie town of Neepawa, Manitoba, she spent two years in what is now Somalia, five more in the Gold Coast (now Ghana), and almost twenty in England, before returning definitively to Canada in 1974. Her fiction reflects this cosmopolitan existence. Somalia inspired the short story "Uncertain Flowering", an anthology of oral literature, and a chronicle of the Somali years entitled *The Prophet's Camel Bell* (1963); Ghana generated *This Side Jordan* (1960), a novel set against Ghana's independence movement, and *The Tomorrow-Tamer* (1963), a collection of stories set in the same country. Laurence's greatest achievement, however, is her so-called "Manawaka" sequence, *The Stone Angel* (1964), *A Jest of God* (1966), *The Fire-Dwellers* (1969) and *The Diviners* (1974), all set in a fictional version of her native Neepawa. Laurence may thus, in theory, be regarded as either an expatriate novelist or a Canadian regionalist. In a study of Nigerian writers (*Long Drums and Cannons*, 1968), however, she notes that successful writing may "sometimes reach out beyond any national boundary", and Laurence – more than most native-born Canadian authors – may justly claim to have done this.

Together with Robert Kroetsch, Laurence is also the Canadian writer most sensitive to extrinsic linguistic issues. Kroetsch's characterization of English as a "mandarin language" unfitted to express the Canadian West has already been quoted. Critic Lee Spinks has commented on the rupture between place and language in Kroetsch's fiction, echoing the novelist's own reference (in the context of the Canadian prairie) to "a pattern of naming that doesn't quite fit". In Kroetsch's more speculative moments, moreover, the language is no more "ours" than the land:

> The Canadian writer's particular predicament is that he works with a language, within a literature, that appears to be authentically his own, and not a borrowing. But just as there was in the Latin word a concealed Greek experience, so there is in the Canadian word a concealed other experience, sometimes British, sometimes American.[2]

Where Kroetsch sees linguistic inadequacy, however, Laurence is more concerned by cultural hegemony. Her perspective was clearly broadened by her years in Africa, for she also regards Canadians – artistically at least – as Third World Writers:

> Canadian writers, like African writers have had to find our own voices and write out of what is truly ours, in the face of an overwhelming cultural imperialism.[3]

For Kroetsch and even Laurence, then, an unreconstructed English language could seem as much the colonial language as the prairies are Native Canadian land. Laurence, incidentally, claims to have addressed the theme of possession in her Manawaka novels through the Tonnerre family, descendants of the Métis "who were once the prairie horselords and were gradually dispossessed of the lands which they and their Indian brothers had lived on" (p. 259).

The unrivalled master in English–Canadian reconstructions of Canadian dispossessions and Canada's dispossessed is nevertheless **Rudy Wiebe**. Born in Fairholme, Saskatchewan, Wiebe grew up in the local Mennonite community of Speedwell-Jackpine. Wiebe's parents were German-speaking Russians who had emigrated to Canada in the 1930s; the novelist's first language was (Low) German and his English was learned in a one-room school in Fairholme, and later at the Mennonite High School in Coaldale, Alberta. Besides having a degree in English from the University of Alberta, Wiebe is also a Bachelor of Theology from a Mennonite Bible College, and his religious faith has an important role in his fiction.

Wiebe's first novel, *Peace Shall Destroy Many* (1962), reflects the moral qualms of the pacifist Mennonites during the Second World War, whilst the documentary fiction *First and Vital Candle* (1966) stems from a visit to a Mennonite community in Paraguay. The epic-like *The Blue Mountains of China* (1970) deals with Mennonites throughout the world, but Wiebe's two major novels are both concerned with other Canadian minorities past and present: *The Temptations of Big Bear* (1973) depicts the Plains Cree Indians at the end of the nineteenth century, while *The Scorched-Wood People* portrays radical leader Louis Riel and the Métis revolt of 1869 to 1885.

The Temptations of Big Bear is a reconstruction of events (from 1876 to 1885) surrounding the implementation of a government treaty, the protagonist being a Plains Cree chief who has refused to sign. Big Bear continues to remain the focal point of the narrative after the outbreak of violence in 1885, in which young Crees kill settlers at Frog Lake, before the whole band escapes, ineffectively pursued by the Mounted Police and Canadian Army Volunteers. The non-violent Big Bear is later found guilty of association with the murderers, and sentenced to three years in the Manitoba penitentiary.

Wiebe's novel is a complex montage of chronicle, journal, commentary, and court transcripts, all confirming the irreconcilable differences between Cree and "Whiteskin" culture. These discrepancies are nowhere clearer than in the final courtroom scenes, the absurdity and irrelevance of which are long anticipated. John McDougall, a Methodist missionary who has spent a lifetime among "the People" and speaks their language fluently, dramatically exposes the ethnocentric Lieutenant-Governor of the territory:

> Has he ever tried to swallow buffalo liver steaming from the carcass, and sprinkled with gall for taste? Has he ever tried to translate a single word into another language? What would he do with "treason", with "the Queen, her crown, and dignity" among a people who have no concept of state and even if they had could not imagine a woman having state dignity, much less a crown, whatever that might be?   (pp. 35–6)

Ironically enough, "treason-felony" is precisely the charge later brought against Big Bear.

The pitfalls of "translation" in various senses are in fact a common theme of the novel, given the recurrent communication barrier between English and Cree speakers. Language is more than mere vocabulary or syntax, however, and Gabriel Dumont, head chief of the mixed-race Métis, understands the power of discourse and the importance of negotiating with Government in their own language, in every sense of the term: "I talk Cree and Blackfoot and Sioux and French, but not white. You have to talk white or it helps nothing" (p. 103). Big Bear, on the other hand, is more wary about the risks of assimilation and comments shrewdly that "it is always dangerous to talk like whites. Soon one might begin to think like them" (p. 120).

The poverty of any white man's translation beside the original is well expressed by a settler's daughter listening to Big Bear's court-room speech: "it is wind rubbing willow branches on a winter night where his voice is the sun now, all golden" (p. 266). But Amelia's comment also highlights another form of "translation"; that between oral and written cultures: to Big Bear, total master of public speaking and a product of oral culture, the authorities are obtuse enough to dispatch *letters*. Asked by a sympathetic Governor Dewdney if he reads the system of Cree syllabics that will help preserve their spoken words, Big Bear replies bluntly that he has abandoned a system monopolized by the missionaries, but will in any case "keep hearing every good word said" (p. 138).

Wiebe clearly feels that a speaker's conceptualization of the world is conditioned by the language he or she speaks, and the novel's more intelligent white administrators obviously share this view. Ultimately, of course, "translation" has an *extrinsic*, as well as an *intrinsic*, dimension in *The Temptations of Big Bear*: for Wiebe – wherever his cultural sympathies lie – has only English, the language of the conqueror and the destroyer, with which to portray a vanished way of life. In this context, however, the consistently skilful "defamiliarization" of white culture (in the manner of such pioneering African novelists as Achebe or Ngũgĩ) adds yet another dimension to what is already a remarkable novel.

The last prairie novelist to demand special attention is **Robert Kroetsch**. Born in Heisler, Alberta, Kroetsch graduated from the University of Alberta in 1948 and worked for six years in the Canadian North-West. His first novel, *But We Are Exiles* (1965), based on working experience on the Mackenzie River, was followed by an Albertan or "Outwest tryptich" consisting of *The Words of My Roaring* (1966), *The Studhorse Man* (1969), and *Gone Indian* (1973). All three novels mythologize Kroetsch's native Alberta in an ironically post-modernist mode. Both *Badlands* (1975) and *Alibi* (1983), on the other hand, are essentially novels based on earlier fictive narratives, and thus emphasize the processes of recuperation and interpretation. Kroetsch's much acclaimed *What the Crow Said* (1978), finally, is a magic–realist version of a mythical place on the border between Alberta and Saskatchewan.

For an author who has offered fine insights into the process of "writing" a new land with an old language, however, Kroestch's novels are not always as receptive as one might expect to the trope of the stepmother tongue. The obvious exception to this broad generalization is *Gone Indian*, although even here, it is the metafictional element that is first apparent. But the narrative is also clearly a genre parody, with a relation to the existential quest novel roughly analogous to that of Reed's *Flight to Canada* to the traditional slave narrative. "Quest" in *Gone Indian*, however, is obviously coterminous with "contact", and the narrative therefore parodies this element, too.

The easiest entry into the context of land and language in Wiebe's novel lies in the curious cultural chiasmus linking the narrator–editor, Professor Mark Madham, and his student Jeremy Sadness. Madham, who now teaches at an American university, was actually "born out there on those wind-torn prairies"; whilst Sadness, who grew up in New York, has a "romantic interest in the northern forests and buffalo plains", and eventually makes the trip to Alberta which generates the text. More significantly still, Sadness's interest in the Candadian prairies had been inspired by his childhood reading of Grey Owl, the pseudonym of the great Canadian conservationist. Although claiming mixed Apache and Scots-American descent, the historical Grey Owl had actually been born Archibald Belaney in Hastings, England, emigrating to Canada in 1905 at the age of seventeen. Here he constructed an imaginary identity for himself, centred on the North American Indian, and wrote four books on the Canadian wilderness. In *Gone Indian*, the immigration authorities are predictably unimpressed by the alleged purpose of Sadness's own trip ("I want to be Grey Owl"); whilst none of the Native Canadians he meets have even heard of the name. For Sadness, however, Grey Owl is the "truest Indian of them all"; and even for the modern reader, his life represents the classic example of cultural appropriation.

In conformity with the conventions of genre parody, of course, Sadness's experiences in Alberta are not what he had expected. Scheduled for a job interview at the University of Alberta, he finishes instead at the 27th Annual Winter Festival in the small town of Notikeewin. His first encounter with a Native Canadian is an ice statue of an Indian on a galloping horse. More ominously, he later witnesses a sled contest, in which the Cree Indian in the lead discreetly throws the race over the final metres. Sadness, on the other hand, wins a long snow-shoe race through manic determination (although he has never worn snow-shoes before), but loses his jacket in the process.

If this could represent a parodic appropriation of the land (twelve miles of it in fact), then the hero's induction into Native Canadian language and culture is hardly less absurd. In his own version of "going Indian", Sadness wears beaded moosehide moccasins, a fringed buckskin jacket and two long braids, prompting an Indian child to whisper to its mother, "Why is his hair that way?" Among the less discriminating clientele of a Notikeewin bar, on the other hand, he passes easily enough ("You fucking Indian") by proffering a few Italian obscenities. This particular occasion predictably ends in a fight, and Sadness is thrown out of the bar, to be rescued by a Cree family. Symbolically, he is provided with a new jacket, although it is ironically one they have long discarded. Sadness's subsequent progress may be read as a mock allegory of assimilation, climaxing in his powerful vision of the returning buffalo, and ending with his disappearance into the Canadian wilderness, much in the manner of his hero, Grey Owl. As a playful interrogation of its master narrative, then, *Gone Indian* – as already suggested – anticipates *Flight to Canada*; like Reed's novel, moreover, it is an appropriate example with which to conclude the section.

After mainstream writing in England and the United States, English-Canadian literature is the oldest and most established anglophone tradition; the process of institutionalization which this implies is perfectly illustrated by the massive three-volume *Literary History of Canada* (2nd edition) assembled by Carl Klinck. Critics and scholars now refer routinely to the "Pre-Confederation Novel" or the "Novel in the New Dominion" – the dividing line being the British North America Act, giving Canada independence in 1867. The first English-Canadian novel is normally considered to be *The History of Emily Montague* (1769) by Frances Brooke, on the basis of the author's six-year stay in Quebec with her clergyman husband in the 1760s; though her novel seems no more (or less) central to Canadian fiction than Leonard Woolf's *The Village in the Jungle* (1913) is to the literature of Sri Lanka. The chief (and perhaps only) claim to fame of both books is that of primacy.

The first genuinely Canadian novel was Julia Catherine Hart's *St Ursula's Convent* (1824); less demands are made on the modern reader, however, in John Richardson's military romance *Wacousta* (1832), or the novels of pioneer chronicler Susanna Moodie. And humourist Thomas Haliburton's *The Clockmaker* (1836, 1838 and 1840) even created, in Sam Slick, Canadian literature's first great comic character; if not as vernacular as *Huckleberry Finn*, Haliburton's sketches are certainly more demotic than Leacock's. It is hardly surprising, then, that editor and publisher Graeme Mercer Adam could complain as early as 1884 of the recent dearth in Canadian literature: "while our great writers are passing away there are few, especially among the masters of fiction ... to fill with acceptance their vacant places"; such a lament at least presupposes an earlier abundance. Adam must have been partly appeased by the fiction of Sara Jeannette Duncan, two of whose eighteen novels – *The Imperialist* (1904) and *Cousin Cinderella* (1908) – have Canadian settings.

The point of this brief excursus should be obvious. The search for an authentic national identity began earlier in Canada than in any other *anz/sac* country; and – in terms of the multi-ethnicity implied by the currently popular *mosaic* trope – might be thought to have come correspondingly further. Canada's literary tradition, and the emerging sense of nationhood to which it is linked, are not incalculably younger than those of the United States; and if the mainstream literary tradition of the United States can be expressed (like that of England) in terms of "our" land / "our" language, then Canada can lay some claim for similar treatment. The stepmother tongue is a rough, even a makeshift, concept, but certainly never a static one; the anglophone writers to whom it might be applied move (if they have not already moved) towards eventual rejection or full naturalization; the step in the latter direction has been taken (or in another sense, perhaps, the *step-* has been taken away) by several generations of modern Canadian novelists. Mother and stepmother are once again indistinguishable.

The Canadian mosaic then, as prevalent in the country's fiction as in its society at large, variously suggests affinities for the country's writers with any of the four combinations of land and language sometimes adopted in this survey. Such a broad overview nevertheless risks numerous omissions, and two of the most obvious in the present Canadian context are Morley Callaghan and Mavis Gallant. But the latter are precisely Canada's most cosmopolitan writers (if of the "outgoing" rather than the "incoming" school); they are therefore discussed with other transnational authors, thus finally confirming the Canadian presence in every category of this survey.

NOTES

1. *World Literature Written in English*, ed. Douglas Daymond and Leslie Monkman (Ottawa: Borealis Press, 1981) vol. 26, p. 112.
2. *Canadian Novelists and the Novel*, p. 239.
3. Ibid., p. 253.

FURTHER READING

The indispensable guide to South African fiction is Michael Chapman's *Southern African Literatures* (Longman, 1996). Chapman has also edited (with C. Gardner and Esk'ia Mphahlele) the comprehensive *Perspectives on South African Literature* (Johannesburg, 1992). A seminal study of various South African writers included in this section is J. M. Coetzee's *White Writing: On the Culture of Letters in South Africa* (New Haven: Yale University Press, 1988).

Since South Africa probably has the least familiar literary tradition of the four *anz/sac* countries, two short prose anthologies – *A Land Apart* (Faber and Faber, 1990), edited by André Brink and John Coetzee, and *Writing for South Africa* (Cambridge University Press, 1995), edited by Anthony Adams and Ken Durham – are worth attention.

Apart from the definitive *Literary History of Canada*, 3 vols, 2nd edn (Toronto, 1976) and vol. 4, edited by W. H. New (forthcoming), there are two useful and easily available literary histories: W. J. Keith's more traditional *Canadian Literature in English* (Longman, 1985) and W. H. New's chronological but thematically structured *A History of Canadian Literature* (Macmillan, 1989). *Survival* (Toronto: Anansi, 1972), Margaret Atwood's highly personal thematic guide to Canadian literature, is a rare example of a bestseller in its genre; more mainstream in approach is John Moss's *A Reader's Guide to the Canadian Novel* (Toronto: MacClelland and Stewart, 1987).

There is generous coverage of Canadian fiction in the *Dictionary of Literary Biography*, vols 53 and 60 (Detroit: Gale Research, 1986, 1987) for Canadian writers since 1960; and vols 68 and 88 (1988, 1989) for Canadian writers from 1920 to 1959. All four volumes, combining anglophone and francophone authors, are edited by W. H. New.

Graeme Gibson's *Eleven Canadian Novelists* (Toronto: Anansi Press, 1973) is a suggestive, if now slightly dated, series of interviews. More recent is the collection *Canadian Novelists and the Novel* (Ottawa: Borealis Press, 1981), edited by Douglas Daymond and Leslie Monkman.

Terry Goldie's provocative *Fear and Loathing: The Image of the Indigene in Canadian, Australian and New Zealand Literature* (Montreal: McGill Queens University Press, 1989) is an important thematic study for both sections of Part III.

Part IV
Old Literatures in Old Worlds

Introduction

The notion of a *stepmother* tongue does not seem applicable to mainstream or metropolitan British fiction, where authors write in what – by any definition of the term – is surely their *mother* tongue. Such assumptions are not unassailable, however, and it is striking how liable the two terms are to contention or erosion. As suggested previously, the incongruously named "King's (or Queen's) English" cannot really have been as self-evident a concept to diglossic provincial authors like Thomas Hardy or D. H. Lawrence as it was for an upper-class Londoner like Virginia Woolf.

In the context of American fiction, the terminological issue assumes other dimensions. Outside Black Vernacular and certain varieties of "tidewater English" off the south-east coast, the number and range of varieties of spoken English in the United States has never been as great as that in the British Isles. The gap between the spoken and written language is therefore typically less for American writers than for some of their British counterparts. This distance was further reduced with the demotic tradition pioneered by Mark Twain. Through the miracle of cultural assimilation which *is* the United States, moreover, nothing might apparently seem more "mainstream" anglophone American than novelists such as Steinbeck, Dreiser, or Vonnegut. And yet, the very names are of course chosen to emphasize a German cultural heritage variously repressed or long absorbed. There is surely no great cultural distance between these three writers and the Canadians Kroetsch and Wiebe, who actually grew up in German-speaking environments, as did the American Henry Miller, although the latter's surname belies the fact. Scratch an American writer, then, and such concepts as "mainstream" or "mother tongue" often become increasingly vague or suspect.

So widespread is the existence of these cultural (and often linguistic) sub-strata amongst anglophone writers, in fact, that even a quintessentially English middle-brow writer like Iris Murdoch can point to an Anglo-Irish background, and claim to feel an exile in Britain. Current suggestions that the marginal has become central, in the sense of normative, while the centre has been marginalized are indeed far more than post-colonial rhetoric. In the present classification, then, it may be wise to recall the original plea of simple expediency: the exclusion of the mainstream British and American traditions has the useful corollary of allowing greater space for other anglophone literatures.

The differences between the British and American traditions may be more obvious than the similarities. The latter, as some critics have suggested, is effectively the first post-colonial literature in English. Time scales apart, it thus has many analogies with the writing of other initially white settler colonies – Australia immediately springs to mind. There is, however, an equally clear analogy with England. For if one allows that the achievements of late twentieth-century American narrative overshadow those of their (native) English counterparts, then one will also recognize the extraordinary progress made since the modest beginnings of Captain John Smith's *A True Relation* (1608) or the *Bay Psalm Book*, almost four centuries ago. But if one then applies a similar perspective to the literature of England and returns to four centuries before the Elizabethan drama (perhaps the one genre and period in anglophone literature as rich and varied as modern American fiction), one is back among the crudities of Layamon's *Brut* and the tedium of English metrical romances. Or one might argue alternatively that all written literatures are post-colonial impositions, but that a point arrives at which a tradition may quite simply and pragmatically be regarded as indigenous. The American one, like its British counterpoint, has surely long reached this stage.

There are, nevertheless, three other more concrete (or less fanciful) parallels to be drawn between the two traditions. First, British and Euro-American fiction each have a major writer of East European origin who has a particular relevance in the context of the stepmother tongue: the Pole Joseph Conrad, and the Russian Vladimir Nabokov. Conrad claimed that on first arriving in England at the age of twenty-three, he knew no English; and because of his early adult years spent in France, the language may never have been more than his third *spoken* tongue, after French and his native Polish. Of Conrad's well-known, quasi-mystical affinity with *written* English ("the merest idea of choice had never entered my head … it was I who was adopted by the genius of the language", etc.), little more need be said. Conrad's assimilation to his new country was swift and thorough, however, and it might seem that he could hardly transform "their" language into "ours" quickly enough, although scholars have found considerable interference from both French and Polish in his writing. Conrad's son, on the other hand, was apparently unable to speak a word of his father's native tongue.

Nabokov, in contrast, is perhaps more genuinely cosmopolitan. After graduating from Trinity College, Cambridge, in Modern Languages, he published nine novels in Russian while living in Berlin and Paris in the 1920s and 1930s (and even wrote briefly in German), before producing his first book in English, *The Real Life of Sebastian Knight (1941)*. Towards the end of his life, moreover, he worked on a *Russian* translation of his most controversial novel, *Lolita* (1955), begun – he claimed – to forestall the problems of future translators. If English remained the stepmother tongue, then, Nabokov paradoxically developed a purely pragmatic mastery of the language that eluded Conrad. This psychologically ambivalent (if more technically assured) relation to English may also reflect the greater social flexibility and cultural hybridity of American society itself, at least in comparison with Edwardian Britain.

Nabokov's background is undoubtedly less extraordinary in an American context than Conrad's in a British one. The United States has at least one other writer of Nabokov's stature and with comparable East European origins: Nobel laureate Isaac Bashevis Singer, who continued all his life to write in his native Yiddish. There may be a small emblematic point in the fact that the next British Nobel Prize winner, William Golding, spent most of his working life teaching at a boys' grammar school in Salisbury. His knowledge of other *living* languages besides English was presumably limited to schoolboy French. The rough hypothetical equivalent of a Singer in insular Britain then – say, a Kipling who wrote only in Hindustani – barely falls within the bounds of fantasy.

A second interesting analogy between British and American fiction is the strong multi-cultural dimension. In Britain, scholars currently refer to Black British writing, whether authors are of African, Caribbean or Asian origin. The category could include Ben Okri (Nigeria), Caryl Phillips (St Kitts) and Hanif Kureishi (Pakistan), the examples chosen to reflect ascending strength in cultural links with Britain. Okri would thus also be widely regarded as a Nigerian writer; Phillips, who left St Kitts at the age of one but maintains close links with the island, uses both Caribbean and British settings; Kureishi is British-born, and his first two novels are classic studies of ethnic Asians in their adoptive country. Critics sometimes quote the protagonist's comment in Kureishi's *The Buddha of Suburbia* about being British from tip to toe ("almost"), whilst forgetting the function of this remark as fictional characteriz-ation. *In propria persona*, Kureishi largely discounts the issue of assimilation, regarding it as the problem of his father's generation rather than his own. But if talented Black British writers assimilate, then the British literary establishment is more than happy to appropriate.

Such cultural tendencies are even stronger in the United States, where African American literature is naturally regarded as indige-nous, and the new multiculturalism therefore emphasizes anglo-phone writers of Chinese, Japanese, Filipino, and South Asian origin. The indispensable source book in this context is King-Kok Cheung and Stan Yogi's comprehensive *Asian American Literature: An Annotated Bibliography* (1988), a work commissioned by the Modern Language Association of America. The reader's only mis-giving here might be the proprietorial attitude with which so many writers are surprisingly classified as "hyphenated Americans". Most of the major Filipino writers in English – N. V. M. Gonzalez, Jessica Hagedorn, Bienvenido Santos and Linda Ty-Casper – are thus included in the Filipino American section of the bibliography. Even Samuel Selvon, who presumably just felt – quite reasonably – that Canada would provide a more hospitable home for his last years than Thatcherite Britain, appears as an Indian American author! Not literally a "hyphenated American", of course, since the Modern Language Association (in the interests of political correct-ness) has abolished the use of the hyphen in these contexts. In view of its cultural appropriation of such writers as Selvon and Santos, however, this move may only illustrate that august body's capacity to swallow a camel but strain at a gnat. The Samoan-New Zealander(!) Albert Wendt noted in his anthology *Nuamua: Pacific Writing in English Since 1980*: "Today some writing considered by Pakeha/Papalagi writers to be post-colonial, we consider colonial" (p. 2). The same might be said of some Anglo-American criticism and theory.

The third and final analogy between mainstream British and American literature concerns the presence in the respective coun-tries of other cultural traditions contemporary with, and sometimes even pre-dating, the mainstream anglophone ones. In the British Isles, this refers primarily to Scotland, Wales and Ireland; in America, to Native Americans and people of Hispanic origin. It is these groups that occupy the remainder of the present section, although it should be stressed that no comprehensive coverage is claimed. Even more than in previous sections, the texts chosen are purely representative.

8

The British Isles

WELSH FICTION

Knowledge of writing from Wales among anglophone readers is normally even sketchier than that from Scotland or Ireland. Many a critic well versed in the subtleties of post-colonial theory would be hard pushed to name a contemporary Welsh novelist writing in *either* of that country's languages. It is a regrettable situation, particularly when Welsh even makes a useful adjectival distinction (unavailable to English) between *Cymreig* (of Wales, the country) and *Cymraeg* (of the Welsh language). The Welsh Academy (*Yr Academi Gymreig*), founded in 1959, recognizes Welsh authors writing in English, even if the latter receive little public or official recognition in England. The term "Anglo-Welsh literature" (current since the 1920s) is, on the other hand, controversial among both English- and Welsh-language writers, who object to the kind of cultural hybridity it implies. But since the prefix "anglo-" has a strictly linguistic rather than a broader cultural emphasis in the present study, it is tentatively retained.

There is, unfortunately, a rather more banal issue that should also be raised at the outset. Most honest readers outside Wales will admit to occasional confusion (even hilarity) over the relatively small number of Welsh surnames, a point that can hardly have improved the already poor reception given to Welsh writers. The surname phenomenon, of course, merely commemorates one of the cruder English interventions in Welsh affairs: the Act of Union in 1536 stipulated that the language of law and administration in Wales should be exclusively English. Welsh names, based on the patronymic system, were summarily anglicized – with many a Siôn *ap Dafydd* (son of David) becoming a John Davies – on the first (colonial) encounter with English bureaucracy.

The Welsh language, virtually banned by the Act of Union then, remained a point of contention ever after. Matters reached a head with the notorious "Welsh Not", a device widely used in the eighteenth and nineteenth centuries to discourage children from speaking their native language. The object in question was a piece of wood or slate bearing the letters W. N. (Welsh Not), hung round the neck of the last child heard speaking Welsh, the pupil wearing it at the end of the school-day being punished by the teacher. The system is identical to that described by Ngũgĩ wa Thiong'o in a classic essay from *Decolonising of the Mind* (1986): in Wales, no less than in Ngũgĩ's Kenya, English could be a particularly cruel stepmother.

Wales has a substantial literature in Welsh, which still thrives, although only about a fifth of the country's population are now native speakers of the language. Meic Stephens suggests that Kate Roberts "is generally regarded as the twentieth century's most distinguished prose-writer in Welsh".[1] Few anglophone readers will be in a position to dispute this; few, sadly, will have even *heard* of Kate Roberts. Most Welsh writers, whether or not technically bilingual, have a good knowledge of Welsh and English, although remarkably few have ever *published* creative writing in both languages: Hugh MacLennan's celebrated trope of the "two solitudes", originally applied to English- and French-speaking Canada, would do equally well for Wales.

Critics often divide twentieth-century Anglo-Welsh fiction into the broad categories of industrial novel and border romance: the former, well exemplified by the massive *Black Parade* (1935) of Jack Jones – with its debt to the naturalism of Farrell and Dos Passos; the latter by critic Raymond Williams's trilogy, beginning with *Border Country* (1960). The most famous single Anglo-Welsh novel, Richard Llewellyn's *How Green Was My Valley* (1939), might be thought to combine both novel and romance in its account of an idyllic mining community (devout, innocent, and quintessentially Welsh) destroyed by an influx of English (and Irish) workers. The novel has nevertheless been criticized for lack of authenticity, and its remarkable success may have owed something to broader notions of nostalgia triggered by the outbreak of the Second World War.

Anglo-Welsh literature provides notable examples of novelists whose Welsh is learned rather than naturally acquired: John Cowper Powys, author of the historical novels *Owen Glendower* (1940) and *Porius* (1951), was English-born but emphasized his Welsh ancestors and mastered their language; the poet R. S. Thomas, another serious student of Welsh, actually published some shorter prose pieces in the language. Emyr Humphreys, perhaps the most distinguished contemporary Anglo-Welsh novelist, also studied Welsh as an adult. His sextet of so-called "Protestant novels", including *Flesh and Blood* (1974) and *Best of Friends* (1978) – for all their sensitivity to Welsh culture and speech rhythms – were none the less written in English.

There are even more comprehensive examples of linguistic re-alignment. Novelist and short-story writer Glyn Jones, born into a Welsh-speaking family but given an English-language education, records first feeling the "power of words" in English and being subsequently unable to write in Welsh. Although a self-styled "for-eigner in the language", Jones illustrates with his fine Lawrentian *Bildungsroman*, *The Valley*, *The City*, *The Village* (1956), that for him, at least, English was not too harsh a stepmother. Moving in the op-posite direction, the versatile and prolific R. M. (Bobi) Jones was raised in Cardiff, in an English-speaking home, and only began to learn Welsh as a schoolboy. His many volumes of poetry, two novels, and five collections of stories are nevertheless all written in that language.

When cross-cultural awareness is reduced to matters of mere lan-guage reproduction, however, **Caradoc Evans**'s early classic *My People* (1915) remains a seminal work. It is customary to regard these fifteen tales of Welsh village life as the beginning of the Anglo-Welsh short-story tradition, but continuities of theme, char-acter, and setting certainly justify their consideration as a single in-tegrated fiction. The savage gusto of Evans's satire, on the other hand, ensures that – for many Welsh readers anyway – it is still difficult to separate technical from ideological issues. The dialogue of *My People* is thus routinely dismissed as totally artificial. Of course it is, since Evans aims at an imaginative, rather than linguis-tically precise, presentation of *spoken Welsh*, and – with *written English* the only means available to him– could hardly have done otherwise.

The exclusively Welsh-speaking environment of *My People* is un-derlined with comic clarity in the eleventh story, "As it is Written", when Dan brings home an English wife to rural Manteg. Evans's version of village speech emerges graphically in the reception by Dan's mother of poor Alice Wite, "daughter of the English":

> Mali came down to her,
> "Our little daughter," she said, "dost her come here to take our son bach away from us now? Let her him be. Shaci will take her back to Camarthen in the old cart."

The woman whom Dan had brought home could not answer a word, because she did not know the meaning of the words Mali had spoken... .

"And tell the rat of a bitch," shouted Mali, "that Dan won't get a red penny after us."

"But, man fach," Dan broke in, "what does that matter? Is not Alice the owner of a nice shop draper?"

Mali now went to Dan, and she called him her own boy bach, and the son of his mother; and she took Dan and his maid into the parlour, and closed the door on them.

Returning to the congregation, she delivered to them this speech:

"There's good you were to come. Dan's maid, dear me, has travelled a long distance. Weary she is. Gracious now, isn't she tidy? English she may be, but has not the Big Man told us to love our enemies? Shop draper! There's wealth for you. Rhys, come you up on a night to speak to her."

(pp. 125–6)

A reader without Welsh may not be qualified to pronounce on the success of Caradoc Evans's dialogue, particularly when Welsh speakers themselves have long been divided on the issue. It is undeniable, however, that the synthesis of Biblical cadences with Welsh phonology, syntax and structures (note, for example, the third person mode of address) at least suggests meticulous attention on the author's part. Evans himself insisted that he had done something for the English representation of Welsh comparable to what Synge had achieved with the Irish of the Aran islanders; and although his intentions are satirical rather than lyrical, he deserves to be taken seriously.

IRISH FICTION

Despite appearances to the contrary, the present situation of Irish is not so remote from that of Welsh. It is thus estimated that in 1851, about a quarter of Ireland's population was Irish-speaking, a figure that would hold good for Wales and Welsh a century later. Irish is, on the other hand, in greater danger than Welsh of following Manx or Cornish to extinction as a spoken language. Novelist Colm Tóibín's lively report from Dublin, entitled "On (Not) Saying What You Mean" (*London Review of Books*, 30 November 1995), reacts scathingly to constitutional claims for Irish as "the first official language" of the country: add the word *not*, he suggests, and "you enter the real world". Critic Declan Kiberd notes in his magisterial *Inventing Ireland* that the country's constitution was drafted in English, and then translated into Irish (with the proviso that the translation should have precedence over the original in any case of linguistic ambivalence).

Kiberd's earlier *Synge and the Irish Language* (1979) is more optimistic about the potential of Irish today. Between the rich Irish-language tradition of the eighteenth century and the extraordinary flowering of Anglo-Irish writing in the twentieth, Kiberd sees a traumatic interlude when – in addition to their material suffering – "the people were painfully shedding one language and slowly acquiring another". The one Irish writer capable of bridging this historical and linguistic gap was playwright J. M. Synge, whose dialogue was shaped by his experiences among the Gaelic-speaking Aran Islanders. Kiberd's book is primarily a well-documented claim that Synge knew Irish far better than is generally allowed, but it is also a plea for a genuine biculturalism (founded on bilingualism) in modern Irish life.

On the choice between English and Irish, Kiberd notes that Patrick (Padraic) Pearse, Brendan Behan, Flann O'Brien and Liam O'Flaherty "wrote with facility and fame in both languages" (p. 7). It should nevertheless be added that Pearse used English chiefly for his political writing; Behan's Irish was largely confined to an early version of his play "The Hostage"; and even O'Flaherty's single collection of short stories in Irish, *Dúil* (1953), was partly a free translation (or "transcreation") of earlier English material. O'Brien, the one internationally recognized Irish novelist to have written in both languages, produced *An Béal Bocht* (1941), translated as *The Poor Mouth* in 1973 and followed by such better-known English originals as *At Swim-Two-Birds* (1939) and *The Third Policeman* (1967). Ironically, much of *An Béal Bocht* is a satire on attempts to revive Gaelic.

Such questioning of Kiberd's arguments for the importance of Irish does not, however, imply that the stepmother tongue is an irrelevant image for Ireland. It rather suggests the full extent of enforced English assimilation. Seamus Deane's standard history of Irish Literature starts from the premise that the anglophone Irish writer was, by definition, "uneasy with the very medium of communication", echoing Thomas Kinsella's comment on the poet not feeling at home in his use of the English language. The classic statement of such linguistic alienation occurs, of course, in Joyce's *A Portrait of the Artist as a Young Man*, when Stephen Dedalus muses during a conversation with the English Dean of Studies:

– The language in which we are speaking is his before it is mine. How different are the words *home, Christ, ale, master*, on his lips and on mine! I cannot speak or write these words without unrest of spirit. His language, so familiar and so foreign, will always be for me an acquired speech. I have not made or accepted its words. My voice holds them at bay. My soul frets in the shadow of his language.   (Penguin edn, p. 189)

Although Dedalus's words cannot be read as unmediated Joyce, other Irish writers have spoken more directly of the language in the same quasi-mystical terms. Flann O'Brien thus writes to Sean O'Casey about the importance of Irish for any kind of literary worker:

It supplies that unknown quantity in us that enables us to transform the English language – and this seems to hold good for people who know little or no Irish, like Joyce. It seems to be an inbred thing.   (quoted by Kiberd, p. 16)

Seamus Heaney suggested quite simply that the Irish language provided a myth of origins. In his poem "The Great Tradition", on the other hand, John Montague evoked the countryside as "a manuscript / We had lost the skill to read": Montague was thinking quite literally of Irish place names, perhaps even "funnier" (in both senses) for some English people than the Welsh surnames already discussed. The strangeness often resides, of course, in the crude English versions of originally meaningful names, a point recalling Brian Friel's inspired allegory of acculturation, *Translations* (1980). Although disqualified by genre from the present survey, Friel's play is so thematically relevant as to require brief comment here.

The action of *Translations* concerns the ordnance survey of Ireland conducted by the British Army Engineer Corps in the 1830s, as the country was mapped and renamed following its recent integration (1800) into the United Kingdom of Great Britain and Ireland. The travesty or obliteration of Irish place-names stands as a metaphor for the destruction of Irish culture at large, and the forced assimilation of Irish people into the anglophone sphere. By a cleverly manipulated convention, virtually all the dialogue of

Translations may be understood as taking place in Irish: *de facto* English is either indicated by a stilted and mechanical delivery, distancing it from the "Irish" speech around it, or else intoned as a kind of "gibberish" parodying the sounds of English speech. Friel's neat reversal of conventional linguistic hierarchies is a potent device met throughout this survey in writers as different as Mudrooroo and Alice Walker.

Of the play's two English officers, the sensitive Lieutenant Yolland would himself happily assimilate – even to the extent of trying to learn Irish – although he remarks sadly to the inhabitants of Baile Beag (now Ballybeg):

> Even if I did speak Irish I'd always be an outsider here, wouldn't I? I may learn the password but the language of the tribe will always elude me, won't it? The private core will always be ... hermetic, won't it?   (Act II, sc. i, line 416)

Ireland has a remarkable crop of contemporary anglophone novelists, although it should be clear from the foregoing that their writing transcends such simple issues as the representation of Irish speech in English, or even the choice of language itself. Neither Brian Moore, John McGahern, nor John Banville, for example, is about to produce a novel in Gaelic.

Born into a Belfast Catholic family, Brian Moore emigrated to Canada in 1948 (acquiring citizenship in 1953), and moved to the US in 1959. He nevertheless still regards himself as an Irish writer, incidentally rhyming his first name with "Ian" rather than "ion". Such Belfast novels as *Judith Hearne* (1955; republished as *The Lonely Passion of Judith Hearne*, 1956), *The Feast of Lupercal* (1957) or *The Emperor of Ice-Cream* (1965) were followed by fiction with an American setting. In the international or transcultural perspective, however, Moore's most significant novels may be *The Luck of Ginger Coffey* (1960), the story of an Irish immigrant in Montreal, and *I Am Mary Dunne* (1968), about a Nova Scotian in New York.

John McGahern was born in Dublin and worked as a teacher in his native city. His initially sombre fiction includes *The Dark* (1965), a partly autobiographical and (as it proved) strangely prescient story of priests and paedophilia: the novel was predictably censored and McGahern was dismissed from his teaching post without further explanation. *The Pornographer* (1970) is a wryly engaging tale of a writer who produces literary erotica to order, but fails dismally in his own sexual relationships. *Amongst Women* (1990) chronicles the life of an elderly farmer with an active republican background.

John Banville, the youngest of the trio, is a Wexford-born journalist currently literary editor of the *Irish Times*. Between *Nightspawn* (1971) – a political thriller set in Greece just before the miltary coup of 1967 – and four novellas studying the creative lives of geniuses – *Doctor Copernicus* (1976), *Kepler* (1981), *The Newton Letter* (1982), and *Mefisto* (1986) – he produced what may be the most significant Irish novel of recent decades: *Birchwood* (1973). *Birchwood* is Banville's comically surrealistic treatment of the classic "big house" theme. English (and anglophone) destinies are prominent here, for the great house in Ireland is always inseparable from the Anglo-Irish "ascendancy" or traditional ruling class.

"The Book of the Dead", the first and by far the longest section of Banville's tripartite novel, is a reconstruction by the ageing Gabriel Godkin of his childhood and youth in the family home of Birchwood. Gabriel's childhood coincides with the imposition on the family estate of collective farming at the time of the great famine. The Anglo-Irish Godkin dynasty is nevertheless supplanted from Birchwood by the native Lawless family, before Joseph, the narrator's father, marries back into the house again. Particularly suggestive here are the onomastics of the rival families: the Godkins, or "God's *kin*", perhaps thus even God's *own* – with two brothers, named Gabriel and Michael like the archangels – are supplanted by the *Lawless*, or "outlawed", upstarts, before a marriage alliance between the two families replaces conflict with complicity. The existence of analogous acts of accommodation in modern Irish history needs no further emphasis.

The eclipse of the Godkin–Lawless dynasty is partly a matter of physical degeneration, but also inseparable from socio-economic decline, as reflected in the increased "boldness" of the peasants (the use of a word with largely negative associations in Irish English is striking):

> As my people knew, and lucky they did, there is nothing that will keep the Irish in their place like a well-appointed mansion. They may despise and hate you, only put a fine big house with plenty of windows in it up on a hill and bejapers you have them by the balls, stunned into a cringing, cap-touching coma.   (p. 49)

The cynical character of Gabriel's retrospective view, together with a new Irishism, conveys the tone of his entire narrative: for here, rather than the drama, the pathos, or even the tragedy of recent Irish history, is black humour and surrealistic farce. Banville refuses categorically to historicize. As political positions harden, and the shrewder family members attempt to anticipate "the new State the revolution would found", Gabriel is finally expelled from his feudal paradise – to join the circus.

The circus is the unifying image of the other two sections of the novel ("Air and Angels" and "Mercury"), suggesting the comic and illusory aspect of the world outside. Gabriel, looking for the omniscient Prospero (maybe God) or his lost sister Rose (perhaps a metaphor for Ireland itself), must content himself with the collapsible kingdom of circus boss, Silas, and ends up as stooge in the latter's fake hypnosis sessions. Exiled from the feudal hierarchy of Birchwood, Gabriel must now unravel ambiguous family relationships within the circus, even while he learns the bombast of the big top. Gabriel eventually manages to find his way back to Birchwood, where, after a night spent sleeping on the billiard table in the ruined house, he sees a group of old women coming to remove dead bodies from the grounds outside. He calls out to them reassuringly ("Look, I am not my father, I am something different"), but predictably, the women remain unconvinced.

The big house is a venerable theme in Irish fiction, and its classic features – declining mansion, dissipated gentry, reckless (often absentee) landlord – are already present in Maria Edgeworth's *Castle Rackrent* (1800). Various novelists often loosely regarded as "English", such as Joyce Cary (1888–1957) and Elizabeth Bowen (1899–1973), were in reality products of this particular culture. There was, in fact, a Castle Cary in Donegal and a Bowen's Court in Cork. Social hierarchies aside, however, the *linguistic* battle in Ireland is apparently won and lost. The poet Michael Hartnett (Micheál Ó hArtnéide), it is true, published his self-explanatory *A Farewell to English* (1975) in a gesture reminiscent of Ngũgĩ wa Thiong'o, but "renegued" with his English-language *Inichore Haku* ten years later. In the absence of explicit linguistic conflict, then, the "big house" becomes the ideal fictional metaphor for an entire (and almost vanished) cultural tradition.

SCOTTISH FICTION

Iain Banks is merely one of a number of talented contemporary Scottish writers; his controversial first novel, *The Wasp Factory*

(1984), routinely grotesque and occasionally repulsive, is also never less than compelling. This quality is nowhere more conspicuous than in the extravagant climax where Frank, the asocial boy narrator, is unexpectedly revealed as a girl, whose true sexual identity has been repressed for years by perverse paternal whim. Such an unexpected reversal provides a fitting conclusion for Banks's masterly debut in modern Gothic. It is also tempting, however, to substitute nation for gender and read the ending as an allegory of the apparently English novel suddenly disclosed as an unambiguously Scottish one. The exact nature of this literary distinction is an important preliminary concern of the present section.

The Welsh contribution to anglophone fiction is relatively small, when set beside that of Ireland; and the number of contemporary writers publishing in Welsh *and* English is even smaller. In the final estimate, however, Welsh and Irish writers could be broadly included in this study's emblematic category of "our land / their language", where an alien tongue (English) is imposed on an indigenous culture (Welsh or Irish). For however paradoxical the claim may sound, there are good reasons for considering Joyce as culturally closer to Achebe and Soyinka than he is to Virginia Woolf: his farewell response to the English language in *Finnegans Wake*, moreover, is not vastly different from Ngũgĩ wa Thiong'o's more literal leave-taking in his essay collection, *Decolonising the Mind* (1986). For the full potential of such cultural and linguistic paradox, one must of course return to Oscar Wilde ("I am Irish by race, but the English have condemned me to speak the language of Shakespeare").

More complex even than Ireland, however, is the case of Scotland, where not *two* but *three* languages are involved: English, Gaelic, and Scots. Of these three, Gaelic – just as it has the overwhelmingly smallest number of speakers – is also the least significant in the context of late twentieth-century fiction. It nevertheless requires passing notice, if only for the remarkable case of a major contemporary writer: Iain Crichton Smith. Born on the island of Lewis in the Hebrides, Smith is not only bilingual in Gaelic and English, but has published fiction and poetry in both languages uninterruptedly for almost forty years. English is undoubtedly the learned language, however, although the author admits that this may even have enhanced its status for him: "the very fact that I had to learn English when I went to school was probably registered in some obscure corner of my psyche as an indication that English was superior to Gaelic".[2]

Smith's keen awareness of the plight of his native language is eloquently recorded in the English poem "Shall Gaelic Die?", from the collection *Lines Review* (1969):

He who loses his language loses his world. The Highlander who / loses his language loses his world.

...

"Shall Gaelic die" A hundred years from now who will say these words? Who will say, "Co their?" Who? The voice of the owl.

[*"Co their" is glossed as "Who will say?"*]

The Irish poet Thomas Kinsella described the death of a language as a "calamity". With rather less than a hundred thousand native speakers, the position of (Scots) Gaelic is by no means assured, although few men have done more for its preservation than Iain Crichton Smith.

With Scotland's other indigenous language, the immediate issue is not that of survival but rather a problem of identification and classification among linguists and literary critics alike. One of the finest accounts of the Scots language in this context is Billy Kay's shrewdly engaging *Scots: The Mither Tongue* (1986). The latter traces the historical process through which the linguistic parity of Stuart Scots and Tudor English (a relation broadly comparable to that of Dutch and German, or Portuguese and Spanish) degenerated to the point where Scots only seemed a suitable vehicle for dealing with the "lower orders". The key historical factors in this process were the shifting of the Stuart court to London, the non-availability of the Bible in Scots, and, later, the rejection of the Scots language by the Edinburgh intelligentsia in the eighteenth century. It was in this period, too, that the modern "fallacy" of Scots as a corruption of English took root.

In mid-century, Lord Mansfield could still write to Alexander Carlyle that "to every man bred in Scotland the English language was in some respects a foreign tongue" (Kay, p. 92). The same kind of cultural split was noted two hundred years later by Edwin Muir in his classic study *Scott and Scotland* (1932/1982), with the famous claim that "Scotsmen feel in one language and think in another". Elsewhere, the novelist Henry Mackenzie, one of those very eighteenth-century figures who turned his back on Scots, suggested that there was a "pure classical Scots spoken by genteel people" which had "nothing of the coarseness of the vulgar patois of the lower orders of the people" (quoted by Kay, p. 109). Kay comments here on the truism according to which dialect or vernacular always seems attractive to speakers of the standard language in inverse proportion to its physical proximity. Mackenzie's sentiment thus differs little from that expressed by Maurice Lindsay two centuries later in his authoritative *History of Scottish Literature* (p. 192), preferring the Aberdonian Scots of Alastair Mackie to the "broken-down *patois* of Glasgow".

The case of Scots is complicated by a question of linguistic perception. Kay rigorously opposes any concept of Scots as a "half-language" or "debased language", but also rejects the condescending, and therefore more insidious, modern view of Scots as a national variety of "World English". In the process, he provides a lucid account of the historical development of Scots and concludes with a brief taxonomy of the modern Scots dialects: Central, Southern, Northern, and Insular. At the same time, he frankly admits the "heavy blow" administered to Scots by the Scottish Education Act of 1872, with the provision of universal primary education in English and the consequent further contamination of Scots.

In spite of these developments, a number of Scottish writers still (in their own estimate and that of many readers) do not write in English at all, but in a distinct language – Scots – although the latter is admittedly very close to its southern cousin. The classification of Scottish fiction in relation to metropolitan English, then, is not simply a matter of whether to place it in the first stepmother-tongue category, as was the case for Wales and Ireland. One should perhaps go for another popular kinship trope entirely, and think of a literary Cinderella long overshadowed by its ugly sister.

Setting aside the recognized historical distinctness of the two languages, however, one is at least justified in asking whether some forms of contemporary "Scots" are not now, in fact, widely perceived as varieties of English. And if this is the case, where would the distinction lie between a language and a dialect? Socio-linguistics is still unhelpful here, and has not really improved on the cynic's definition of an army and a few frontier posts. The latter elements are certainly significant in the process of political and cultural autonomy that has allowed the Norwegian language (in two versions, moreover) to distinguish itself from Danish and Swedish in the course of the twentieth century. It is interesting to speculate what the same institutions might have done for Scots.

The present study, however, is concerned more with literary criticism than with socio-linguistic theory or nationalist ideology. In the context of modern Scottish fiction, the primary concern is the *written representation* of vernacular forms (rather than the forms themselves), together with the relation of this fiction to literary traditions beyond the British Isles. It is these questions that now require attention.

The question of linguistic classification will never of course disappear entirely, since the Booker Prize, Britain's most prestigious literary award, was recently won by a novel written in precisely the "broken-down *patois* of Glasgow" deplored by Lindsay: James Kelman's *How Late It Was, How Late* (1994). Kelman caused a further stir at the award ceremony by making his acceptance speech in Scots, to the consternation of most of his middle-class London audience. If Scots really is a distinct language, then there is a certain irony that Britain's most prestigious literary award should be given to an author with such ambivalent relations towards English. The point must certainly have amused Kelman. According to an increasingly popular hypothesis, moreover, Middle English (the predecessor of the modern language) is not a direct linear descendant of Anglo-Saxon, but rather a "creolization" of Norman *French*. In this light, Kelman might have been happy to go for the *Prix Goncourt*, too!

In practice, Kelman is (initially at least) quite lenient on the standard English speaker, as the opening lines of his novel illustrate:

> Ye wake in a corner and stay there hoping yer body will disappear, the thoughts smothering ye; these thoughts; but ye want to remember and face up to things, just something keeps ye from doing it, why can ye no do it; the words filling yer head; then the other words; there's something wrong; there's something far far wrong; ye're no a good man ...   (p. 1)

This is clearly a subtle suggestion rather than a narrow transcription of demotic Glaswegian, and as such may be usefully juxtaposed with another literary response to four centuries of colonial domination and linguistic conditioning, discussed in a previous section:

> One grim winter evening, when it had a kind of unrealness about London, with a fog sleeping restlessly over the city and the lights showing in the blur as if is not London at all but some strange place on another planet, Moses Aloetta hop on a number 46 bus at the corner of Chepstow Road and Westbourne Grove to go to

Waterloo to meet a fellar who was coming from Trinidad on the boat-train.   (p. 23)

The beginning of *The Lonely Londoners* (1956), Samuel Selvon's classic study of the immigrant experience, is also based on a fairly attenuated representation of demotic speech. Both novels limit themselves to suggesting a few select linguistic features: glottalization for Kelman, absent tense markers for Selvon, and non-standard pronominalization in both passages.

Of related interest here is the possible realization of two such highly *colloquial* narratives. The two passages would obviously be *read* quite differently by a metropolitan English-speaker (ironically, both novels were first published in London) and a Scot or Trinidian respectively. It is in fact doubtful whether someone possessing only standard English could do full justice to either novel. *The Lonely Londoners* was a fairly self-conscious literary experiment in the sense that it was virtually the first Caribbean novel to use dialect consistently throughout the narrative, and not merely in the dialogue. *How Late It Was, How Late*, on the other hand, is largely indifferent to questions of register, once stylistic parameters are established. The language of the protagonist is accepted unquestioningly as a kind of linguistic given throughout the course of the narrative. Kelman calls little further attention to the voice itself, and his novel is far more remarkable for its surrealistic distortion of everyday life in the manner of Beckett or Kafka, and its oppressive slow-motion and repetition reminiscent of Pinter.

The writing of Kelman is obviously related to the tradition of representation established by "Lewis Grassic Gibbon" (James Leslie Mitchell). Gibbon prefaced *A Scots Quair* (1932–4), his classic trilogy of Scottish rural life, with a famous plea for linguistic indulgence:

If the great Dutch language disappeared from literary usage and a Dutchman wrote in German a story of the Lekside peasants, one may hazard he would ask and receive a certain latitude and forbearance in his usage of German. He might import into his pages some score or so untranslatable words and idioms – untranslatable except in their context and setting; he might mould in some fashion his German to the rhythms and cadence of the kindred speech that his peasants speak. Beyond that, in fairness to his hosts, he hardly could go: to seek effect by a spray of apostrophes would be both impertinence and mis-translation.

The courtesy that the hypothetical Dutchman might receive from German a Scot may invoke from the great English tongue.

In practice, the "score" of untranslatable words is a glossary of some five hundred items, but *A Scots Quair* is never heavy reading for an English speaker. For Gibbon actually achieves a genial linguistic compromise: by remaining within the conventions of standard English orthography, he produces a text that an Englishman will read as a variety of English, and a Scot as some form of Scots. Kelman, in *How Late It Was, How Late*, follows this example, and for this reason alone, his novel provides an important point of reference in the cultural–linguistic divide at the heart of modern Scottish fiction.

On the one side of Kelman, in the anglophone corner as it were, are such contemporary writers as Janice Galloway (*Foreign Parts*, 1994) or A. L. Kennedy (*So I am Glad*, 1995), where it may be argued that gender is normally more significant than ethnic issues. For a more established writer such as Allan Massie, on the other hand, a post-colonial paradigm is sometimes useful (but just as often not), in much the same way as it is for the Australian novelist Thomas Keneally. Massie was in fact born in Singapore, although this is not of any great relevance to his writing; his Scottish background, on the other hand, is particularly important in *The Ragged Lion* (1994), his freely dramatized biographical study of Scott, or in *These Enchanted Woods* (1993), with its Scottish reworking of the Gatsby myth. In some analogous examples, Keneally's *The Playmaker* (1987), a bicentennial re-creation of the first dramatic performance ever produced by white Australians, or his earlier *The Chant of Jimmie Blacksmith* (1963), a classic narrative of contact between Euro-Australians and Aborigines, are also recognizably post-colonial novels. On the other hand, Massie's Roman trilogy on the lives of Augustus, Tiberius, and Julius Caesar has no more direct relevance to post-colonial fiction than Keneally's best-seller set in Nazi Germany, *Schindler's Ark* (1982).

The one novelist who could be placed unhesitantly in the other corner, however, in that reflections on the trope of the stepmother tongue are inevitable, is **Irvine Welsh**. Welsh's first full-length novel, *Trainspotting* (1995), is a cleverly stitched series of episodes from Edinburgh drug culture, arranged in groups under the seven sub-headings, "Kicking", "Relapsing", "Kicking Again", "Blowing It", "Exile", "Home", and "Exit". It remains consistently self-conscious about questions of register. Welsh has also written extensively in English and an occasional section of narrative in *Trainspotting* (although virtually no dialogue) uses this language, too. Rather than abandon standard English entirely, then, like Kelman's *How Late It Was, How Late*, *Trainspotting* merely overturns conventional linguistic hierarchies by marginalizing the language. Welsh's metropolitan Scots is actually far more impressive in range and variety than the more homogeneous Glaswegian demotic forged by Kelman. Welsh thus uses several voices besides that of his shrewd protagonist, university drop-out and periodic heroin-user, Mark Renton: these include the sensitive but barely articulate Danny (Spud) and the chemically clean but psychopathically violent Begbie.

There are also occasional reminiscences of a more traditional kind of Scottish writing, recalling Scott, Stevenson, and even Smollett, where Scots dialogue alternates with English narrative. These sections include "Growing Up in Public" (a family gathering on the death of an uncle), "Grieving and Mourning in Port Sunshine" (a story of club funds lost with the premature death of a club member), "The First Shag in Ages" (the protagonist's unforeseen involvement with an under-age schoolgirl), and "Bad Blood" (the revenge fantasy of the serio-positive Dave on the person by whom he has been infected).

The linguistic epicentre of the narrative, however, is Mark Renton, whose mastery of register has few rivals among anglophone fictional protagonists, as may be illustrated by two brief episodes. In the first of these, Mark and Spud carefully botch job interviews in order to remain unemployed. Spud achieves this by an ecstasy-induced manic enthusiasm, which successfully frightens off prospective employers; Mark, on the other hand, maintains a quietly articulate Scots, before lapsing into English at the crucial moment with his pseudo-sanctimonious confession:

> Yes. I've had a long-standing problem with heroin addiction. I've been trying to combat this, but it has curtailed my employment activities. I feel it's important to be honest and mention this to you, as a potential future employer.   (p. 65)

There is an even finer virtuoso performance when Mark and Spud appear in court charged with stealing books. Questioned by a sceptical magistrate about the appeal of Kierkegaard, one of the authors stolen, Mark again unexpectedly switches to English:

– I'm interested in his concepts of subjectivity and truth, and particularly his ideas concerning choice; the notion that genuine
choice is made out of doubt and uncertainty, and without recourse to the experience or advice of others. It could be argued
with some justification, that it's primarily a bourgeois, existential
philosophy and would therefore seek to undermine collective
societal wisdom ...   (pp. 165–6)

before breaking off deferentially with a silent reflection ("As an
educated man ah'm sure he kens far mair aboot the great philos-
ophers than a pleb like me" (p. 166). The two episodes are
symptomatic of a general undermining of linguistic hierarchies in
Trainspotting, whereby English loses both authority and reliability.
This process is accelerated by Mark's frequent comic subversion of
conventionally established meanings: objecting to the efforts of the
local Drug Squad, for example, Mark identifies himself as a "classic
liberal" who is "vehemently opposed tae state intervention in any
form" (p. 53); his complex giro fraud, on the other hand, involving
five different addresses between Edinburgh and London, is described as an exercise in "management skills" (p. 146).

The discussion of Scottish fiction began with the climax of a
novel (Banks's *The Wasp Factory*) that could well symbolize the psychological conflict of the Scottish writer long expected to masquerade as an English one (Robert Burns himself was once featured in
John Morley's *English Men of Letters* series). Such figurative readings are also tempting for the major contemporary Scottish novelist
not mentioned to this point: Alasdair Gray.

Gray has responded positively to Kelman's encouragement to
write in Scots, but his most interesting novel in the present context
is *Poor Things* (1992), a hilarious pseudo-biographical and
metafictional extravaganza entirely in English. Within the traditional framework of the editor and the discovered narrative, *Poor
Things* fantasizes the life of Bella Baxter (or Victoria McCandless),
daughter of a crass industrialist, protégée of medical pioneer
Godwin Baxter (but wife of Archibald McCandless), and first
woman doctor to graduate from Glasgow University. Bella's (or
Victoria's) first husband had been the brutally sadistic General Sir
Aubrey de la Pole Blessington, hero of half a century of English
colonial campaigns. Victoria leaves the general when he is unwilling to give her either a child or even any form of sexual satisfaction
(activities that would have dissipated his imperial energies).

McCandless apparently supplies both of these needs, but his idyllic (and posthumous) account of the marriage is followed by a twenty-five-page rebuttal from his widow, before the pseudo-scholarly apparatus of the original editor.

To return to the allegorical approach applied to *The Wasp Factory*: Bella (Victoria) is dominated by her father (through the institution of patriarchy), tyrannized by her first husband (by a process analogous to colonialism) and merely rewritten by the second (a benign but insidious example of neo-colonialism). *Beautiful* and *victorious* both in name and in fact, however, she ultimately finds both fame and glory in the course of a long and successful career. One might wish the same fate for the contemporary Scottish novel!

9
North America

NATIVE AMERICAN FICTION

Neither of the two smaller American literatures discussed below has a long written tradition comparable to that of Wales, Ireland, or Scotland. Native American literature, and (less obviously) Chicano literature (produced primarily by the Hispanic culture of the American South-West) nevertheless have strong oral traditions. Two minor historical details, on the other hand, have a certain emblematic significance in this context: the oldest continuously occupied site in the United States (approximately a thousand years old) is Oraibi, a *mesa* village of the Hopi Indians in the middle of the Navajo reservation in north-east Arizona; similarly, the oldest surviving public building in America is the *Casa de los Gobernadores*, or Palace of the Governors (1610), seat of successive Spanish-speaking administrations in Santa Fe. Here, in a nutshell, are dramatic symbols of "our" land and "our" language respectively, both of which pre-date any significant English influence in the United States.

Native American fiction is an appropriate context, initially, to raise once more the curious anomaly by which the term "American" is normally applied exclusively to citizens of the United States: Native (North) Americans by definition, however, are variously from the United States or Canada. The main focus of *The Stepmother Tongue* is on anglophone writers with an ambivalent relationship towards the English language, and Native Americans, whatever their modern national allegiance, fall naturally into this category.

In the massive Gale Research Guide, *Native North American Literature*, editor Janet Witalec makes an excellent point about who has traditionally been considered "Indian" or "Negro", respectively. For centuries now, any person with African ancestry has been described as Black (or in more recent terminology, "African American"), and the attempt to conceal that ancestry is described, generally with disapproval, as "passing for white". The classic example is the author Jean Toomer, who is normally considered an Afro-American writer, but wished to remain outside racial classification, which in practice meant living as white. And since Toomer's first name (his own contraction of Eugene) is commonly used for a woman, whilst his major work *Cane* – with elements of autobiography, reportage and poetry – regularly defies novelistic expectations, this writer is ambivalent in terms of genre and gender, too.

A Native American with any non-Native ancestry at all, on the other hand, has traditionally been referred to by the disparaging term "half-breed". The Canadian *Métis* writer Maria Campbell (of mixed Scottish, Indian, and French descent) wrote a best-selling autobiography with precisely this title. Campbell's *Halfbreed* (1973) was even an attempt (with admittedly limited success) to remove the stigma from the term; Janet Witalec also discusses the popular perception according to which the proverbial "drop of African blood" made one black, while a "drop of white blood" disqualified one from being Indian:

> Since Africans were brought to the Americas as slaves and Native peoples were here on land which Europeans have continued to take from them, it seems clear who it benefits [sic] by making one person's African ancestry so powerful that it makes them nothing but "Black" and another person's Native ancestry so weak that it can be nullified by any other racial mix.   (p. xiv)

The logic, if not the syntax, of the claim is unassailable; and Witalec's comment also helpfully returns the focus to the issue of *land*. Loss of land was in many cases preceded by loss of *language*, and the two recurrent motifs of this study thus surface yet again.

Basil Johnston, N. Scott Momaday, Martin Cruz Smith and Louise Erdrich are invariably reckoned among the major Native American writers, although the relative significance of the ethnic designation clearly varies from case to case. The four authors are also representative by being born in successive decades – although this chronological sequence is not always apparent from publication dates. Momaday's novel *House Made of Dawn* (1968) won a Pulitzer Prize for fiction in the same year (1969) as protesting "Indians of All tribes" occupied Alcatraz Island in San Francisco

Bay, a landmark in Native American awareness. Other works by these writers date almost exclusively from the 1980s and 1990s.

Basil Johnston is an Ojibway (or Chippewa), born on the Parry Island Indian reserve in Ontario, Canada. A respected ethnologist and educator, he is also a native Ojibway speaker who has published a language course and lexicon in that language. His only fiction, *Moose Meat and Wild Rice* (1978), republished in 1993 as *Ojibway Tales*, consists of twenty-two stories set on the fictive Moose Meat Point Indian Reserve near "Blunder Bay" (a presumed reference to Thunder Bay, Ontario). The stories are all in English, although great care is obviously taken with language presentation, as may be seen by an excerpt from "A Sign of the Times" when Big Flossie confronts Olga Shaposhnikoff, a government health worker bringing advice on birth control:

> "... Now. How many kids you got?"
> "None," Miss Shaposhnikoff spluttered.
> "Dats bedder! You married, you?" Big Flossie examined.
> "No," Miss Shaposhnikoff answered in a quivering voice.
> "You take dem pills, you?" Flossie interrogated.
> "No," Miss Shaposhnikoff replied, quaking.
> "Den, how come youse gonna teach us dis family planning. Youse aint married; youse ain't got kids, youse don' take pills; youse dont hab a house. How you gonna teach us dem tings? Eh? Eh? Eh?"
> "I read and do research," Miss Shaposhnikoff returned.
> "Well, me, I don't hab no education. I raisit ten kids. I keep house, I keep clean. I feed my husband. I happy me. You happier, you, wid no kids? Is womens who hab no kids happier? Only time us take pills and medicine is w'en wese sick. Is dat de bes' your Department can do? If dat's de bes', den we don' need you dammed help." Big Flossie sat down. The interpreters went to work. Miss Shaposhnikoff blanched and paled.   (p. 56)

It is interesting to compare Johnston's technique with that of Caradoc Evans in *My People*, quoted above. Most obviously, phonology (i.e. pronunciation) now receives greater attention than syntax or cultural reference. In generic terms, on the other hand, all satirists – whether benign like Johnston, or more abrasive like Evans – risk accusations of stereotyping or pastiche, and *Moose Meat and Wild Rice* has not escaped them. Biographical details nevertheless suggest that, if Evans was an Anglo-Welshman who knew a lot of Welsh, then Johnston is actually an Ojibway speaker who has mastered English.

For the other three authors, however, the trope of the stepmother tongue has a less literal application: Momaday (Kiowa father/ part-Cherokee mother) and Erdrich (German-American father/ Chippewa [Ojibway] mother) became successful mainstream academics as well as novelists, whilst Cruz Smith (Papago–Yaqui mother) emerged as an international best-selling author, all in what is effectively their *first* language – English.

N. Scott Momaday's *House Made of Dawn* is a Native American *Bildungsroman* whose protagonist, Abel, returns alienated from World War II to the South-West pueblo of his childhood. Here, he kills "the white man", a mysteriously evil albino, and is sent to prison for six years. On release, he is relocated to Los Angeles, and becomes involved with an Indian Rescue Mission. He eventually returns to his pueblo, however, and finds peace in the traditional Indian world. Such reductive summary clearly fails to convey the complexity (and occasional obscurity) of Momaday's novel, or even the author's particular relation to the English language. The latter can be illustrated by just two details: the first word of Momaday's prologue is *Dypaloh* and the final word of the novel is *Qlsedaba*, both apparently appropriate formulae for oral tales in the Jemez Pueblo of Momaday's childhood, thus hinting at traditional orature as one interpretive key for the entire narrative. And when Abel is on trial for murder, he experiences a sudden confusion at the white man's language: "Word by word these men were disposing of him in language, *their* language ..."; the sadden stab of alienation is identical to that felt by Joyce's Stephen Dedalus. The last word on language, however, is supplied by Abel's Los Angeles friend Ben:

> They have a lot of *words*, and you know they mean something, but you don't know what, and your own words are no good because they're not the same; they're different and they're the only words you got.   (p. 193)

Frequently in the narrative, then, English is figuratively (even literally) the stepmother tongue, within a broader theme not limited to Momaday: the erosion of Native American culture by mainstream Euro-American life. *House Made of Dawn*, together with Momaday's historical study *The Way to Rainy Mountain* (1969), his autobiographical *The Names* (1976), and a second novel, *The Ancient Child* (1989), are heroic attempts to arrest this decline.

Martin Cruz Smith was actually raised and educated in the American North-East, and spent only a brief period as a small child on a New Mexico reservation. He was a prolific writer of thrillers (under various pseudonyms), before the international success of *Gorky Park* (1981) and their sequels, famous for their Russian detective, Arkady Renko, and what were assumed to be authentic re-creations of Soviet life. Before *Gorky Park*, however, Cruz Smith had published two other novels, still under his own name, including *Nightwing* (1977), a gruesome extravaganza set on the Hopi Indian reservation in Arizona, where a mad medicine man conjures up a tribe of plague-bearing vampire bats. Cruz Smith was strongly criticized for the inaccurate portrayal of Hopi life (he admitted to never having been near the reservation). He has spoken elsewhere of his wish to avoid being a "professional Indian"; in *Nightwing* he runs the risk of becoming an amateur one. His fiction, in fact, is probably better approached from the thriller genre rather than through Native American ethnicity.

Louise Erdrich, the last writer of the present quartet, was brought up near the Turtle Mountain Chippewa reservation in North Dakota, where her parents both worked for the Bureau of Indian affairs. It is worth noting here that Erdrich's father was in fact a German-born American, so that the novelist's marginal relation to mainstream American culture had, from the very outset, a double thrust. All of Erdrich's novels, from *Love Medicine* (1984), through *The Beet Queen* (1986) and *Tracks* (1988) to *The Bingo Palace* (1994), focus on a fictional community of Chippewas; all except *The Beet Queen* are set on a reservation. Both Erdrich's initial regionalism and her capacity to transcend these geographical limits have routinely encouraged comparisons with Faulkner. The easy availability of her novels, not least, makes Erdrich an ideal choice for further discussion here; *Love Medicine* (1984), whose thirteen interlocking narratives were increased by five in a new expanded edition (1993), is arguably Erdrich's central text.

The first (and longest) of the eighteen sections of the revised novel, "The World's Greatest Fisherman", depicts a family gathering in 1981; the remainder weave back and forth over fifty years and through three (or marginally five) generations of the Kashpaw family. From this multitude of personal histories, one may extract a chronological sequence, beginning with Margaret, or Rushes Bear, who had married the original Kashpaw and received a territorial grant in the North Dakota wheatlands. The contrasting lives of Margaret's children, Nector and Eli – subsequently twin patriarchs of the Kashpaw clan – represent with emblematic simplicity the cultural conflicts of the Native American consciousness:

> She had let the government put Nector in school, but hidden Eli, the one she couldn't part with, in the root cellar dug beneath her floor. In that way she gained a son on either side of the line. Nector came home from boarding school knowing white reading and writing, while Eli knew the woods.   (p. 19)

Whilst Eli remains unmarried, Nector leaves his first love, Lulu Nanapush, for Marie Lamartine – daughter of poor whites – and eventually becomes tribal chairman. Lulu, who had repeatedly absconded from the government school, becomes the lover of unassimilated Moses Pillager on his island, before returning to more conventional marriage with Henry Lamartine. Nector and Marie have several children, and it is their granddaughter, Albertine Johnson (fathered by a local Swedish immigrant), who describes the gathering with which the novel opens.

Land and language are prominent motifs of *Love Medicine*; the Chippewas' hold on both is tenuous. Nector, who had negotiated astutely with the government to retain the special Indian status of the reservation, later signs away the land of his ex-lover, Lulu, for the white men to build a factory. On or off reservation, Chippewa identity is equally precarious, a point ironically suggested by the youthful ramblings of the statuesque Nector. In a series of reminiscences ("The Plunge of the Brave"), he thus recalls appearing in a Western movie, where he is expected to fall off a horse, and posing for an old white woman artist, who paints him leaping from a cliff. Cultural expectations are minimal in both contexts; or, as the narrator wrily observes, "Death was the extent of Indian acting."

Nector's contemporary, Beverly Lamartine, peddles word-enrichment books for the children of ambitious working-class parents in Twin Cities (Minnesota–St Paul), although he has neither house nor family of his own; and in the next generation Henry Lamartine returns shattered from the white man's war in Vietnam (much like the protagonist of Momaday's *House Made of Dawn*) – amongst other emotional baggage, he carries the poignant words of a dying Vietnamese woman: "'You, me, same. Same.' She pointed to her eyes and his eyes: the Asian, folded eyes of some Chippewas."

At the heart of Chippewa cultural impoverishment is the loss of language. English is occasionally the subject of comic misunderstandings, as when Nector explains to his mother about *Moby Dick*'s big white whale, only for her to wonder what the white man has to wail about; or when Lipsha Morissey, the young man with special gifts who gathers the "love medicine" of the title, lives in fear of a malpractice *suit*, which he assumes to be a compulsory item of clothing for root-doctors like himself. Other linguistic references are more serious. Chippewa itself is referred to repeatedly as "the old language": it is what the recluse, Moses Pillager, speaks on his island; it is what Lulu pines for in her government school ("I lived by bells, orders, flat voices, rough English. I missed the old language in my mother's mouth", p. 68). It is what the old Chippewas return to in their twilight days at the Senior Citizens' home.

Erdrich nevertheless avoids naive sentimentality on this issue. Basil Johnston has suggested that only three of fifty-three original Native Canadian languages are not in current danger of extinction; Chippewa is one of these, although the younger generation's knowledge of the language in *Love Medicine* seems limited to drunken requests for a cigarette. On a broader level, language (and its loss) is the most obvious emblem for the slow and painful assimilation process which *Love Medicine* describes. The full social, political, and religious implications of language are evoked unforgettably in Lipsha Morrissey's meditation on Christian and Chippewa gods:

> Our Gods aren't perfect, is what I'm saying, but at least they come around. They'll do a favor if you ask them right. You don't have to yell. But you do have to know, like I said, how to ask in the right way. That makes problems, because to ask proper was an art that was lost to the Chippewas once the Catholics gained ground. Even now, I have to wonder if Higher Power turned it back [sic], if we got to yell, or if we don't speak its language. (p. 236)

The single word "language" is the obvious metonym for a whole vanished way of life. Erdrich's insights make *Love Medicine* – together with Momaday's *House Made of Dawn* – a lasting monument to Native American culture.

The history of Native Americans provides dramatic material for the theme of land and language. The Gale research guide lists almost three hundred "Major Native Nations", including fifty in Canada. It is debatable whether one is more struck by the small-ness of the territory ceded to three hundred nations, by the general inhospitality of the same, or by the fact that nearly three hundred other self-proclaimed Indian communities are not officially recognized in the United States, alone. More chastening still are the data for native speakers of Indian languages. According to the 1990 census, only a quarter of 1,800,000 Native Americans speak an Indian language at home, with Navajo (*c*.150,000 speakers) being by far the most important.

Among younger major Native American writers, Canadian dramatist Tomson Highway, who spoke Cree until sent to an Indian Residential School at the age of six, can speak most literally of English as a stepmother tongue. Within the twentieth century, incidentally, Native American children in both Canada and the United States have routinely been forcibly separated from their parents and sent to Indian Residential Schools where they were forbidden to speak English. The spirit of the "Welsh Not" lives on.

CHICANO FICTION

The beginnings of Chicano literature may be dated from the Treaty of Guadalupe Hidalgo in 1848, signalling the end of the so-called Mexican War. As a result of this agreement, the size of Mexico was halved, when California, New Mexico, and Texas north of the Rio Grande were ceded to the United Sates. The "Mexican Cession" eventually formed the states of Texas, New Mexico, Arizona, Nevada, Utah, and even parts of Wyoming and Colorado. It also provided the starting-point for Chicano literature, created by:

> writers of Mexican descent born in the United States, living here permanently, or having lived in the country which until 1848 was part of Mexico.[3]

Many of these are predictably bilingual, and heirs to an established Spanish culture. The *Dictionary of Literary Biography* cites novels from the 1940s and 1950s, such as Luis Pérez's *El Coyote the Rebel* (1947) and José Antonio Villareal's *Pocho* (1959), but the great flowering of Chicano writing is a phenomenon of the following decades. It coincides partly with the establishment of a literary prize, the *Premio Quinto Sol*, first awarded to Tomás Rivera's *"... y no se lo tragó la tierra"* in 1971. Rivera's novel documents the plight of Chicano migrant workers (the National Farm Workers Association was formed by the legendary César Chávez six years earlier), and stands comparison with Steinbeck's *The Grapes of Wrath* (1939). It was translated immediately by Herminio Ríos as *"... and the Earth Did Not Part"*, although this version was partly superseded by a new translation from **Rolando Hinojosa**, entitled *This Migrant Earth* (1985).

Hinojosa is a major Chicano novelist in his own right. The son of a Mexican-American and a bilingual Anglo, he maintains a complex literary dialogue between two languages. His novels all form part of the so-called "Klail City Death Trip Series", an ongoing saga of life in the fictional Belken County, Texas, in the lower Rio Grande Valley. The series began with the *Estampas del valle* or *Sketches of the Valley* (1973) – later published in a freely revised English translation as *The Valley* in 1983. Hinojosa's second novel, *Klail City y sus alrededores*, was translated by the author as *Klail City* in 1976. The English versions of both of these works thus provide yet another perspective on the discourse of the stepmother tongue.

The Valley, as its Spanish title implies, is quite literally a series of "prints" – vignettes of Texas *mexicano* life in the perpetual shadow of the all-powerful Texas Anglos. Hinojosa's portrait of Belken occasionally emulates the Faulkner of Yoknapatawpha County, whilst its lighter episodes recall the Steinbeck of *Sweet Thursday*. Or, to suggest a Spanish analogy, the historical rivalry of the *mexicanos* with *los rinches* (or Texas rangers) has something of the timeless conflict between Lorca's gypsies and the *guardia civil*.

By the twentieth century, however, physical confrontation has been superseded by ethnic discrimination – or just about: for life in Belken, as Hinojosa's narrative *persona* Rafe Buenrostro points out, "is fairly cheap ... and if you're a Texas Mexican, it's even cheaper than that" (*The Valley*, p. 44). In more recent times still, the novels suggest, cultural marginalization and conflict are regularly viewed in linguistic terms, a point that Hinojosa makes frequently, whether with humour or with more biting irony. The sober Emilio Tamez is thus presented as a man who, against appearances, reads and writes English *and* Spanish, although to little avail ("a tee-total bilingual ... but with all that going for him he's still a damfool"

(p. 100). There is, on the other hand, a more scathing portrait of the bilingual *coyotes*, self-appointed Chicano mediators at the county courthouse who exploit visitors unfamiliar with English. Fluency in English is not everything, however, particularly if it entails a corresponding loss of self-esteem. When, in *Klail City*, the children from the North Ward Grade School move on to junior high, they find *mexicanos* from the city's South Ward more fluent in English, but lacking a cohesive social identity: they are referred to disparagingly as "the Dispossessed".

In the Klail City series, language, class and ethnicity are related issues. But Hinojosa's own position as a completely bilingual writer, who yet writes a novel in English with characters who would naturally be Spanish-speaking, also raises interesting extrinsic questions. One of several techniques for overcoming this anomaly is skilful speech presentation, in the case of the Michigan-born *mexicano* evangelist Brother Imás, or the Texas Anglo Sheriff, Big-Foot Parkinson. Elsewhere, Hinojosa uses a number of other techniques for creating authenticity: in *Klail City*, for example, the three articulate narrators all often imply that their English versions are a mere concession to the reader, and certain culture-specific concepts or idiomatic phrases are left in Spanish, with or without glosses. Examples are the words, *curandera, vecindades, or resacas,* roughly translatable as "healer", "neigbourhoods", and "dried-up creeks", respectively. And what English phrase, one wonders, would convey the almost self-explanatory Spanish expression *hombre de bien*.

In the case of Hinojosa, it is meaningless to suggest that economic factors have had much influence on his choice of language: he is an established academic, not financially dependent on his creative writing, beside which he is obviously capable of translating or recreating his own work at will in either direction. Hinojosa himself is most informative on the issue of his bilingualism: the third novel, *Korean Love Songs*, was thus written directly in English, a fact conditioned – the author explains – by its setting in that rigidly anglophone institution, the United States Army. This was followed by *Mi Querido Rafa* (1981), an epistolary novel translated by the author in 1985 as *Dear Rafe*. The latter was preceded by *Rites and Witnesses* and succeeded by *Partners in Crime* (1985), both English originals owing much to the formulae of the detective story. Hinojosa's ninth novel, *Claros Varones de Belken/Fair Gentlemen of Belken*, breaks new ground by offering parallel Spanish and English texts.

Hinojosa is only one among a number of fine Chicano novelists. Rudolfo A. Anaya – whose *Bless Me, Ultima* (1972), about a *curandera* or folk-healer, is a minor classic – was not, however, as linguistically privileged as Hinojosa. As he ruefully explains in Jussawalla and Dasenbrock's *Interviews with Writers of the Post-Colonial World*:

> I didn't have a choice. I was educated in the American school system, and this school system teaches English. So very quickly I moved from my native tongue, which is Spanish, into the English language both written and spoken. So the choice was not there to make.   (p. 250)

Another canonic novelist is Ron Arias, whose interest in *mestizaje* or racial hybridity in *The Road to Tamazunchale* (1971) recalls the multiculturalism of Wilson Harris. Like Anaya, however, Arias writes exclusively in English, in spite of a Spanish-speaking childhood.

Among the younger generation of Chicano writers, there is an interesting parallel with Afro-American literature in the special prominence achieved by women novelists. Ana Castillo's *The Mixquiahuala Letters* (1982) an exchange of forty letters between two women, and Sandra Cisneros's *The House on Mango Street* (1983), extending the scope of Chicano literature with its depiction of north Chicago's Latino section, are notable examples of this new writing. With his unique extrinsic position, however, together with the intrinsic linguistic interest of his novels, Hinojosa remains the most interesting Chicano writer in the present context.

The linguistic position of Spanish-speakers in the United States (if not always their socio-economic one) is healthy. There are officially 17 million Spanish-speakers, ten times as many as for any other language besides English. The most convincing evidence for the healthy position of Spanish may emerge indirectly from *Language Loyalties* (1992), James Crawford's highly revealing source book on the "Official English" controversy. In a national survey of 1987, two-thirds of the respondents revealed that they assumed English to be the official language of the United States; the Constitution is of course silent on the subject. Since that date, a number of state legislatures have passed language statutes and amendments codifying the *de facto* primacy of English. This is not the place for a full discussion of the status of Spanish in the United States, but many of the documents in Crawford's collection suggest that whereas the anglophone mainstream can afford a belated largesse to a decimated Native American population, it perceives a cultural threat from a far larger Hispanic minority, often unwilling to assimilate. According to this survey, many Hispanic speakers, and particularly the Chicanos of the South-West, – unlike the Native Americans, for whom the battle is virtually already lost – thus regard the transition from "our" to "their" language (or from the *mother* to the *stepmother* tongue) with fear or resentment.

There are good grounds for including Native American and Chicano authors with indigenous writers of other more recent ex-British settler colonies; there is a case, too, for placing at least Welsh and Irish writers in the same category. The configuration of "our land/their language" could be applied variously to them all as well as to their African and Asian contemporaries. The main justification for discussing Native American (or Chicano) authors here, then, is the new perspective it offers on "mainstream" American culture; it is to be hoped that the brief review of Welsh, Irish, and Scottish ones achieved something similar for the literature of the British Isles.

NOTES

1. *The Oxford Companion to the Literature of Wales* (1986) is highly informative. Stephens is illuminating, for instance, on Welsh writing in Patagonia. The colony in Southern Argentina still has about five thousand Welsh-speakers, including several notable writers who are typically bilingual in Welsh and Spanish.
2. *Iain Crichton Smith: Critical Essays*, ed. Colin Nicholson (Edinburgh: Edinburgh University Press, 1992), p. ix
3. The definition is taken from the *Dictionary of Literary Biography*, whose volumes 82 and 122 offer the most informative account of Chicano writers.

FURTHER READING

British Isles

For Wales, Meic Stephens's *Oxford Companion to the Literature of Wales* (1986) is extremely useful. Raymond Garlick's *An Introduction to Anglo-Welsh*

Literature (Cardiff: University of Wales Press, 1970) is partly superseded by Roland Mathias's *Anglo-Welsh Literature: An Illustrated History* (Bridgend: Poetry of Wales Press, 1986). Caradoc Evans's *My People* exists in a modern edition (Bridgend: Poetry of Wales Press, 1987), with a helpful introduction by John Harris.

For Ireland, a good starting point is Seamus Deane's *A Short History of Irish Literature* (London: Hutchinson, 1986), which may be supplemented by Norman Vance's *Irish Literature: A Social History: Tradition, Identity and Difference* (Oxford: Blackwell, 1990). Declan Kiberd's most useful books are his *Synge and the Irish Language* (Basingstoke: Macmillan, 1993) and the magnificent *Inventing Ireland* (London: Jonathan Cape, 1995).

For Scotland, Maurice Lindsay's authoritative *History of Scottish Literature* (London: Robert Hale, 1992) is obviously helpful, but not as useful as Trevor Royle's *Mainstream Companion to Scottish Literature* (Edinburgh: Mainstream, 1993). There is a valuable collection of essays on contemporary Scottish fiction: *The Scottish Novel since the Seventies* (Edinburgh: Edinburgh University Press, 1993), edited by Gavin Wallace and Randall Stevenson. Most illuminating of all, however, is Robert Crawford's remarkable *Devolving English Literature* (Oxford: Clarendon Press, 1992), a study that moves far beyond Scottish literature and discusses some of the issues raised in *The Stepmother Tongue*.

Billy Kay's *Scots: The Mither Tongue* (Edinburgh: Mainstream, 1986) is a partisan but extremely lucid account of Scots, memorable for occasionally resorting to that language when it simply expresses a point more pithily than English.

North America

For Native American fiction, the large research guide *Native American Literature*, edited by Janet Witalec and published by Gale Research Incorporation (New York, 1994), is indispensable. Volume 175 of the *Dictionary of Literary Biography* (Detroit: Gale Research, 1997), edited by Kenneth M. Roemer, covers Native American writers of the United States. This may be supplemented by Penny Petrone's *Native Literature in Canada: From the Oral Tradition to the Present* (Toronto: Oxford University Press, 1987).

Also of interest are *Our Bit of Truth: An Anthology of Canadian Native Literature* (Winnipeg: Pemmican Publications, 1990), edited by Agnes Grant, and Hartmut Lutz's *Contemporary Challenges: Conversations with Native Canadian Authors* (Saskatoon: Fifth House, 1991).

Invaluable aids for Chicano fiction are those volumes (82 and 122) of the *Dictionary of Literary Biography* (Detroit: Gale Research, 1989 and 1992) which deal with Chicano writers. Both are edited by Francisco A. Lomeli and Carl R. Shirley.

Houston A. Baker produced the informative *Three American Literatures: Essays in Chicano, Native American, and Asian-American Literature for Teachers of American Literature* (New York: Modern Language Association, 1982). Other helpful guides are Martin A. Lewis's *Introduction to the Chicano Novel*

(Milwaukee: University of Wisconsin, 1982) and *Contemporary Chicano Fiction: A Critical Survey* (Binghamton, NY: Bilingual/Editorial Bilingüe, 1985), edited by Vernon E. Lattin. Denys Lynn Daly Heyck's collection *Barrios and Borderlands: Cultures of Latinos and Latinas in the United States* (New York: Routledge, New York, 1994) has much background material, while *Memory and Cultural Politics*, a volume in the New Approaches to American Ethnic Literatures series (Boston: Northeastern University Press, 1996), edited by Amritjit Singh et al., has essays on Chicano fiction.

Bruce Novoa's *Chicano Authors: Inquiry by Interview* (Austin: University of Texas Press, 1980) is an important collection.

Extroduction

A number of novelists do not easily fit in any of the categories proposed so far: some, like South Africans William Plomer or Pauline Smith, are essentially colonial novelists covering their traces; others, like Shirley Hazzard of Mavis Gallant, are difficult to attach (or even actively resist attachment) to any particular national tradition; a third group, including Margaret Laurence or Ruth Prawer Jhabvala, change subjects, settings, and even personal circumstances quite dramatically in the course of their careers. There are finally those – like Joyce – for whom exile becomes a vital precondition for creative work: two examples of the latter tendency are the otherwise so disparate writers V. S. Naipaul and Salman Rushdie.

The title of the final section also requires comment, if only to pre-empt accusations of affectation or obscurity. Apart from a harmless touch of symmetry in relation to the Introduction, the heading draws on a (perhaps) wishful piece of morphological thinking. The rough, but often suggestive, notion of the stepmother tongue elaborated in the *Intro*duction led quite literally *into* the present model; a dozen almost random texts (examples might be multiplied almost indefinitely) could provide the "*Extro*duction" leading *out of* it. For the crucial point here is that the stepmother tongue, with or without its even rougher corollaries of land and language, is a fluid and impermanent concept. It can be applied to much anglophone literature at the end of the second millennium; but changing cultural and linguistic norms suggest it may not last very long into the next. For the stepmother tongue, as many examples in this study suggest, is either eventually naturalized – or, in rarer cases, finally rejected. In most contexts, then, the stepmother cannot ultimately be distinguished from the mother; for, as in the world of fairy-tales which provided the trope, the two are ultimately identical.

The *extro*duction therefore posits two broad categories, not mutually exclusive or even strictly comparable, but intended to cover the outstanding novelists (in both senses) reserved from previous sections. A large number of these writers are linked by by stylistic or generic criteria, according to which they have produced novels with a moral or psychological dimension in an international setting (almost invariably, the writers themselves belong to this milieu). The great precursor here is Henry James. Other writers are related by cultural or ethnic criteria, which identify them with an international diaspora from more ambivalently anglophone countries. Many of the first group – typically of Australian, New Zealand, Canadian, or even South African origins – are practitioners of what, in the Jamesian context, would be called "the international novel"; most of the second – of whom a remarkable number are of Asian origin – have been described by Salman Rushdie as tellers of migrant tales. The two categories are therefore distinguished here by the appropriately broad designations of *The Last Jacobites* and *The Asian Diaspora*.

THE LAST JACOBITES

For a number of authors in the early twentieth century, the pull to what was seen as the metropolitan centre was understandably strong. The trajectories of Henry Handel Richardson, or William Plomer and Pauline Smith, have already been noted. Another significant international writer of the period is Katherine Mansfield, generally seen outside her own country as a European modernist rather than a New Zealand realist. A yet more striking example is the Canadian writer Sara Jeannette Duncan, who spent two decades in India (where she met E. M. Forster), but subsequently lived and worked in the United States; she actually corresponded with James, was consciously cosmopolitan – within well-defined imperial parameters – and became a fluent practitioner of the "international romance".

Canadian novelist Morley Callaghan is not a writer easily confused with James, the more obvious literary association being Hemingway. Callaghan spent a year (1929–30) in Paris, like many other North American intellectuals, and subsequently lived briefly in the United States. He always rejected nationalist movements, however, regarding himself as an internationalist for whom Canada remained "part of the British North American pattern". Callaghan may, of course, have been making a virtue out of a necessity, since it is well known that his British and American publishers resisted the idea of a narrative set in Montreal or Toronto: the novelist was therefore reduced to giving fictionalized Canadian cities an American name.

If there is a Canadian heir to James, however, it is surely Mavis Gallant. Born in Montreal, Gallant attended a Jansenist boarding-school from the age of four, followed by sixteen more schools in Canada and the United States. One of Canada's few major writers who is genuinely bilingual in English and French, she has lived for almost half a century in Europe, whether London, Rome, Paris, or Madrid. Her preoccupation with the "international theme" of Anglo-Saxons abroad is quintessentially Jamesian. Known primarily as a writer of short stories, Gallant also published two novels – *Green Water, Green Sky* (1959) and *A Fairly Good Time* (1970). Like Callaghan, Gallant is generally dismissive of nationalisms, and defines herself simply as "a writer in the English language".

Christina Stead grew up in Sydney, but left for England in 1928; she subsequently spent nearly fifty years in Britain, France, and the United States, before returning to Australia in 1974. Only *Seven Poor Men of Sydney* (1934) is set in her native country. Stead's other major novels are *The Man Who Loved Children* (1940), placed in America but inspired by a conflictual relationship with her own father, and *For Love Alone* (1944), about her struggle to get to England. *Cotters' England* (1967; published in the United States as *Dark Places of the Heart*) is a portrait of Britain during the Cold War. *The House of All Nations* (1938) is set in Paris, whilst three other novels, *Letty Fox: Her Luck* (1946), *A Little Tea, A Little Chat* (1948), and *The People with the Dogs* (1952), have an American background. As the record of an international novelist, Stead's *vita* speaks for itself.

The antecedents of Doris Lessing are also certainly international. Born to British parents in Persia, she grew up on a farm in Southern Rhodesia (now Zimbabwe) and moved to England in 1949. The specifically Southern African element in Lessing's writing is clearest in her first novel, *The Grass is Singing* (1950), and in the first four volumes of the sequence – *Martha Quest* (1952), *A Proper Marriage* (1954), *A Ripple from the Storm* (1958), *Landlocked* (1965) and *The Four-Gated City* (1969) – collectively known as *Children of Violence*. Lessing's range and versatility are illustrated (to give only a sample) by the experimental feminist novel *The Golden Notebook* (1962), the five-part "space-fiction" series of *Canopus in Argos: Archives* (1979–83), and a study of urban terrorism, *The Good Terrorist* (1985). Another ex-colonial who grew up among a small white elite was Jean Rhys. *Wide Sargasso Sea* (1966) is her only work with an exclusively colonial setting, although it still arouses greater critical interest than anything written by Lessing. Dan Jacobson, a South African based in England since the late 1950s, has also long abandoned African settings. All three authors thus have a good claim to transnational status.

Some novelists, however, whether enforced exiles or voluntary expatriates, remain engrossed (even haunted) by their native country: a good example again is Rushdie, who may have started out in the second of the above categories but gradually wrote himself into the first.

In more recent Australian fiction, there are clear analogies with James in the case of Shirley Hazzard, and rather more distant ones in that of Janette Turner Hospital. Born and raised in Sydney, Hazzard lived with her family in both Hong Kong and Wellington, and later worked ten years for the United Nations in New York. She now divides her time between the United States and Italy. Hazzard's earliest novels, *The Evening of the Holiday* (1966) and *The Bay of Noon* (1970), follow their heroine's moral and spiritual quest in the classic Jamesian manner; her most acclaimed work, *The Transit of Venus* (1980), embodies the grand international theme in its account of two Australian sisters on an English odyssey.

Janette Turner Hospital, who was born in Melbourne and graduated from the University of Queensland, spent four years in the United States and now divides her time between Australia, Canada and the United States. Her novels, variously set in all of these countries and India, include *The Ivory Swing* (1982), *The Tiger in the Tiger Pit* (1983) and *Borderline* (1985). Transnational existences, like Hospital's own, are a staple of this fictional output.

In *Charades* (1989), Hospital's most complex work, each of the novel's four sections is focalized through a major character, and concluded by the narrator–protagonist's own speculations. The opening section (entitled "Charade") establishes an intertextual pattern for the novel, as Charade Ryan, fringe-student at MIT and compulsive story-teller, insinuates herself first into the bed and then into the life of Professor Koenig, distinguished theoretical physicist and inveterate womanizer: for Charade is nothing less than a modern Scheherazade, and Koenig (the "king") is her latter-day Caliph. Charade's nightly instalments in the professor's Cambridge apartment reveal tantalizing but often contradictory glimpses of a rural Australian childhood with nine siblings under the loving care of Bea, the earth-mother figure. Further in the background hovers Aunt Katherine (Kate or Kay), Bea's superficially more conventional stepsister, and other more shadowy figures from Bea's own past.

The second section ("K: The Variorum Edition") revolves around Auntie Kay; the third ("The 366th Night and Thereafter") concentrates on Koenig, as the professor presents his own halting account of a broken marriage and two resentful children; the fourth returns to episodes from the life of Bea. The final section offers a solution to the question of Charade's origins, but remains pointedly open on her future relationship with Koenig.

It is worth noting that the protagonist's name is Charade, although the title of the novel is *Charades*. The Oxford English Dictionary helpfully defines "charade" as a kind of riddle, where a word to be guessed is "enigmatically described" or even "dramatically represented", and the book's title may gloss both features. On the one hand, the heroine *enigmatically describes* not one but several versions of key events in her life, creating a number of "Charades" rather than a single autonomous figure. Or alternatively, the other characters in the novel, *dramatically represented* through this fragmented intelligence, are even more obviously illusions. In the spoken language, of course, the two dimensions are indistinguishable, since none of the shifting characters have an existence beyond the narrator's controlling intelligence: or, more economically expressed, the *charades* are always *Charade's*.

Such ambiguity and paradox is matched by the more explicit wordplay that structures Hospital's gently ironical assault on the assumptions of realistic fiction. By name and nature, Bea suggests some transcendental female essence (whether being or *bea*-ing), although she is elsewhere reduced to the scientific impersonality of *Bea*-particles. The quietly imposing Aunt Katherine (or Kate, or Kay) is similarly fragmented in Part II ("K: The Variorum Edition"), a clear reference to Kafka's disembodied cypher; Koenig is ironically allowed to begin his story on the model of Chaucer's non-existent "kynge's tale".

To this point, Hospital's novel passes as a highly sophisticated essay in metafiction. What allows it to transcend mere cleverness is the incorporation into the novel of the real-life Zundel trial in Toronto, where the defendants had tried notoriously to depict the Holocaust as a mere fiction; here, surely, is a narrative beyond subversion.

It hardly needs adding that the fictions Turner so ingeniously deconstructs remain as utterly compelling for the reader as

Scheherazade's ever were for her Caliph, or Charade's are for Koenig. There is a broader Jamesian analogy, however, in the sense that European aristocracy and American meritocracy are supplanted in *Charades* by the new tenured nobility of the university – who read these kinds of novels, analyse them and often actually write them. Technically, *Charades* is a dazzling performance, although one is sometimes prompted to ask if there really is a life beyond the campus. Happily for Hospital, whose remarkable recent novel *Oyster* (1996) is a study in millennial sects, the answer is clearly yes.

James has undoubtedly lost stature as a novelist, although perhaps not to the extent once envisaged by Forster's devastating (but ultimately shrewd) appraisal in *Aspects of the Novel*:

> Maimed characters can alone breathe in Henry James's pages – maimed but specialized. They remind one of the exquisite deformities who haunted Egyptian art in the reign of Akhnaton – huge heads and tiny legs, but nevertheless charming. In the following reign they disappear.   (p. 162)

In the fiction of recent decades, however, the grand international theme embraced by James has acquired a new post-colonial perspective. A good example of this tendency is the fiction of **Ruth Prawer Jhabvala**, another exemplary transnational writer. Born in Germany of Polish parents, Jhabvala moved to England in 1939, but migrated to India after her marriage in 1951. Her novels draw on thirty years' experience of that country (before she moved to the United States in the early 1980s), and deal typically with the clash between Indian and Western cultures. *Heat and Dust* (1975) has been compared to Forster's *A Passage to India* (a patronizing analogy), whilst Jhabvala herself is sometimes presented as an Anglo-Indian Jane Austen (another unhelpfully ethnocentric comparison). The parallel with James, whose Americans must come to terms with Europe just as Jhabvala's English struggle with India, is more useful.

The young female narrator of *Heat and Dust* has come to the country to learn more of her grandfather's first wife, Olivia, who had left her Anglo-Indian husband to live with a local Nawab in 1923. Her account alternates regularly between the past (constructed with the help of surviving letters) and the present (in the form of a journal); this arrangement produces a strong sense of *déjà vu*, as the lives of the two women increasingly overlap. In one section of "present time", for example, the narrator visits a *suttee* shrine, whilst the complementary "past time" passage has a group of colonial ad-ministrators discussing *suttee* over dinner. In another section, the narrator becomes the lover of her Indian landlord, whilst Olivia is seduced by the Nawab (the two scenes actually share the same physical setting). Later, the narrator's pregnancy is immediately in-tuited by local midwives, whilst Olivia announces hers to both husband and lover: each woman undergoes an "abortion massage", although only Olivia finally terminates her pregnancy.

Such parallels also reflect the subtler realities of caste and class, Indian or British. Some local *dacoits* or robbers (time past) thus face execution impassively, except to inquire anxiously about the caste of the hangman; the narrator (time present) is also hampered by caste divisions. The medical superintendent's wife (time past) does not speak socially acceptable English; the young white *sadhu* Chid (time present) still talks with an incongruous "flat Midlands accent".

As might be expected from a meticulous realist who works in an Indian setting, moroever, other languages besides English are also significant social markers in *Heat and Dust*. As the narrator's knowl-edge of Hindi increases, she can speak with Indian *women* of all classes, and is no longer limited to educated professional *men* who wish to practise their English. In 1923, on the other hand, the Collector's wife speaks Hindustani out of duty rather than plea-sure, whilst Olivia's husband, Douglas (the District Officer), only values the language as an instrument for "deliver[ing] deadly insults with the most flattering courtesy" (p. 38). Husband and wife both understand the significance of this faculty ("'It's a man's game, strictly.' 'What isn't?' Olivia said").

At the centre of the narrative in time past stands the Nawab, whose attitude to things English suggests corrupt complicity rather than reluctant assimilation. One may feel some sympathy for his witty comment on British imperial attitudes: "you like rough people who fight well and are mostly on a horse. Best of all you like the horse" (p. 45); and yet the same man can only finance his own reactionary feudalism by contributions from *dacoits* who murder or mutilate local villagers to obtain them.

The Nawab's command of English is never at issue, of course, al-though if language is regarded merely as metaphor for an entire culture, then he immediately becomes a target of satire. The mountain residence, described as "a Swiss chalet with a dash of Gothic cathedral" (p. 74), may be a harmless folly, but the collected bric-à-brac in the Nawab's cellar suggests a Western shallowness to complement an intrinsic Indian decadence:

> There was an immense amount of camera equipment which, though already rusting, did not seem ever to have been used; some of it was still in its original packing. The same had happened to some modern sanitary equipment and an assortment of games such as a pinball machine, a croquet set, a miniature shooting gallery, meccano sets, and equipment for a hockey team. (p. 86)

Only in such flair for metonymic detail used for ironic or satirical ends are comparisons with Austen perhaps justified.

For all her skilful observation, however, Jhabvala remains an outsider in the Indian context. She thus differs from Anita Desai, who is more genuinely poised between two worlds, and is even further from such genuine insiders as Shashi Deshpande or Kamala Das. After her move to the United States in the 1980s, moreover, Jhabvala's links with India grew even remoter, as she embarked on a new career in cinema. Her scripts for *Autobiography of a Princess* and *Shakespearewallah* helped win these films international acclaim, although there is some irony in the fact that Jhabvala's most recent successes in this field are adaptations of both James and that earlier dabbler with India, E. M. Forster.

THE ASIAN DIASPORA

If Jhabvala moved initially towards India, then a far greater number of writers have moved away from it (or from other Asian countries). The number of talented Asian (and above all Indian) writers who live outside their country of origin is astonishing; from a Vassanji, whose ancestors arrived in East Africa over a century ago, to the latest bird of passage on a North American campus, the range of individual transnational destinies is equally impressive. So varied are these, in fact, that it is worth trying briefly to refine the original broad category of diasporic writing. On the basis of hints scattered throughout this study, and material available in Emmanuel Nelson's invaluable research guide, *Writers of the Indian*

Diaspora (1993), it is possible to make a broad division. There are, in fact, *two* diasporas.

For the many writers who have moved from India, one may speak in terms of expatriation or *exile*; for others, whose ancestors emigrated to the Caribbean, East Africa or the South Pacific, but who personally moved on to Britain, North America or Australia, a more appropriate term would be *double exile*. The previous sections have already mentioned many writers from each category. But not all of this twentieth-century double diaspora is Indian. The United States, above all, has significant writers originating from Japan, China or the Philippines; and the first of these East Asian cultures has a remarkably precise set of terms to designate an immigrant's relation both to country of origin and to new home.

All people of Japanese origin in North America (and, by extension, other countries, too) are called *nikkei*; the generation that immigrated from Japan are known as *issei*. Second-generation immigrants (the children of *issei*) are described as *nisei*, although *nisei* who lived in Japan for a large part of their childhood or adolescence are also known as *kibei*. Third-generation Japanese immigrants (the children of *nisei*) are called *sansei*. The Anglo-Japanese novelist Kazuo Ishiguro, who was born in Nagasaki in 1954 but moved to England at the age of six, could therefore be called a *nisei*, but might also qualify as a *kibei*: his first two novels, *A Pale View of Hills* (1982) and *An Artist of the Floating World* (1986), are set partly and entirely in Japan, respectively, before the shift to an English *milieu* in the better known *The Remains of the Day* (1989). On a related theme, Ishiguro once told me that his Japanese was fluent, but had never progressed beyond the expressive level of a small child. His fine *oeuvre* nevertheless suggests only fruitful and harmonious relations with the stepmother tongue.

The Japanese classification could of course be used with other countries of origin in the great Asian diaspora. Most of the writers here are effectively *issei* who emigrated from India in their early twenties, such as Kamala Markandaya (Britain), Bharati Mukherjee (the United States in the first instance) and Rohinton Mistry (Canada). A smaller number of well-known writers could be classified as *nisei*, or second-generation *nikkei*: notable examples here are Hanif Kureishi and Amy Tan. Kureishi, who depicted a young Asian boy's assimilation process in *The Buddha of Suburbia* (1987), has spoken with great honesty of his own situation: "People think I'm caught between two cultures, but I'm not. I'm British; I can make it in England. It's my father who's caught." Similarly, in Amy Tan's *The Joy Luck Club* (1989), it is the four *issei* mothers (first-generation Chinese–American immigrants) who struggle to come to terms with a new identity.

Ismith Khan (Trinidad), Ahmed Essop (South Africa) and V. S. Naipaul himself, on the other hand, are examples of *sansei*, or third-generation Indian immigrants. Khan's Pathan grandfather came independently, rather than as an indentured labourer, to Trinidad at the beginning of the twentieth century: his first novel, *The Jumbie Bird* (1961), is the classic Indo-Caribbean account of three generations of immigrants. Essop, whose grandfather came from Surat, is the chronicler of South Africa's Asian "coloured" community in his short stories including *Hajji Musa and the Hindu Fire-Walker* (1978), and the two novellas, *The Visitation* (1980) and *The Emperor* (1984).

In a number of cases, novelists of the diaspora write about the trauma of immigration itself, and two very different novels on this theme are Mukherjee's *Jasmine* (1991) and Mo's *Sour Sweet* (1982). **Bharati Mukherjee** provides an interesting challenge to classification. Born and educated in Calcutta, she is enshrined in the *Dictionary of Literary Biography* as Canadian, but would now certainly consider herself American (straight and unhyphenated). Unlike most other exiled or expatriate Indian writers, moreover, she consciously uses American rather than British-based forms of English. Her fiction, on the other hand, remains a searching examination of the immigrant experience, in terms of language and identity, or of cultural loss and adjustment.

The two opening chapters of Mukherjee's third novel, *Jasmine*, contrast Jyoti, a young peasant girl from a Punjab village, with Jane Ripplemeyer, daughter of a country banker in Iowa. Jyoti and Jane are, of course, the same person, and the major transformations in the heroine's life are each marked by a change of name as she "shuttles between identities": from Jyoti to Jasmine, on marrying a local boy at the age of fifteen; from Jasmine to Jazzy, in Lilian Gordon's Florida safe-house for illegal immigrants; from Jazzy to Jase, to work as "caregiver" for an academic family in New York; from Jase to Jane, after running away to become a bank-clerk in rural Iowa.

Throughout Jasmine's harsh childhood, brief marriage, early widowhood, and illegal residence in the United States, moreover, language is the most conspicuous marker of cultural identity.

Although a "whiz in Punjabi and Urdu" from elementary school, and a Hindi speaker, Jasmine pursues English to escape the "feudal" values of her Punjabi-speaking family. When Masterji, the Sikh teacher, begs Jasmine's father to let his daughter continue school (although she is nearly thirteen and grandmother Dida has found a suitable match), the issue is fortunately discussed in English, and Dida is therefore reduced to marginal comments in Punjabi.

Following the murder of her husband by Sikh terrorists, Jasmine begins her long odyssey right through Europe and over the Atlantic, and then from Grand Cayman to the Gulf Coast of Florida. This entire section of the novel is a tribute to all "outcasts and deportees, strange pilgrims visiting outlandish shrines", acquiring much of its force through sharp linguistic observation: the Filipina nurse and Tamil auto mechanic; hollow-eyed Muslims making long-winded advances to Jasmine in Farsi or Pashto, and then in broken Urdu; secure young Australian students (only briefly reduced to "international vagabondage") singing the praises of Perth. In Florida, Jasmine acquires a new identity with which to elude the immigration authorities, and leaves for New York, where she acquires a forged green card and economic independence. From her marginal position, Jasmine is well qualified to appreciate the rationalism and flexibility of American life, although she is correspondingly quick to expose naively condescending attitudes born of insularity and ethnocentrism. She thus reacts angrily to a teacher's patronizing comments ("doing so well, isn't he, considering") on Du, the young Vietnamese boy she adopts with her banker husband:

> *Considering what?* I want to say. Considering that he has lived through five or six languages, five or six countries, two or three centuries of history; has seen his country, city, and family butchered, bargained with pirates and bureaucrats, eaten filth in order to stay alive; that he has survived every degradation known to this century, *considering all those liabilities,* isn't it amazing that he can read a Condensed and Simplified for Modern Students edition of *A Tale of Two Cities?*   (p. 214)

In the final chapters of the novel, Du becomes something of a counterweight to Jasmine in his attitude towards the immigrant experience. Whereas Jasmine (who has not spoken Hindi or

Punjabi since leaving New York) has thoroughly embraced American life, Du (always maintaining contact with the local Vietnamese community) finally abandons his surrogate parents to rejoin his one surviving sister in California. In terms of cultural adaptation, Mukherjee distinguishes here between a virtually "genetic" and a merely "hyphenated" transformation: American and Vietnamese-American.

The cultural analogy between Jasmine and her creator is obvious. As a writer, Bharati Mukherjee, too, sees herself as American *tout court* rather than "hyphenated-American" or Indian. But with her fine psychological re-creation and sharp linguistic observation of the immigrant experience (much of it presumably first-hand), she also ultimately transcends more simplistic notions of a stepmother tongue to become a truly transcultural writer. Mukherjee's gifts are particularly evident in her more recent and ambitious historical novel, *The Holder of the World* (1993).

Timothy Mo belongs to the minority of the Asian diaspora who are not of Indian origin. Born in Hong Kong to an English mother and Cantonese father, Mo was educated in England and now lives in London. He speaks some Cantonese, but does not write Chinese, and cannot usefully be considered a "Hong Kong" writer. His first novel, *The Monkey King* (1978), nevertheless has a contemporary Hong Kong setting, although the massively ambitious *An Insular Possession* (1986) has the broader historical backdrop of the first Anglo-Chinese opium war. At an exact midpoint between the two, *Sour Sweet* (1982) is set in London's Chinese community during the sixties, whilst *The Redundancy of Courage* (1992) depicts a guerrilla movement in a barely disguised West Irian, and *Brownout on Breadfruit Boulevard* (1995) explores the existence of Chinese Americans in California. Mo's cultural hybridity, doubtless instrumental to his broad literary range and multi-cultural perspectives, also assures his place among Rushdie's transnational writers of "migrants' tales".

Sour Sweet depicts the life of a humble Chinese waiter, Chen, together with his wife, son and sister-in-law, whilst examining the criminal activities of the Hung family, or Hong Kong *triad*. Both elements are recorded with a precision characteristic of nineteenth-century realism (one need only recall the account of the Chen family's dress on their expedition to find premises in South London, or the society's street-fighting school in the Church Hall at New Cross). The two plot components fuse when Chen contracts a debt with the society, and is later wrongly suspected of cheating them.

In terms of "land" and "language", Mo's narrative of London is viewed entirely through Chinese eyes, and – despite the English-language medium – even through the Cantonese language. Chen has little English, his wife Lily even less, and only Mui the younger sister (after an unvaried diet of English television) makes any genuine headway in the new language. No-one is concerned by these issues, however, and there is actually some alarm at the son's "disturbing tendency to speak English as well as Cantonese", a fault which not even parallel education at a Chinese primary school can entirely remove. For the rest, the Chen family is content to possess the minimal English necessary to sell the bastardized Cantonese food that appeals to the *faan gwai* (or "foreign devils"), from their South London Chinese takeaway.

Such details suggest a fairly light-hearted, even satirical, account of a London Hong Kong family, although much of Mo's satire, direct or indirect, is reserved for the host population. The irony is more ambivalent, however, with Lily's delight at the "tea song" little Man Kee learns at school (the English are "quite civilised for once"), or indignation when her English guests thank the deity for food she herself has provided. In matters of language presentation, Mo apparently shows great skill. A reader without Cantonese cannot pass judgement, but the presumably literal translations of forms of address, formulae of ritual humility, and occasional Cantonese aphorisms sound convincing. More subtly, too, Mo notes the difficulty of reproducing finer nuances in a foreign language:

> Her voice, so expressive and live in her native Cantonese, became shrill, peremptory and strangely lifeless in its level pitching when she spoke English. She would have sounded hostile and nervous; a cross between a petulant child and a nagging old shrew, neither of which descriptions adequately fitted the mature and outward-going young woman who was Lily Chen.   (p. 135)

But *Sour Sweet* is more than socio-linguistic fieldwork, for language in the novel is simply the most obvious correlative for an entire culture: it is, as Margaret Atwood remarked, "everything you do". For all her wisdom and tolerance, Lily is outraged, for example, at her young son's expressed wish to be a gardener when he grows up (rather than an accountant as she dreams, or even a restaurant owner – the limit of father Chen's ambition); the thought of Man Kee becoming merely another kind of "coolie" provokes her to tear up his carefully cultivated mangrove tree. Cultural values are as deeply engrained as language.

In mere terms of plot, the narrative ends tragically when Chen is erroneously "washed" by the Triad society. Lily, who assumes the absence is a temporary one with a view to improving the family economy, mistakes the society's monthly compensation payments for remittances from a dutiful husband. In broader symbolic terms the conclusion may be even more poignant, however, as sister Mui leaves to marry the elderly Lo (the family's only male friend), takes out naturalization papers, and opens a fish 'n chip shop. By a final stroke of irony, moreover, this cultural (and perhaps linguistic) surrender will occur in the very premises which Chen and Lily had once rejected as too grand for their own requirements.

One of the major novelists of double exile is **V. S. Naipaul**, a much anglicized Trinidadian of Indian ancestry now based in Britain: to compound this transnational element, *A Bend in the River* (1979) is also an Indo-Caribbean writer's portrait of Indians in Africa. The novel provides a dystopian account of a newly independent African state, clearly based on Mobotu's Zaïre. Salim, an Indian trader and the novel's protagonist, leaves his family on the East African coast for a business opportunity in the interior, incidentally retracing in reverse direction a traditional route of the slave trade.

Naipaul then follows the attempts of a small group of individuals to construct or reconstruct their lives in an unstable post-colonial environment: these include Salim's assistant Metty (actually a hereditary family servant or slave); the energetic village *marchande*, Zabeth; the latter's ambitious son, Ferdinand; and Father Huismans, the Belgian principal of the local *lycée*. The squalor of the environment is partially eclipsed by the new "Domain", the great residential showpiece on the edge of the newly emerging city by the "bend in the river". This false idyll is the home of the beautiful Yvette and her husband Raymond, European intellectual and history professor at the model polytechnic housed there. But the domain itself, of course, is a hoax and a sham, just as Raymond personally has become an empty shell, without the influence he once possessed over a now increasingly autocratic president. For Salim, too, the twin appeal of the New Africa and of Yvette herself quickly fades: the former with a gradual realization of the domain's "shoddy grandeur", the latter in the bitter aftermath of a passionate affair.

The theme, setting, and even the mood of the novel are thus Conradian, replacing the Dickensian humour and pathos of *A House for Mr Biswas*. But Naipaul's style has nothing of Conrad's verbosity, and his sharp vignettes of futility and despair in distant places are closer to Graham Greene. Also reminiscent of Greene is the growing convergence of author and protagonist, as Salim's lucidity and detachment increasingly resemble the characteristic pessimism of Naipaul himself. Portrayed as a man with "no family, no flag, no fetish" or, alternatively, as a "man without a side", Salim might seem a rather self-indulgent projection of the author. Like Naipaul, moreover, he carries a British passport and at one point moves to England. But he soon returns to Africa, and falls victim to the new economic policy of "radicalization", with his government-expropriated store passing into African hands.

In addition to its disenchanted account of a newly independent African state, *A Bend in the River* is also a fictive history of the double exile experienced by so many Indians, whether in East Africa, the West Indies, or the South Pacific. Salim himself is the descendant of a Gujarati trading family from North-West India, while his friend and confidant, Nazruddin, is the grandson of a Punjabi who had worked as a contract labourer on the East African railway. But Naipaul is no more tolerant towards a certain Indian mentality than he is towards what he regards as the African character: "our civilization", he has Salim suggest, "has always been our prison", referring to the passivity and fatalism that usually kept expatriate Indians aloof from their adopted countries. Ultimately then, *A Bend in the River* may be as memorable for its portrayal of deracination and double exile among Indians, as for its harsh indictment of post-colonial Africa. And it is in this sociological sense that Naipaul is most obviously a teller of "migrants' tales". In Naipaul's case, moreover, the theme of physical and cultural displacement is as relevant to the tale (Salim's story) as it is to the teller (Naipaul himself).

Another double exile is **Moyez Vassanji**, although the author's background is Indo-African like Salim's rather than Indo-Caribbean like Naipaul's. Vassanji's novel *The Gunny Sack* (1989) uses the device of the title, an old bag bequeathed to the narrator by his great-aunt, as a metaphor for the narrative imagination, or (more explicitly) as the "storehouse of memory". The contents of the sack enable Vassanji's narrator (another Salim) to re-create a chronicle of Indian life in East Africa over four generations and almost a hundred years.

The three parts of the novel are each centred around a prominent female character. The first of these is the great-aunt herself, brought from India as a wife for the pioneering Dhanji Govindji, who has already shocked his family by setting up house with an ex-slave-woman and producing Afro-Indian offspring. Historically, this section covers the German colonial period in Tanganyika, the native Maji Maji revolt, and the effect of the First World War on the colony.

The second part, "Kulsum", focuses on the narrator's mother, introduced (by a characteristic chronological leap) as a decrepit old woman. The ensuing flashback to her early married life with Juma, son of the renegade Huseni, then records the successful attempt of the couple to escape the tyranny of the Indian extended family. It also depicts both the relative idyll of life in Nairobi before the Mau Mau emergency, and a subsequently harsher existence in Dar-es-Salaam, with all of Salim's childhood tensions and traumas. In a broader historical perspective, these chapters describe the independence of the ex-German (and then British) colony, a political coup and riots in Zanzibar, followed by further rioting in Tanganyika. They end with the unification of the two ex-colonies in the modern state of Tanzania, and the subsequent process of Africanization.

The third part of the novel deals with the narrator's youth, beginning with military service on Lake Victoria in the heart of Africa, where he meets and falls in love with a fellow conscript, Aminta, who gives her name to the section. When Aminta is later arrested for political conspiracy, the highly compromised Salim makes a rapid escape to the United States.

The gunny sack itself has varied functions within the narrative, ranging from a simple metaphor for memory, to a kind of psychological screen to cover traumatic childhood memories exorcised by the act of narration. Vassanji's novel was opportunistically launched as the African answer to *Midnight's Children*, but the analogy is misleading, since the book contains relatively little metafiction or magic realism. Far from suggesting the magic of the Arabian Nights, the celebrated sack often seems little more than a simple framing device, like that of Scott's "Tales of My Landlord" or Dickens's "Master Humphrey's Clock". The novel's ultimate

literary interest may lie elsewhere: in its imaginative re-creation of
an entire diaspora relegated to the margins of colonial history; and
in its sensitive analysis of a social group that largely lost its links
with Mother India, without ever truly integrating itself in its new
African home. In both respects, the closest literary analogy is less
Rushdie's *Midnight's Children* than Naipaul's *A Bend in the River*.

Two other novelists who defy most attempts at classification are
Lindsey Collen and Zulfikar Ghose. Utterly disparate in ideology
and intellectual formation, the two writers paradoxically approach
each other in the examples considered here, with their clear post-
colonial parameters and respective Shakespearean subtexts.

Lindsey Collen grew up in South Africa, has lived in London
and New York, but is now settled in Mauritius. She thus mirrors
some of the cultural diversity of Mauritius itself, with its long colonial history (including a century of French domination before 150
years of British rule) and its present multi-ethnic character. The
island is considered part of East Africa, although a majority of its
population is of Indian origin, a historical legacy of the same institution of identured labour that has conditioned the ethnic balance
of Trinidad, Guyana, or Fiji.

Mauritius has produced indigenous anglophone novelists such
as Deepchand Beeharry, with his wide-ranging studies of the
island's ethnically Indian population, from *Never Good Bye* (1965) to
The Heart and Soul (1983). Its best-known novelist, on the other
hand, is arguably the francophone writer Malcolm de Chazal.
These are significant points, since over half of the island's 1.09
million population speak a French-based *Créole*, whilst just under
half speak some Indian language, predominantly Bhojpuri – regarded in turn as a kind of Hindi creole; the number of official an-
glophones is tiny (2,000 according to the 1983 census). Predictably
then, the implied linguistic medium of Collen's *The Rape of Sita* is
Créole alternating with Bhojpuri, whilst Collen's English narrative
also explicitly thematizes both languages. Notions of a "stepmother
tongue" are suggestive here, then, although the concept may mean
different things to the cosmopolitan South African-educated Collen
and her predominantly Indo-Mauritian characters.

The most striking features of the novel are its incorporation of
oral techniques, its fusion of Western and Indian myth, and its explicit linkage of sexual violence with (post-)colonial exploitation.
Collen's highly self-conscious narrator, Iqbal the Umpire, thus
recites the story of Sita: daughter of political activists, partner of the

radical Dharma, and protégée of the old stonecutter Ton Tipyer, she is raped during a stopover on the island of Réunion on the way home from a conference in the Seychelles. In imitation of oral history, Iqbal begins his story with the traditional Mauritian formula *Sirandann* – "shall I begin" – and receives the response *Sanpek* or "go ahead". His painstakingly assembled account of Sita is also supplemented by the oral traditions of the community, right back to the heroine's great-great-grandmother, Olga Olande, who in turn recalled the burning down of the Dutch East India Company's headquarters in 1695.

The novel's intertextual links are partly Shakespearean, although not *The Tempest* but *The Rape of Lucrece* (Sita's assailant, the *kolom* Rowan Tarquin, even shares the name of the historical Lucretia's violator). Sita's own name, however, is that of Rama's wife, abducted by the King of Lanka in the Indian epic of the *Ramayana*. Her modern avatar is the Indian radical populist Phoolan Devi. The physical rape of Sita is also an obvious allegory of the historical experience of colonization, a parallel underlined most emphatically by the heroine in a telling variation of the "land" and "language" motifs. The rape thus occurs on Réunion (unlike Mauritius, still a colonial possession), where the independent Sita feels disoriented in both politico-geographical and cultural–linguistic terms: "*She was out of her geography. He was in his. She didn't know the language here. He did*" (p. 152; my emphasis).

The final section of the narrative features a long internal monologue by Sita, developing more fully the historical and psychological parallels between sexual and colonial violation, from the overseer's abuse of his female workers on the sugar estate to America's rape of Iraq in the Gulf War. It is the latter implications of Collen's novel, as much as the author's own background, which allow it to transcend narrower regional categories.

Zulfikar Ghose was born in Sialkot, India (now Pakistan), and moved to Britain after partition, before making an academic career in the United States. A native speaker of Punjabi, but also heir to the rich Urdu legacy of the subcontinent's Muslims, he records his "first broken attempts to speak English" after moving with his family to Bombay in the early 1940s. In a lively but tantalizing interview with Jussawalla and Dasenbrock (*Writers of the Post-Colonial World*), he describes himself as "British" rather than "multi-cultural": "I'm really more Anglo-Saxon than the Anglo-Saxons" (p. 187). And yet, however playfully he treats constructions of identity here, it is significant that Ghose has always published in English ("the only language that I have").

Figures of Enchantment (1986) is the Ghose novel most easily related to post-colonial paradigms. The first and third of its five sections follow the life of Felipe Gamboa, a humble government clerk in a nameless South American country, dismissed from his job, wrongly arrested, and exiled to a remote island. The second and fourth sections follow the destiny of Federico Chagra, boyfriend of Gamboa's sixteen-year-old daughter Mariana, as he acquires the cloak and magic amulet from Popayan's theatrical costumes shop which make his wishes come true. The novel's social and magical realism are conflated in the final section, when Federico arrives as a surveyor on the island where Felipe is being held. *The Tempest* now becomes an increasingly insistent subtext as an allegorical drama is played out between the unrecognized Federico (suggesting Shakespeare's Ferdinand), the elderly Felipe (Prospero), his new daughter Herminia (Miranda), and the monstrous islander Balthazar (Caliban).

The true significance of *Figures of Enchantment*, however, may lie in its being quite untypical of the novelist's *oeuvre*. In the interview already quoted, Ghose refers disparagingly to contemporary writers so concerned with sociological and political content that they succeed only in producing "new versions of the nineteenth-century novel" (p. 185): perhaps a valid comment on some post-colonial fiction founded on what Wilson Harris refers to as the "realist fallacy". He insists that he is not a "content novelist", and believes in the total primacy of language, a view reflected in a versatile series of a dozen novels and a number of significant critical works, including *Hamlet, Prufrock, and Language* (1978) and *The Fiction of Reality* (1983). His early novels, *The Contradictions* (1966), on the clash between British and Indian culture, and *The Murder of Aziz Khan* (1967), set in the newly created Pakistan, were followed by the major trilogy *The Incredible Brazilian*, consisting of *The Incredible Brazilian: The Native* (1972), *The Beautiful Empire* (1975), and *A Different World* (1978). The latter follow four centuries of Brazilian history in the various reincarnations of their picaresque hero Gregório Peixota da Silva Xavier.

Where uncompromisingly political content is concerned, Ghose could well have included *The Rape of Sita* in his strictures, although the latter can hardly be related to the conventional nineteenth-century realist novel. In its use of myth and the fantastic to explore post-colonial positions, in fact, Collen is by no means remote from Ghose's own explicitly political *Figures of Enchantment*; in this context, then, there may be good reason yet again for trusting not the teller but the tale.

Ghose also produced an early autobiography, *Confessions of a Native-Alien* (1965), notable for its development of the "triple" exile theme (India/Pakistan, Britain, and the United States); while his most sympathetic critic, Alamgir Hashmi, has repeatedly emphasized his author's Kroetsch-like quest to create a language for a hitherto "uncreated" land.

If there is a single writer who represents the break-down of national and ethnic divisions, however, it may be **Michael Ondaatje**. A product of Sri Lanka's tiny *Burgher* minority – a group that is English-speaking, although of predominantly Portuguese or Dutch descent – Ondaatje attended school in England, before emigrating in his late teens to Canada, where he now lives. It may be significant, therefore, that the quartet of solitary, marginalized major characters in Ondaatje's *The English Patient* (1992) includes no Englishman or Sri Lankan, but two Canadians.

The setting of the novel is the war-torn *Villa Girolamo* near Florence, behind the advancing Allied armies at the end of the Second World War. Here, the horribly burned and anonymous "English patient", survivor of a plane crash in North Africa, is tended by Hana, his Canadian nurse. Journal extracts and conversations gradually reveal the patient's previous life as a desert explorer, before his rescue by a Bedouin tribe and internment by Allied security forces. Traumatized by her own war experiences (including the recent death of her father), Hana lives in a state of mental suffering equivalent to the physical one experienced by her patient.

The isolation of the couple is broken by the arrival of David Caravaggio, an Italo-Canadian attached to the Allied forces, and Kirpal Singh (Kip), a British-trained Sikh sapper sent to defuse land mines at the villa. With a courage and sensitivity that had made him volunteer for one of the few humane occupations in modern warfare, he is also the one person capable of penetrating Hana's solitude.

The English Patient is not principally a love story, however, but a novel about transcending spatial, temporal, and – above all – national boundaries. The patient is described as: "A man with no face. An ebony pool. All identification consumed in a fire." No amount of interrogation by suspicious military intelligence can identify him as anything but another of those "international bastards". Details nevertheless later emerge of an extraordinary career in the deserts of North Africa: a life spent in friendly rivalry with fellow explorers and peaceful co-existence with local communities is now lyrically evoked:

> There were rivers of desert tribes, the most beautiful humans I've met in my life. We were German, English, Hungarian, African – all of us insignificant to them. Gradually we became nationless. I came to hate nations. We are deformed by nation-states.   (p. 138)

This existence had, of course, been interrupted by Europe's war between these very nation-states. *The English Patient* thus belongs to a group of narratives which takes a personal stand against the insanity of war (*All Quiet on the Western Front* is often quoted here). But with its Italian setting, and growing love (here non-physical) between nurse and patient, the novel also inevitably recalls another major example of the genre: Hemingway's *A Farewell to Arms*. Ondaatje's main characters, like Hemingway's, also make their individual peace. Hana finds consolation in the care of her patient and her love for the young sapper; Caravaggio discovers the wounded man's real identity, but sacrifices political loyalty to personal friendship; even Kip, who has constantly risked his own life for the elimination of evil, withdraws in bitterness after the atomic attack on Japan ("They would never have dropped such a bomb on a white nation").

The English Patient owes much to its romantic subtexts of the spy story and the explorer's tale. A more lasting impression of the novel, however, is that of a timeless and endlessly repeated folly: the Italian campaign of 1943–4 is described as the last medieval war to be fought in Europe; Allied attempts to dislodge the Germans are compared to the efforts of Crusaders against Saracens; the faces of modern soldiers resemble those on frescoes by Piero della Francesca. The tragic ironies of history are always present. It is hard not to see a silent judgement at the end of the novel, when Kip and Hana each withdraw from a European world of so much promise but so little fulfilment. In its broadest terms, their gesture reflects a rejection of the national for the *supra*- or *trans*national. It is a gesture implied, moreover, by all tellers of migrants' tales.

The most prominent case of single exile in the Indian diaspora, however, is probably that of **Salman Rushdie**, the first to discuss tellers of migrants' tales. Although Rushdie is often described as an Anglo-Indian writer, it is surely the second element that predominates in *Midnight's Children*, a novel saturated with the sights and sounds of the subcontinent, and structured by the major events of its recent history. The account of the Aziz-Sinai family moves from Kashmir to India, to Pakistan and Bangladesh (and back again to India), but also proceeds from the Amritsar massacre (1919), to Independence and Partition (1947), the assassination of Gandhi (1948), the Sino-Indian conflict (1962), the war over Kashmir (1965), and the birth of Bangladesh (1971), ending with Indira Gandhi's State of Emergency (1975–7).

The central conceit of the novel, however, is the group of one thousand and one children, all with special talents, born within an hour of India's independence on 15 August 1947; the narrator, Saleem Sinai, and his alter ego, Shiva, being born closest to the magic hour, possess the greatest powers of all. The number of potential narratives now available is only the novel's most obvious echo of the Arabian Nights. The MCC (or Midnight's Children Conference) also gives the novel its cyclical pattern. This group declines steadily right up to the declaration of the State of Emergency (that longer and more sinister form of "Midnight"), when only four hundred and twenty members can be mustered by nervous authorities for compulsory vasectomy or hysterectomy (or both in one spectacular case). But the adult Shiva has by now impregnated half the wives of Delhi society, and it is these children, together with Saleem's son Aadam, who will form a new Midnight's Children Conference.

If both groups of children offer a kind of microcosm of India, then the novel itself also provides a metafictional commentary on the process of writing. As Saleem increasingly assumes the role of Scheherazade, his servant Padma (the lowest common denominator of the *narratee*) plays a low-brow Caliph with a preference for linear narrative. Elsewhere, authors are implicitly compared to the illusionists of the Delhi magicians' ghetto, to Lifafa Das the "dekho-dilli" or peepshow man, and (most ingeniously of all) to the Bombay chutney-makers. For as he completes his thirtieth chapter (like one more jar of *Special Formula*), Saleem aspires to nothing less than the "chutnification of history; the grand hope of the pickling of time!" Within these parameters, Rushdie has an evocative power unequalled in the *English novel* since Dickens (or even in the *novel in English* since *Ulysses*). Certain accounts of Bombay are as meticulous as any representation of Joyce's Dublin.

The narrator–protagonist is also the novel's main reference point in terms of linguistic sensibility. In his exclusive English-speaking enclave, the young Saleem has little to do with Bombay's vernacular languages; by another unlikely coincidence, however, it is the fictional Saleem who sparks off the very real language riots between the city's Marathi and Gujarati speakers in 1957. And when Saleem acquires his capacity for "supernatural ham radio", his first impression is of linguistic incomprehension: "… from Malayalam to Naga dialects, from the purity of Lucknow Urdu to the Southern slurrings of Tamil. I understood only a fraction of the things being said within the walls of my skull" (p. 168). Later, in Bangladesh, the "vendor of notions" will offer him a magic belt whose wearer will automatically be able to speak Hindi (p. 372), a presumed dig at India's drive for a "national language". A command of foreign languages, whether English, or even (in earlier sections) German and Persian, is often the main indicator in *Midnight's Children* of a secular, humanist and cosmopolitan outlook, as opposed to an enclosed, traditional, and even obscurantist one: the old matriarch Naseem Aziz's idea of Hell is thus a place as hot as Rajasthan where everyone must learn seven languages; or if God had expected us to speak several tongues, she remarks elsewhere, why did he only give us one? Familiarity with foreign languages (or cultures) should not, however, preclude knowledge or understanding of indigenous ones. For if India is the mythical land, the great "collective fiction", then Rushdie is presently its greatest explorer in English. Saleem's boast towards the end of *Midnight's Children*, "to understand me, you'll have to swallow a world" (p. 383), remains a fitting epigraph for the novel, its protagonist, and its author.

The earlier analogy between Rushdie and Joyce is fruitful. For if Joyce's writing presents the paradox of a man who spent almost forty years in exile, but creatively never left Dublin, then Rushdie has a similar (if not quite so all-absorbing) ambivalence towards his native Bombay (described elsewhere as "my lost city"). Admittedly, Rushdie's early *Grimus* (1975) is an American-based fiction that Thomas Pynchon might have written (and possibly suppressed), while *Shame* (1983) is a fantastic treatment of Pakistan. The joint protagonists of *The Satanic Verses* (1988) are both from Bombay, however, while the city even dominates the Da Gama–Zogoiby family saga of *The Moor's Last Sigh* (1995).

Bombay's centrality is defined by its protean energy and diversity, although the freedom generated by these forces is undermined by language. When Saladin Chamcha, the quintessential mimic-man of *The Satanic Verses*, returns to India, he realizes that he is now "caught in the aspic of his adopted language" (p. 58). More disturbingly, Bombay's very tolerance is threatened in *The Moor's Last Sigh* by the Hindu-fundamentalism (together with the linguistic separatism) of Raman Fielding and his Mumbai's Axis (a savage caricature of Bal Thackeray's Shiv Sena party).

Rushdie writes more explicitly of land, language and cultural identity in several essays of *Imaginary Homelands* (1991). In the title piece, for example, he credits the writer who is "out-of-country and even out-of-language" with an enhanced ability to "speak properly and concretely on a subject of universal significance and appeal" (p. 12). In a later essay, he refers to himself as a "minute-man", a late product of Macaulay's arrogant demand for an anglicized Indian elite. In another colonial context, of course, the "minute-men" were the American revolutionary militia named for their ability to deploy at short notice against British troops; latter-day "minute-men", finally, are missiles used by America to defend its own empire.

The idea of the "minute-man" who is "out-of-country and even out-of-language" is a particularly suitable concept with which to conclude this section. For Rushdie, one of the giants of contemporary anglophone fiction, seems to anticipate in these and many other comments from *Invisible Homelands* all the connotations proposed in the Introduction for the "Stepmother Tongue": simple linguistic imposition (in however attenuated a sense); cultural asset (for the enlarged perspectives it offers); vehicle of subversion (in its challenge to native English complacency); and – ultimately – an agent that is inseparable, and indeed indistinguishable, from its cultural analogue of the mother tongue.

Afterword

POST-POST-COLONIAL

While distinctions between mother and stepmother tongue continue to be eroded, current post-colonial paradigms face a similar threat of obsolescence. The aim of this postscript, then, is to attempt another kind of "extroduction", and suggest how, or to what extent, post-colonial theory could also be displaced in the near future.

The present study is arguably under-theorized – in the context of *extroduction* – and it may be objected that it is hard to lead readers *out* of a field which they were never properly led *into*. My lukewarm response to theory does not imply that, for the student of new anglophone fiction, addresses of good bookshops in Delhi and Manila (or even a Maori–English dictionary) are more useful than Homi Bhabha's *Nation and Narration*; it must be admitted, however, that the lack of space in this study for post-colonial theory is not even my primary regret. More troubling, for example, was the arbitrary restriction to *novels*, the literary form privileged by contemporary Western discourse, not to mention contemporary Western publishers. This has occurred at the expense of other literary genres or even other discursive forms. In the first context one need only remember those writers who choose the short story as their natural vehicle of expression (from Canada's Mavis Gallant to Jamaica's Olive Senior); or the autobiographical tradition so central to African American writers (from Langston Hughes to Maya Angelou), black South Africans (Peter Abrahams's *Tell Freedom* or Esk'ia Mphahlele's *Down Second Avenue*), and Caribbean authors (C. L. R. James's *Beyond a Boundary* or Austin Clarke's *Growing Up Stupid Under the Union Jack*). And where other discursive forms are concerned, there is little space for the oral tradition or its modern corollary of narrative in contemporary performance arts.

It is nevertheless important to remind the general reader once again of what else is missing from this study. The most useful theoretical introduction to post-colonial literature is widely regarded as being the collaborative effort of Bill Ashcroft, Gareth Griffiths and Helen Tiffin, *The Empire Writes Back* (now complemented by a *Post-*

Colonial Studies Reader from the same team). It is with these two works that theoretical study should begin.

The Empire Writes Back covers a wide range of issues connected with the theory and practice of post-colonial literatures; it ends with a critical bibliography and suggested study programme (even complete with recommended reading order). The massive *Post-Colonial Studies Reader* offers brief extracts from many of these works: all one ever wished to know of the subject, perhaps, between the same two covers. Such sheer convenience made one Caribbean scholar dismiss the combined project as the *Windows 95* of post-colonial studies. The analogy is not, however, as damning as was clearly intended: *Windows 95* is an immensely helpful tool (this book, for example, owes much to it), although such software packages date rapidly. In the same way, *The Empire Writes Back* – without a second edition in the near future – may soon be chiefly remembered for an admittedly snappy title and the typographic idiosyncracy that launched the egalitarian concept of "world englishes".

For all their innovation or much-needed revisionism, moreover, Ashcroft, Griffiths and Tiffin still define modern anglophone writing (if only ironically) in terms of *Empire* (essentially the British one): there is no serious consideration of other imperialist tendencies, particularly those of the United States, whilst one of the most complex post-colonial arenas of all, Ireland, hardly receives a mention.

In certain respects, the *Post-Colonial Studies Reader* is even more helpful than *The Empire Writes Back*. The anthology is split into fourteen large sections, ranging sensibly from such headings as "Issues and Debates" through "Nationalism", "Hybridity" and "Language" to "Product and Consumption". The collection is also admirable for its inclusion of oppositional voices. Here, for example, is W. J. T. Mitchell's "Postcolonial Culture, Postimperial Criticism" with its thesis that post-colonial discourse is "a coloniser in its turn", adding value to the literary "raw material"; here is Kwame Anthony Appiah's "The Postcolonial and the Postmodern", describing the *comprador* intelligentsia "mediating a trade in cultural commodities"; here is Ketu Katrak's "Decolonizing Culture: Toward a Theory for Post-colonial Women's texts", regretting the lack of attention to the theoretical productions of post-colonial writers themselves, deploring the role of texts as raw materials for theory producers, and lamenting theoretical production as an end in itself; here, finally, is Barbara Christian's "The Race for Theory", adopting the stance of the traditional critic against the hegemony of theorists.

The *Post-Colonial Studies Reader* contains good theory, bad theory, and even incomprehensible theory, but theory it always remains. Among over eighty extracts in the reader, moreover, barely a dozen are by creative writers (most notably, Achebe, Ngũgĩ and Kroetsch); and elsewhere, as Barbara Christian points out, post-colonial theory itself is less suggestive of scientific discourse than of Biblical exegesis, with its ritual obeisance to its own prophets. There is a particularly clear example of this in an essay (which had better remain unidentified) where consecutive paragraphs begin "As Diana Brydon has illustrated ..." and "As Stephen Slemon has demonstrated ..."; the reader's misgivings are increased by the fact that Brydon herself is only recapitulating what Deleuze and Guattari have earlier "illustrated". It does not seem excessive to describe this kind of academic atavism as incestuous.

Creative writers themselves have often expressed similar reservations towards some post-colonial theorists. Wole Soyinka, for example, was remarkably prescient in a comment written more than twenty years ago:

> We black Africans have been blandly invited to submit ourselves to a second epoch of colonialism – this time by a universal-humanoid abstraction defined and conducted by individuals whose theories and prescriptions are derived from the apprehension of *their* world and *their* history, *their* social neuroses and *their* value systems.

Ironically, this passage may also be found in the *Reader* (p. 256), for – like any respectable grand narrative – post-colonial theory can tolerate and absorb most kinds of intellectual challenge, although it remains vulnerable to irony, ridicule, or plain indifference.

Zulfikar Ghose thus asked recently: "Is there anyone left who loves literature more than some imbecile theory that can be woven around it?" Whilst Bharati Mukherjee, in an Indian context, refers even more scathingly to the position of certain "assassins of the imagination":

> people who desperately need a political theory to which they reduce the quirkiness and interrogativeness of fiction. Aijaz Ahmed [sic] has questioned the right of people like Edward Said and his *chelas* to speak for critics here when they are permanently

located in their privatised world of lucrative Chairs. They've refashioned themselves, given themselves false biographies of marginalised peoples.   (*Times of India*, 31 December 1995)

Elsewhere in the article, Mukherjee refers explicitly to Homi Bhabha and Gayatri Spivak, widely regarded, together with Said, as the three most significant figures in the field of post-colonial theory.

Bhabha, whose writing has concentrated on such issues as marginality, hybridity, mimicry and subalternity, remains best known for the collection *Nation and Narration* (1990) – where he is editor and a major contributor. His own intellectual formation is itself a powerful hybrid; it includes Fanon's pioneering studies of marginalization, *The Wretched of the Earth* and *Black Skins, White Masks*; Foucault's emphasis on the power residing with those who control discursive practice; Derrida's decentring of cultural and epistemological formations; and certain aspects of modern psychoanalysis. There is nevertheless a paradox at the heart of Bhabha's work: the theorist who made his reputation by deconstructing the centre and revalidating the marginal has in turn become part of an academic establishment, the authoritative centre of his own discipline. Among theorists, Bhabha may be the natural leader of that small group of Western (or Westernized) scholars, castigated by Mukherjee and others, who have literally *expropriated* literary discourse.

Gayatri Spivak, on the other hand, is a feminist-Marxist-deconstructionist who later extended her interests to post-colonial studies. Originally winning acclaim for a virtuoso translation of Derrida's *Of Grammatology* (1976), with its important prefatory essay, she is ultimately a less eclectic figure than Bhabha, and in fact owes most to Derrida. Her seminal work remains the collection of essays published under the title *In Other Worlds* (1988). Widely berated for her obscurity by readers and critics alike, she is normally more appreciated by a small band of fellow theorists.

The third seminal figure in post-colonial studies is Edward Said, a writer quite distinct from Bhabha or Spivak in his ability to engage theorist, critic and general reader alike. His early monograph, *Beginnings* (1975/1985), used structuralist and even formalist approaches in a broadly philosophical disquisition on the creative intentions of writers; the essay collection *The World, the Text, and the Critic* (1983) then introduced the central concepts of "secular criticism" and the "worldliness" of texts (neither of them simple assumptions in the light of Said's Palestinian background);

Said's mentor here was Foucault. The key texts for post-colonial studies, however, are *Orientalism* (1979) and the more accessible *Culture and Imperialism* (1993), examining the discursive practices underlying Western contructions of the Orient and Empire, respectively. The achievements of Said raise the question of whether there could be a powerful new critical discourse capable of absorbing the whole field of post-colonial theory, before applying it usefully to a major literary tradition. That the answer is a ringing affirmative emerges from the finest response yet to this challenge: Declan Kiberd's *Inventing Ireland* (1995).

Kiberd's central thesis in his survey of Irish (and Anglo-Irish) literature from Spenser's *View of the Present State of Ireland* (1598/1633) to Brian Friel's *Translations* (1980) is the mutual dependence of Ireland and England in their constructions of self and other. As such, his book reflects a new mood in post-colonial criticism, exemplified, at a purely theoretical level, by Aijaz Ahmad's *In Theory* (1992), or, in monograph form, by Sara Suleri's *The Rhetoric of English India* (1992). The two latter books, superficially so different, share the common revisionist aim of eroding the binary oppositions of colonial discourse, rather than merely inverting them, in the manner of many earlier theorists. Ahmad's original target is the rigid division of literary discourse into First and Third Worlds by the American Marxist critic Fredric Jameson; Suleri's is the more general obsession with "otherness" that characterizes post-colonial critical orthodoxy.

The question of what might transform or even supplant post-colonial paradigms is complex. In general terms, one may envisage a "post-post-colonial condition" by simply drawing analogies from other quite disparate theoretical fields. Few scholars today, for example, would describe themselves unreservedly as either "narratologists" or "deconstructionists"; and yet it is clear that key insights from each approach (say the formers' analysis of narrative temporality or the latters' concept of textual indeterminacy) have been absorbed into the critical mainstream. A similar process will doubtless occur with post-colonial theory.

To predict the last independent advances on the road to assimilation is even more difficult. The present study has consistently emphasized issues of language and identity, which – together with the concept of cultural hybridity – seem likely to remain key concepts. There is, for example, a marked tendency in certain areas of contemporary anglophone fiction to become more rather than less national(ist) or regional in character. Kenyan author Ngũgĩ wa Thiong'o still remains an extreme case, with his categorical rejection of the English language; Jamaican short-story writer Olive Senior, on the other hand, explicitly regards herself as bilingual (in English and Creole) and, like a number of her colleagues, wishes to write primarily for a Caribbean audience; Samoan novelist Albert Wendt distinguishes carefully between indigenous and neo-colonial writing in the South Pacific, while stressing the need for an anthology in the vernacular languages of the region; the Maori novelist Witi Ihimaera still registers bemusement at the idea of being read by an American or European audience. Examples could be multiplied endlessly. For all these authors, *dialect* and *sociolect* (whether conceived as creole, patois/"patwoh", nation language, or some other language variety) remain central issues.

With many other writers in the stepmother tongue, however, transcultural characteristics make it difficult to place them within a national tradition. In economic jargon, these tellers of migrant tales might be called multinational enterprises; in older humanist terms, they could be seen as constituting a single indivisible "republic of letters". The latter phrase is not as antiquated as it sounds, incidentally, for within the context of the modern academy, it acquires a new resonance. One might, in fact, propose a literary continuum here, whose two poles are formed by university teachers who write novels and novelists who teach at universities (predominantly American, British, or Australasian)! More seriously, the accompanying process of institutionalization undergone by these writer–academics generates a cultural hybridity, even as it promotes a certain homogenization of the English language. By a curious paradox, then, the cosmopolitan novelist may ultimately become a "country of one", where *idiolect* (i.e. the linguistic system of an individual speaker) rather than dialect or sociolect is now the key concept.

In a related context, it may be significant that the mushrooming of literary theory since the 1960s has developed many text-based, reader-oriented and above all, politically determined approaches, but – with regard to the author – has made little progress beyond traditional Romantic-humanist assumptions. Even psychoanalytical theory, as exemplified by, say, Peter Brooks's *Reading for the Plot* (1984), was more interested in the psychodynamics of the text than in that of the writer. It is not far-fetched, then, to predict for the near feature a major new theoretical initiative by way of a writer-oriented approach. From what synthesis of linguistics and modern life-sciences this might emerge, however, is a question beyond the scope of this study.

FURTHER READING

Extroduction

Two books mentioned in the context of Indian fiction, *Writers of the Indian Diaspora* (1993) and *Reworlding: the Literature of the Indian Diaspora*, respectively edited and authored by Emmanuel S. Nelson, are highly relevant here.

Simon Gikandi's *Writing in Limbo: Modernism and Caribbean Literature* (Ithaca: Cornell University Press, 1992) consistently emphasizes the theme of exile.

Various contributions to the New Essays in American Ethnic Literatures series, particularly in the volume *Memory, Narrative, and Identity* (Boston: Northeastern University Press, 1994), edited by Amritjit Singh et al., are suggestive. Certain essays in Salman Rushdie's *Imaginary Homelands: Essays and Criticism, 1981–1991* (London: Granta Books, 1992) are seminal.

Afterword

Bibliographical details of a number of works mentioned in this section are given at the end of the Introduction (p. 26).

Works Discussed

The following eighty novels are discussed more fully in *The Stepmother Tongue*, in the order in which they appear here. The list is intended as a simple reference guide rather than a formal bibliography; it thus includes author, title, original publication date and edition used in this study (an accessible paperback imprint where possible). Unless otherwise indicated, the latter's place of publication is London (or Harmondsworth in the case of Penguin UK).

1 NEW LITERATURES IN OLD WORLDS

India

Mulk Raj Anand, *Untouchable* (1935; Penguin).
Raja Rao, *The Serpent and the Rope* (1960; Orient Paperbacks/ Delhi).
R. K. Narayan, *The Guide* (1958; Penguin).
Kamala Markandaya, *Nectar in a Sieve* (1954; Signet/New York).
Khushwant Singh, *Train to Pakistan* (1956; TBI/New Delhi).
Anita Desai, *Baumgartner's Bombay* (1988; Penguin).
Shashi Deshpande, *The Binding Vine* (1992; Virago).
Rohinton Mistry, *Such a Long Journey* (1991; Faber and Faber).
Amitav Ghosh, *The Shadow Lines* (1988; Black Swan).
Shasi Tharoor, *The Great Indian Novel* (1989; Viking).
Vikram Seth, *A Suitable Boy* (1993; Phoenix).
Rukun Advani, *Beethoven Among the Cows* (1994; Faber and Faber).

Other Asian Fiction

K. S. Maniam, *The Return* (1981; SKOOB).
Bapsi Sidhwa, *Ice-Candy-Man* (1988; Penguin India/New Delhi).
Yasmine Gooneratne, *The Pleasures of Conquest* (1995; Penguin, India/New Delhi).

West Africa

Chinua Achebe, *Things Fall Apart* (1958; Heinemann).
Cyprian Ekwensi, *Jagua Nana* (1961; Heinemann).
Wole Soyinka, *The Interpreters* (1965; Heinemann).
Ayi Kwei Armah, *The Beautyful Ones Are Not Yet Born* (1968; Heinemann).
Buchi Emecheta, *The Joys of Motherhood* (1979; Heinemann).
Ben Okri, *The Famished Road* (1991; Vintage).

East Africa

Ngũgĩ wa Thiong'o, *A Grain of Wheat* (1966; Heinemann).
Nuruddin Farah, *Sardines* (1981; Heinemann).

Southern Africa

Esk'ia Mphahlele, *Chirundu* (1979; Ravan/Johannesburg).
Tsitsi Dangarembga, *Nervous Conditions* (1988; Women's Press).

South Pacific

Mudrooroo [Colin Johnson], *Doctor Wooreddy's Prescription for Enduring the Ending of the World* (1983; Hyland House/Melbourne).
Patricia Grace, *Potiki* (1986; Women's Press).
Albert Wendt, *Leaves of the Banyan Tree* (1979; Talanoa/Honolulu).
Russell Soaba, *Maiba* (1979; Three Continents Press/Washington, DC).

2   NEW LITERATURE IN NEW WORLDS

Afro-America

Claude McKay, *Banana Bottom* (1933; Harvest).
Ralph Ellison, *Invisible Man* (1952; Penguin).
Zora Neale Hurston, *Their Eyes Were Watching God* (1937; Virago).
Alice Walker, *The Color Purple* (1982; Washington Square Press/New York).
Gloria Naylor, *Mama Day* (1988; Vintage).

Toni Morrison, *Tar Baby* (1981; Picador).
Paule Marshall, *Praisesong for the Widow* (1983; Virago).
Ernest Gaines, *The Autobiography of Miss Jane Pittman* (Bantam/ New York).
Ishmael Reed, *Flight to Canada* (1976; Atheneum/New York).

Caribbean

George Lamming, *In the Castle of My Skin* (1953; Longman).
Sam Selvon, *The Lonely Londoners* (1956; Longman).
Earl Lovelace, *The Dragon Can't Dance* (1979; Heinemann).
Shiva Naipaul, *A Hot Country* (1983; Penguin).
Caryl Phillips, *Crossing the River* (1993; Picador).
Zee Edgell, *Beka Lamb* (1982; Heinemann).
Erna Brodber, *Jane and Louisa Will Soon Come Home* (1980; New Beacon).
Wilson Harris, *Palace of the Peacock* (1969; Faber and Faber).
Jean Rhys, *Wide Sargasso Sea* (1966; Penguin).

3   OLD LITERATURE IN NEW WORLDS

Australia

Patrick White, *A Fringe of Leaves* (1976; Penguin).
Peter Carey, *Oscar and Lucinda* (1988; Faber and Faber).
Robert Drewe, *The Savage Crows* (1976; Flamingo/Sydney).
Thomas Keneally, *The Chant of Jimmie Blacksmith* (1972; Penguin).
David Malouf, *Remembering Babylon* (1993; Vintage).
Randolph Stow, *Visitants* (1979; Minerva).

New Zealand

Janet Frame, *The Carpathians* (1988; Vintage, NZ/Auckland).
Maurice Shadbolt, *Monday's Warriors* (1990; Sceptre, NZ/Auckland).
Keri Hulme, *The Bone People* (1983; Picador).

South Africa

Nadine Gordimer, *The Conservationist* (1974; Penguin).
André Brink, *A Dry White Season* (1979; Minerva).

John Coetzee, *Life and Times of Michael K* (1983; Penguin).
Christopher Hope, *Kruger's Alp* (1984; Minerva).

Canada

Margaret Atwood, *Surfacing* (1979; Penguin).
W. O. Mitchell, *The Vanishing Point* (1973; Macmillan / Toronto).
Rudy Weibe, *The Temptations of Big Bear* (1973; NCL / Toronto).
Robert Kroetsch, *Gone Indian* (1973; New Press / Toronto).

4   OLD LITERATURE IN OLD WORLDS

Wales, Ireland, Scotland

Caradoc Evans, *My People* (1915 / 1987; Poetry of Wales Press / Bridgend).
John Banville, *Birchwood* (1973; Paladin).
Irvine Welsh, *Trainspotting* (1995; Minerva).

North America

Louise Erdrich, *Love Medicine* (1984; Flamingo).
Rolando Hinojosa, *The Valley* (1973; Bilingual Press / Tempe, Arizona).
Rolando Hinojosa, *Klail City* (1976; Arte Público / Houston).

5   EPILOGUE: EXTRODUCTION

Janette Turner Hospital, *Charades* (1989; Virago).
Ruth Prawer Jhabvala, *Heat and Dust* (1975; Penguin).
Bharati Mukherjee, *Jasmine* (1991; Virago).
Timothy Mo, *Sour Sweet* (1982; Vintage).
V. S. Naipaul, *A Bend in the River* (1979; Penguin).
M. G. Vassanji, *The Gunny Sack* (1989; Heinemann).
Lindsey Collen, *The Rape of Sita* (1993; Minerva).
Zulfikar Ghose, *Figures of Enchantment* (1986; Bloomsbury).
Michael Ondaatje, *The English Patient* (1992; Picador).
Salman Rushdie, *Midnight's Children* (1981; Picador).

Author Index

This index covers anglophone authors of imaginative literature in the twentieth century (including non-fictional works). There are also separate references for the eighty *Works Discussed* (listed on pp. 339–41)

Abrahams, Peter (1919–), 110, 177, 180, 332
Abruquah, Joseph Wilfred (1921–), 87
Achebe, Chinua (1930–), 2, 3, 17, 82, 87, 88, 124, 125, 127, 138, 164, 207, 240, 254, 263, 285, 334; *Things Fall Apart*, 4, 81, 84–6, 104, 124, 165
Advani, Rukun (1955–), *Beethoven among the Cows*, 61–3
Aidoo, Ama Ata (1942–), 81, 95
Alexander, Meena (1951–), 59
Ali, Ahmed (1910–94), 63
Alkali, Zaynab (1950–), 14, 72, 79–80
Allfrey, Phyllis Shand (1915–86), 192
Aluko, T. M. (1918–), 17, 88
Amadi, Elechi (1934–), 17, 44, 87, 93, 96
Amis, Kingsley (1922–95), 11, 91
Anand, Mulk Raj (1905–), 4, 38; *Untouchable*, 5, 16, 33, 36–7
Anantanarayanan, M. (1907–), 48
Anaya, Rudolfo (1937–), 304
Anderson, Jessica (1923–), 215, 227
Angelou, Maya (1928–), 136, 332
Anthony, Michael (1932–), 166, 182
Arias, Ron (1941–), 304
Armah, Ayi Kwei (1939–), 80, 88, 91, 95; *The Beautyful Ones Are Not Yet Born*, 93–4
Ashton-Warner, Sylvia (1908–84), 234
Atwood, Margaret (1939–), 4, 10, 253, 254, 320; *Surfacing*, 255–6, 258, 284
Awoonor, Kofi (1935–), 80, 101

Bail, Murray (1941–), 227
Baldwin, James (1924–87), 140, 143, 156, 165
Ballantyne, David (1924–86), 230
Banks, Iain (1954–), 284–5, 292
Banville, John, 282; *Birchwood*, 283–4
Baraka, Amiri (LeRoy Jones) (1934–), 154–5
Beckett, Samuel (1906–89), 23, 289
Beeharry, Deepchand (1927–), 324
Behan, Brendan (1923–64), 280
Bekederemo, J. P. Clark (1935–), 80
Bennett, Arnold (1867–1931), 241
Bhattacharya, Bhabani (1906–88), 16, 33, 36, 43
Bissoondath, Neil (1955–), 190, 191, 250
Bond, Ruskin (1934–), 36
Bontemps, Arna (1902–73), 136
Bosman, Herman Charles (1905–51), 21, 208–10, 240
Bowen, Elizabeth (1899–1973), 284
Boyd, Martin (1893–1972), 200, 211
Bozic, Sreten; *see* Wonga, Banumbir
Brathwaite, Edward Kamau (1930–), 19, 20, 137, 162
Brew, Kwesi (1928–), 80
Brink, André (1935–), 240, 244, 248; *A Dry White Season*, 113, 245
Brodber, Erna (1940–), 14, 200, 254; *Jane and Louisa Will Soon Come Home*, 185–7
Brookner, Anita (1928–), 10
Brooks, Gwendolyn (1917–), 150
Buchan, John (1875–1940), 240
Bulosan, Carlos (1913–56), 72, 75

Cade Bambara, Tony (1939–95), 150
Callaghan, Morley (1903–90), 200, 266, 300
Campbell, Maria (1940–), 295
Carew, Jan (1925–), 169
Carey, Peter (1943–), 232; *Oscar and Lucinda*, 216–18
Cary, Joyce (1888–1957), 84, 229, 284
Castillo, Ana (1953–), 304
Castro, Brian (1950–), 215
Chatterjee, Upamanyu (1959–), 51, 55
Chatterjee, Debjani (1952–), 13
Cheney-Coker, Syl (1945–), 101
Chesnutt, Charles (1858–1932), 136
Chimombo, Steve (1945–), 115
Chinodya, Shimmer (1957–), 115, 116, 200
Cisneros, Sandra (1954–), 304
Clarke, Austin (1934–), 133, 136, 165, 167, 177, 250, 332
Cliff, Michelle (1946–), 134, 180
Coetzee, J. M. (1940–), 2, 200, 230, 240, 241, 244, 245; *Life and Times of Michael K*, 246–7
Collen, Lindsey (1948–), *The Rape of Sita*, 324–5
Collins, Merle (1950–), 183
Conrad, Joseph (1857–1924), viii, 4, 11, 23, 84, 103, 168, 225, 251, 272–3, 322
Conton, William (1925–), 78, 87
Cooper, J. California, 152
Cope, Jack (1913–91), 242
Courage, James Francis (1903–63), 228
Cross, Ian (1925–), 229–30
Cruz Smith, Martin (1942–), 295, 297, 298

Dabydeen, Cyril (1945–), 41, 190, 191
Dabydeen, David (1956–), 173, 190
D'Aguiar, Fred (1960–), 165, 180
Dangarembga, Tsitsi (1960), 115; *Nervous Conditions*, 116–17
Dark, Eleanor (1901–85), 215
Das, Kamal (1934–), 315

Dathorne, O. R. (1934–), 118, 169
Davies, Robertson (1913–95), 207, 229, 253, 254, 257
Davin, Dan[iel] (1913–90), 228
De Boissière, Ralph (1907–), 163
De Lisser, H. G. (1878–1944), 163, 179
Desai, Anita (1937–), 16, 36, 49, 315; *Baumgartner's Bombay*, 50–1
Desai, Boman (1950–), 34, 51, 52
Desani, G. V. (1909–), 43
Deshpande, Shashi (1938–), 36, 315; *The Binding Vine*, 52–3
Dhondy, Farrukh (1944–), 34, 59
Diesco, Joseph (1955–), 114
Djoleto, Amu (1929–), 81, 87
Dos Passos (1896–1970), 277
Drabble, Margaret (1939–), viii
Drayton, Geoffrey (1924–), 192
Dreiser, Theodore (1871–1945), 143, 271
Drewe, Robert (1943–), 120, 122; *The Savage Crows*, 218–19
Duckworth, Marilyn (1935–), 230
Du Fresne, Yvonne (1929–), 230
Dunbar, Paul (1872–1906), 136, 137
Duncan, Sara Jeanette (1861–1922), 265, 309

Edgell, Zee (1940–), *Beka Lamb*, 183–5
Ekwensi, Cyprian (1921–), 17, 88; *Jagua Nana*, 89–91
Ellison, Ralph (1914–), 137, 140, 142, 156, 190; *Invisible Man*, 143–5
Emecheta, Buchi (1944–), 4, 17, 80, 92, 95; *The Joys of Motherhood*, 96–8
Erdrich, Louise (1954–), 295, 297; *Love Medicine*, 298–300
Essop, Ahmed (1931–), 317
Evans, Caradoc (1878–1945), 22, 296–7; *My People*, 278–9
Ezekiel, Nissim (1924–), 34

Farah, Nuruddin (1945–), 2, 5, 4, 102, 103, 105; *Sardines*, 106–7
Farrell, James T. (1904–79), 277
Faulkner, William (1897–1962), 10, 149, 179, 190, 298, 302

Fernando, Lloyd (1926–), 68, 69, 76
Findley, Timothy (1930–), 253, 254
Forster, E. M. (1879–1970), 42, 58, 62, 229, 309, 313, 315
Fowles, John (1926–), 216
Frame, Janet (1924–), 10, 230; *The Carpathians*, 231–2
Friel, Brian (1929–), 23, 281–2, 336
Furphy, Joseph (1843–1912), 212

Gaines, Ernest J. (1933–), 140, 154; *The Autobiography of Miss Jean Pittman*, 155–6
Gallant, Mavis (1922–), 266, 308, 310, 332
Galloway, Janice (1956–), 290
Galsworthy, John (1867–1933), 211
Gamalinda, Eric (1956–), 74
Garner, Helen (1942–), 204
Gee, Maurice (1931–), 206, 207
Ghose, Sudhindra (1899–1965), 30, 38
Ghose, Zulfikar (1935–), 2, 63, 288–90, 324, 325, 334; *Figures of Enchantment*, 326–7
Ghosh, Amitav (1956–), 36, 51, 55, 59, 66; *The Shadow Lines*, 56–7
Gibbon, Lewis Grassic (1901–35), 22, 44, 289–90
Golden, Marita (1950–), 152
Golding, William (1911–), 10, 273
Gonzalez, N. V. M. (1915–), 72, 75, 274
Gooneratne, Yasmine (1935–), 66; *The Pleasures of Conquest*, 67
Goonewardene, James (1921–), 68
Gordimer, Nadine (1923–), 1, 10, 113, 248; *The Conservationist*, 242–4
Grace, Patricia (1937–), 17, 119, 126, 129, 228; *Potiki*, 122–4
Gray, Alasdair (1934–), 292–3
Greene, Graham (1904–91), 178, 219, 229, 322
Grenville, Kate (1950–), 226–7, 228
Grove, Frederick Philip (1879–1948), 20, 251, 257
Gunesekera, Romesh (1954–), 66
Gurnah, Abdulrazak (1948–), 102

Hagedorn, Jessica (1949–), 74, 274
Hanrahan, Barbara (1939–), 216
Harris, Wilson (1921–), 137, 163, 188, 304, 326; *Palace of the Peacock*, 189–90
Hartnett, Michael (Micheál Ó hArtnéide) (1941–), 284
Hau'ofa, Epeli (1939–), 17, 120, 127
Hazzard, Shirley (1931–), 227, 308, 311
Head, Bessie (1927–86), 109, 112–13
Heaney, Seamus (1939–), 1, 281
Hearne, John (1926–94), 178–9
Herbert, Xavier (1901–84), 212
Heath, Roy A. K. (1926–), 2, 167, 173
Heller, Joseph (1923–), 248
Hemingway, Ernest (1898–1961), 309, 328
Herbert, Xavier (1901–84), 22
Hercules, Frank (1917–96), 134
Highway, Tomson (1951–), 250, 301
Hilliard, Noel (1929–), 22, 235
Himes, Chester (1909–84), 145
Hinojosa, Rolando (1929–), 304; *The Valley* and *Klail City*, 302–3
Hodge, Merle (1944–), 14, 18, 182
Hodgins, Jack (1938–), 257
Hope, Christopher (1944–), 249; *Kruger's Alp*, 247–8
Hosain, Attia (1913–), 46
Hospital, Janette Turner (1942–), 227; *Charades*, 311–13
Hove, Chenjerai (1956–), 115, 116
Hughes, Langston (1902–67), 136, 143, 332
Hulme, Keri (1947–), 18, 21, 19, 22, 122, 129, 228; *The Bone People*, 236–7
Humphreys, Emyr (1919–), 277–8
Hurston, Zora Neale (1903–60), 18, 23, 133, 136, 137, 139, 140, 148, 149; *Their Eyes Were Watching God*, 145–7

Ihimaera, Witi (1944–), 17, 18, 119, 122, 129, 228, 235, 337
Ireland, David (1927–), 226

Ishiguro Kazuo (1954–　), 316
Iyayi, Festus (1947–　), 93, 95

Jacobson, Dan (1929–　), 242, 311
James, C. L. R. (1901–89), 136, 163, 332
Jhabvala, Ruth Prawer (1927–　), 49, 308; *Heat and Dust*, 313–15
Joaquin, Nick (1917–　), 72, 73, 75
Johnson, Colin; *see* Mudrooroo Narogin
Johnson, James Weldon (1871–1938), 136
Johnston, Basil H. (1929–　), 250, 295, 296–7
Jones, Gayl (1949–　), 152
Jones, Glyn (1905–　), 22, 278
Jones, Jack (1884–1970), 277
José, F. Sionil (1924–　), 2, 71, 72, 73–4, 75
Joseph, M. K. (1914–81), 228–9
Joshi, Arun (1939–93), 36, 48, 49
Joyce, James (1882–1941), 11, 22, 35, 57, 60, 158, 186, 281, 297, 330

Kahiga, Sam (1943–　), 107
Kanga, Firdaus (1959–　), 34, 51, 52
Kauraka, Kauraka (1951–　), 127
Kayira, Legson (1942–　), 115
Kelman, James (1946–　), 288, 289, 290
Keneally, Thomas (1935–　), 22, 200, 218, 290; *The Chant of Jimmie Blacksmith*, 220–2
Kennedy, A. L. (1965–　), 290
Khan, Ismith (1925–　), 18, 19, 69, 174, 191–2, 317
Kidman, Fiona (1940–　), 230
Kincaid, Jamaica (1949–　), 11, 19, 133, 138, 173
King, Thomas (1943–　), 250
Kinsella, Thomas (1928–　), 280, 286
Kipling, Rudyard (1865–1936), 206, 273
Klein, A. M. (1909–72), 251
Koch, C. J. (1932–　), 227
Kogawa, Joy (Nozomi) (1935–　), 252
Kreisel, Henry (1922–91), 251

Kroetsch, Robert (1927–　), 21, 200, 252, 260, 271, 334; *Gone Indian*, 263–4
Kunene, Mazisi (1930–　), 109, 112, 148
Kureishi, Hanif (1954–　), 63, 173, 273–4, 316–17

Ladoo, Harold Sonny (1945–73), 250
La Guma, Alex (1925–85), 109, 110, 112
Lamming, George (1927–　), 84, 136, 164, 170, 172, 177, 179, 240; *In the Castle of My Skin*, 165–7
Larsen, Nellie (1891–1964), 136
Laurence, Margaret (1926–87), 253, 259–60, 308
Lawrence, D. H. (1885–1930), 10, 24, 80, 241, 271
Lawson, Henry (1867–1922), 21, 205–6, 210, 212
Leacock, Stephen (1869–1944), 21, 207–8, 210, 265
Lee, Dennis (1939–　), 20
Lessing, Doris (1919–　), 24, 192, 241, 242, 310
Liang, Lee Kok, 68, 69
Llewellyn, Richard (1907–83), 277
Lo Liyong, Taban (1939–　), 108
Lord, Audre (1934–92), 133
Lovelace, Earl (1935–　), 10, 18, 174, 161, 240; *The Dragon Can't Dance*, 175–7

McAlpine, Rachel (1940–　), 230
McDonald, Ian (1933–　), 192
McGahern, John (1934–　), 282–3
McKay, Claude (1889–1948), 44, 133, 140, 163; *Banana Bottom*, 141–2
MacLennan, Hugh (1907–90), 253, 257, 277
McNeish, James (1931–　), 234–5
Maillu, David (1939–　), 108
Mais, Roger (1905–55), 173
Malgonkar, Manohar (1913–　), 48–9
Malouf, David (1934–　), 21, 22, 200; *Remembering Babylon*, 222–4

Mangua, Charles (1942–), 107
Maniam, K. S. (1942–), 68, 61–2,
    77; *The Return*, 69–70
Mansfield, Katherine (1888–1923),
    21, 192, 309
Mapanje, Jack (1944–), 115
Marachera, Dambudzo
    (1952–1987), 115
Markandaya, Kamal (1924–), 316;
    Nectar in a Sieve, 44–6
Marshall, Paule (1929–), 134, 135,
    139, 140, 150, 152; *Praisesong for
    the Widow*, 153–4
Masiye, Andreya (1922–), 115
Massie, Allan (1938–), 290
Mathers, Peter (1931–), 226
Mbise, Ismael (1944–), 108
Mehta, Ved (1934–), 48
Mendes, Alfred H. (1897–), 163
Miller, Alex (1936–), 24
Miller, Henry (1891–1980), 252, 271
Millin, Sarah Gertrude (1888–1968),
    241
Mistry, Rohinton (1952–), 34, 51,
    52, 250, 316; *Such a Long Journey*,
    54–5
Mitchell, W. O. (1914–), 22, 253,
    257; *The Vanishing Point*, 258–9
Mittelholzer, Edgar (1909–65),
    163–4, 179
Mnthali, Felix (1933–), 115
Mo, Timothy (1950–), 317; *Sour
    Sweet*, 319–21
Momaday, N. Scott (1934–), 295,
    297–8, 300
Montague, John (1929–), 23, 281
Moore, Brian (1921–), 282
Morrieson, Ronald Hugh (1922–72),
    229
Morrison, Toni (1931–), 1, 18, 134,
    138, 139, 140, 148, 150, 137–9, 187;
    Tar Baby, 151–2
Mphahlele, Es'kia (1919–), 109,
    332; *Chirundu*, 110–12
Mudrooroo (Narogin) (1938–),
    17, 119, 240, 282; *Dr Wooreddy's
    Prescription for Enduring the
    Ending of the World*, 120–1
Muir, Edward (1887–1959), 23, 286

Mukherjee, Bharati (1940–), 16, 51,
    250, 316, 334–5; *Jasmine*, 317–19
Mulaisho, Dominic (1933–), 115
Muller, Carl (1935–), 67
Mungoshi, Charles (1947–), 115
Munonye, John (1929–), 87, 92, 96
Munro, Alice (1931–), 253, 254
Murdoch, Iris (1919–), 271
Mwangi, Meja (1948–), 107

Nabokov, Vladimir (1899–1977),
    viii, 24, 272–3
Nagarajan, K. (1893–1986), 42
Nahal, Chaman (1927–), 36, 46, 51
Naipaul, Shiva (1945–85), 190; *A
    Hot Country*, 177–8
Naipaul, V. S. (1932–), 1, 19, 24,
    48, 69, 93, 102, 137, 163, 165,
    167–9, 176, 177, 178, 179, 188, 190,
    308, 317; *A Bend in the River*, 321–2
Namjoshi, Suniti (1941–), 14, 204
Nandan, Satendra (1939), 19, 129
Narayan, R. K. (1906–), 4, 5, 16,
    33, 36, 206; *The Guide*, 40–2
Naylor, Gloria (1950–), 138, 140,
    148, *Mama Day*, 149–50
Nazareth, Peter (1940–), 108
Ngũgĩ wa Thiong'o (1938–), 11,
    23, 95, 105, 107, 138, 148, 277, 284,
    285, 334, 337; *A Grain of Wheat*,
    103–4
Nichols, Grace (1950–), 183
Nkosi, Lewis (1936–), 112
Nwapa, Flora (1931–), 5, 17, 92, 95
Nyamfukudza, Stanley (1951–),
    115

O'Brien, Flann (1911–66), 22, 280,
    281
O'Casey, Sean (1880–1964), 281
O'Flaherty, Liam (1897–1984), 22,
    280
Ogot, Grace (1930–), 107–8
Okara, Gabriel (1921–), 17, 80, 92
Okigbo, Christopher (1932–67), 92
Okpewho, Isidore (1941–), 87, 92
Okri, Ben (1959–), 93, 95, 98, 273;
    The Famished Road, 99–101
Omotoso, Kole (1943–), 80, 92, 98

Ondaatje, Michael (1943–), 24, 66, 250; *The English Patient*, 327–8
Orwell, George (1903–50), 248
Ostenso, Martha (1900–63), 251

Park, Ruth (1923–), 216
Paterson, A. B. (1864–1941), 212
Paton, Alan (1903–88), 240, 241
Patterson, Orlando (1940–), 173
p'Bitek, Okot (1931–82), 108
Pearse, Patrick (Padraig) (1879–1916), 280
Pearson, Bill (1922–), 229
Penton, Brian (1904–51), 212
Persaud, Lakshmi (1951–), 183, 190
Petaia, Ruperake (1951–), 127
Peters, Lenrie (1932–), 78, 87
Philip, Marlene Nourbese (1947–), 183
Phillips, Caryl (1958–), 19, 165, 273; *Crossing the River*, 180–2
Phiri, Gideon (1942–), 115
Pinter, Harold (1930–), 289
Plomer, William (1903–73), 240, 241, 308, 309
Porter, Hal (1911–84), 215
Powys, John Cowper (1872–1963), 277
Prichard, Katherine (1883–1969), 215
Pynchon, Thomas (1937–), 248, 330

Rajan, Balachandra (1920–), 47
Rao, Raja (1908–), 3, 16, 34, 35, 36, 38–40; *The Serpent and the Rope*, 30, 34–5
Redcam, Tom [Thomas Henry MacDermot] (1870–1933), 163
Reed, Ishmael (1938–), 137, 140, 263, 264; *Flight to Canada*, 156–8, 237, 238
Reid, V. S. (1913–87), 18, 180
Rhys, Jean (1890–1979), 190; *Wide Sargasso Sea*, 192–4
Richardson, Henry Handel (1870–1946), 21, 211, 309
Richler, Mordecai (1931–), 251, 252
Rive, Richard (1931–89), 113

Rosca, Ninotchka (1946–), 74
Ross, Sinclair (1908–), 253, 257
Rotimi, Ola (1938–), 80
Roy, Namba (1910–61), 180
Rubadiri, David (1930–), 115
Rushdie, Salman (1947–), viii–ix, 1, 2, 14–15, 23, 24, 51, 59, 99, 106, 216, 308, 309, 331; *Midnight's Children*, 35, 60, 323, 329–30

Sahgal, Nayantara (1927–), 36, 48
St Omer, Garth (1931–), 174
Salinger, J. D. (1919–), 226
Salkey, Andrew (1928–), 169
Salverson, Laura Goodman (1890–1970), 251
Santos, Bienvenido (1911–), 72–3, 74, 274
Sargeson, Frank (1903–82), 21, 205, 206–7, 210
Saro-Wiwa, Ken (1941–95), 17, 92–3, 98–9
Scott, Lawrence (1909–83), 192
Scott, Paul (1920–78), 58
Sealy, I. Allan (1951–), 36, 51, 52
Selvadurai, Shyam (1965–), 66
Selvon, Sam (1923–94), 19, 164, 167, 168, 188, 191; *The Lonely Londoners*, 170–2, 288–9
Senior, Olive (1941–), 18, 136, 166, 182–3, 332, 337
Sepamla, Sydney (1932–), 113–14
Serote, Mongane Wally (1944–), 17, 109, 113, 200–1
Seth, Vikram (1952–), 35, 59; *A Suitable Boy*, 60–1
Seymour, A. J. (1914–), 163
Shadbolt, Maurice (1932–), *Monday's Warriors*, 233–4
Shinebourne, Janice (1947–), 183, 190
Sidhwa, Bapsi (1938–), 2, 46, 63, 77; *Ice-Candy-Man*, 64–6
Singer, Isaac Bashevis (1904–91), 273
Singh, Khushwant (1915–), *Train to Pakistan*, 46–7
Smith, Ian Crichton (1928–), 22, 285–6

Smith, Martin Cruz (1942–), 295, 297, 298
Smith, Pauline (1882–1959), 192, 240, 241, 308, 309
Soaba, Russell (1950–), 17, 119; *Maiba*, 127–9
Soyinka, Wole (1934–), 1, 2, 17, 79, 84, 88, 207, 285, 334; *The Interpreters*, 91–2, 93, 94
Stead, C. K. (1932–), 122, 200, 230, 232
Stead, Christina (1902–83), 227, 310
Steinbeck, John (1902–1968), 241, 271, 302
Stow, Randolph (1935–), 21; *Visitants*, 224–5
Subramani (1943–), 120, 129
Such, Peter (1939–), 259
Sutherland, Efua (1924–), 80
Synge, J. M. (1874–1909), 279, 280

Tan, Amy (1952–), 316–17
Tharoor, Shashi (1956–), 35, 51; *The Great Indian Novel*, 57–9
Themba, Can (1924–68), 17
Tiempo, Edilberto (1913–), 72, 75
Tlali, Miriam (1933–), 113, 114, 254
Tóibín, Colm, 279
Toomer, Jean (1894–1967), 136, 295
Tutuola, Amos (1920–), 11, 17, 83–4, 204
Ty-Casper, Linda (1932–), 74, 274

Vassanji, M. G. (1950–), 18, 102, 250, 315; *The Gunny Sack*, 332–47
Venkataramani, K. S. (1891–1952), 42
Vonnegut, Kurt, Jr (1922–), 271

Walcott, Derek (1930–), 1, 2, 161
Walker, Alice (1944–), 18, 22, 137, 138–9, 140, 282; *The Color Purple*, 147–8
Washington, Booker T. (1856–1915), 136
Watson, Jean (1935–), 230
Watson, Sheila (1909–), 257
Waugh, Evelyn (1903–66), 211
Wedde, Ian (1946–), 232–3
Weller, Archie (1957–), 119, 120
Wells, H. G. (1866–1946), 33, 70, 143, 168, 248
Welsh, Irvine (1957–), 22; *Trainspotting*, 290–2
Wendt, Albert (1939–), 17, 120, 127, 201, 274, 337; *Leaves of the Banyan Tree*, 124–6
White, Patrick (1912–90), 22, 212; *A Fringe of Leaves*, 213–15
Wiebe, Rudy (1934–), 20, 22, 200, 251, 252, 271; *The Temptations of Big Bear*, 261–3
Williams, Denis (1923–), 188
Williams, Raymond (1921–88), 277
Wilson, Colin (1931), 120
Wilson, Ethel (1888–1980), 257
Wiseman, Adele (1928–92), 251–2
Wolfe, Tom (1931–), 219
Wongar, Banumbir (or Birumbir) (1932), 121–2
Woolf, Leonard (1880–1969), 265
Woolf, Virginia (1882–1941), 107, 271
Wright, Richard (1908–60), 127, 130, 140
Wynter, Sylvia (1928–), 169, 173

General Index

Abrahams, Lionel, 208
ACLALS (Association for
  Commonwealth Literature and
  Language Studies), 2
Adam, Graham Mercer, 265
Adams, Anthony and Ken Durham,
  266
Africa
  African dictatorships, 106, 112
  African languages (historical), 18
  African literature, 3
  anglophone Africa, ix, 2, 15, 16
  linguistic complexity of region,
    77
  relations with Afro-America, 133
  see also East, Southern, and *West*
    Africa, as well as single
    country entries
Afro-America, 294–5
  Afro-American fiction, 8, 18, 22,
    23, **133–58**
  relations with Caribbean, 133–4
Ahmad, Aijaz, 13, 334; *In Theory*,
  26, 336
Allende, Isabel, 74
Althusser, Louis, 62
Amerindian peoples, 162
anglophone literature (definitions,
  etc.), 6–7, 10, 11
Antigua (and Barbuda), 4, 161, 162
anz/sac, 201–2; vernacular pioneers,
  202–10
apartheid, 109, 110, 239
Appiah, Kwame Anthony, 333
Apuleius, 25
Arabian Nights, The, 84
Arabic literature, 7, 80, 98
Ashcroft, Bill *et al., The Empire
  Writes Back*, 26, 202, 332–3
Asia
  Indian fiction, ix, **31–63**
  other Asian fiction, **63–75**
  see also single country entries

Asian–American literature, 23
Ausonius, 25
Austen, Jane, 206, 313, 315;
  Mansfield Park, 4, 179
Australia, x, 15, 17, 52, 119, 120,
  192, **211–27**, 309
  Aborigine writers, 117, 119–22
  Aborigine languages, 219, 221–2,
    223
  anz/sac, 201–2
  contact novels, 212–15, 218–19,
    220–5, 226
  European tradition, 19–20, 21
  historical novels, 215–16
  "white writing", ix, 192, 199

Bahamas, the, 161
Baker, Candida, 237
Baker, Houston A., 143, 146, 306
  *Blues, Ideology, and Afro-American
    Literature*, 137, 138, 158
Bangladesh, 47, 49, 55, 63, 66, 77, 201
Barbados, 161, 162
  Barbadian writers, 133, 134, 152,
    165, 166, 172, 177
Bay Psalm Book, The, 272
Beacon, The, 163
Beatson, Peter, 130
Belize, 133, 160, 161, 183, 184
Bell, Bernard W., 159
Bettelheim, Bruno
  The Uses of Enchantment, 14
Bhabha, Homi K., 3, 26
  Nation and Narration, 332, 335
Bhagavad Gita, The, 35, 76
Bharucha, Nilufer E. and Vilas
  Sarang, 75
Bible, the, 104
Bim, 163
Birbalsingh, Frank, 194
Birch, Eva Lennox, 159
Black British writers, viii, 10, 64,
  273–4

350

Boehmer, Elleke, 26
Botswana, 113, 114, 115
British Raj (India), 5, 42, 43, 65
British Isles, 10; *see also* single
    country entries
Brontë, Charlotte: *Jane Eyre*, 192–3
Brooke, Francis, 265
Brooks, Peter, 337
Brown, William Wells, 135
Brydon, Diana, 334
Bunyan, John, 241, 247, 248
Burns, Robert, 205, 292

Cameroon, 78
Canada, 4, 66, 127, 179–81, **249–66**
    Caribbean links, 133, 167, 172
    contact novels, 257–66
    francophone literature, 2, 20, 253
    international novelists, 309, 310
    literary pioneers, 207–8
    Métis writers and culture, 295
    multi-ethnicity, 20–2, 249–52
    Native Canadian languages, 261,
        295–6, 300–1
    Native Canadian peoples, 232
    Native Canadian writers, 224–5,
        250
    Ontario novelists, 253–4, 257
    prairie fiction, 192, 251
    "white writing", ix, 15
Caribbean, the, ix, 18–19, 82, 84,
    160–94
    experimental novelists, 187–90
    fictional autobiographies, 182–7
    "home and away", 167–77
    Indian diaspora, 190–2
    literary precursors, 163–7
    politics and history, 177–82
    "white writing", 192–4
Carriacou, 153, 154
Cervantes, Miguel de, 138, 212
Chamberlin, J. Edward, *Come Back*
    to Me My Language, 161, 195
Chapman, Michael, 108, 113, 118,
    266; *Soweto Poetry*, 113
Chaudhuri, Nirad C., 47–8, 66
Cheshire, Jenny, 26
Chicano fiction, 23, 294, **301–5**

Chinweizu *et al.*: *Towards the*
    Decolonization of African
    Literature, 118
Cheung, King-Kok and Stan Yogi,
    75, 274
Christian, Barbara, 333, 334
Coleridge, Samuel Taylor, 45–6, 190
Collymore, Frank, 163
Columbus, Christopher, 13, 19, 148
Commonwealth (British), viii, 6, 7;
    Commonwealth literature, 1–2,
    10
Cook Islands, 126, 127
Craig, David, 44
Crawford, James: *Language*
    Loyalties, 304–5
Crawford, Robert, 306
creole (Caribbean), 18, 142, 162,
    184, 337
    creole continuum, 19, 160–1
    plantation creole, 139, 240
    written representations, 191–2
Cuba, 160, 161
Cudjoe, Selwyn, 194

Dabydeen, David and Nana
    Wilson-Tagoe, 194
Dance, Daryl Cumber, 169, 194
Davies, Carol Boyce and Elaine
    Savory Fido, 194
Daymond, Douglas and Leslie
    Monkman, 267
Deane, Seamus, 280, 306
defamiliarisation, 77, 85, 99, 116,
    120, 237
Defoe, Daniel, 82, 89–90; *Robinson*
    Crusoe, 4, 246
Derrida, Jacques, 335
Devy, G. N., 75
diaspora, 18, 77, 129, 309
    Asian, 309, **315–31**
    Filipino, 74
    Indian (South Asian), 129, 192
    Nigerian, 77
Dickens, Charles, 55, 60, 70, 168,
    171, 213, 322, 323, 330
Dictionary of Literary Biography, ix,
    118, 159, 175, 267, 306, 317

Dillard, J. L., 159
Dominica, 161, 162, 192
Dominican Republic, 160, 161
Donne, John, 9
Donnell, Alison and Sarah Lawson
    Welsh, 195
Dostoevsky, Fyodor, 143
double exile, 19, 142, 316
Douglass, Frederick, 134, 135, 136,
    150

East Africa, 18, 70, **101–8**, 322, 323
Edgeworth, Maria, 284
Eliot, George, 60, 241
Empire Day celebrations, 165, 184
English language
    Middle English, 8–9, 288
    Modern English, 9–10
    Old English, 7–8
"English literature", 3, 22, 24, 25–6
English renaissance, 25
Equiano, Olaudah, 19, 82, 134–5,
    137, 179
Evans, Mari, 159
Evans, Patrick, 230, 238

Fagunwa, D. A., 84
Fanon, Frantz, 3, 117, 335
Fielding, Henry, 57, 82, 138, 212
Fiji, 19, 127, 129, 324
Filipino fiction, **71–5**, 274
Filipino American fiction, 74–5, 274
Focus, 163
Foucault, Michel, 335
francophone literature, 3, 6

Galang, Zoilo, 71
Gambia, the, 78, 82, 87
Gandhi, Indira, 54, 57; "State of
    Emergency", 35, 58
Gandhi, Mahatma, 35, 37, 38, 51, 57,
    58, 65: *Quit India* movement, 34
Garlick, Raymond, 305
Gates, Henry Louis, Jr: *The
    Signifying Monkey*, 137–8, 158
Ghana, 78, 82, 87, 93–4, 101, 259–60
    indigenous languages, 80–1
Gibson, Graeme, 267
Gikandi, Simon, 118, 338

Gilkes, Michael, 194
Goetzfridt, Nicholas J., 129
Goldie, Terry, 267
Gomes, Albert, 163
Goodwin, Ken, 237
Gramley, Stephan and Kurt-
    Michael Pätzold, 26
Grant, Agnes, 306
Gray, Stephen, 13
Grenada, 133, 153, 154, 161
Grey Owl (Archibald Belaney),
    263–4
Griffiths, Glyne, 194
Guyana, 160, 161, 163, 167, 169, 188,
    189, 190, 324
    historical fiction, 164
    multi-ethnicity, 19, 136, 162
    political dystopia, 177

Haggard, H. Rider, 240
Haiti, 133, 145, 160, 161, 177
Haliburton, Thomas, 207, 265
Hardy, Thomas, 24, 44, 126, 141,
    142, 166, 271
Harlem Renaissance, 133, 135, 138,
    142
Harrow, Kenneth W., 118
Hart, Julia Catherine, 265
Harte, Bret, 205–6
Hashmi, Alamgir, 327
Hawthorne, Nathaniel, 203
Hergenhan, L., 237
Heyck, Denys Lyn Daly, 307
Howells, William Dean, 203, 204

indenture system, 19, 77, 162, 167,
    190
India, 2, 4, 6, 15, 16, 77
    Indian English, 32–3, 59
    Indian fiction in English, 15,
        31–63
    Indian history, 329
    Indian languages, 31–2, 60–1,
        318, 330: Bengali, 15, 33, 47,
        48, 49, 61, 63, 250; Gujarati,
        50, 54, 64; Hindi, 16, 33, 49,
        52, 54, 61; Hindustani, 16, 33,
        37, 40, 51; Kannada, 16, 33,
        34, 38, 40, 52; Marathi, 48, 52,

53, 54; Punjabi, 16, 32, 37, 38,
40; Tamil, 16, 32, 40, 42, 66,
68, 70; Urdu, 16, 49, 61, 63
Indian religions, 34, 46, 64
Iqbal, 65
Ireland, 8, 22, 23, 234
"big house" theme, 283–4
Irish fiction in English, **279–84**
Irish language (Gaelic), 10, 22,
239, 279, 280, 281–2
Ulster, 9

Jacobs, Harriet, 136, 146
Jamaica, 141, 142, 160, 161, 162, 173,
177
historical writing, 135, 180
precursors in Caribbean fiction,
163
links with Afro-America, 134,
140, 145
political fiction, 179
James, Adeola, 79, 81, 118
Jameson, Fredric, 336
JanMohamed, Abdul, 118, 138
Japanese kinship terms, 316
Jayasuriya, Wilfred, 76
Jinnah, Muhammad Ali, 58, 65
Jones, R. M. (Bobi), 278
Journal of Commonwealth Literature,
x, 2
Juneja, Renu, 194
Jussawalla, Feroza and Reed Way
Dasenbrock: *Interviews with
Writers of the Post-Colonial
World*, 27, 34, 118, 235, 304, 325

Kafka, Franz, 143, 246
Katrak, Ketu, 333
Katzner, Kenneth, x, 26–7
Kay, Billy: *Scots: The Mither Tongue*,
286–7, 306
Keats, John, 200, 223
Keith, W. J., 267
Kenya, 43, 82, 110, 250, 277
indigenous languages, 102–3:
Acoli, 108; Gikuyu, 25, 103,
104, 105; (Ki)swahili, 79, 102,
105, 108; Luo, 108

Kenyan fiction in English, 107–8
Land and Freedom Movement
("Mau Mau"), 101–22, 103,
104, 107, 116
Kiberd, Declan, 280, 306, 336
Killam, G. D., 118
King's (Queen's) English, 24
King, Bruce, 194
Kiribati, 126
Klinck, Carl, 265
Kunapipi, x
Kyk-over-al, 163

Labov, William, 138
Lal, P., 58
land and language, 12
Latin
language, 8, 10, 207
literature, 25–6
Lattin, Vernon E., 307
Lawson, Alan, 13
Layamon: *Brut*, 272
Leavis, F. R., 240
Leeward Islands, 161
Lesotho, 108
Lewis, Martin, 306
Lewis, Matthew "Monk", 179
Liberia, 78, 71, 147, 181
Lim, Shirley Geok-lin, 73, 76
Lindfors, Bernth, 84
Lindsay, Maurice, 287, 288, 306
little magazines (Caribbean), 163
Long, D. S., 129
Long, Richard and Eugenia Collier,
159
Longfellow, Henry, 207
Lucan, 25
Lucretius, 25
Lutz, Hartmut, 306

Mackenzie, Henry, 286
Mackie, Alastair, 287
Mahabharata, The, 35, 39, 57–8, 76
Malawi, 108, 115, 201; indigenous
languages, 114
Malaysia, 25, 63, 77; Malaysian
(Malayan) fiction, 68–70
Malta, ix

Mansfield, Lord, 286
Maori writers, 18, 122–4
    language and culture, 119, 127,
        231, 233–5, 236–7
Márquez, Gabriel García, 74, 233
Martial, 25
Mathias, Roloand
Mauritius, 19, 129; indigenous
    languages, 324
McGregor, Graham and Mark
    Williams, 238
Mead, Margaret, 125
Melville, Herman, 143
Memmi, Albert, 3
Menon, Krishna, 33
"migrants' tales", 309, 319, 322
Mitchell, W. J. T., 333
Moodie, Susanna, 255, 265
More, Sir Thomas: *Utopia*, 25
Moss, John, 267
Mozambique, 244
Mukherjee, Meenakshi, 36, 76

Naik, M. A., 75
Namibia, 108, 114
Native America
    Native American ethnicity, 295,
        301
    Native American fiction, 23, 250,
        274, **294–301**
    Native American languages,
        300–1
nation language, 19
Nehru, Jawaharlal, 61, 65
Nelson, Emmanuel S. (ed.), *Writers
    of the Indian Diaspora*, 75,
    315–16, 338
New, W. H., 266, 267
"New Literatures in English"
    (definitions), 5–6, 15
new literatures in new worlds
    (scope), 18–19
new literatures in old worlds
    (scope), 15–18
New Zealand, 15, 202, 227–37
    contact novels, 233–7
    European tradition, 19–20
    Maori writing, 17–18, 119, 228,
        231

realist tradition, 227–30, 309
vernacular voice, 199–201, 206–7
"white writing", 192
Newfoundland, 9
Nigeria, 1, 2, 4, 105, 108, 110
    attitudes to English, 77–80
    literary tradition, 6, 17, 102
    Civil War, 83, 87, 89, 98, 99
    indigenous languages: Hausa,
        14, 78, 79, 96, 100; Igbo, 78,
        79, 80, 97, 135; Ijaw, 80;
        Yoruba, 25, 78, 80, 90, 96,
        100
    see also West Africa
Niue, 126
Nobel Prize (literature), 1
North America, 19, 294
    see also Native American and
        Chicano fiction

O'Brien, John, 159
Odyssey, The, 35
"Official English" controversy, 304
Ogunbiyi, Yemi, 118
old literatures in new worlds
    (scope), 19–22
old literatures in old worlds
    (scope), 22–4
Onitsha market, 17, 89
oral culture: African, 81, 84, 87, 105;
    Afro-American, 146, 155;
    Mauritian, 325; Native
    American, 297
Owomoyela, Oyekan, 118

Pakistan, 2, 6, 16, 35, 51, 76
    Pakistani fiction, 63–6
Papua New Guinea, 17, 119, 126,
    224; indigenous languages,
    128–9, 225
Parry, J. H. *et al.*, *Short History of the
    West Indies*, 195
partition (India and Pakistan), 35,
    46, 51, 65, 325
Penguin History of India, The, 76
Pérez, Luis, 301
Petrone, Penny, 306
Petronius, 25
Phaedrus, 25

Philippines, the, ix, 16, 56, 63, 77, 316
  recent history, 71
  indigenous languages, 70–1
  see also Filipino
Pidgins, 78, 90, 91, 94, 99
Planters' Punch, 163
Poe, Edgar Allan, 157, 190
Post-colonial literature
  definitions, 1, 2–5
  surveys, 333–4
  theory, 332
Pringle, Thomas, 200
proverbs, 37, 81, 87
Puerto Rico, 160
Pushkin, *Eugene Onegin*, 59

Rahman, Tariq, 63, 76
Rajagopalachari, C. R., 58, 76
Ramayana, The, 35, 39, 76, 325
Ramchand, Kenneth, 194
Ramraj, Victor, 194
Richardson, John, 265
Richardson, Samuel, 82, 138, 146–7
Ríos, Herminio, 302
Rivera, Tomás, 302
Rizal, José, 71
Roberts, Kate, 277
Romaine, Suzanne, 27, 238
Royle, Trevor, 306

Sahitya Akademi, 35–6, 52, 75
Said, Edward, 3, 26, 179, 234, 335–6
St Kitts (& Nevis), 161, 180
St Lucia, 1, 161, 162, 173, 174
St Vincent, 161
Samoa, 17, 124; Samoan language, 119, 126, 127
Sander, Reinhard, 118
Schreiner, Olive, 240
Scotland, 8, 10, 22, 274
  Scots Gaelic, 10, 239, 285–6
  Scots (language) 8, 22–3, 35, 285, 286–8, 290–3
  Scottish fiction, **284–93**
Scott, Sir Walter, 22, 164, 291, 323
Second World War, 34, 97

Seneca, 25
Senn, Werner and Giovanna Capone, 238
Shakespeare, William, 25, 62, 285, 315; *The Tempest*, 4, 9, 103–4, 152, 164, 225, 325, 326
Shelley, Percy Bysshe, 223
Shiv Sena, 54
Shoemaker, Adam, 129, 130
Sierra Leone, 78, 82, 87, 101; indigenous languages, 81
Simms, Norman, 129
Singapore, 16, 63, 77; Singapore fiction, 68–9
Singh, Amritjit, 307, 337
slave narratives, 134, 156
Slemon, Stephen, 3, 334
Smith, Captain John, 272
Smollett, Tobias, 248, 291
Sollors, Werner, 7
Solomon Islands, 126
Somalia, 102, 259; Somali language, 2, 102, 105, 106, 107
South Africa, 1, 2, 13, 20, 77, 102, 199, 309
  anz/sac, 201–2
  black South African fiction, 15, 17, **109–14**, 208–10, **240–9**
  contact fiction, 21–2
  South African languages: Afrikaans, 2, 20, 109, 208, 209, 239–40, 243, 244, 248; other languages, 108–99
  white South African fiction, 208–10, **240–9**
  "white writing", ix, x, 192, 200
South Asia, 15, 17
South Pacific, 15, 17, 18
  Aborigine fiction (Australia), 118–22
  indigenous languages, 316
  Maori fiction, 122–4
  other South Pacific fiction, 125–9
  see also single country entries
Southern Africa, **108–17**; *see also* single country entries
Soweto, 113

Spanish language, 23, 160, 294, 302–3, 304
Spenser, Edmund, 336
Spivak, Gayatri Chakravorty, 3, 26, 62, 335
Sri Lanka, 16, 55, 63, 250, 265
  English in Sri Lanka, 66–7
  other languages, 66
  Sri Lankan fiction, 66–8, 76, 239, 327
Stephens, Meic, 227, 305
stepmother tongue, 26, 144–5, 204, 308: definitions, 11–15
  Africa, 77, 277
  Afro-America
  India, 16, 50
  Ireland, 280
  Native American culture
  Scotland, 287
  Wales, 277
Sterne, Lawrence, 212
Stevenson, R. L., 22, 126, 291
Story of English, The, 6, 26
Sturm, Terry, 238
Subramani, 129
Suleri, Sara, 26, 336
Swaziland, 108
Swift, Jonathan, 82, 248

Tanzania, 101, 102, 108, 250
Tatar, Maria: *The Hard Facts of the Grimms' Fairy Tales*, 14
Tennyson, Alfred, Lord, 157
Thackeray, W. M., 70
Thieme, John, 5
Tonga, 17, 119, 127
transnational writing, 24–6, 311, 315, 319, 321
  "The Last Jacobites", 309–15
Trinidad (& Tobago), 161, 162, 163, 170, 174
  carnival, 175
  expatriate writers, 250
  links with Afro-American writing, 134
  multi-ethnicity, 19, 129, 136, 164, 190, 324
  political fiction, 168, 176

Trinidad (magazine), 163
Twain, Mark, 21, 166, 206, 207, 208, 271
  Huckleberry Finn, 204–5, 210, 265

Uganda, 101, 102, 108
Upanishads, The, 39, 76

Valeros, Florentino B. and Estrelita V. Gruenberg, 76
Vance, Norman, 306
Vanuatu, 126
Vedas, The, 39
vernacular (etymology), 138–9
  BEV (Black English Vernacular), 18, 23, 139, 144, 271
  "dialect novel", 145, 147, 170, 180, 204
  Gullah, 139, 240
Villareal, José Antonio, 301

Wales, 8, 22–3, 274
  Welsh fiction, 276–9
  Welsh language, 10, 239, 276–7
  Welsh Not, 276–7
Wallace, Gavin and Randall Stevenson, 306
Wasafiri, x
West Africa, 16, **78–101**
  custom and tradition, 83–8
  new voices, 95–101
  (Nigerian) Civil War, 92–3
  post-independence adjustment, 88–92
  post-independence disillusion, 93–5
West Indies, 162; *see also* Caribbean
"white writing", ix, 13, 199, 200
Wilde, Oscar, 285
Wilkes, G. A., *The Stockyard and the Croquet Lawn*, 212, 237
Wilkinson, Jane, 118
Willbanks, Ray, 237
Williams, Gavin and Randall Stevenson, 306
Williams, Mark, 238
Wilson, Harriet, 135
Windward Islands, 161

Witalec, Janet: *Native North
    American Literature*, 294–5, 301,
    306
World literature in English
    (definitions), 1, 5–6
*World Literature Written in
    English*, x

Zaïre, 178, 108
Zambia, 108, 110, 114, 115, 242
    indigenous languages, 114
Zell, Hans, 118
Zimbabwe, 82, 105, 108, 115, 116
    Chimurenga, 102, 115
    indigenous languages, 115, 116